I.T. Wars

DAVID
SCOTT

I.T. WARS:
MANAGING THE BUSINESS-TECHNOLOGY WEAVE IN THE NEW MILLENNIUM

2006

IT WARS: Managing the Business-Technology Weave in the New Millennium.
© 2005 by David Scott. All rights reserved. No part of this book may be used or reproduced in any manner whatsoever without written permission, except in the case of brief quotations embodied in critical articles or reviews.

ISBN: 1-4196-2763-5
LCCN: 2006902076

To order additional copies, please contact us.
BookSurge, LLC
www.booksurge.com
1-866-308-6235
orders@booksurge.com

Notes from the Author:

In referring to "Business" with a capital "B," we're discussing groups of business people. When referring to "business" (small "b"), we're referring to conduct of business – the operations and managing that an organization performs in getting the job done.

When referring to "Technology" with a capital "T," we're discussing groups of technology people. When referring to "technology" (small "t") we're referring to equipment or methodologies. When referring to "IT," we generally mean IT staff, unless followed by a qualifier, such as "IT procedure," "IT priorities," etc.

This book can be seen as a "Weave" of its own. Chapters, concepts, and details are self-reinforcing. Because today's Business-Technology Weave is so tightly interwoven, it can be difficult for some discussions to begin – where to start when there are so many dependencies and reinforcements? Which foundational understandings come first, when they themselves require simultaneous understandings of other areas?

In fact, this is what impedes discussion, understanding, and qualification in many organizations. Either discussions are made without solid understandings, or, appropriate discussions are avoided through the simple challenge for where to begin.

Organizations will have differing strengths and weaknesses. Therefore, what may be a logical progression of chapters for one organization may not be suited to another. For this reason, a comprehensive reading of the book will serve best, with a return and focus where and as necessary.

Thanks to:

Family & friends,

and

Tom Wolfe: A great friend; invaluable counsel.
Gary & Joyce
Sajid
Roger "Who has more fun than bookkeepers?" Rinebolt: Thanks for all.
Ralph & Jackie Featherstone: Friends and encouragement.
Ruth Williams & The Writer's Circle: For standing early on the path, pointing the way…
Marilyn: Steadfast friendship and encouragement.
Max: A best-buddy; the best little cat in the world. I miss you, Max.

… and lastly (but only for emphasis), *Misha's Coffee House*: Best coffee and jazz. What a coffee house should be… and a writer's dream…

… to all who believe.

ABOUT THE AUTHOR

David Scott began his association with the Business-Technology Weave in the U.S. Army, and grew to manage networks, infrastructures, and eventually large business-IT enterprises. He has directed Information Technology endeavors for many Washington DC Metro organizations, to include private business, government agencies, and associations, and has consulted on a contractual basis. He has helped to emplace, restore, and grow operational IT/business success and planning in several global Fortune 500 companies in leading areas such as public relations, patient care, laboratory accreditation, direct-mail marketing, telecommunications, and food safety. He has also assisted several organizations in their dispense of human and environmental services.

CONTENTS

Foreword   xi

CHAPTER 1   **The Challenge**   1
The Challenge Writ Large; The "Local" Challenge; Meeting the Challenge; The Challenge in Knowing "Where We Are"

CHAPTER 2   **Today's Business-Technology Environment – Where Are We?**   7
A More Comprehensive Understanding; Two Types of Organizations; Knowing Where You Are

CHAPTER 3   **Tomorrow's Environment – Where Are We Going?**   15
The People Prism; Sanction and Support; Determining Where You're Going

CHAPTER 4   **Getting There: Qualifying the Organization for Change**   21
Moving Business Forward; (Not Just) Another Team; The Business Implementation Team (BIT); Selling BIT; Change–An Easy "Sell"– A Difficult Buy?

CHAPTER 5   **Change - the Basics**   27
A Basic View to Understanding Change; A Basic Model for Change

CHAPTER 6   **Planning and Managing Change**   37
High Level Plans; IT's Onus; Three Plan Types; The Five-Year Plan; The One-Year Plan; The Individual Action Plan; Leveraging Your Plans; The One-Year Plan's Support to Projects

CHAPTER 7   **Delivery - Project by Project**   45
Don't Appliqué "Good" On Top of "Bad"; The General Project Requirement; The Danger in Divides; An Association's Experience; Project Janitoring; Pushing (Reacting) vs. Pulling (Leading); A View through the Weave; Making Better Projects; Be Qualified to "Look at Yourself"; Defining Your Project; Leadership; The Project Manager; Project Management Necessities; Timelines

CHAPTER 8	**False Solutions - and How to Avoid Them**	83

Automation is Good – Right?; Beware Adding Layers to Business Process; Automating Poor Process is Wasteful; Real Solutions in Plain Sight; Out with the New, In with the Old; The False Solution Writ Large; False Projects

CHAPTER 9	**Business and IT: Who Does What, Why, and When?**	97

The Filing Cabinet Analogy; The "Why" for Who Does What; Empower Business, Free IT; A Business Deficit; An IT Deficit; Putting Activity Where it Belongs; When

CHAPTER 10	**Managing People in the Weave - The Challenge to IT**	107

A View to Managing Those Around You; Classes of People in the Weave; WorkOns, WorkWiths and WorkFors; Reward/Recognition; Emphasizing the Future; Edge and Balance; Maintaining Morale; Discipline; TechnoShines, TechnoFinds, and TechnoBinds

CHAPTER 11	**The Power Prism**	131

A WorkOn's Temporary Shift; The WorkWith- Squeezed in the Middle; When a WorkWith Requires a WorkOn Approach; WorkFors in the Prism; The Emperor has Clothes; Discretion and Sensitivity; The Prism's View

CHAPTER 12	**Managing People in the Weave, Part II - The Challenge to Business**	141

Positioning Jobs-Positioning People; An Accrual of Returns; The Plug-and-Play of Positions; Frankensteins; Today's Expediency-Tomorrow's Emergency; Practices and Support; Setting Structure

CHAPTER 13	**Ignorance – A Posture Business Can No Longer Afford**	151

What Business Doesn't Know Can Hurt It; Two Basic Understandings; The IT Enlightened Organization; The Index of User Awareness; The 'Soft Bed' of Ignorance Closes; A Close Mesh; From Ignorance to Enlightenment; The TAP Policy; IT's Obligation in Getting Business "There"

CHAPTER 14	**Ignorance, Part II – The IT Conceit**	179

Who's Challenged?; When IT is Immersed and Myopic; IT's Obligation to Business' Needs; IT Leadership's Obligation; Duty has No Room for Conceit

CHAPTER 15	**The Criticizing of Excellence (How to Dispense and Handle Criticism)**	193

In Defense of Criticism; Maintaining a Balance; Examining Criticism; Justified, Unjustified and Cloaked Criticism; Motivations; Delivery; Follow-up; Receiving; Handling; Responding; Criticism's "Win-Win-Win";The Weave's Vulnerability; The Dividing Force of Unmanaged Criticism in the Electronic Age

CHAPTER 16	**The Success Culture**	229

Define -Or Be Defined; Groomed to Assume; The Stark Relief of Success;Creating the Success Culture-Groomed to Know; Missions, Values, Beliefs and Standards; The Excuse Factory

CHAPTER 17	**Content: Leveraging Information; Limiting Liability; Managing Documents and Retention**	243

A Growing Divide; A Basic Understanding of Need; Business and Non-Business Content; Appropriate and Inappropriate Content; Getting It, Using It, Re-Using It, and Getting Rid of It; Leveraging Content; Limiting Liability; Content Policy vs. Acceptable Use Policy; Retention; Forms of Content; The Proliferation of Unstructured Data; Structured Data; The Repository; A Document's Life; Content's Dark Side-Managing Liabilities; Identifying a Solutions Partner; Sizing the Solution; A System of Content Management

CHAPTER 18	**Security: Managing Protection, Reliability, Risk…and Recovery**	283

A Deadly Serious Business; Security in an Imperfect World; Risk-Unmanaged Possibilities become Probabilities; Zero Risk; Awareness; Prevention -a Mission, Value, Belief, and Standard; People -The Greatest Challenge; Areas of Security; The Acceptable Use Policy; Monitoring; Disaster; Natural vs. Deliberate Harm; DAPR -Disaster Awareness, Preparedness, and Recovery; Policy and Plan; Harming Events and Circumstances; Key Documentation; Plan Fundamentals; Preventions; Priorities and Resources; Various Loss and Contingency; Managing the Routine; The Edge; Managing, Swapping and Zeroing Burdens; Ensuring Survival

CHAPTER 19	**The Users Group: The Power Within**	353

Content and People; The Users Group Leader; The Users Group Meeting; The Guest Leader; A Grassroots Aid to Success and Security

CHAPTER 20	**The Heart of It All: Turning the Crank Day-by-Day**	359
	Today -and All Our Todays; Defining the Handle; Identity; Service Levels; Problems; Platforms; Events; Assets; Configurations; Resources and Provisioning; Solutions Partners; Discover, Act, and Manage	
CHAPTER 21	**What's At Stake: Lessons of the Business-Technology Weave – The 4-1-1 on 9/11, Katrina & Beyond...**	377
	Background to Where We Are; A Sobering Reliance; New Realities, NewAwareness; Terror Attack; Natural Disaster; Qualifying and Advancing the Discussion; IDRU -Inadequacy, Disaster, Runaway, Unrecoverability; EMP-Electro-Magnetic Pulse; An American Perspective; National Security; Where We Really Are; The Best We Can Do?; On the Precipice of Runaway; Comprehensive Failure on Comprehensive Cycle; The Right Questions; An Answer; Business Security -BizSec; BizSec=Privatization?; The Goal and the Whole of the Plan -Prevention; Repurposing Past Examples	
AfterWord	**The Big Conundrum – The Simple Solution**	401

Foreword

Why *I.T. Wars*?

I.T. Wars helps to identify and overcome inefficiencies created by a divide between Business and Information Technology (IT). In today's environment, the divide occurs because IT and Business frequently talk to the other in their own respective "language." Neither understands the other's language, and domain, particularly well so there is misunderstanding or misreading of the other. There is a subsequent spiral into inefficient methods of engagement.

Negotiating the divide is costly to any project or initiative and therefore to the organization as a whole. There is a tax on morale, motivation, mission, security, profit… anything you care to name in the realm of business. This is true whether an organization is private, for-profit, non/not-for-profit, a government agency, or anything else. Indeed even the sole-proprietor suffers this divide if conducting business with inefficient technical fit to his or her business practice. In all instances we'll define *business* simply as the managing and operations you conduct in support of your desired outcomes.

Basically, it is time to acknowledge a tax on success in the form of extra efforts, or in outright failures, requiring regrouping and subsequent stabs at success as the divide is broached in each case. In fact, the divide we speak of spawns many others that are suffered in most business-technology endeavors. They arise because the organization doesn't know how to prevent them, or how to close them once existing. Many evolve slowly over time. Some are not even readily identifiable to the untrained eye, and it can be difficult to tie specific divides to related, and diminished, outcomes; their influence is none-the-less powerful.

Divides also manifest themselves inside the two general groups: If Business cannot effectively communicate needs, or if IT cannot hear, Business suffers divides within – limping along on poor business-supports as it struggles to remain productive. IT too suffers these internal divides, as it sometimes struggles to define needs within the decipher of business expectations.

The importance of getting it right – and keeping it right - has never been more important. Creative ideas for managing technologies effectively and meshing the right solutions for business have never been more in demand. The requirement for an educated, talented technical staff is not in doubt. But now, more than ever, an organization's technological endeavors require an IT visionary partnered with a strong, technology-aware, Business leadership. We also know that staff must be trained to the optimal degree of effectiveness for ultimate return-on-investment from the increasingly powerful technology at their fingertips.

In these regards, the organization must align business and technology to a whole new standard. In capturing the best fit and use of technology, it's often like making a jigsaw puzzle - except several people have their hands on the pieces, and the pieces change size and color as you go along. To further the analogy, often times someone or something upends the table halfway through the puzzle's completion – and you start over. It often seems impossible!

Yet within this climate, many organizations' senior management, governance, and board level engagement on technical management issues is actually declining. According to a recent Price Waterhouse Cooper Global Management Survey, roughly half of respondents believe that senior management is not placing enough emphasis on data quality. Consider that this is in spite of important changes to global business operating environments – changes driven by major corporate scandals and new regulatory compliance requirements. Beyond that, consider the risk in a lack of involvement regarding simple business-intelligence by this level. The quality of your products or services, the margin of your profits, the quality and quantity of help you provide to others, *your reputation*, is directly influenced by the quality and effective use of appropriate technology and the associated fruits.

We must also squarely face the major challenge to governments and the private sector as they build, manage, and grow systems to effectively secure their constituents (us) from harm. In this realm, not only must many formerly discreet systems operate in effective unison, but these systems and their agencies have a requirement for effective sharing of data and resources. Their goal is a cohesive, sustained mission that leads and trumps each new challenge to our safety and security. Divides to effectiveness, sustained by protectionism, jealousy, or other impediments, in an efficient lead in security will be fatal.

Why *"War"*?

For many organizations and individuals, the overall divide leads to a low-grade war that percolates between technology and the larger business at-hand. War may seem a strong word, but when you consider the cost of flawed communication, erroneous expectations, and poorly mounted "solutions," you may as well have a good excuse. Let's consider what war generally means: two sides that have failed at communication, have real or seemingly diametric interests, and who likely haven't taken the time to understand each other very well – all leading to conflict and negative consequence.

Our war heats up during times of stress – outside change, fluctuations in business, technical implementations, futures planning, budget negotiations, competition for resources, fault finding, the quash of performance with politics, and so on. War seems a pretty good explanation for the state of business-technology affairs in, and across, many organizations.

The war leads to divides of diminished engagements, and actual avoidance. We risk generating "silos" that surround individuals, whole departments, and even organizations. Often the yield of these divides is business application systems that fail to follow the flow for the way business is actually conducted. Efficiency suffers because disparate systems don't "talk," or worse, generate competing data (content). Business results are lowered because information of similar and enhancing content is dispersed and hidden. Liabilities of information's content are not exposed and managed. A proper return on investment is not achieved through staff's effective utilization of business automation. Security lags and weakens in the face of new challenges. Bars for performance and quality of service are not upheld.

If your organization has experienced divides and undesired yield - problems in implementation, effective use, and alignment between technology and the business of *getting the job done* – you're in large company. But even in the best of circumstances there is room for improvement and imaginative ideas. With the increase in sophistication involving both Business and IT (their respective missions and supports) the requirements for an effective business-technology partnership grow ever more important and challenging. In these circumstances you will not be able to afford the "War." In this war there can be no single winner: Both sides win, or both lose. You must get on the proper footing now.

In this book, the challenge is understood. So too are the ways to meet this challenge. Through the establishment of a common language understood by IT *and* Business, we'll begin to build a new level of awareness. We'll take unusual views in finding and determining the lesser known, but emerging and increasingly important, disciplines that support better cooperation and better business.

We will provide the means to dismantle fractured methods of engagement so that we can regroup for common purpose. When we do, it will be important for Business and IT to read all areas of the book - particularly sections that seem targeted to the other. In this way each will gain a better understanding of the other. The appreciations gained will give you new perspective and will yield a more effective team.

Something this book won't do: We won't bother regrinding old grounds to hope for better coffee. Any organization can hire someone to put a network together. Anyone can snap together various technical platforms, business applications, and "solutions." Too, any company can hire business managers well-steeped in respective business knowledge. Organizations are full of competent technical and business people. What is difficult is leveraging disparate groups of people in effecting a balance of visionary outlook, the pragmatism, and the qualification to manage today's Weave with its acceleration of coming demands.

There is a dire need to eliminate the ineffective and costly methodologies that have woven themselves into your organization's culture. It is time for a different weave. It is time to create a modern arena for smart planning and the execution of smart solutions. *Solutions that support better business*.

1

The Challenge

The greatest challenge to any thinker is stating the problem in a way that will allow a solution.

Bertrand Russell

Business is increasingly sophisticated. Business is routinely conducted twenty-four hours a day, seven days a week. Organizations are increasing their global outreach. Travel no longer means that people are out-of-the-loop. Because people can stay connected to their work they often find, or at least feel, that they must stay connected. The requirement for effective business and information systems, their proper utilization, and the pressure for the most return possible has never been greater.

As we consider the increasing requirements for immediate access to data, the security of data, the management of data's content (that is, the treatment of business information as a leveraged advantage), and the growing demand for time in maintaining the highly technical back-end of business information systems, we realize that we face an increasing risk to a most important asset. At risk is business information itself - or business *intelligence* – and its effective management and use. In addition to the business reliance on steady information, we must realize too - whether factory, farm, hospital, distribution point, port, etc. – that operations, process, production and delivery are increasingly or completely dependent on technology.

Everyone must gain a thorough understanding for managing the combination of business and technology now, and for what is coming in future burdens. To illumine the problem another way - without a remedy to current inefficiencies, the divides of communication and understanding will compound exponentially during the coming demands of any business-technology environment. With accumulating vulnerabilities, not always readily seen, you can face a very real danger to your continued business existence.

At the same time, whether it be core mission-critical business applications, association management systems, accounting systems, e-mail systems, content management systems, shelf applications, etc., *all* organizations are challenged to implement, upgrade, or change outright these systems on a periodic basis. There is an ongoing requirement to expand systems' capabilities for services and deliverables while sustaining support of daily business operations.

The fruits of this technology, for example the ability to mine, analyze, and deliver data in providing useful information to Business with accuracy, speed, and efficiency, is not only desirable, it is an absolute necessity. In tandem, you need an attendant, informed, user class that can leverage technical business tools and their output for maximum effect. For organizations of today it is now your business to jump, perform, and deliver with an immediacy that wasn't necessary ten years ago – or even five.

Organizations also must anticipate and build accommodation for whatever the future of business holds: changing markets; new products; faster deliveries; improved services, increased competition; and rising security challenges. In the case of governments and aligned agencies (with mutually reinforcing and united missions) there are new and emerging requirements to work together. Their objectives and success in achieving them affect safety and security of entire nations. We can fairly ask: Will governments achieve the necessary agility in responding to the accelerative change of threats? For all of these reasons, we realize that we must emplace a culture that supports ultimate outcomes.

THE CHALLENGE WRIT LARGE – AND LESSONS FOR US ALL

We don't have to look far for examples of divides that rise to national consciousness – and consequence. We can also inspect them for lessons and obligations for the "local" organization. In these pages, we'll examine the FBI's recent, failed, project to implement the Virtual Case File (VCF) tracking system. This project was to replace a paper-based system, and to automate the collection and sharing of critical data in the post-9/11 world. The four year, $300 million, project failure presents potent lessons. It also allows divides to ride for several more years: that between the FBI's need - and its ability - to track terror suspects effectively. Its need – and its ability - to share data on a leveraged basis with other organizations in the united purpose of preventing harm.

Because the U.S. Justice Department's after-action report says that the FBI's ability to "connect dots" effectively will not be achieved for "several more years," we must examine the larger failures to show specific vulnerabilities to your organization's security posture – and what you can do about it. We can also inspect the FBI's related project in this instance, and examine it against areas for your own organization's improvements.

We'll also look at a case involving natural threat - the recent flooding of New Orleans, and the compounding of disaster from Katrina. Here was a tragic yield due to divides between awareness - and reality. Between diminished action - and desperate need for action. Between standards of prevention - and the discount, or dismissal of prevention as a necessary standard and value. Ultimately, the best know-how and technology in the world failed the simple business of implementing a proper system of protection. Our yield here was the loss of many lives. Our yield also included the loss of New Orleans itself - recoverable only through great expense. But our yield here too is an important lesson – for many, including your organization.

Because any organization's security requires the larger security of the public environment, we'll see why it is imperative for us to discuss perils to entire nations posed by these divides. Divides have achieved a new scale of unaffordability due to the challenge of rapidly changing asymmetric threats. We will show how a new interaction between Business and Technology can contribute to the removal of certain perils to society.

THE "LOCAL" CHALLENGE

For organizations of all sizes, divides of communication and effective cooperation go well beyond impact to the immediacy of various needs, initiatives, and their fulfillments. These divides give rise to the war of negative expectations regarding cooperation. There can be a diminished character of engagement, and often the actual avoidance of engagement. This creates a compartmentalizing of people and groups who are supposed to be working as a collective whole on the organization's ultimate aims. This is what contributes to many organizations' reactive posture to change, and the increasingly difficult transitions in meeting the future's challenge. On this local scale, your organization's culture suffers with each success deferred, with each "success" diminished.

An Important Awareness: Because Business must sponsor and support changes in this arena, for its own betterment, the requirement for knowledge - and the acknowledgement of that requirement - is increasingly important. In fact, your organization's IT strategy needs to be a Business-driven IT strategy, with all necessary qualifications. Business understands that IT exists at Business' pleasure; IT serves business. But Business must realize that for this very reason, IT requires sanction and sponsorship for that which it does.

Business must lead, granting permission and exposing the length and safe channel of IT's own lead. Senior management must swim in a new stream of technology awareness for truly effective business planning. This is not to suggest there be a duplication of knowledge, but rather that Business be qualified to discuss its own requirements, priorities, and available resources for best exposure and understanding. There must exist a knowledge on Business's part for what is available in the technical arena, and their engagement on how it can be utilized for better and future business.

On the IT side, there is the need for a better appreciation of business: What are the business requirements; are needs being met; and how effectively are we charting future needs? How effective is staff's use of the current technology? How effective is training, practice and policy? How do we best measure, assess, and make effective response to these things – for now, and for the future? IT should be as exact a fit to its specific business-berth as it can be. IT is not a swappable appendage between organizations.

On both sides, there is that requirement for vision as well as an appreciation for the practical component of getting today's job done.

Let's also consider some other realities. Increasingly, an organization is challenged to do more with less - to be as efficient as possible, while remaining as effective as possible. And so, therefore, are you challenged. To manage cost. To remain within budget. To reduce overhead. To identify requirements - accurately. To effect and execute a one-year plan. To effect a long-range plan. To simultaneously plan, produce and deliver solutions that are the *right size*, while remaining scalable for the future's requirements. Herein lies the challenge to the IT leader and to the Business leader alike: How to effectively and efficiently maintain today's systems, to mesh them with business, and how to maneuver successfully into the future through delivery of results.

Meeting the Challenge

Today's main challenge, in support of all others, is to create and maintain the Business-Technology Weave. It is a tight fabric of mutual support and reinforcement that won't tear, shrink, or strangle anybody: respectively, an effective business-technology environment that won't break; that will increase, not diminish, in effectiveness as time moves forward; and that won't bring harm to those attempting to manage it, or allow harm to those relying on it.

In the coming chapters, we'll explore effective, efficient ways to do that – we'll expose systems of management and implementation that have yielded the secret to identifying appropriate solutions for support. We'll lay some general groundwork and understandings in the early chapters. As we go along, we'll get increasingly detailed as we explore real world situations and solutions.

Those things that can be made routine *must* be made routine, so that the more challenging and emerging aspects of the Business-Technology Weave can be attended to with the proper time and attention. Consider: The more energy it takes for you to manage your present, the less energy your organization has for managing the future. The resultant, poorly crafted future becomes your new ill-managed present – with ever-diminished attention to the increasingly ill-managed future. And the cycle continues. Your present must be made solid, reliable, and effective.

So, for the manager at any level, we'll show how to identify and size best practices and emerging practices. We'll establish effective ways to work within larger management. We'll identify effective methods for managing projects, short and long-term, and for calming the waters in the most challenging endeavors. We'll establish incentives, set triggers for rewards, and map discipline. We'll identify ways to overcome obstacles, to push through or past difficult people (while maintaining the integrity of permissions and authorities), to make the sale, to achieve sanction and sponsorship, to break through organizational silos, and to communicate across, up, and down the hierarchy.

We'll set beliefs, values, and standards in creating a culture of success, in support of defined missions. We'll discuss how to select people, promote people, hire people, fire people, rate people, balance work, balance jobs, create effective job descriptions, set goals, and manage tasks according to the merits necessary in support of those missions – in general, we'll keep the train on the tracks and lay *new* tracks.

For the IT leader, we will expose ways to increase your recognition and contribution to the organization. Most importantly, we'll identify ways to increase the standing and prestige of the IT department in your organization. For the Business leader, we'll help to identify the mysteries of technology as it may stand in your organization, and show ways to partner in bringing better technology, and better *use* of technology, to your needs. You can have the best fit to your business in the selection of raw technology, but if your business staff doesn't make effective use of it, you have the bottom-line equivalent of a poor system. We'll help you discuss your requirements and ideas with IT in building better support to business.

We will expose ideas that can be leveraged to dramatic effect. Obvious, or familiar, areas needing improvement have been well documented – often with tired and worn "solutions." So, we'll bring new appreciations and perspectives to those areas. In addition, we'll develop fresh ideas, with matching imagination, for modern, forward-looking solutions. There is no attempt here to create a one-size-fits-all approach to diverse organizations and their challenges. Instead, we'll leverage the power of simple examples and fundamental approaches. From there, your own creativity and imagination can size and shape the ideas in this book to your organization's best advantage – regardless how large, irrespective of mission. Your goal should be to achieve the possible, so as to expand the possible – in maintaining *continuous improvement*. Always seek a proper return on your efforts.

THE CHALLENGE IN KNOWING "WHERE WE ARE"

We must gain an appreciation: Effective business will require our best use of people and resources, inside an accelerating environment of change and challenges. We'll require proper identification of needs, correct application of will, targeted effort, and fulfillment. Further, business will require new awareness for the best practices regarding management of threat, risk, and liabilities.

Today - City, State and Federal government; private business; and all manner of organizations, associations and agencies, have infrastructure, business applications, vast amounts of data, robust resources, and assets. Organizations depend on these things, and that dependency brings central vulnerabilities to business. The central support of technology to business, paired with the overall risks and vulnerabilities in today's rapidly changing world, means that any organization has to uncover and leverage the Business-Technology Weave in all regards.

How do we influence individual attitudes, and consequently, the organization's culture in order to close divides? How can we bias the most challenging endeavors not only for ultimate success, but for all the incremental successes necessary in bringing timely solutions to bear in the most efficient manner?

First, we must understand "where we are"… - where are you?

2

Today's Business-Technology Environment – Where Are We?

Begin where you are; work where you are; the hour which you are now wasting, dreaming of some far off success may be crowded with grand possibilities.

Orison Swett Marden

Know where you are. In examining where we are, we're going to begin with your organization's knowledge, its confidence, its values – its culture.

It's also good to know where you're going, especially if you're endeavoring to get someplace. But in order to begin, you must know *where you are now*. Certainly any route you map for a car trip starts with your current location – try planning a route to a destination without a start point. Think of it this way: Someone is driving all around the USA, to experience America. This person calls you from the road, asking for a route to Chicago. What is your first, primary, requirement in delivering on that need for a route? You must know the point of departure: the "where are we" of this person's location.

We generally think we know where we are, but too often truly knowing this involves the understanding of things that we may not even be considering. Often, organizations mount grand plans to destinations without knowing their point of origin. Under these circumstances, there can be no real route - merely a false route, with no tether to reality. As the project meanders, signs pop up and conditions expose themselves to essentially help uncover just where the organization *is* – with the attendant scramble to adjust. This is a very expensive way to discover or adjust a start point, and to correct a route that should have been planned in accordance with reality. Because you cannot map a destination without a starting point, it is little wonder that many projects and initiatives seem to wander all over the place - before failing and starting over.

A More Comprehensive Understanding

Some of the most important "where are we" factors may be ones that you've never really thought about. For the business manager, part of knowing where you are in the Business-Technology Weave involves a solid understanding of the relationship between mission, business process, and your organization's technical supports and solutions. It's increasingly important for the business manager to not only understand his and her immediate domain, but to appreciate the surrounding whole of the business and its supports so as to effectively help plan, steer, and *use* the mesh of technology and business. As but one example, the balance and effective use of resources becomes less a competition and squeeze, and more of a properly sized and distributed set of assets, when Business and Technology make a qualified measure of mission, process, and support.

Knowing where you are also involves knowing your organization's potential. For example, you know that the implementation of new computer solutions poses challenges to each department, and specifically to yours. Therefore, part of knowing where you are would be to understand staff's potential and ability to rise to the challenge of a new system. Who are your users and how do they work? It is their technical comfort, their knowledge of existing applications, their current workflow, and their aptitude that will be major factors in the success or failure of any new system. This knowledge influences the design of the system, the speed of the rollout and the level of training necessary. Does your organization have the caliber of people necessary for effective use of the selected system? How will you set and pace your training for staff members? IT reports to Business, so it must be asked: Is your IT staff capable of project managing, delivering, and supporting this solution? Will Business need to make and direct changes to IT in anticipation of this implementation?

For the IT leader, knowing where you are certainly involves the obvious things: you can document systems; you can know your IT staff's capabilities; you should know your user population and their capacities; you have an approved budget; you have some ongoing projects and some upcoming ones. But you must know the business of your organization – thoroughly. By extension, the IT department and any aligned technical agencies, such as vendors or contractors, must know what it is your organization does, and endeavors to do in the future. An IT department is not a swappable block on an organization chart. Your IT department should be a hand-in-glove fit, over time, to the organization's business: It should understand the daily requirements, the near and long-term objectives, the strengths, and vulnerabilities. IT should understand the organization's position in whatever market or justification you occupy. To this end, IT should be the strongest possible partner in advancing the business aims of the organization.

But for you, the IT leader, there are other extremely important things to know regarding "where you are" – particularly if you are entering a new organization, are experiencing new governance or management in an existing organization, or if you are just now entering IT management. Fully knowing where you are is the understanding of your governance: your board, your top management, and any outside regulators – even the influence of customers and members. You cannot only consider what you'd like to do – you must fully understand what you are *allowed* or *able* to do. That is part of the condition for where you are. Be fully aware of the limits of your authority. Anyone, IT or Business, who has inadvertently exceeded the limit of their lead will understand that they *didn't* understand "where they were" when they did that.

To truly know where you are, you must expose your business environment - its culture - to the light of day. How are expectations communicated? How strong and accurate is the identification of need? How reliable is any communication in your organization? Is there a best faith engagement by all parties? That is, is there a sincere engagement on issues and projects? Do these enjoy full support, being viewed as a part of the business day, rather than an interruption to it? Is there accountability? Do those charged with making change enjoy necessary, full, and ongoing sponsorship and sanction?

Is IT in the senior management circle in your organization – or does IT rely on some representation in that circle? That is, does the IT leader - be it Chief Technology Officer, Chief Information Officer, Director or Manager - have direct, steady, participation in the arena where business is decided? If so, is IT a full player? Does the organization understand and respect IT's modern role? If IT is not present in this arena, who sponsors IT? For the IT leader, those providing supervision and oversight will be your sponsor(s); those that will represent you and your department's initiatives and issues in the senior-most decision making circles.

Regardless of IT's formal standing in the organization, there will always be conversations and maneuvers external to IT regarding business directions and objectives… even discussion regarding IT itself. In any considerations where IT is not there to represent itself, it would be nice to have sponsors, formal or informal. That is, someone to advocate for IT. How effective will that sponsorship, or advocacy, be? Will your interests and issues be translated effectively? Will all of the things you think important even be presented? Will the impact of IT issues be *fairly* presented? What filters, either inadvertent or deliberate, will your sponsor (and listeners) employ? What is senior management's capacity, and *willingness*, in understanding the issues? In short, will sponsorship be effective? You must know – it is part of knowing where you are.

Many people manage for many years and don't always know where they are – as silly as that can sound. For the IT leader, don't rely on trial and error to determine where you are within the organization. It's easy to speak about status of things that are empirical – easily measured through direct observation: server capacities; faculty of infrastructure; level of staff training and ability; a budget. A bit more difficult are those things that are less tangible: who partners effectively across the organization? What is my level of support? How do we resolve conflict? Where are the fulcrums and levers for best advancing business?

For Business and Technology leaders, you must know: Is it worth striving for excellence here? Who stands to lose, and who stands to gain, through any successful measure? (Or, as importantly, what are those perceptions?). *Where are we?*

TWO TYPES OF ORGANIZATION – WHERE ARE YOU?

In today's business environment, from the Weave perspective, there are two types of organizations. Simply put: those that understand how to manage business-technology endeavors, and those that do not. In order for the IT leader to effectively manage - to maximize that department's support to business - the organization as a whole must be able to effectively manage IT. It's a partnership – but a partnership that *Business* manages.

A frequent complaint from IT leaders, and quite a few business leaders, translates as "my organization doesn't understand technology." The follow-on from Business is that systems are cumbersome, don't deliver as expected, and that IT help is frequently ineffective. The IT follow-on is that senior personnel and managers don't understand IT, and many simply care not to. Within these circumstances, Business and IT fail to set an example, which means that staff fail to understand, or seek how to effectively use, the technology at their disposal. The result is that many of us simply don't understand technology's true role in the organization, and our modern responsibility within that.

On one end of the extreme is the organization that thinks of IT as a sort of glorified typewriter repair. Plans and success for optimal alignment between business and technology suffer here, but so too does the day-to-day. In other words, people at all levels of the organization first and foremost think of IT as a place to call when their PC acts up. Theirs is a rather benign, naïve view of the technology lever – and therefore they don't grab that lever and use it to maximum effect. The organization does not reap the best return on its technical supports and investments. In this realm too are those that resent technology – they have an adversarial relationship with it and the people who support it. At best is a view that technology is a necessary evil of sorts – there is a diminished and delayed engagement on the planning and execution of solutions, as this engagement is viewed as a difficult, unrewarding, endeavor.

At the other extreme is the organization that gets it: IT occupies a place at the organization's planning table – there's not a relevant business decision made without IT's knowledge, and where necessary, it's recommendation. People respect technology's contribution, and they value the professionals who work within this important support endeavor. In these environments, people explore, poke, and expand systems' capabilities. They are more likely to self-motivate in expanding their knowledge, and in contributing to the forward momentum of the Business-Technology Weave. Most organizations fall somewhere in the middle. No matter where your organization falls, there is always room for improvement.

Surprisingly, in many organizations, discussions regarding the direction or support of business frequently take place without proper consideration of technology's role. Support may be taken for granted, or technology's applicability is overlooked, or perhaps it's assumed to be sized as some out-of-the-box remedy. Consider a mid-size organization that chose to implement an "automated" performance appraisal software for managing the annual review of individual staff members. IT was directed to procure a software solution. Here, a business decision was made without IT involvement because the business folks in the organization didn't want to "waste IT's time" - not until a decision was made to change the appraisal process.

A very fine software application was dutifully procured and implemented. But, the solution turned out to be more work and trouble than the former method, which employed readily available software application tools the organization already owned. The real problem in this organization's production of employee appraisals was a *human* one - no one enforced the schedule for the submission of the appraisals – a situation that continued with the new software application. And, people weren't utilizing currently installed office automation effectively – nor being required to use it.

We'll revisit the appraisal example in detail in a coming chapter, as it reveals many important lessons – lessons that can be applied to the largest endeavors. But remember that bringing an effective technical solution or support element to business requires early involvement of the technology department. For the IT and Business leader, your organization's effectiveness in employing IT for relevant business planning is part of *where it is,* and consequently, a part of *where you are.*

Other elements that establish where you are involve a thorough understanding of the organization's culture, and your position in it: an establishment and understanding of your authority; your knowledge of responsibilities and ownerships (yours and other's); knowledge of your sponsors and their limits; knowledge of partners; knowledge of resources. In discussions, be certain to clarify things. Where there seems to be a lack of commitment, allow for a certain ambiguity in evolving situations – but don't ever build *your* commitment to something without a proper foundation. That is, get the commitments you need from others clearly agreed to; get the expectations and all support elements clearly defined and clearly stated, so that you're providing your own *qualified* commitment.

In examining where we are, we can provide a common qualification for the Business and IT leader alike. Both groups will see that things such as equipment and infrastructure are on the list. Some may wonder at a Business qualification to know anything about these. If you are one of those wondering, be patient. In the coming chapters we'll show where knowledge is required, just how much, and where the lines are in preventing diminishing returns.

KNOWING WHERE YOU ARE:

- Understand and establish your authority
- Identify your sponsors
- Determine the limits to which sponsors can back you
- Understand the people
- Identify and know your resources
  - Staff
  - Budget
  - Time
  - Equipment: platform, infrastructure, systems, ...
  - Vendors, contractors
  - Etc.

- Understand your sanction
  - You must know where the organization wants to go
  - Understand the limits of your lead
  - Agree to levels of participation
  - Agree to rates of progress

- Get "their" commitments first, when needed for your commitments
- Document commitments, agreements, etc.

In establishing where you are, don't forget the status of readily observable and, relatively speaking, easily measured systems, infrastructures, and procedures – the state of those things also factor into where you are. Anything that is poorly maintained, yet easily measured, shows a problem in managing *routine things*. There's a clue: Imagine the problems you'll encounter when there are challenges in arenas that may have more subjective, and even political, considerations. So look to these empirically measured areas as an overall barometer to the organization's effectiveness and success – its *success culture*.

Understand "where you are" to effectively plot where you're going.

3

Tomorrow's Environment – Where Are We Going?

It would appear that we have reached the limits of what it is possible to achieve with computer technology, although one should be careful with such statements, as they tend to sound pretty silly in 5 years.

John Von Neumann (ca. 1949)

Where *are* we going - and how do we get there? We know that IT, Business, the Future - involves change. However, it's obvious from John Von Neumann's statement above that trying to predict the future with detailed certainty is not only impractical – it's not possible. In fact, it's unnecessary. Why? Because you merely need to establish the model and methodologies that will serve to help your business expose needs, partner on identifying solutions, and collaborate on implementing/making effective use of those solutions, in order to serve the future. In other words; the best way to predict the future is to create it.

Because IT is always about change, the IT leader should be staying abreast of the latest technology and scanning the horizon for new and innovative business solutions - you must be ready to weigh in at any time with paths for progression and suitabilities to corresponding business practices. Equally, for the Business leader, you should be considering support technology as you plot your future from the business perspective. For you, it's easy enough to talk to your business counterparts in other organizations to gain a sense of what works for them, and what doesn't. Additionally, most newspapers, magazines, and many online forums feature articles about technology that are written specifically for business eyes. Read these articles and begin to swim in this stream of awareness.

Do these things and the future becomes much more manageable. We'll also be developing a kind of model that will suit any business/technical endeavor well – a general, high level view of things that eases the organization into an upcoming change. This general model can then be tweaked to your various projects.

Von Neumann also missed something that's crucial – what's possible with a computer, or technology, is not determined by limits inherent in the computer's potential – processing power, "intelligence," storage capacity, data-density, bandwidth, etc. – it is determined by the limits of *human potential*. And we hope that human potential is limitless. We will demand of the computer that which we desire and need, and we will create technology to fulfill those desires and needs. Therefore, let's talk about *people*.

THE PEOPLE PRISM

Always view your organization through the people (Business) prism first, and mold the technology to those needs. True, there will be times when evolving technology will drive business practice to a degree, but you must *always* consider the business requirement and impact to people. This will come naturally to the Business leader, so let's concentrate our attention for awhile on IT's necessary awareness in getting the organization to where it's going.

Developing a model for identifying needs, finding potential solutions for support of those needs, and exposing the organization to the choices requires cooperation. Subsequently, choosing the best solution, managing its implementation, turning on the solution, and ensuring its effective use requires your ability to effect the best collaboration among people. Of course, the biggest challenge in any endeavor, technical or not, involves human beings. Managing people - not just the formal management of those that report to you, but to include the informal managing of those around you, above you, and even external to your organization – can be difficult. Maybe you think it's always difficult, only varying by degrees. It doesn't matter – the fact is that you want to manage as effectively as possible. You have to build teams. These teams will comprise business partners and technology partners.

You want to get along with everyone, but you must get the best from everyone – not just your staff but also your boss, your board, your fellow managers in other departments, your solutions partners (vendors and contractors), and associates in other organizations. In other words, we want everyone's best game. You want to contribute to everyone's potential to bring his and her best game to the mission each day - particularly when partnering with you. That's a weave that's mutually reinforcing – the better you get people to partner with you, the greater your success and standing. Much, if not most, of what you do depends on others. The larger an endeavor, and the more comprehensively it affects the organization, the more people you'll have contributing to the success of the endeavor (and therefore to your success).

At the same time, you'll have more people who have potential to limit your success. There will be those who will resist change of any kind. The people who resist change most effectively are the people with the power and means to do so – unfortunately. But that is the sense of it – they'll have the weight to throw around in resisting and stalling projects. They won't contribute unless pushed and forced to contribute. Part of your success in contributing to an organization's evolution – its ongoing successful transition into the future – will be to know when to do the pushing yourself, and when to defer it to another – your boss, for instance, or another authority (for instance his or her boss, etc., on up the line depending on the level of the person who needs the push, and the critical nature of lags). When necessary, you'll have to know how to present the deferment.

You'll need to use the appropriate language, tone, reasoning, and degree of brevity or detail. Remember to speak to your audience – for example, keep technical details away from top management, unless solicited, and rather expose the business facet of issues. Obviously always start with your direct supervisor. Remember that for any technical arena, on any technical project, in any IT department, you are wrapped in a business environment - *people* determine where you're going, *people* will determine your level of success, and *people* will always be your biggest challenge.

SANCTION AND SUPPORT

Another important concept in piloting your way into the future is understanding your sanctions – it's a huge part of where you are. That is, upon approval of anything, understand your sponsors and their limits. Understand your consensus: who is fully on board? Who is lukewarm, or even hostile to the project? Who gains, and who loses – or - who harbors those *perceptions*? What documentation exists to spell out the needs, expectations, authorizations, duties, and measures of success? Is the undertaking springing from a known point of origin? Is any part of "where we are" not known to the organization – or to those who are sponsoring and sanctioning projects? If any of these sponsoring/sanctioning bodies are serving expectations that are in excess of where the organization is (that is, the organization is not suitably prepared for a project's demands), then adjustments must be made.

At this point, we can summarize some points for detailed discussion later. We have two very simple, yet sometimes difficult, concepts: knowing *Where You Are* and *Where You're Going*.

From Chapter One, we have these important concepts in knowing Where You Are:

- ◆ Know *Where You Are*:
    - Understand and establish your authority
    - Identify your sponsors
    - Determine the limits to which sponsors can back you
    - Understand the people
    - Identify and know your resources
        - Staff
        - Budget
        - Time
        - Equipment: platform, infrastructure, systems, ...
        - Vendors, contractors
        - Etc.
    - Understand your sanction
        - You must know where the organization wants to go
        - Understand the limits of your "lead"
        - Agree to levels of participation
        - Agree to rates of progress
        - Get "their" commitments first, when needed for your commitments
        - Document commitments, agreements, etc.

Further, once you've identified where you are, you're in a position to begin the identification of where you need to go.

You must know where you're going before you can plan the "getting there." You must expose the destination, which will help to evidence the necessary change, and its associated planning, initiatives and projects:

DETERMINING WHERE YOU'RE GOING

- ◆ *Where You're Going* – Determining the means to reach your destination:

    - Survey the requirements
    - Expose needs
    - Participate in planning
    - Define projects and goals

- Recognize major milestones
- Create and maintain documentation
- Make clear assignments
- Establish incentives
- Establish discipline
- Survey progress on a defined basis
- Provide regular status reports
- Adjust alignment – the fit to business – as necessary
- Develop methods of conflict resolution
- Seek help when necessary
- *Manage change in "getting there"*

Getting There: In getting there, we'll see that we need to identify, size, and manage change. We'll see that the smaller, near-term projects can be managed more simply and less formally. The longer, more complex, projects will require a formal management style and tool set. We'll leave the detailed discussion of methods for project management to a later chapter – first, we must emplace some fundamental supports to "where you're going." We must understand how to get there - how to plan and manage change. In order to do this, we must qualify the organization itself for change.

REMEMBER ~

The truth in knowing Where You Are can involve many hidden things that must be exposed and defined. The truth in knowing Where You're Going is not necessarily where you (the reader) *want* to go, but rather where you are *able* or *allowed* to go – but certainly where you *need* to go. Getting where you need to go won't happen if you exceed the limit of your authority or lead, and proceeding without appropriate sanction and support is imprudent.

Remember that no one person can know exactly where all of the longest-term destinations are. As information comes, and as you participate in planning, it's up to you to have the model in place to interpret needs and circumstances in a timely fashion, with accuracy, and in a way that allows Business and Technology to work together.

This effective partnership, a part of the weave, is a qualified, defined, team – as we shall see. For, if knowing where you're going is important, *getting there* is imperative – and you'd better have the qualification for making it happen.

4

GETTING THERE:
QUALIFYING THE ORGANIZATION FOR CHANGE

In the modern world of business, it is useless to be a creative original thinker unless you can also sell what you create. Management cannot be expected to recognize a good idea unless it is presented to them by a good salesman.

    David M. Ogilvy

Getting to where you're going involves a sale. It's true: If you can't sell your creation to the organization - your idea, your vision, your direction for the organization - you've labored in vain. There must be a belief in a business idea, or a technical solution, or any combination – and that belief is sold to other believers. In a larger sense, the organization must sell itself and its own objectives to its staff. Selling, whether believing in a proposal, product, solution, service, new method, etc., means effectively communicating to those who can help you and who can partner with you to achieve the aims. In doing this, we can ask: "How do we qualify to sell?" and "Where do we sell?"

For an effective partnership, we need to create a sales-ready environment into which appropriate people can direct those energies, and vet these ideas. When we talk about identifying, planning, and selling change here, we're really talking about achieving a shared vision and consensus – a belief - between Business and Technology for achievement of *best* change. "Best change" means that we deliver something suitably sized, based on proper expectations, in the most effective manner possible. We need an effective teaming: one that minimizes the opportunity for mistakes; wrong impressions; erroneous expectations; wasted time, money, and energy; and delivery of wrong, or diminished, things. An enterprise that structures itself for efficiency and delivery of success through effective communication, mutual understanding, and collaboration. The kind of collaboration that is positive so as to move business forward. Let's repeat that: *to move business forward.*

MOVING BUSINESS FORWARD

Whatever your organization's mission, product, service, desired accomplishments (its *business*), all effort should be directed to that regard. Any suspect activity can be illuminated by the simple question: "Does this move business forward?" (Or, thought of another way, "Does this have *business value*?" There can be many versions to this question, but they all essentially expose an answer that must meet the qualifier of advancing business' interests). Any answer short of "yes" is unacceptable. Just to be clear, we're talking here about exposing inhibitors to good faith partnering in conducting sound business. *Anything* that moves business forward is not necessarily appropriate – your organization's ethics and good legal standing are assumed to be in place.

(NOT JUST) ANOTHER TEAM

So, to help us remain within a proactive, forward thinking, and positive posture, we're going to lay the groundwork for a qualified partnership between IT and Business. In short, we're going to create a team.

We're not just creating another team – we're going to create a special team in crafting and maintaining the Weave: *the* team. This team will have as its prime goal the perfect storm weave of *People, Policy and Process* when crafting, steering, and delivering success for your business-technology investment. We're going to need some rules for the team. We're going to define the structure and means for interaction by members within the team. And, we'll show how best to communicate the team's concerns, conclusions, and recommendations to other management – for sanction, sponsorship, and delegated action in achieving results.

It's amazing how many organizations make ill-informed decisions. Whether they leave out major business players that have a stake in the decision, or build a business solution independent of the most reliable and effective technical mesh to business, this poor decision making process is costly: in terms of budget, morale, productivity and, increasingly, security. Exacerbating the problem is a common reliance on poor, even ad hoc, communications to the organization itself regarding important central, core, business changes.

It's also confounding that IT frequently finds itself on the coattails of the decision-making process, often being the recipient of an approved "solution" with orders to "make it happen." Once IT is in the game, IT is frequently the unhappy participant who discovers all the other unsurveyed entities that have a shared interest in the change, and who now have major, legitimate, and sometimes competing concerns. None of this is good. All of this is avoidable.

In order to collaborate effectively, IT and Business must first communicate. In order to communicate effectively, there needs to be an identified group of qualified communicators – people who will help to identify, plan, and support change in a knowledgeable fashion. Do not waste time by putting unqualified persons on this team, such as those who do not appreciate policy and business objectives; who may not understand process; or those who do not utilize technology well (or who even may have an adversarial relationship with technology). Do not waste time replicating some other dysfunctional team, or teams, in your organization.

The participants must come from those parts of the organization that effectively manage business and manage IT. Individuals from both areas must understand the means by which business is conducted – these are the middle and upper middle managers, and as necessary those visionaries and planners who are identifying emerging business and practices. That is, those privy to the organization's direction: they who can bring timely notification to the group of new business directions, emerging requirements, and technical developments. This group will become that special team, and we'll call it the Business Implementation Team (BIT). You can call it what you wish, of course, but here we'll refer to it as BIT.

THE BUSINESS IMPLEMENTATION TEAM (BIT)

The creation and successful launch of the BIT team will require your ability to sell the concept to your supervision: your boss, his or her boss, and any other necessary approval authorities, and subsequently, you must sell the concept to the other managers in the organization. If your organization already has some sort of regularized or formal meeting between IT and Business that is *successful*, you are largely set, and can glean from this discussion those things that will enhance your team. If, however, you don't have something like BIT, or if you have a somewhat dysfunctional or poorly defined version of BIT, you'll want to launch a newly defined team and meeting to fill the void in the case of the former, or to emplace an effective table in the case of the latter.

The BIT team provides a forum for interaction by IT and Business. The participants, schedule, and agenda flexes according to many things: business cycles, budget cycles, periods and locations of heavy implementation, periods of relative inactivity. Ideas can be debuted and discussed in the BIT forum: new, upcoming business postures can be exposed for discussion and planning; a business-delegate can impart desires from a governance committee; IT's supervision can sit in when desired or necessary, exposing the organization's leaders to new technology planning and impact, or announcing major, upcoming changes that require Business' involvement. This is where business leaders can effectively expose department needs and solicit ideas. As necessary, other staff members with specific job functions and specialized job knowledge can participate when necessary. Solutions partners, in the form of vendors or contractors, can be invited to participate.

For example, during major software implementations, the BIT team would comprise those department heads affected by the new software. During budget planning, the BIT team would want to pull in all major department heads to discuss common needs. Changes to the web or e-Commerce would involve the relevant people. In these examples, all proposed needs should be identified – vetting them can ordinarily transpire in BIT. However, there will be times where sensitive vetting takes place later between the IT leader and her supervision, and in-turn the necessary senior-most Business individuals.

Depending on the organization, the BIT team may meet quarterly, it could be monthly, sometimes weekly, and it will meet off-schedule sometimes. The schedule and participants will be determined by the needs. Generally, it should be IT's lead to make these determinations, as the BIT team should be seen as an IT-hosted and lead endeavor *in service to business*. The agenda should be assembled by IT, with input from Business. However, at times and as necessary, anyone on the team can suggest a meeting and agenda.

SELLING BIT

Hopefully IT can see the need and utility for the BIT team – but if one doesn't exist in your organization, it's likely because Business has not understood the need for one. How to sell it to Business? A sponsor – a believer - needs to debut the idea with its direct reporting authority first. A Business and an IT person can pair and best sell BIT to an immediate authority, who will in-turn sell it to the highest possible authority for sanction at the very top. Perhaps the biggest selling point to BIT is that it is, in addition to other things, a *mindset*. The BIT team will be about moving business forward. BIT will be proactive, prudent, positive and empowered. A successful sell, launch and exercise of a BIT team in your organization will not only make the managing of business better, it will change your organization's culture. We can predict this because we are going to do something with the BIT team that is unusual for many organizations. We are going to make it effective, efficient, and accountable – collectively, the team will account, and the individuals on the team will account.

We are going to ask for and engage everyone's best game. We're going to create a point of pride - and we're going to stamp this team with excellence. People are going to be proud of what this team produces, and people are going to hold their membership on this team in high regard. This is largely why, if you have a similar but less effective team in place now, you must sweep it away with BIT. BIT will have a discipline in attitude, subtle yet strong, that will sway the most negative players into a zone of increased positivity. Why? Because they will be required to engage that way when they participate on this team. That requirement will be delivered and backed by a power greater than the IT leader or any laterally situated Business leaders – that's for certain.

As we stated, the sale of the BIT concept must be made at the highest possible level, and you must receive sanction there. Once you make that sale, you will leverage your sale and explanation of the BIT team to the other players by having its debut and related importance communicated by that power. We are going to have the team's culture defined and sanctioned by the level of power in your organization that can require adherence to a set of principles, and dedication to good faith efforts. Thus, we create a zone within your organization's culture. It may be an island at first, or it may fit your organization's current culture reasonable well, but regardless its influence will be felt – and in more ways than one.

CHANGE: AN EASY SELL – A DIFFICULT BUY?

We can smooth the sale for BIT by defining and selling the benefits of effective change management – just as importantly, *we expose the rising risk and rising cost of ineffective change management* - in an overall world environment of accelerating change.

We can call change an easy sell because, if you think about it, you're going to buy some kind of change whether you plan to or not. Change is a default setting – you can't uncheck that box and remain static – in any endeavor. You're going to acquire change no matter what position you're in, and you'll either change as a reaction to other changes, or you'll lead your necessary changes. As the world at large is going to force you to "buy" changes, you want to buy (to identify, lead, and emplace) the best changes – you don't want any difficult buys. You must get into a position to leverage that default change dynamic to your advantage.

It is important to understand the environment that carries change to its successful destination. We can have the best BIT team in the world, identifying all necessary and correct change – but what happens if even prudent, appropriately sized, change is improperly managed? What if we attempt to change too fast? What if some elements of the organization aren't ready? What if BIT misses some important "where we are" factors?

We need a close interaction of Technology and Business within our Weave to ensure a basic understanding from both directions in defining, tracking and managing change. Further, this interaction goes beyond management and BIT: this involves the whole of the organization.

Therefore, we must have a basic understanding of change - in simplest terms, and from anyone's perspective…

5

CHANGE - THE BASICS

It must be remembered that there is nothing more difficult to plan, more doubtful of success, nor more dangerous to manage, than the creation of a new system. For the initiator has the enmity of all who would profit by the preservation of the old institutions and merely lukewarm defenders in those who would gain by the new ones.

Machiavelli

Change happens.

It would seem pretty obvious that change is a routine part of life. However, you wouldn't know this by observing some people. To them, change is an outrageous imposition. A bolt of lightening out of the blue. To them, when a rare occurrence of major change does come down the pike, it should be something that poses no special challenge, no obstacle to be overcome, and somehow those effecting the change should make it transparent to them.

Change is challenging – there's no getting around that. Under the best of circumstances it will involve everyone's best game – therefore, it is important to get everyone possible on board in support of the agenda for the change. For those who are determined to drag their feet, or even undermine the agenda (and there will always be those), you must be prepared to neutralize their impact. Certainly there are ways to work on negative people to bring them aboard, or to at least gain a measure of cooperation from them – and we will discuss those ways. But the larger the change, and the larger the organization, the more likelihood that you'll have people that will simply require outright neutralization. We'll define that later (it's probably not what some of you are hoping for).

Change must always support business, enhance business, and keep business current and moving. Change cannot, and does not have to, impede business –

either situationally, or through delivery of unanticipated harm. Remember too that outside change (change external to your organization) demands internal change. Because change is coming anyway, you *must* get on a footing to welcome it by being ready for it.

Also, we must gain an important clarity. Today's organization should keep foremost in mind that most IT-managed change (save for hard technical projects) has true origination outside of IT. Everything germinates through the conduct of business. A department may need a new module added to the organization's core business application to accommodate new business, practices, or regulations. You may begin or expand an e-Commerce initiative. Perhaps your organization needs a new e-mail system that supports more capacity, better security, and easier user administration. Even seemingly technically-driven episodes can have a business motivation. For example, a vendor may have a new release of software that requires immediate implementation for security purposes. In this case IT notifies Business of this upcoming implementation, and negotiates schedule and necessary support. We could view this as IT-driven change. But even here, we're really speaking about a business genesis; we're accommodating the business of the world's demands to our own business security posture. In other words, we're never really implementing software or dispensing change at some IT whim, or pure IT instigation.

A Basic View to Understanding Change

In examining a basic understanding of change, we're going to look at simple change that has a direct impact on Business, and the way business is conducted. That is, we'll leave aside for the moment the pure IT initiatives, as these should be transparent to business: updates to applications, networks, infrastructure, operating systems, the changing of Internet service providers, etc. These sorts of computer room, or backend, things certainly enhance business in important ways. But the model for handling change that we're going to discuss here is for use when changes affect large groups of users in your organization. That is, front-end change – stuff that hits the desktop and creates a challenge for Business. Change that influence people's *day*.

Also, we're going to qualify change as being appropriately sanctioned – approved in accordance with all other requirements. At the first sign or plan of a necessary change - be it major upgrades to core business platforms, or more mundane things such as rollout of new PCs, upgrades to peripheral shelf software, etc. - IT and Business must always review the organizational calendar for obvious times that don't offer themselves as good periods to support a particular change. It would not be good to implement a new e-mail system during the run up to the annual conference, for example. Talk to executive schedulers and key department heads; there is a wealth of information to be considered, formal and informal, regarding general schedules and burdens to the organization. Know the organization's general calendar.

Also explore those demands that may *not* yet be documented – we're back to knowing "where you are." Then, through the BIT team, further survey departments and discuss their internal calendars regarding their major activities. When determining where best to place change, be sure that you view requirements through the people prism. After all, the priority and goal is to serve business – not to impact business. People need, and are entitled to, a period of adjustment even regarding relatively small initiatives that affect them. They will need to adjust and size their attitude – managers will need time to inform their staff.

Sometimes certain business schedules can make allowances to accommodate implementations. It may very well be that IT will have to adjust because of some unforeseen cycle of business. It's a give-and-take. Also remember that departments aren't silos operating independently of all other departments (although occasionally they may try to operate that way). Elements of change will need to be negotiated between many departments, and there must be appropriate lead-time to allow for this.

For the IT leader, most change can be negotiated and driven from your participation with the BIT team. Whether change originates through a debut within the team, or needs are identified elsewhere and subsequently brought to the team, the BIT team should be where most of the sizing gets done. That is: negotiations, agreements, sponsorships, schedules, ownerships, identification of metrics, standards of delivery, etc.

A BASIC MODEL FOR CHANGE

Before discussing specific change, and how it is identified and sanctioned through requirements for fulfillment, lets build a simple understanding. This understanding also must precede a discussion of large-scale projects, and such things as project management software, and tools and metrics associated with complex change and its delivery. Let's first consider the *appearance* and *enactment* of change - in the simplest terms - to the organization and the individual.

We are going to put Business first in this discussion – where it belongs. The following two chapters will get around to the discussion of, first, a general plan structure in support of change, and second, the specifics of identifying needs, which in-turn drive specific change.

Here, we'll consider a very simple model for presenting change to an organization – to Business. Once we understand this model, we can keep it in mind; we find that even at the outset of the largest projects, with the most detailed plans and tools, there remains utility in this simple model. We can use it to anticipate and fulfill needs that are often overlooked.

The appearance of sanctioned change to any organization should come from this simple model:

1. Announce the change
2. Train for the change
3. Implement the change
4. Support the change

Let's understand this basic model so that we can employ it to its best advantage in support of your organization's change. This model is at the heart of the most sophisticated projects. Let's examine each point in turn:

Announcing the change: Barring security concerns, IT staff will have early knowledge of upcoming changes. Once a business decision is made to effect a change, the IT leader should alert the IT staff: they are the ones who will implement and support it, and in virtually any circumstance they deserve to know about it before general business staff. For this reason, IT staff must be held to a special standard regarding confidential business knowledge and change information. They must maintain a strict confidence in not allowing planning information to disseminate prior to proper announcements. A timely notification to IT staff is generally a natural communication within a closed IT staff meeting.

When announcing change to the organization at large, view the announcement from an individual staff person's perspective. Here, consider what your concerns have been during times of change:

- "What is it?" *What's changing?*

- "Why?" *Why are we doing this?*

- "When is it?" *How soon is this all happening?*

- "How will it affect me?" *Will my job change? Will I have more work? Will my work be harder?*

- "What do I have to do?" *Is anything required of me in advance?*

- "Will I know how to do what's required upon the change?" *Will I be trained? How will I stay informed? Who do I see with questions?*

- "What if something doesn't work?" *What if I can't do my job? Who do I go to with problems?*

Viewing concerns in an imaginative way from the other person's perspective can serve both IT and Business well when engaging the other. Further, by examining questions form an end-user's perspective, we can build a much better announcement and discussion regarding forthcoming change. In fact, early examination of these questions can lead to a better overall plan and implementation.

Initial presentations of change should be handled as face-time – as opposed to e-mail or memo notifications. An initial announcement of change can present a rough schedule for the change – however, detailed timelines with major elements such as training, user actions, and go-live dates can be presented later. Using a new e-mail system as an example, you want an initial announcement to get the concept of the new e-mail system on the table so that people can digest that, and give them a rough idea as to when the organization would like the change to be in place. For example: "end of June." Avoid getting too detailed in the initial announcement. Make it known that a memo will follow with more detail about training, user actions, and a firm schedule. We'll talk in detail about timelines, milestones, and project management in the next chapter, but remember that this initial announcement is the first that the organization is hearing about the upcoming change – keep it simple. Keeping it simple allows the organization to acclimate itself to the idea of the change. A simple presentation will be less threatening than a blizzard of detail and a lot of discussion.

Integral to the announcement of the change are the reasons for the change and how the change will lead to better business. A good forum for the aforementioned face-time is the organization's all-staff meeting. This serves a couple purposes: It obviously provides an opportunity for questions and answers. It also profiles the IT leader in front of the group – as an *organizational* leader. The change is accorded the appropriate importance; it takes its place on the organization's agenda, and is not seen as a sole IT agenda - or worse, an IT imposition. The IT leader should profile the benefits to be had (which helps to support the view that IT understands the organization's business), with a follow-on by a Business sponsor (showing an engagement by Business on technical issues and supports, and an understanding of their relationship to process). It is important that relevant supervisors, senior management, and sanctioning authorities and sponsors weigh in on the importance of change and why it is being undertaken. Particularly in the case of a powerful sanctioning authority, you help establish acceptance of the change on the part of the organization: Change is a one-way ticket, and you get onboard or get left behind.

As examples: If your organization has customers (likely), and is changing the customer management system (CMS), have one or two department leaders weigh in with the advantages of the new system from the business perspective. They can explain how the new CMS will facilitate better workflow, better manage and serve customers' needs, and improve delivery of timely business information. If your organization is redesigning its website to increase online sales, have someone from Business explain the changes and how they will facilitate the desired increase in sales.

You can plan these brief presentations in the BIT meetings. Try to show benefits of change to several areas of the organization or process – too often change is delivered as some obtuse requirement, and thus suffers the generic label: Imposition. Have a questions and answers period. Make it known that meetings and training will be forthcoming.

A follow-up correspondence to the organization with some details is also used in announcing the change. The memo should be detailed enough to answer most questions, but should be brief and stick to the main points. The memo should have a schedule of the major activities supporting the change; the memo should also reference forthcoming, periodic e-mails that will alert staff to necessary actions. When crafting this memo, ensure reinforcement of the original face-time announcement by writing it as if for someone who missed the meeting. This not only provides a reinforcement of information, but also takes care of those who were not present.

So, now the organization knows about the change, is aware of the reasons for it, and accepts that it's coming.

Training for the change: We'll talk about IT staff training in another chapter – we're still putting Business first - so we'll establish that IT staff is ready to support the change. Here we'll talk about user training - training the organization. Getting the staff ready for the changed environment must be completed before the change is implemented for any group of users. It's helpful to train not too far in advance of the change – users get complacent and forgetful if trained too far in advance. But, you should train far enough in advance to allow training to sink in - to give time for questions to germinate. Remember, your users will exit training and discuss it amongst themselves – they'll attend their own departmental meetings and begin to leverage their questions and concerns through this interaction.

Also, leave enough time and resource to allow a certain percentage of users a return-training engagement. Make allowance in advance for reinforcement training - some folks will need a return session. Also, employ the "train the trainer" concept where possible. Identify a strong user – a volunteer - from each department and turn that person into the department's internal resource for questions, answers, and informal one-on-one training. This person can even lead small group training. Find a way to provide recognition to these people: mention their good work in the all-staff meeting; send a letter of thanks to their supervisor; perhaps accelerate them on the schedule of new computer implementations.

Implementing the change: We'll talk about larger project management in detail in the next chapter; here we must understand some common guides for change. Essentially any implementation involves clear definition of duties and responsibilities, knowing exactly what to expect upon change, proceeding at the right pace, keeping everyone informed, and making allowance for fallback. Let's look at each of these:

<u>Definition of Duties and Responsibilities</u>: Make sure that each individual IT staff member understands their duties and responsibilities in implementing the change. Each person owns their respective piece of the project, and their success overlaps and supports everyone else's. For example, in the case of the e-mail change, there may be a schedule for users to delete unnecessary e-mail prior to a migration of mail from the old system to the new. Clearly define expectations and communicate these to the users with a date for having it done. Reinforce this requirement by communicating to managers what is required of their staff. For any upcoming change, have managers survey their staffs to make certain each staff member is in compliance regarding necessary actions. The structure for this can be negotiated and agreed to in the BIT meetings.

IT's responsibilities are generally well documented, and many common methodologies apply from change to change. Here, don't miss the fact that IT members are ambassadors for change during this period. That is, they engage with users in a positive manner when they are queried about the change. IT members support the change by promoting it as good for business. IT addresses concerns about challenges and reinforces the sale regarding the upcoming change. The positive tone is set by the IT leader within the IT staff meetings. IT enacts change in support of, and at the behest of, Business – once change is sanctioned and coming, IT is fully "in."

Know Exactly What to Expect Upon the Change: Ensure that the IT staff is ready for the support burden upon implementation (more on this below). Be sure that the Business staff, the user body, is ready: trained, comfortable, and fully aware of when the change takes effect and what's required of them. Make the users aware of their support options.

Proceed at the right pace: Be sure to establish a schedule that allows for the unforeseen. Each part of a larger change should be completely vetted before going to the next stage. Where possible and as necessary, test the changes in a test environment, and then transfer to your production (actual business) environment. Whenever possible, make an IT individual, and subsequently the IT department the first test of a change in the production environment. That way IT can get a direct feel for any problems and fix them before rolling the change to the next part of the organization. When ready to implement outside of IT, choose a specific, qualified user: Have them work in the changed environment so as to provide useful feedback to IT. We can call this person a LeadUser. If all is well, roll the change out to a small department, then to more LeadUsers and respective departments.

Keep everyone informed: Make timely communications regarding each phase of change. Business and IT leaders can make notifications – so long as they are coordinated, and not duplicated or opposing. Coordination, timing, and content of communications can be easily planned in BIT meetings. Many of these messages can be handled through e-mail. You want to steer the project and maintain your contact with the organization – but don't overdo it. Make sure communications are necessary – and clear. Group any small announcements that you can. When you have a major announcement or situation, don't dilute it with smaller, relatively inconsequential ones. You want messages regarding change to be seen as timely, as important, and as a necessary read.

You'll also want to provide updates at all-staff meetings when major projects are ongoing and spanning several months. Provide an in-person brief even if you sense a well-informed staff – in this case, be brief – but it is important to maintain change's profile (as well as those people who are managing it).

Make allowance for fallback: In any change you must plan for the worst outcome: that the change fails to deliver as expected, or just plain doesn't work. If this happens, you must fall back to the prior environment, or status, in order to maintain continuity of service. In the case of our e-mail example, you would put the prior system back online in order to maintain the organization's e-mail capability. Don't burn any bridges! You then have time to troubleshoot the new environment and plan another go-live date for the new system. In situations such as these, and assuming good-faith teamwork and best efforts, it is not necessary to dwell on failure or to make an overage of apology. In the proper Business-Technology environment, it will be well known that everything anticipatable was done to effect success – and that success will come.

Supporting the Change: IT staff is at the ready for support to change once it is in the business arena. The HelpDesk supports the new system or endeavor, obviously, but beyond, every member of IT should be in a special state of awareness, readiness, and service. Support also means sustaining a positive attitude regarding the change. The IT team must be seen as approving of the change – the change is good for business and the change has merit. There is no room on the IT staff for grumbling along with users as to why changes were made, or in complaining about new systems. IT supports positive change and seeks ways to bring users over the bridge, and into effective use of new technologies and systems.

Because the change supports better business, develop informal leaders amongst Business and develop a self-reinforcing weave. Too, sanctioning authorities and sponsors should maintain an engagement, and ask how things are going. There can be no fear of negative feedback here; exposure of inefficiencies, difficulties, or breakages must be made and dispatched.

A Users Group is ideal for this, and we'll talk about leveraging knowledge within the organization in a later chapter. For now, also remember that you can expand your formal HelpDesk activity with effective utilization of LeadUsers in your organization.

REMEMBER ~

Because change happens, we can easily see that it will happen with or without our engagement. For the appropriate view, realize that IT suggests, responds, partners on, rightsizes, and implements the appropriate solutions – but IT doesn't do this for its own sake. It's done on Business' behalf. When proper change comes to an organization from any source or motivation, it is important that appropriate departments and individuals help to make the sale, and to participate in sponsorship and support of the change. This awareness goes a long way to setting an appropriate Business-Technology Weave and associated culture.

For those charged with it, there is nothing more rewarding, and more perilous, than managing change. Therefore change can be exhilarating or anxiety inducing – it's all a matter of control. Control is power. If you've achieved effective sponsorship, set your sanctions, and established your authority, you should have some measure of power. Use your power to control and mete out change. Proper change always brings better ways to accomplish business. In these circumstances, change will be exciting, and a healthy Business-Technology Weave will welcome it.

6

PLANNING AND MANAGING CHANGE

What do you want to get done? In what order of importance? Over what period of time? What is the time available? What is the best strategy for application of time to projects for the most effective results?

Ted W. Engstrom

Change is a continuum. For the organization, something is continuously changing that affects it: change is happening within, and it is happening in the surrounding environment. All change must be weighed and assessed for impact, and there must be a ready posture for doing this. Too many organizations think of change as something mounted in a burst; "now we can rest." This is why so many organizations seem to take action at the back edge of the envelope, if you will: change for them is constituted as an addressal of problems under pressure-filled and even desperate circumstances. When change is mounted under pressure, there is usually a failure to fully survey *where you are*, therefore the route to destination is a broken one - reaching the destination is painful, inefficient, and sometimes not even achieved.

The smart organization doesn't disengage from change - nothing around them stands still if they do. Therefore, the management of change isn't just some reaction to what is happening internally, or some engagement that is forced by outside change. You must present a position of readiness, so that you have the muscle in place to exercise change. You must be able to forecast, develop, and schedule. This requirement for readiness presents itself to the individual, to groups, and to the organization in equal measure, as we'll see.

And now we need to realize and acknowledge that even *change* changes. How does change change? Consider: While we're busy implementing a documented, sanctioned change, some of our assumptions, support products, regulatory requirements, business practices, etc., haven't done us the courtesy of standing still. Further, various projects and their change can compete for common resources; they can shift in schedule and crash into one another; they can have interlocking dependencies and impacts that must be carefully coordinated. Any time you make a course correction, an accommodation, an expansion in scope, etc., you are making a change to change. Circumstances such as these, and the quality of planning in your organization, either yields a house of cards, or a solid structure of mutually reinforcing initiatives and projects.

Because things are shifting and evolving around us all the time, we need plans that have enough structure to guide us effectively, but that are not so rigid as to straightjacket us. We don't want to be implementing so-so or broken solutions today that looked great yesterday. We don't want the organization to be thrashing as it attempts to mount major changes without regard to prudent sequence, or that are even in direct competition with each other.

HIGH LEVEL PLANS IN SUPPORT TO DETAILED PLANS

From a high level view, we need to plan support to the Business-Technology Weave. High-level plans should identify, guide, assist, and facilitate that which you wish to accomplish. They provide the general documentation and a calendar position for a collective of projects and initiatives, the sum total of which represent the organization's forward thrust, and each of which have their own detailed, operational plans as separate documentation.

Aligning an organization's detailed plans, projects, and initiatives is similar to tuning a car: you want all of your cylinders firing in proper sequence and timing. When properly tuned, your car not only has maximum power in "getting to where you're going," it is making the best possible use of resources (in the form of highest gas mileage, and with minimal wear to the engine). Your organization's individual operational plans are like cylinders – each contributing to the organization's forward movement relative to time and circumstances. You must ensure that each of these plans fires in proper sequence, so as to assist the next plan – or at the very least not impinge upon it. You must get the collective of projects and initiatives making a concerted best-use of resources.

At the same time, the higher-level plan must have some flexibility in order to make allowance for an adjustment in schedule or direction. Yet, they can't be so ill defined as to provide no structure at all. And, we have to preserve order: an order in change, and the order of the organization. How do we effectively manage this trick?

IT'S ONUS

We've already discussed the importance of communication between Business and IT. And we know that it's wise today for Business to make known its planning and direction for early participation and contribution by the organization's technical investment. Certainly Business must facilitate IT's understanding of required support to business initiatives, evolving technology needs, and changing environmental factors (such as security, expansion, new regulatory requirement, etc.). But realize that whether this happens effectively or not, IT still exists for, at the pleasure of, Business. The onus is on IT to support, align with, and enhance Business' plans for business. IT must dig where and as necessary.

There is plenty of chance to do that, so recognize your opportunities: There will be the obvious occasion for plans' creation and adjustment within specific, formal, plan meetings – but also formally and informally in the course of budget meetings, staff meetings, board meetings, etc. The exercise of snapping them into focus happens largely in the BIT forum, and in specific IT plan meetings: but anywhere that there is a discussion of futures planning contributes to the overall opportunity to assess change, and to effect the gel of a plan.

Further, in a changing world, there is the onus on IT to hear everything as a weigh against possible change requirements.

THREE PLAN TYPES

IT's general support to the Business-Technology Weave can be effectively planned and managed through three major plan types. These are the high-level, across-the-board support plans – which acknowledge and mark the upcoming projects.

We'll refer to these IT-Business support plans as the *Five-Year Plan,* the *One-Year Plan,* and the *Individual Action Plan.* You may wish to label these plans differently in your organization; you may need to look further into the future with a ten-year plan – or more. But here we'll use these generic names for ease. Let's take a brief look at each plan type, how it relates to the other plan types, and how together they help maintain your adjustment.

The Five-Year Plan

The Five-Year Plan begins with the upcoming (next) calendar year, and extends through each of the upcoming five years. The upcoming first year becomes the organization's detailed One-Year Plan, upon the turn of that new year. Therefore, the first year of the Five-Year Plan should contain everything you intend to do in the upcoming year. Because the One-Year Plan is the near-term focus for what needs doing, it should be as detailed as necessary – it is executable in that it has been vetted and sanctioned, is budgeted, has been announced, and all preparatory steps have been taken for each element of the plan. It matches the organization's business expectations, needs, and overall business plan for the year. Also, the One-Year Plan spawns all of the detailed project plans and individual action plans as necessary for the organization's various managed projects and changes. The organization's overall project management benefits from the coordinated tracking on the Five and One-Year plans, as supports, dependencies and competition for resources can be adjusted in maintaining optimal results.

The Plan's Progression: Years Two, Three, Four and Five are progressively less detailed, respectively, as you consider periods of time that are further out from "now." Looking out to Year Five, we can see that in a year's time, its detail and plan moves into the Year Four slot; the former Year Four is now Year Three, and so on. At each turn-of-year, a new Year Five is added to the back of the plan. As each year of the *Five-Year Plan* marches toward you, it is massaged into better focus; adjusted according to changing business priorities or objectives; availability of resources; advancing technology; changing environment; and new methods and practices. There is an ongoing maintenance for the organization's alignment of business and technology. Eventually, our original Year Five clicks forward, having evolved and focused according to needs, until it moves into position as the One-Year Plan. In this manner, we find that a properly maintained Five-Year Plan can efficiently generate a comprehensive, executable, sanctioned, and aligned One Year Plan. This means that an organization's staff is fully informed and qualified to tackle the forthcoming changes, and changes align with business needs in fulfilling expectations accurately, comprehensively, and efficiently.

At any given time, we can expect that Year-Two doesn't have quite the focus or detail as Year-One - however, most major initiatives are known and a fair amount of detail is present. The more distant years will have large bullet items without a lot of detail, because technology and business factors change, sometimes radically, over a period of years. Your Years-Four and Five may even contain rather whimsical wish-list type of items, just to keep them on the radar. Your organization may have potential mergers or acquisitions under consideration, which will require different technology and business practices – these considerations can call for placeholders on the plan, ensuring some exploratory discussion and gathering of pertinent information. These efforts establish and define a "where we are," they project a "where we're going," and ensure the start of a bona-fide, progressive, route for future actualization.

The Plan's Direction and Flexibility: Planned items can go one of two ways: Some things become certified as bona-fide objectives, and additional detail is accumulated and added to the plan. Just as importantly, other things may be dropped due to a change in business priorities. Likewise, other things may pop on as completely new items. The flexibility of the plan means that you may bump back certain items over the course of a couple months, or even years - maintaining them as placeholders – perhaps until a return-on-investment threshold is reached. Other things may heat up and slide forward.

At the same time, the Five-Year Plan cannot simply be a receptacle for every crazy brainstorm or trendy practice that comes along. It must represent a managed plan that adheres to the true needs of the organization.

The Five-Year Plan (or any long range plan) also does something else that's very important: it should not only expose dependencies, but should also show vulnerabilities and strengths. For example, if your plan is to implement a new content management system in the course of the next few years, you may need to consider an upgrade to your hardware platform and infrastructure. Your plan may have to accommodate new fileservers and workstations, for example. You'll have a significant training and support burden. Once that decision is made, it may be evident that another project that was waiting for these upgrades can now move forward. The preparation and timing for implementation of many things will coordinate nicely through the plan.

Remember: As the first year of the Five-Year Plan becomes the current year, that part becomes the new year's One-Year Plan. The Five-Year Plan adds a year at the end of its range, is populated as necessary over the course of time, and all years are updated and tuned accordingly. A properly maintained Five-Year Plan not only means that you *know where you are*, and *where you're going*, but also means that you'll always have your One-Year Plan ready at the beginning of each year. In fact, you'll have one-year plans under development for each of the next five years. That is managing change as a continuum. Also keep in mind that you can project further if you feel you need to. Just remember to match your time and effort to the likelihood that a particular plan objective will actually be undertaken.

THE ONE-YEAR PLAN

A properly maintained Five-Year Plan means that your One-Year Plan is being worked on and readied not only in a near-term advance; technically, you've been working on it to one degree or another for five years! Again, this plan drops into place from the front of your Five-Year Plan. It outlines all of your major objectives for the year with just enough detail so as to present an efficient, informative overview of each objective. Items on the One-Year Plan are broken out and assigned to individuals and, as necessary, groups, to manage as projects for the larger endeavors and as tasks for the smaller initiatives. Hence each item on the One-Year Plan is on at least one person's Individual Action Plan; some items on the One-Year Plan will be on several individuals' action plans, as they will require a team, or project, effort. Group initiatives will show on the Individual Action Plans as a specified role and set of responsibilities for that individual.

THE INDIVIDUAL ACTION PLAN

Each IT staff member's Individual Action Plan is a roll down from the department's One-Year Plan. Each item on the One-Year Plan is on various Individual Action Plans, with expanded detail and specific expectations. Here are the actual projects, tasks, duties, and ownerships – indeed this plan is one of the most effective levers for getting things done. Sure, you've got goals listed in each of your employee's appraisals, and you may have a professional development document somewhere – these are generally filed away until a mandated annual review. But the Individual Action Plan is drafted and maintained by the individual IT staff member, and approved by the manager. It has projected dates for completion of items. It is reviewed quarterly at a minimum, and on an ad hoc basis as necessary. Items are marked as completed or pending as appropriate.

If an item is not to be undertaken - for example if something cannot be funded as anticipated - it is removed. Initiatives that were not originally planned, but which have been added to the year's objectives, are assigned and added to an appropriate person's action plan as necessary. A well maintained Individual Action Plan is a ready reference come review time, and makes the preparation of each employee's appraisal much easier – it also makes for great supporting documentation.

A current year's Individual Action Plan can also include items from any year of the Five-Year Plan. For example, a somewhat distant future initiative may need researching now. However, the Individual Action Plan is primarily a "get it done" document for achieving the near-term objectives of the coming year.

The "Who" of Getting Us There: Further, as we consider the importance of where we are, where we're going, and how we're getting there, consider the "who" of getting there. Who exactly is doing what? Within the organization, the Individual Action Plan is the ultimate setting, documenting, and control as to who is doing what.

LEVERAGING YOUR PLANS

Toward the middle and end of each year, a major focus shifts to year-one of the Five-Year Plan. It is now the upcoming One-Year Plan, and it should be on the agenda in the BIT meetings. It should be raised in budget meetings, all-staff meetings, and IT staff meetings: anywhere futures discussion and planning is happening. The IT leader must be sure to do a final survey of Business regarding all of their needs, real and imagined, and the various Business teams must vet and justify each. It is also very important for Business to make their own effort: to make needs known to IT on a timely basis, particularly as regards changing needs that evolve between formalized meetings or understandings. The fourth quarter of the year is a good time for IT's sponsor(s) to attend a BIT meeting or two. Getting everything on the table and identified as a "need," "want," and "wish-list" type of item is very important.

Once the year starts, remember that the current One-Year Plan is a living document. As the BIT team meets and issues are raised or fine-tuned, relevant items add to the plan and get tracked. Some items may drop. There should be very few surprises in a properly maintained plan environment. IT works within its supervision to make sure the BIT-developed and other work is on track with the organization's goals and expectations.

THE ONE-YEAR PLAN'S SUPPORT TO PROJECTS

As a One-Year Plan approaches actualization, specific items take shape as separate, defined, and detailed plans in support of managed projects. As the bulk of the work is viewed from a requirements standpoint and a budget perspective, and as work is discussed and balanced in terms of load to departments and individuals, it starts to become apparent what can be supported - and perhaps what cannot. In other words, the overarching One-Year Plan becomes fairly steadfast, and becomes a catalog of sanctioned projects and initiatives – pointing to detailed plans that are under development or ready for execution. As importantly, any delayed or disapproved work will be known to all participants – expectations and requirements are now being satisfied according to the *organization's* authority and sanction, with everyone's full knowledge.

REMEMBER ~

Any specific IT plan should have a match to a business plan or objective in the organization. The Five-Year, One-Year, and Individual Action Plans must support sanctioned business initiatives. IT's plans help to establish where you are, where you're going, and the route for how you're getting there. As importantly, direct responsibility is assigned through the plans; the specific "who" of getting you there.

Remember to leverage BIT and its agenda in support of managed change according to plan.

7

DELIVERY - PROJECT BY PROJECT

The art of progress is to preserve order amid change and to preserve change amid order.

Alfred North Whitehead

From a grassroots view, as we sight along the line where daily business is conducted, we can understand the importance for communication of upcoming change. We need to ready the organization for change. We must have an effective way to implement change, and we must support change. Hence the basic *Announce, Train, Implement,* and *Support* model. This helps us to preserve order amid change.

We can also see the importance for understanding and emplacing the general structures for near-term, longer-term, and individual action planning in support of change – the One-Year, Five-Year, and Individual Action Plans, respectively. In this regard, we're preserving change amid order – in other words, we don't allow ourselves to become complacent and rusty. Things are less likely to catch us off guard. We find that readiness keeps our change muscles toned – we don't allow ourselves to atrophy. This is necessary because, with or without our engagement, change is a continuum. Events, requirements, and motivators are streaming into our face.

Conversely, when we preserve change amid order, we're not really talking about conducting or experiencing large change at each moment in time – that would be a pretty good definition of chaos. But we're staying cognizant of, and ready for, all of the necessary changes that the organization will have to undertake as it identifies, schedules and plans to undertake them within the world at large. Being cognizant and ready is a way of "preserving" change. Being ready means that we can position any change to the organization's best advantage. Whether suiting the organization's larger schedule, its fiscal burdens, its availability of resources, or workloads of individuals, the optimal change has at its disposal the change-ready organization.

There will be increasing peril to the delayed, too-far spaced, and expensive lurches into the future that are characteristic in too many environments. Delays, whether due to fear, ignorance, lack of will…or just general procrastination, are increasingly dangerous. Whereas the future won't stop its sponsored change, we recognize that change is ongoing, comprehensive, and accelerative in nature. It must be handled for accurate delivery on properly sized, business case, needs – all the while preserving order. And so we come to "the project."

It may seem that we've put the cart before the horse here - all of this change qualification and management – with no germinating change in the first place. However, carefully evaluate your own feeling, and your organization's stance: If it seems this conversation's order is reversed, it is likely because your organization has an overly *reactive* philosophy regarding change. Certainly there will be times when you must react to things, but to serve the future effectively you must create, lead and control your change to be highest degree possible. You must be *ahead* of change – even when it is driven by outside influencers. In order to lead change you must have some measure of the disciplines and structures we've been discussing solidly in place.

The character of your organization will influence the project: the organization's size; its business; the number of concurrent projects; project dependencies; qualifications of staff; budget, and so on. These things will also influence your measure and selection of project tools; your assessment and mitigation of change's undesired impacts to business; and your assemblage of teams for defined projects. But any organization has very fundamental vulnerabilities and problems when mounting projects. We can safely say that all organizations suffer certain inefficiencies and undesirable impacts to business during any project's course: varying only by degree. We know things can *always* be better: In order to make best change to the organization, we must make positive change to *change management.*

For this, we must thoroughly understand the problems faced by projects, and the often unwitting contribution to problems by organizations and individuals. As we discuss projects, their general difficulties, and their improvements, we will see that the two most important elements in success (and failure) are: *project definition* and *leadership*. Keep these two things in mind as we examine common mistakes and misperceptions regarding projects. Assess your own organization's application of leadership, and measure your organization's project definitions. We will come back to leadership and definition after a thorough exposure of "bad." Exposing the bad in the face of projects is also key to where you are.

Don't Appliqué "Good" on top of "Bad"

Without a thorough understanding of common problems and their sustenance, you will drag "bad" along with your efforts to install "good." Too often the good is merely an appliqué on top of bad – something looks and smells good for a while, but continues to rot underneath. Eventually, the top layer is infected by the bad, and you find that nothing has really changed. This explains the failures of many reorganizations and shakeups – that is, the failure of their objectives – they don't go all the way to the true heart of the matter. In addressing the true heart of project problems, you must, again, know where you are. All projects and allied systems of management, no matter how good, have room for improvement. But particularly if your organization struggles with change, you must understand the "where you are" factors that are contributing to difficult projects. Therefore, be patient with a necessary, *thorough*, exposure of "bad."

Project management is a large discipline; we could devote the entire book to it. But most organizations have some familiarity with project management and, even for those that feel very inadequate in this regard, there already exist many fine books and references. If your organization's IT efforts need help surveying business, reviewing products, conducting a fit analysis, etc., there are many fine, fundamental guides. On the other hand, if your business elements have difficulty defining their business practices and subsequent needs, there are many gurus, self-surveys and assessment packets to ferret and expose what your organization is doing – or thinks it's doing. In fact, the amount of quality free material on the web is quite good. Therefore, projects and their management don't go awry for a lack of advice, tomes, detail, and tools. They don't even go awry for a lack of quality effort. So what precisely is it that can drive even the best intentions to frustration? Overall, we can pinpoint any project's vulnerabilities, risks, divides, and deferred success by understanding the requirements of the Business-Technology Weave. When an organization fails to adhere to the Weave's requirements, you cannot approach the modern standards necessary for best projects and change.

The General Project Requirement

As needs are identified or evidenced they must be acted upon: they must be serviced and met. If a need is big enough, comprehensive enough, and complex enough, it requires contribution from a collection of people - usually reporting to different lines of authority. As you would expect, these people and respective authorities are in both the technical and business areas of the organization, and some may even report beyond the organization. Delivery on a large need requires an occurrence over time. Arriving at this delivery entails a careful orchestration of people, schedules, and resources in managing a bundle of hierarchical tasks and sub-deliverables. Needs such as these may be debuted and exposed in your BIT sessions – driven by emerging markets, new products, changing technology. Or, perhaps needs have evidenced themselves through new regulatory requirements, or new demands from customers, members, or clients. Needs can also arise from shifting environmental factors, and the organization's emerging alignment to new risk.

THE GENERAL PROJECT "BAD"

Keep in mind that with project management - as in many other things - less is often more. Ironically, it is the over-management of the process that frequently blurs the project's objectives, as well as the project's actual standing: the taxing burden on participants as they pour effort into a zone of diminishing return. Too often a project employs competing tools, conflicting advice, and duplicitous standards of measure. More effort often merely means: more effort. Realize that it's not always the strength of your grip that determines success: even effort has a diminishing return. Overwork leads to mistakes, disruption of schedules, problems with morale, and burn-out. Over-survey of activity, riding people for results, or constantly looking over shoulders is counter-productive here too. Another way to think of it: You reach a point where you're squeezing a wet bar of soap - squeezing harder does not secure your grip; it does the opposite. Likewise, over-managing projects does not secure your grasp on the project or its success. It is the constitution of the "soap" that best determines the security of your grip (that is, the constitution of the project best ensures successful management to conclusion).

What happens when we've got the "wet bar of soap" equivalent of a slippery project? People find themselves laboring under a requirement to deliver on ambiguous demands. Report of real deliveries slows, so there is an over-survey of negligible progress – which is then inflated to show "advancement." This clouds the standing of the project, lowers standards of reporting on it, and opens the door to all kinds of busy-work. The output of busy-work can be all manner of graphs, charts, reports, and justifications. The inefficiency is not just in the generation of this material – someone has to spend time presenting it, and others have to spend time looking at it. This is usually so much fodder – it doesn't contribute to traction or results. The real traction in the *poorly* mounted project comes from painful exposure of ambiguity, the scramble to cobble together agreements under pressure and deadline, and constant realigning of the solution to each day's updated understanding of the main Need.

These adjustments mean that people within the project find that they have to run after other people in finding someone to handle exigencies and emergencies. There is simply no way to plan for unexpecteds to the same grade as expecteds; people begin to mire in escalating effort and cost as they realign the solution to the reality of business. "Settled" items require a resurvey and rescale of expectations. Too, frequently there is the juggling and reshuffling of schedules in trying to accommodate people who are supposed to be prioritizing their commitment to the project – but don't. Competition for poorly managed resources and people can mean that milestones, due dates, and critical deliverables are missed. Too often, the ultimate go-live delivery of a solution is missed. Sometimes projects completely stall and crash, as they are consumed by conditions of *runaway*. Runaway in this case would be escalating effort that is being directed at cleaning up mistakes, focusing fuzzy ideas, and fixing erroneous expectations, thus robbing the effort to move forward. Once the focus blurs between what should be past, and what you should be doing to advance, the project is in jeopardy.

Project Janitoring

In these circumstances, project managers become project janitors. Are you one? Are you someone who is turning a project manager into a project janitor? Poorly mounted projects can turn everyone involved into a janitor. This is certain: Projects that are managed on a janitorial basis are inefficient, and take too long. Projects that take too long hurt business. And projects that fail are very damaging.

The Project Janitor handle is a powerful one. There is certainly value in janitorial activity – no question. But that should not be the bulk of the effort in *managing*. Yet, this is what many people actually feel *is* project management: streaming identifications, slow-moving definitions, pop-up negotiations, and an awkward, off-balance set of ongoing cleanup activities. The project manager is thought of as someone who straddles difficult divides: bridging groups of people who don't often cooperate or even communicate with each other; mediating between groups who should be aligned; listening to and acting on complaints; and mopping up problems. All this, as the PM stokes the illusion that he or she is leading this comparative rag-tag effort in accordance with the disciplines of project management.

Because many organizations think that the *project as a whole* is meant to tease out details, or because they at least operate that way, the project's definition at its outset is not fully realized. There is a failure to understand "where we are." Without this imperative, solid definition of project, there is no hope for true project management or any efficiency in a project's sponsored implementation of change. Needs aren't fully exposed or understood: therefore it follows that expectations are lacking; agreements cannot be complete; true specifications have not been made; and the overall project clarity goes lacking. The result is the divide whereby a project's course deviates from the murky business case that is supposed to support it. If you're lucky, the project's assumptions and ill-fitted deliverables slowly tighten with the slowly focusing business need – until we achieve a "match." This is part of our understanding for why so many projects feel like an off-balance lurch and stumble – with an eventual arrival at the base we're seeking.

In the course of this lurch, many relationships suffer, and even become forevermore diminished. Your luck in this case is a final deliverable at the expense of a frustrated staff, damaged relationships, and a broken budget. The organization itself may suffer matters of impaired or diminished trust and credibility going forward. We're not only impacting a success culture in the immediate sense, we're driving the quality of the organization's culture down by setting and fulfilling negative expectations. The result: Every project will lurch out of the gate, with diminished expectations, dread, delays, an overage of cost, and at further expense to relationships and general business efficiency. The organization may even suffer a damaged reputation amongst the public.

The Danger in Divides

Poorly defined projects represent a divide between full understanding of need, and the exact methodology for bringing satisfaction to the need. As with most divides, other divides are spawned. There can be no real hope that responsibilities, schedules, resources, and "solutions" will be adequate: they cannot reflect the reality for what's about to unwind. When projects are poorly defined, they actually become a sponsor of competing "understandings," definitions, and requirements between people or groups. Because nothing fits together as effectively as it should, the organization spends a precarious amount of time putting things right along the way; now no one can do a proper job within the distracting pressure to deliver on objectives. This pressure compounds itself on a team effort. When project participants end up juggling parts that won't fit as desired, it becomes very expensive to re-engineering the project's components. This robs everyone's energy and momentum for ratcheting the project forward.

Let's look at some other impacts that you may not normally consider, but which are extremely affecting. In problem circumstances, the project's schedule, or timeline, becomes less of a guide and risks becoming something that makes everyone look (and feel) bad. Risk of mistakes rises as project participants scramble to maintain the cohesion of a managed project. Resurvey, overwork, and mistakes impact not only the project and project team, but they affect other business staff that has to over-engage on the project – crashing into their contribution in the daily business sphere. This all rolls up to a general organization impact – more effort, yet delay, and a necessary solution that is still in the distance. These circumstances will put you on the back edge of the wave – slip too far and you cannot possibly paddle fast enough to get back on the crest.

Soon, competition takes priority over cooperation as various units of the project attempt to protect their performance and solvency. It's important to note that people within the project labor mightily to present a positive picture of progress to stakeholders and "outside" eyes: senior managers, governance, the board, shareholders, clients, customers, members, etc. There can be peril in reporting problems on projects – which makes people hesitant to do so. This impacts the truthful assessment for status, and therefore helps to manifest further problems. This yields an intensification of the back edge, reactive, addressing of issues.

A HELPFUL ANALOGY

When we define a project, we can think of its support to change as being similar to those plans and schedules that support the construction of a home. We can well imagine the expense and frustration if we did not completely specify the home to be built, with all of our materials, contractors, plans, and schedules fully identified and defined. If our foundation is brick, we need to specify those bricks at the very beginning. We expect delivery of the bricks that we defined and ordered. If upon delivery of our supplies, we find that someone made errors or assumptions that do not reflect the reality of requirements, we begin the divide.

If instead of bricks of our size, someone delivered those of another, we must re-engineer the foundation, or burn time procuring the originally specified bricks. What would happen if, instead of hardwood flooring, we find that the desire (requirement) suddenly changed, and is now for carpeting throughout? Or, instead of a natural yard, comprising trees, lichen, moss and rocks – a lawn is now required. What if entirely new requirements were introduced, such as a pool and a guesthouse? In any of these circumstances, we suddenly need different expertise, different personnel, additional resources and budget. There can be no efficient project management. The project is being redefined as we go. Here we can see the need for accurate identification and delivery on each area of expectation, because they support another area or phase of the project.

We can go further with this analogy – such as knowing where we are. Is there a homeowner's association that limits our plans in the build of our new home? Are there hills that require special drainage for runoff of water during heavy rain? How will surrounding "where we are" factors affect the project?

PUSHING (REACTING) VERSUS PULLING (LEADING)

Managing a shifting project becomes something that is less leading (pulling forward the objectives), and more *pushing* (standing behind problems, and handling them on their back edge once they are in full sway and influence). When you pull (lead) anything, you have the advantage of pulling in the direction you have set (the one you've defined). It's easier – like pulling a wagon. Because you're leading the wagon, it is continually coming into the incremental positions you're pulling it into and through – known and desired positions. When you push something, you lose your advantage – it is much more difficult to steer. When we consider pulling and pushing in relation to people, we realize that we can best lead when people know what to do. When people know what to do within a defined project, they are constantly moving forward by virtue of this knowledge. From the leader's perspective, this represents a positive bias, and pulling people (and the project) forward is an effective achievement. The project manager is able to lead on an efficient, macro (vs. micro) basis. When the project is poorly defined, people aren't sure what to do, or they take mistaken action within their ignorance. In this circumstance, the leader must push people back into alignment, or push them forward by constantly collecting and dispensing knowledge that should have been better defined at the outset. Much like anything else, with project management you tend to push *toward* a desired destination (which is inexact) instead of pulling *into* a destination (which is exact).

Here we can provide two potent visualizations: one for the successful project, and one for the foundering project. Think of the successful project and its pull as a triangle: the point at the top is the ultimate project destination: a go-live date of a system, or a date for any deliverable. At the bottom of the triangle is the wide, diverse body of planning, initiatives, tasks, and incremental changes that gradually narrow and converge to success as you lead your efforts to the top – a point of successful conclusion.

Now think of the poorly defined project as one that is pushed along, with leaders' and participants' *reactions* providing too much of the effort. In extreme cases, this project looks like a trapezoid: wide at the bottom, and wider at the top! Everything is pushed, not into alignment, but into diverging lines of "progress" – teams within the project may even work at cross-purposes. You may have paths that cross rather than support: duplication of work and even effort that cancels other effort.

When we push, why do things tend to diverge? It's because people begin to compartmentalize; problems narrow individual focus. Problems focus attention such that a problem's particular fix may not integrate into the whole of the project. Now we start to see why so many project elements are done – and redone - and redone again. When you operate on the back edge of problems, the collective view forward is not clear: if there are enough problems, the view is completely blocked. The destination is now murky, as project participants actually reverse direction. Frequently, they have to go further back, to discover problems' genesis, and where each problem has impacted other areas. Obviously, the deferred advance toward a project's destination is not a prudent part of project management – as it is avoidable. Project management, and project performance, is about looking forward, moving forward, and reaching the forward destination. Moving back is not only counterintuitive here; it is simply the wrong direction. Now, this isn't to say that there can never exist a necessity to look back, or go back, in putting something right. No project will be perfect – but any sort of revisit activity should be minimal. If you're running a project as a janitor, and if you find yourself doing more pushing than leading, the project will be all over the place.

Therefore, when you lead fully defined project initiatives, you find that things line up because you and others pull knowns together toward a common point – the project's defined destination. You are also able to stand ahead of what's happening for a comprehensive view of your leading front, across the entirety of the project. You should be able to watch and monitor elements as they fit and snap into place, with minor adjustment along the way. Because your departure, route, and destination is known (the "where you're going"), your entire posture is biased toward the lead, your efforts are spent on the forward momentum - carrying you to the fore of the forward destination.

Turning the Project Corner: If a project's efficiency and success are set at the beginning, we can fairly ask: "What goes wrong so early?" And – "Why?" This is a pretty easy understanding to be had. We're back to some people's resistance to, and fear of, change. They only engage when absolutely necessary, and often on a half-hearted basis. We also know that everyone is busy, and often times a project is not a welcome intrusion to the routine. Many people with direct assignments and tasks are not fully engaged at the outset of the project. Too, people can view the planning and defining phase as something other than "the real project" (but only if the organization lets them). There is sometimes an unwillingness to hold people accountable to the project to the same standard as their daily activity. The emphasis is on the day-to-day, where natural attention falls because we're focused on the present: we occupy the present.

Therefore, know now that there is an increasing necessity to hold people accountable for the effort and value in their futures planning and delivery. Not just the leaders: This will become a high profile requirement of *everyone* in the modern organization, sized according to their specific role and whatever authority they may exercise. We will examine this requirement further in *Managing People in the Weave*, but the sense is essentially this: For each jobholder, define and set the expectation that they will help pilot that job into the future in accordance with our understanding of change. The aggregate of these efforts and awarenesses will set a collective forward bias in your organization. This awareness and effort in service to the future will then be well emplaced in your culture, leading to a natural support and readiness for projects. This natural support mounts the view that projects and change are a part of business, as opposed to an intrusion to it.

GOOD PROJECTS MAKE THINGS BETTER;
POSITIVE COMMUNICATION MAKES BETTER PROJECTS.

At your project's conception, you'll have many clues as to the successful definition and mount of the project. The preliminary quality of communication and effort between Business and Technology should be one of enthusiasm. As the project engagement between Business and IT is defined (the who and the how – think BIT), the team must expose needs accurately, slay ambiguity, match solution to expectation, gather commitment, assign and *acknowledge* responsibility - and shape not only the project, but also the project supports. Note that the poorly defined and overlooked things will create expanding deviations over time. (It's not so much the metrics, the measures, the tools, the reporting, the attention to issues, etc. Those things force themselves, if nothing else). Remember that unexposed divides - between project definition and business reality - rarely fail to yield a disproportionate effort in closing divides that ride - and get wide. These divides generate inefficiency, instill confusion, and rob the forward momentum of any project. They require an expanded effort in closing them, making people prone to mistakes, or errors in judgment: risky short-cuts become more attractive in these circumstances. The focus goes to closing divides in the schedule, instead of to the quality of the underlying work.

Most project problems are not necessary – from the high-level business view, they're primarily self-inflicted wounds. Therefore, do not fail to expose all needs, accurately. Understand *where you are* at the project's beginning. (An understanding for where you are is a requirement that serves the Business-Technology Weave at-large; lacking this understanding in the face of projects is indefensible). Be aware of some perils: lacking this large understanding in support of the project realm, the divide between where you really are - and the point from which you're actually leaving - means that you'll almost certainly craft a false route to your anticipated destination (the project's delivery on the objective). Bear in mind the additional divides between all of the incremental needs, expectations and deliveries. Each divide will push laterally across the project, and cascade through the project's projected course. Thought of another way, problems touch and begin to compact themselves into snowballs – and the snowballs will compact into snowboulders. They crash against milestone dates, and bump them back. You may not readily see how an issue Y affects an issue X – until they surface, combine, and leverage.

BE QUALIFIED TO LOOK AT YOURSELF

In fact, the unqualified organization cannot see or predict the damaging, interwoven, yield. Organizations that don't manage change and projects well generally don't know that they lack focus – that's the best that they're seeing at the moment. They believe that their foggy picture of themselves is the best resolution to be had. But - it's similar to our view of a 36" television: great picture. Until we saw HDTV. Organizations need the "HDTV" granular detail of *where they are* if they hope to define, mount and conduct projects in the best way possible: with an efficient, reality based, route to success. That ultimate success is a properly sized solution at the destination of the project's conclusion.

It can be hard for many organizations to see themselves as they really are. Projects are always launched to make something better, so there's usually some discomfort, lag, or even broken process in the mix. You must identify any instance of non-cooperation, inefficient process, and breakage. If you don't, a new project won't fix your real problem. You're back to appliquéing good on top of bad. This can yield two fundamental, ultimate project divides:

Ultimate Project Divides:

>1) The yawning chasm between the solution's original delivery date, and the one that actually happens,

>- and -

>2) The divide between the solution you need, and the "solution" you get – or in extreme cases, the "solution" that is abandoned.

Today, the flat-out unaffordability of missteps is evident – but unaffordability is quickly assuming a new definition: one of peril to business existence. Virtually anything that your organization does in the conduct of business is supported by technology. Therefore, the qualified organization must look at itself from the business and technology perspective – and effectively meet at the table of improvement. It can do this by tasking project participants, business stakeholders, and any individual of standing to bring at least one, but hopefully more, improvement(s) to the table that *they or their department need to make* in support of better business (and in leveraging the project's delivery).

This aids in establishment of a positive, forward, bias on the project. Realize that in any circumstance, everyone in the organization has a theory about what someone else's culpability and contribution to problems is when things are less than optimal. This essential nature won't change in the loom of a project. There's usually not enough self-reflecting before communicating at the common table of project definition and launch. Therefore, the Project Manager should task everyone at the project's outset to define an area for improvement that is central to them, their department, their work – and to bring their solutions and commitments for bringing improvement.

An Association's Experience

We can consider an actual association, which was in dire need of a new association management system (AMS). Upon implementation of their last AMS, they had failed to survey and define their real requirements. They had mounted a project that delivered an AMS of limited service and support to business. They had been living with the results for several years.

As time moved on, and as business grew, their AMS became increasingly inadequate. It couldn't be scaled for growth. Searches for information were taking too long. The application had a poor flow – too often one had to "back out" of one business process to reference necessary information elsewhere in the application. After either printing it or writing it down, a user had to then restart the original process. At the same time, the vendor had fallen on hard times, and the product was poorly supported. The AMS' product suite was no longer growing and aligning to even general business considerations. Customizations to the core product were increasingly exorbitant.

Whatever the reasons, we can see that an upcoming change in AMS is a major project affecting virtually every department and person in the organization – and all lines of business. The general system tracks membership, maintains member demographic information, triggers membership renewal notices, maintains benefit levels, manages sales such as subscriptions to publications, sales of educational material or courses, provides reports and statistics, helps the organization identify and enter new markets, interfaces and delivers information to the accounting system, and essentially tracks and manages all business for the association.

In managing an effective Business-Technology Weave, we would want to avoid the selection of systems lacking service and longevity (an ability to remain in the market, as well as an ability to serve business). A new system needs an overall ability to adapt to new operating systems, new scales of hardware architecture, and new interoperability with other emerging software products, etc. It also means an ability to grow with us; we want solutions that effectively support our ever-changing business on a long-term basis.

Why Projects Really Suffer or Fail

In these circumstances, however, we should realize that project management does not, generally, fail. *Projects* fail. This is an important realization: Nothing that is ill defined or poorly constructed can be effectively managed to success. *You have to have something worthwhile to manage.* Therefore, it is a project's very *definition* that is at the crux of success or failure. Or - any measure of failure, such as inefficiency, costliness, or incomplete fit.

For those who manage the project managers, you must understand the parity of the following necessity: you need the ultimate in project management, and you need the ultimate in project definition. So for that association, for anyone, let's make life easier.

DEFINE. YOUR. PROJECT.

When we define projects, it's important to understand a comprehensive requirement for projects' definitions: we're not just articulating, examining, and defining a business need. We're defining the support structure for managing and executing the project, within a defined situation (where we are), and a defined destination (where we're going; our project objective) and the project's defined course (how we're getting there).

Think of any project's definition as the foundation upon which your project rests. Nothing will succeed or stand on a weak foundation; therefore your project definition must be as strong as you can possibly make it. It will serve as the understanding between all parties regarding business expectations, participation, objectives, and final results. The project manager drafts the project definition, but all key participants in the project provide input, and the definition is an agreement between all relevant parties, sponsors, and stakeholders of the project – it's like a contract. It's also like a Constitution. Imagine questionable areas, ambiguities, and even personalities raising questions, during the project's course. Now imagine referencing your Project Constitution for answers and interpretations – *that's* the definition you want to build. As with all content, a proper project definition can be leveraged for future projects – it sets precedent; it provides illumination for what worked and what didn't,

Consider and define these elements when defining any project:

- Project name: The project needs an official name. It should be descriptive, but short. Think of it as the project's brand name – it should be attractive, in some sense.
- Project statement: Create a sentence that describes the situation being addressed and its resolution.
- Project Description: Create a brief narrative of the background leading to the project, and the project's context and goals. (Think of *divides*, the *closing of divides*, and *a projection through and past the hard project – to the ultimate, ongoing, benefit to the organization*).
- Solutions partners (vendors, contractors, products)
- Risk and management of risk
- Project manager
- Project sanction and sponsorship
- Project team/organization
- Responsibilities, assignments and tasks: expectations within the project, and for other staff and the organization at-large

- Objectives
- Deliverables
- Timeline: start, schedule, finish
- Resources/support requirements
- Budget/Costs
- Related requirements: dependent projects; infrastructure requirements; the overall organization schedule of activities and events; etc.
- Surveys
- Measures
- Reports

You may know of other areas in your organization that impact your project: make certain to define and attain the relevant agreements on any areas that can impact the project, or that need the project's addressal.

The sponsorship, sanction, leadership and confidence in the project – and therefore its ultimate success – spring from proper project definition. The project is already a success or failure the day you begin its implementation. The project's efficiency is already determined the day you start it. Your solution is either both aligned and fitted, or not - the day you finish your definition and plan. Proper project definition stems from everyone's best game. This is where the BIT philosophy is leveraged, as you want everyone on a "moving business forward" engagement – projects don't have time to waste. Let's weave in an understanding of the upcoming *Success Culture*: Your organization has either established the larger disciplines surrounding any effort (such as the bars for performance, achievement, excellence, quality, and success), or it has not. Your project is birthed, lives, and concludes in the sway of your organization's overall culture and expectations.

It is also important to understand that a project's definition, and all that is contained within it, must unambiguously define all that is expected from the project – and define what is expected from project participants and general staff. We can easily see here the necessity for a Business-Technology *Weave*. The weave itself is a need and fulfilled requirement that precedes all others. It is a necessity for matching all subsequent business needs and expectations to business solutions.

When defining projects, think about what will *constitute* them. We spoke of a Project Constitution – and why not? This goes beyond the mere "what are we doing, why, where, who does it, and when?" - and establishes standards, values, rights, authorities, and appropriate paths for resolution and accomplishment. Remember - your particular project constitution will be partly dictated by your organization's culture, and how effectively your organization manages in general. Your project constitution should bear some earlier things in mind:

- Understand the people – know their capabilities, their strengths, their weaknesses:
    - IT staff
    - Business leaders
    - The user body
    - Senior management

Here too it is helpful to examine the "Where You Are" and "Where You're Going" review from Chapter Three. Consider the aspects listed there, and apply them to your project definition as you deem fit. The important thing is to leave no area unexposed – at least examine these aspects and, as necessary, add them to your project definition and identify all detail and support as necessary – in constituting and defining your project. If you're able to define a project according to the organization's true need, in accordance with true sanction, and in alignment with a few important sponsors, you are in a position of strength. Once the strength of your project is defined, you can then load that project into any of those wonderful templates and tools that are available.

STRENGTH

We can close a divide by considering any vulnerability as an opportunity – an opportunity for strength. By adopting this view, we readily expose these areas for positive potential (at the same time, this outlook brings a "moving business forward" approach to them). When we examine the environment for vulnerabilities, we can present the vulnerability to decision makers in a powerful way: we not only show the strength to be had, but we should be able to articulate the risk in allowing a vulnerability to remain. Particularly in cases where a vulnerability impacts a pillar of the project, you should be able to indicate to the decision maker a balanced assessment of risk. But the ultimate aim is to close the divide as you drive toward the positive in outlining what is necessary to turn this vulnerability into a strength.

We've discussed the liability and vulnerability of poor project definition, and the strength to be had from solid project definition: We know that we must have something worthwhile to manage. We should know now that the worthwhile project requires worthwhile management. It requires leadership: Beyond definition, the modern project's other main vulnerability is a lack of leadership.

LEADERSHIP, LEADERSHIP, LEADERSHIP

Just as we understand real estate's three most important factors - location, location, location - project management's factors can be thought of as *leadership, leadership, leadership*. As an otherwise great property can suffer in a bad location; an otherwise great project can suffer from poor leadership. And, as an otherwise diminished property can benefit from a great location, a poorly defined project can benefit from a great project leader. In these limited pages, we can effectively address virtually any organization's project challenges by helping you to identify and emplace the *right project leader (or leaders)* as matched with a proper project definition (and the right sponsorship and sanction, of course). We can then outline and bullet some high level concepts for the attention of your leaders. The right project leader can do many things for us, but here in these pages we will rely on a project manager (PM) to *define* the project properly, to take advantage of existing guides and practices in *leading* the project to success, and in helping all participants maximize their contribution along the way.

When we establish leadership for a project, we not only require the obvious PM, and any other necessary project leads, but the project itself must have the weight of a larger, sanctioning, authority. This sanctioning person, or body of people, will represent sponsorship as well. But unlike other sponsors who merely facilitate the project's forward momentum, and contribute to the goodwill surrounding the efforts, this authority has *power*. For most organizations, this means an Executive Director, a President, a governing council, a Board, etc. For any size of endeavor, there must be a trumping authority above all others who are within the project's influence. An overarching authority must express their engagement and belief in the project – as sanction – and it is helpful to express that commitment on a regularized schedule (such as during monthly staff meetings).

This authority must also understand the project's definition, obviously, and have some measure of understanding for the project's structures and supports. It is their responsibility to do that as the ultimate project sponsor. When the organization throws its full weight into the success of the project, no one can hold back "in case this thing doesn't go," or because they harbor a selfish agenda that can jeopardize the project's success. Later, we'll talk about the IT Enlightened Organization, which qualifies senior-most authorities to help vet projects and solutions, so as to have their own *self*-assurance in committing their authorization and leadership to these endeavors.

From a project point of view, too often projects and their leaders seem orphaned or abandoned: it becomes difficult to garner engagement, and the project comes to be seen as an interruption to work. All projects are a part of work, and their priority should be known and respected. The "leadership" and "best effort" components to defined projects is another self-reinforcing Weave, and is necessary to conduct and conclude successful projects. The project has to be saleable, and sold, to everyone involved – not only direct project participants, but to the whole of the organization. The organization must believe in it. Our later discussion in *The Success Culture* helps here, and it can certainly be helpful at this point to jump ahead to that chapter, and return. But for now, we need senior-most management clearly conveying their sanction of the project, and sponsors must be known, engaged, and setting the example. Leadership, as defined within the project, means powerful, committed, and believing authorities that will drive all other leaders and lesser authorities toward the project's successful conclusion. As we get to the project manager's level, we see the necessity for a strength of position: We can easily see that a project leader has to *qualify* to fill that position.

THE PROJECT MANAGER

If we've defined a project, we should be able to believe that an effective leadership will align effort and deliver success. Projects demand a special kind of leadership, so let's discuss the special qualifications of the Project Manager (PM). These qualifications extend too to the entire project team, and it is the PM's example that helps to develop and maintain an overall project character. The PM is a person with solid qualification, but as importantly, is the kind of person who will quickly add to her or himself what's necessary to be qualified for any aspect of the project's management. As no one can know everything, it is important to select a PM with impeccable self-start ability, and a capability for learning quickly. The right PM will emplace the necessary success factors to all areas of the project.

Consider that implementation of the new association management system. Obviously the implementation of a new AMS, and the transfer of the history and daily conduct of business to the new system, is a challenging endeavor. It involves a lot of people, and lots of sensitivities. It will require effective communication at all levels of the organization. Just as importantly, the project's sponsors and leaders must manage perceptions and emplace their version of reality – one that reflects the actual status of the project, and one that incorporates excellence in all phases. Here too our greatest challenge will be the people – Technology and Business staff alike. Project management's main efforts will be communication and the coordination of schedules, knowledge, activities, and resources. In these regards, the objective is to leverage and maximize a collective human effort in delivering a solution.

In extremely large endeavors, some of which bridge organizations, agencies, and outside solutions partners, a very large team will be involved. But whether extreme-scale endeavor or basic project you need people with certain, common, strengths of character. For this reason, we can start with the attributes of a good project manager. Everyone associated with the project should have these qualities – but the project lead's character *must* harbor these traits in very strong measure, as this lead will be expected to set an example, and also to surmount any shortcomings in the technical or business realm with civility, tact, and result.

Recognize that business systems, even shelf applications, are very sophisticated and complex today. The expected deliverables from these systems is increasing, and the reliance on this fulfillment is sometimes overwhelming organizations and their staffs. The planning, selection, sizing, customization, management, and maintenance of these systems – *as an appropriate fit to business* - is an art as well as a science. Finding the right people to address the burden in effectively matching these systems to business requirements is imperative – therefore, you must not "under spec" your PM.

THE ATTRIBUTES OF A PROJECT MANAGER

The efficiency and success of any project requires a lead person with these leadership attributes and abilities:

- Patience
- Judgment
- Communication Skills
- Seeks Responsibility
- Takes Ownership
- Gets Along with Difficult People
- Can Handle Pressure
- Has Technical Knowledge
- Has Business Knowledge
- Stays Informed
- Possesses Sound Judgment
- Knows How to Push
- Knows When and What to Delegate
- Knows When to Seek Help

- ♦ Is Proactive
- ♦ Follows-up

If you get the right manager for a project, you're 90% of the way home. If that seems an overstatement, think to projects where you may have had the wrong person managing. If that's happened to you, you know how costly that can be. This chapter can help you identify the best person for project management (and by extension, the project management team), but no less importantly, this chapter helps you to groom that person through the identification of what can be expected of them and the requirements they'll be asked to fulfill. If you are a PM, consider these attributes in depth and relate them to project management:

Judgment: For extremely large projects in large organizations, or projects that are spanning and influencing different, yet aligned, agencies, there will be almost a diverging set of priorities here. Project stakeholders that are well above PMs, and those who provide report of survey and measure of progress to even higher authorities, will have a heavier political and diplomatic approach to project progression – frequently at the expense of hard realities. Individuals at very high levels soften focus and often buffer their communication at the expense of the message that best serves the project. These situations require a very tight tether between those high level leaders, and those who are dealing with the realness of aligning and progressing the project.

Under these circumstances, those in the direct realm of the project square should not succumb to an overage of political sensibilities – the "politicians" can soften and blur, but you must ensure that they are doing so with full knowledge of any risks and possible project penalties that can arise; such as when hard and fast issues and need for settlements are not effectively addressed. The PM's judgment here must be finely tuned, so as not to create false alarm, but yet focus attention where it needs to be: to highlight the gaps between true attention, action, and results.

Having said that, we can keep this relatively simple – any project manager, at any level, is going to employ judgment in a variety of disciplines and circumstances, no matter the project. Unless you're willing to have someone running to you seeking your guidance for each nuance outside the ordinary, or seeking your approval for that which is going to be done anyway, find someone with judgment. Someone who possesses good judgment will have confidence. Confidence is contagious, and the PM should radiate confidence.

The PM will employ judgment when assessing the success of each project element, and whether it is prudent to progress to the next step. Very importantly, the PM is going to choose, or assist in choosing, the project management team.

The PM will be employing judgment when choosing people for assignment of tasks and delegating responsibilities. Not only must the PM judge people according to who can best handle an assignment according to education and training, the PM must posit tasks and responsibilities in accordance with workload. The project requires a delicate balance of all resources.

At the same time, the PM must keep everyone informed: The PM must judge information regarding the project and separate that which is newsworthy from that which is routine – and report accordingly. Therefore, another area of judgment involves cases where the PM has to go up the line to get an overarching authority to facilitate movement on the project. The PM must know when to seek out this authority, and must also keep her or his supervision and sponsors informed. The PM must understand balances of power, and political sensitivities – or at least be able to suspect where these things lie, so that they come to you for guidance at the appropriate times.

Patience: The project manager must have an abundance of patience – in fact, patience in excess of the demands of the project. Look for the person that does not make it a habit to complain. The PM must never lose his or her "cool." Never. It's been said that a bad first impression is only overcome through six subsequent positive episodes. Some feel that a bad first impression can never be overcome. In the challenges of a project, one moment of anger, even one episode of negativity will not only impact the PM – it will cloud the project in a degree of negativity that we don't need.

The project manager will be the anchor – the person to whom everyone else looks to for confidence. This person will provide the assurances that the project is moving along, that obstacles can be and are being overcome, and that expectations are being met. The PM will always rotate any problem to present the plan for solution, and will remain in control regarding outcomes. That way, regardless of specific challenges, the rest of the project team, peripheral players, and the organization will have nothing but confidence that the PM will surmount all problems, and that the project will succeed. It's that simple. It may not be easy, but it is that simple. The PM really becomes the living embodiment of the project. Recognize that this makes the PM the target of criticism and the recipient of complaints. Therefore, this person cannot take things personally, and must maintain a business perspective through all challenges. Select this person and groom them such that *nothing* knocks them off their base. If you are the PM, become this person.

Communication Skills: The PM must be selected for an ability to speak to different audiences, or ears. In other words, the PM must talk to different groups in their own language. Remember that this person will be speaking to non-technical business representatives, the IT team, vendor PMs, the vendor's technical teams, and on occasion upper management. The PM will also be doing a lot of listening. Make sure this person is able to listen completely, and to digest what is being said. The PM will be listening to all sorts of people who may not have good communication skills themselves, but who are nonetheless important to the project – therefore it is incumbent on the PM to listen and to ferret out the important information. Also, the PM must be able to weigh the quality of communication between others, to ensure understanding in all directions. The PM must also gauge that what she or he is communicating is accurately understood. Verbal acknowledgements and nodding heads mean nothing without the PM's complete satisfaction that everything is properly understood all around.

The PM will be collecting business requirements from business members and translating those to the project team for vetting and for crafting of solutions. The PM will also be translating technical matters and requirements back to business staff in the course of testing and delivering on expectations. In this diverse mix, it is more than likely that the PM will provide or assist in status presentations to staff, management, and possibly board members, governance, and other oversight committees. This person must know when to speak, the degree of detail or brevity required by the audience, and what to convey. No less important, the PM must be able to control and steer conversations. Where a meeting or an agenda starts to drift off-topic, or into non-productive areas (such as over-plow of the same ground, or the airing of ungrounded fears and consequences), it is time for the PM to exercise some discipline in bringing the discussion back to the positive. Again, remember our question: "Does this move business forward?" A "no" answer means the PM must bring the conversation back into the zone of productivity. Far from being merely smart, or articulate, your PM needs a comprehensive balance of communications skills.

Takes ownership: The PM owns control of the project – this person has a vested interest in the successful outcome of the project, and in the successful management of the project to meet stated expectations. The PM believes in their own expectations, such as the achievement of milestones by expected dates, cost control, and ultimately an on-time delivery of the business-ready solution. The PM also steps up and assumes ownership for ambiguous tasks, or steps in and identifies a delegate. Nothing languishes and all variables are identified and assigned for identification and solution.

For example, let's say that within our new Association Management System project, the senior director of the Expositions department needs to identify finance codes used for her department; these codes help track revenue and expense in relation to conference booths, hotel rooms, and services, etc. Subsequently, the Chief Financial Officer needs to approve the codes. The IT department can then test them. Ultimately, Expo will have the authority to edit and configure their own codes.

The project manager has asked the Expositions director to create the codes, submit them, and to meet with the CFO and PM by a certain date in order to have an approved set of codes ready for IT's input. However, the Expo director has failed in this task, missing several adjusted dates for completion. It is now incumbent on the PM to make this happen by setting a meeting for these two and ensuring that they do actually meet and hammer out the codes. It matters not whether the Expositions director has valid reasons for missing the assignment or not. It matters not whether the CFO has made himself available for consultation as requested.

It is the PM's responsibility to move the process along in ensuring that the codes get created for input. Regardless who owns each incremental task – the PM is the ultimate owner and will answer to each success.

Knows when and what to delegate: This area lies very close to the project manager's overall level of judgment. The PM, in conjunction with the appropriate manager, must delegate tasks and requirements not only according to what is *appropriate* to delegate, but must delegate things in accommodation with the *resources available*. This is very important, so let's break it down. First, appropriateness: The PM can only delegate that which makes sense. Keep efficiency in mind. Don't delegate something to a person who will require more of someone's time in shepherding them through a process than if you simply delegated it to the "shepherd" in the first place. (An exception to that would be in the case where the shepherd is in a training role – but many project initiatives, and many projects themselves, are not the best situations for training).

Be certain that delegates are qualified by knowledge and experience – that's obvious. But keep in mind too that delegates must possess the requisite confidence and judgment. No less important is the balance of overall work: the PM must ensure that some are not overtasked, and some under. Keep in mind that inefficiencies ripple out... inefficiency is seldom contained. It spreads and steps on others: any body that has to do anything to overcome another department or person's inefficiency becomes less efficient themselves. Determining where this ends is difficult – just whack inefficiency at its source.

An example of an appropriate delegation might be as follows: The PM has determined that test-data has been migrated into an order-entry module of the AMS in a test-environment. The data supports the order history for products purchased by members. There is now a requirement to run reports on the test-data to show that the data in the test-environment reflects the actual data in the production system (the system that will be replaced). The PM can delegate these reports production to an appropriate IT staff person. Once IT has verified the data and the performance of the module, the PM should also task a business person to review various member records for accuracy in the test-environment – and indeed must do this in order to receive a sign-off from business indicating that the data is acceptable. Where appropriate, business staff can also run their own reports, and should check data in the system to their own satisfaction.

The PM must also delegate according to resources available: We have a task that needs to be delegated – who has the knowledge, time, and necessary access to other resources? Here is where the *when* as well as the *what* comes into play. Hopefully the PM has built an appropriate timeline that makes effective use of everyone's time. Things that can happen in parallel do, and elements of the project that depend on other things are sequenced properly. The PM may have to wait until an appropriate person's schedule opens up to handle a task or requirement. The PM must not overburden delegates, and must balance the load –dispersing it amongst individuals *and* dispersing it over time.

Is not afraid of responsibility: A good project manager enjoys having responsibility. This person takes pride in knowing where things stand that are under his or her purview. They ensure that things are accomplished according to standards and on time. At the same time, they perform their direct duties and tasks to the same standards: production of status reports, scheduling of meetings, publishing of agendas, etc. Because project management involves a myriad of things in various stages of development, this is the type of person who can flex… someone who can ramp up to the exigencies of the day. Also, emergencies are handled with the same balanced behavior. Whether it be a bad data conversion that needs to be reconverted, a meeting that needs rescheduling, an adjusted date for completion of a major milestone, the PM takes it in stride as a part of business, rather than as an exception to business. Within project management, the *non-routine* is part of the routine. The PM knows this, accepts it, and embraces this as part of the job.

Gets along with difficult people: This is of critical importance and may seem obvious – but in large-scale implementations things can get testy. There is almost an exponential increase in the risk for misunderstanding and friction as you increase the number of people involved in any endeavor. Therefore you must *manage* and *control* to limit this risk. The PM must always be seen as the measured voice of calm in any situation. The PM is the go-to person for all concerns, problems, answers and solutions – their credibility must be solid. The PM is one of the most important constants in the project.

Difficult, or unreasonable, people can be handled in a variety of ways depending on circumstance. Some ways to work with, through, and where necessary around difficult people are discussed in the chapter *The Criticizing of Excellence*. For now, remember that any conversation with any person involved anywhere near the project is always positive on the side of the PM, with a steerage back to the business at-hand, and an eye on solutions. Any objection that cannot be overcome by the PM's limited authority will be politely escalated, through an identified channel to handle any episode – as we'll talk about in detail in subsequent chapters. For now, remember to handle criticisms and to identify paths for resolution with simple, obvious questions: "What can I do to help you?" "How do you see this issue being resolved?" A good one is: "How do you see yourself contributing to the solution? Can I count on you to _____?" Get a commitment.

Most of the difficult people in this world rely on ambiguity and things that are poorly defined as their fertile arena for criticism. So – nail down what needs to happen, in their view, and who will do what to achieve that which needs to be done. Anything that is unreasonable in their view becomes immediately apparent, and can be handled. That which is reasonable gets identified and assigned for resolution. Remember to ask: What can each of us (including the difficult person) do to move business forward? Hold the difficult person accountable. Some people will respond better to a very business-like demeanor. By that, we don't mean that they prefer it. They may prefer a friendly demeanor - someone they can push around. But they may respond, that is perform, better if you keep things brisk and business-like.

Difficult people may then sense that if they lighten up, the other people in the project are likely to be a little friendlier, and the difficult person may therefore decide to play nicer for the duration of the project. This is especially true if you have a strong sponsor who will back you in placing requirements on the difficult person. That person will begin to focus more on fulfilling their requirements, and will have less time and energy to devote to being difficult.

Can handle pressure: The project manager is a person who handles stress well. The PM generally knows who is doing what at all times. Whatever specific information is required is gathered by the PM according to need. If the vendor's technical team is doing a test-migration of data to a module of your new AMS, the PM has to know how the migration went immediately after the performance of that migration. There are people waiting to test the data in the AMS test-environment. If something doesn't go according to plan, for example if the wrong data is migrated, the PM must again align resources and reschedule that project element with the same attendant care. The PM will also have to adjust other requirements based on the part of the project that is being redone. If any parts of the project lag, the PM must find the reason and facilitate progress.

The PM will often be dealing with people who feel the squeeze, as will the PM – so, again, choose this person wisely. The PM will frequently be reporting progress made by teams comprising people over whom the PM has no direct control. That is, there will be internal business staff, and outside contractors and/or vendors, and maybe even IT teammates that under usual circumstances have no reporting requirements to the PM. The PM does not rate these people or supervise them in the usual formal sense. And while each member of a project team's performance will factor in an appraisal, reward, and discipline process of some sort, these are not usually dispensed directly by the PM – particularly to those outside solutions partners. Therefore, some management levers that one would normally have at one's disposal are not available here. The PM cannot grant compensatory time to a vendor staff, for example. Nor can the PM discipline a business person for failing to put proper attention to a project element. The PM will find that there are some weak levers employed at times in getting the job done – humor, charm, or negotiation to get or keep something moving.

Here the greatest stress comes from the feeling that there is a lack of control for outcomes. However, the PM need never plead or grovel for cooperation. The PM need merely go to the chain of authority that is charged with judging situations within the project, and with dispensing the necessary guidance and discipline in bringing people to account. Generally speaking, it is the even temperaments and the even personalities who can handle and work through this stress, seeing the way clear to imaginative ideas and solutions in getting the job done under this kind of pressure situation.

Technical knowledge: We know that the project manager will have a degree of technical knowledge, and that any IT-Business project demands it. How do we determine the level of technical knowledge, and more importantly, technical aptitude, necessary for the project? Remember, any project is likely to require the acquisition of new knowledge both within and outside of a person's primary area of expertise. The question regarding technical knowledge should be satisfied by accommodating a few main considerations: Determine who is best suited by virtue of their usual job function – and, when several people meet this first criteria, determine who is best suited according to disposition, workload, and general aptitude. In our example of the new AMS system, it might be logical to select one of the programmers, someone who works on a regular basis in updating and modifying the current AMS system. Such a person already has experience with the evolving business end of software requirements, and has experience in satisfying these needs on the technical end.

Assuming there are several programmers supporting the AMS, we would look for someone who met the other criteria that we've established in defining a good project manager. People sometimes lobby to lead a project, offering to step outside their area of expertise in the hopes of gaining more experience – not the seeking of project management experience, but rather the seeking of new technical knowledge and experience. Projects are not good training grounds for the acquisition of new knowledge. Always utilize someone who is very grounded in the technical knowledge and best practices that will be supporting the project.

Business knowledge: The project manager must have a solid understanding of the specific business and its conduct under present circumstances. Certainly the PM can't understand a business element as well as the business associates who are in the day-to-day routine and who may have years of experience conducting this business – but – the PM must have a common reference for understanding most of the concepts for the conduct of this business. You want someone who can grasp concepts quickly and accurately. The PM will be meeting with business elements to do requirement surveys and to familiarize the project team with the business element. Because Business is, well, conducting business, their time is extremely valuable. Your PM *must* be as efficient as possible in grasping concepts and in building a solid understanding of business.

A general understanding of like-business elements can be leveraged here: an astute PM will be able to pick-up the details of business modules quickly, and this is the quality to look for in this regard. It is also a boon if your PM has the business acumen to suggest better ways of conducting business – you can really leverage the implementation of new software applications to build the accommodations for better business routines. Keep an eye out for someone with vision as well as knowledge. Again, a programmer already has a relationship and rapport with Business through the satisfying of program requests, and is a logical selection for project manager in the case of our AMS implementation – but in any case, look for an open mind and sound judgment.

Stays informed: To say that a project manager stays informed may seem obvious – how else to know the status of a rapidly changing environment? But here we speak of, perhaps, a less obvious state of being informed. What we need to look for is the IT professional that not only knows her or his chosen area of IT, but also stays current in his or her surface knowledge of *other* areas of technology.

The best computer programmers stay abreast of server and network developments and capacities, etc. – just as an example. Network engineers not only know about infrastructures and connectivities, but also should be knowledgeable about databases and their requirements, etc. We want overlap. We want talent, and a pride in staying informed about... the *weave* of all of these elements. This person should be informed about your internal business practices, and also the general best practices affecting your industry, trade group, partnerships, and so on. Obviously the better informed your lead player, the better that person is positioned to pull everyone's best game.

Knows how to push: Projects generally involve pressure situations. Indeed the entire project by nature is a pressure situation. A project is not a permanent situation – it must be mounted and resolved so that an organization can focus on business. The more you can safely compress a project's timeline, the better you are in terms of resources like money, time, staff availability – and other peripheral influencers such as evolving operating systems, business cycles, competing projects, etc. And let's not forget the obvious: we want the project's benefit to apply to business as soon as possible. Therefore, there's generally a need to get things done quickly, get them done correctly, and to fix things fast that don't go as anticipated. The PM has to know how to overcome obstacles: from objections by staff who may squawk about tight deadlines, to challenges by vendors regarding schedules – the PM must be able to *negotiate* and *sell* in successfully leading, but inevitably pushing too, the project along to meet objectives on time. Therefore the PM must be a person who can be resolute without being overbearing, insufferable, or unrealistic.

Knows when to seek help: We touched on seeking help when discussing a project manager's need for good judgment. As the PM manages the project, there will come times when forward momentum is put at risk. Negotiating with an individual, or even one department is fairly straightforward. But issues are compounded when they cross various departments and interests. This is when the PM will need to seek help from the appropriate authority – it's either his or her supervisor, or a level beyond that supervisor's - where the authority has ultimate dominion over those departments and individuals amongst whom the issues develop. The PM must have the judgment to posit the problem with the supervisor – not just in the interest of keeping their supervisor informed, but also in passing the judgment to the supervisor for the appropriate escalation of the issue. If you're the person project managing, remember to report the problem factually and to have some ideas for solutions. The reverse of the question "How does this move business forward?" can be used to expose the problem in the appropriate light: "How is this hindering business?" - that is, what is the hindrance to the business of the project's forward momentum?

Along with pushing the project, the PM has to know when a required push is too heavy. Just as you would seek help in pushing or lifting a very heavy object, the PM must know when to seek help in pushing an issue that is too heavy for the PM alone. In the heat and details of the project it can be very easy to cross the line and try to affect an area beyond authority. Be very careful. The PM can hurt their standing in the organization if the project tunnels their view to the exclusion of appropriate behavior or sanctioned action. An attempt to push resolution to an issue, particularly in cases where a specific lag is generating risk for putting the project at-large behind schedule, can be tempting and obfuscating. Be aware of all sensitive escalations and necessary increments in matched, sponsoring, authority.

Follows-up: This is of critical importance. The obvious point here would be to say that it's necessary to follow-up on elements of the project to ensure that they are progressing and being completed. Not so obvious may be the level of care about the end-user experience. Not just a care and necessity to survey and satisfy the business community, but in how you go about that. In our example, users will be testing and approving software modules in our AMS, and providing feedback along the way. Follow-up with these customers is not only necessary, it is important that the entire project management team ally themselves with the users – from the top down - President to administrative assistant. They do this by showing themselves to be involved with the user community's cares and concerns - their experience.

In addition to formal surveys and meetings that solicit this feedback, the PM should cycle through departments occasionally, visit with critical users, and associate with staff on an informal basis in collecting feedback. Not only will the PM, and by extension the project management team, be seen as caring – but the PM will receive important feedback and details during this kind of follow-up that may not tease out in a more formal setting.

PROJECT MANAGEMENT NECESSITIES

Now that we've identified what a good project manager is and does, let's list some project management necessities for support of any good project. Everyone and every organization has their own style in handling people and projects, of course, but there are some very fundamental things that must be done. Best practices in this regard have been identified and developed - make use of them.

It's surprising how many people who mount major projects are unaware of many simple concepts, tools, and practices. Some of these practices are a reinforcement and an expansion to our basic model for handling change. In addition, we need a reminder to employ some things that are common to managing any work experience: discipline, accountability, and recognition.

As we list things here, we can gain some important perspective. First of all, realize that there will be some items that are already contained in our Project Definition list from earlier. These items are not redundancies – rather, these will be items both central to project definition, as well as to the project's management. For example, a project will be partly defined according to the finite money available to it – the overall budget. But the budget factors in another obvious way – that other way is in the management of the budget. It is crucial to apportion the budget appropriately as a resource to various efforts and goods within the project. Don't suffer the divide between a robust project budget, and the squander of it through poor exercise of it; it must be managed.

At the end of our list, we'll examine some specific areas in detail. We can show how to apply our increasing understanding of the Business-Technology Weave so as to influence the examined areas in a positive way (and by extension, you can model your insight to the other areas).

Project Management Necessities:

- ♦ The Project Manager
- ♦ The Project Management Team, comprising elements of:
  - Sanction
  - Sponsorship
  - Business
  - IT
  - Solutions Partner(s) – Vendors, Contractors, etc.
- ♦ Project Management Tools
  - Agreement
  - Use
  - Measures
- ♦ Full Disclosure and Discovery of Needs
- ♦ Determined and Documented Expectations
- ♦ A Project Definition
- ♦ Commitments
  - Establishment and agreement to success factors

- 'Rules' of engagements
- Rules of escalation and resolution to problems
- Fully exposed, understood, and agreed to responsibilities in all areas and phases of the project.
- An acknowledgement of flexibility and cooperation by all parties in deference to the project's ultimate success.

♦ Resources
- Budget
- People
- Equipment
- Time

♦ Project Timeline
- Start
- Schedules
- Milestones
- Training
- Deliveries
- Tests
- Go-Live or End-delivery Date

♦ Information (think of content management principles; apply them to the project).
- Reference material and guidance
- Reporting of status
- Overall project standing
- Issues tracking and resolution
- Ongoing Analysis and Alignment, as necessary
- ID of Key Personnel:
    - Special expertise
    - 'Go-to's for various exigencies; emergencies (this is also supported by the Project HelpDesk)
    - Establishment of proper liaisons

♦ Project HelpDesk
- Service and support
- Eliminate and prevent silos, and obstructions to accomplishment
- Issues resolution, or coordination and escalation as necessary
- Liaison between Business, IT, outside contacts, as necessary and as assigned.

- The HelpDesk is "Keep Moving Central" – that is, it does everything it can to keep things moving; by ticketing, tracking, and dispensing issues for resolution. As in any HelpDesk, everyone is a customer, and if an issue is not squarely within the HelpDesk's ability or authority to resolve, it will still do everything it can to steer issues and personnel to the correct area for resolutions.

Your PM, associated team, and anyone involved in the project needs to understand the project's definition and supports. Part of the PM's initial contact with ALL direct project participants should be an expository training on the items we've listed above. The PM will explain the various project supports and how the pieces fit together for a total reinforcement to a forward momentum.

PROJECT MANAGEMENT: A VIEW THROUGH THE WEAVE

As we mentioned, let's look at some areas from above in greater detail, from a *Business-Technology Weave* perspective. Let's examine:

- The project management team;

- Information (the information required for, and generated by, the project);

- The Where We Are, Where We're Going and How We're Getting There concepts.

A Project Management Team: This is very similar to setting up the BIT team – follow that model as developed in our Weave, and run the team according to that ethic of engagement. It is likely that most of the project management team is to be comprised of BIT people. There may be other people from respective areas of business that the project is influencing, and from which the project is drawing input. In comprehensive cases where a project affects the organization at large, you can simply use the BIT sessions in piloting the project, with the addition of any necessary additional internal business staff, IT members, and any necessary outside solutions partners. Additional personnel resources may in fact be from any level; they can be people who are directly involved in the granular details of business functions and process, to higher-level stakeholders in the project.

Remember that when we talk about the team's definition, we're not only speaking about who comprises the team. We're establishing the members' responsibilities, and the expectations for their contribution. We're also defining the conduct of the team as it executes its responsibilities in reporting on and in steering the project. For example, you may find yourself vetting activity or behavior by asking the question: "Does this move the project forward?"

Project Information: Information – whether paper based or electronic, and whether representing plans, reference material, e-mails, and so on - should be managed as project *content*. Content Management is the ready identification of information's worth; exposure and understanding of specific information's relevancy to business use and relevancy to *other* information; and an ability to find and get what you need efficiently (among other things). The upcoming chapter, *Content*, is helpful here and should be referenced. Basically, we want to leverage all project-specific information across the entirety of the project – nothing should stall because someone can't find a permission that's already been granted, locate an existing file that's needed but can't be found, or find or even know about the existence of published instructions, etc. The Weave defines content as a leveraged information *asset*. Make sure all project participants know where to find needed content, make sure all necessary information is made readily available.

Content can also pose a liability. Make sure project content is *up-to-date*! Be sure that it is a clear, concise and accurate reference. Also – be certain that access to specific content follows the organization's security guidelines. It should be obvious that not everyone is authorized to all information. Sensitive project information must be managed and secured in accordance with the governing policy for all of the organization's content and security measures.

Where We Are, Where We're Going, and How We're Getting There: Manage the project in accordance with our previously discussed concepts: Know where you are. Be certain of sponsorship and sanction. You must plot the route of the project from a known start point – understand the lay of the organization – all strengths and all weaknesses. Examine the organization's weaknesses for vulnerabilities to the project: do everything you can to turn vulnerabilities into strengths. Chances are these vulnerabilities are things that are overdue for attention – the organization may as well address them now, in the face of the project. Understand the destination. When you plan the route - the assignments, tasks, deliverables, metrics, reports, and ultimate arrival – be certain to create a timeline and milestone achievements that are reasonable. Make certain you arrive at the organization's desired, required, destination – not some approximation.

A Perspective on "Arrival": We recognize that there is a delivery (fulfillment) that any project must make. But further, once you're at the destination of the project's conclusion, you must realize that there is a success-qualifier that is only measured through satisfaction over time. Keeping this perspective in mind helps project participants, and all project contributors, to avoid a myopic view of the delivery, or go-live date, as the end of the project. Viewing a project too much in terms of its end, and a "thank goodness that's over with" attitude, can diminish a standard of effort. The standard of effort must view the project's utility and value to the organization's future.

Here, our understanding is again aided by viewing our goals as a road trip: once you reach your destination, you don't evaporate. Nor do you touch a "base" and turn around and leave the destination. You inhabit that destination – at least for a time. You *do* something at that inhabitation. If it's a vacation, the success of the planning and trip (the project) will not just be in the mere arrival. The success is really measured in the things that you are able to do on vacation, and the satisfaction and enjoyment they bring. If you've moved to a new community, the trip and "project" is to establish a new home and way of life. Is life good? Is it what you expected and are you well satisfied? In other words, you are now in your new home, and immersed in your new way of life – but *that* is not the real measure of your success. It is whether you are doing and living the way you intended when you planned and managed your change to this new life. It is the meeting of expectations, and fulfillment of needs over time, as you go about living.

Any project's hard and fast management ends at the "arrival" of its delivery but, in essence, the project *projects* through and past the delivery to influence the organization for a long time. A project's influence only ends when the delivered solution is subsumed or replaced by another. Viewing the project beyond its mere delivery date helps participants to focus on true value in all areas of the project - for the living that will go on after the hard project's end. This helps those within the project to avoid an insular experience and to avoid a division: A loss of vision for what the actual needs and goals of the organization are - and the project's expected contribution to those.

In the upcoming chapters there will be ideas and models that provide help beyond the three specific areas of project management we just looked at. These chapters are as self-reinforcing as your Business-Technology Weave, as are your organization's departments and disciplines to the whole of your business goals. Just as we've explored some areas here, and applied concepts of the Weave to them, you can bring each area of the book to bear on the others. When you begin your next project, think about all areas from the perspective of the Weave.

A Word About Timelines: Doing Things Right, Right on Time

In discussing a major project, someone once said: "We're not going to finish this project by a specific date, we're going to do it *right*." This statement was delivered with the spirit that this was an enlightened concept. However, finishing a project according to a stated expectation, and doing things right, are not mutually exclusive. In fact, if we're speaking of a true managed project, we must operate according to a fundamental understanding: By definition, project management means *doing things right, right on schedule*.

Now of course some things are going to occasionally slip off schedule. But we're speaking in reasonable terms here, and we must strive to make deliveries and achievements on time. In fact, the well-run project can do this with amazing regularity. Doing things *right* is going to come from the standards, disciplines, and accountabilities we emplace according to defined practices. These practices are established and maintained in managing any department or group of people, and are supported by Human Resources policies, standard business practice, best IT practice, and common sense. This is all part of the Weave too. Doing things *right on schedule* comes from effective project management. In order to manage cost and to make effective use of resources you must have a schedule for completion of the project, and you must manage according to the schedule.

Whether you use a project management software such as MS-Project, MS-Solomon, spreadsheets, documents, templates, other proprietary project applications, in any combination, it is also helpful to have a representation of a timeline, a summary, of the sort we're about to examine.

Focus: A Very Basic Timeline

In the very early stages of your project, get a 6' x 4' whiteboard – one that you can dedicate to the project. The whiteboard is extremely helpful in planning the timeline early on. Later, the whiteboard serves as a snapshot of the timeline as a readily accessed, seen, and digested representation of the project status. How many times have you been involved in a project, sitting in a meeting, looking at all kinds of status reports, project timelines, spreadsheets, etc., and wondered to yourself "what the heck is really happening?" Don't be afraid to go simple. At any time, participants should be able to look to the whiteboard to see what should be happening when - on a macro scale for sure, but that is very important. You will be amazed at how this simple device keeps everyone on track and feeling secure. Individual departments and cells of the project can have whiteboards, but here we're speaking of a main whiteboard for big-bullet project status. Larger organizations will have rooms that have entire walls that are whiteboards. Their projects can *use* an entire wall – but keep the main board to one wall, and depict as best you can the major milestones on *one line of time*.

If you're not able to take someone in five minute's time - a visitor, a new hire, a new vendor, etc. - from a cold-start to a fairly solid feel for your project and its goals – *you're in trouble*.

In roughing out a timeline, pick a start date and a go-live date (that date by which you hope to have a new solution in place, fully implemented in your production environment, in use by users and fully supporting business). In roughing out the start and go-live dates, pick dates which make sense, but don't be too concerned with pinpoint accuracy. Early discussions within the BIT environment will yield dates that are realistic if not yet fully sanctioned. What we're looking to do is to establish the life of the project – that period of time under which the project will bloom and yield, delivering permanent "fruit" – the new solution. Once that proposed bracket is on that board, begin to hang some major milestones on the timeline to see where things fall. You will begin to quickly shuttle dates, sliding them forward or back along the timeline as you estimate how long things will take, and which things are dependent on other things. You'll also notice that many things can happen in parallel.

This simple, graphic depiction of the timeline is very effective in exposing the areas you can tighten up – as well as ones where you'll need to dedicate more time: You'll see where things that can happen in parallel from a strictly technical point of view can in fact not happen that way due to a stretch of staff or budget. Remember that the whiteboard is for the larger, more visible milestones – things that would be understood by the BIT team and other management, or understood with some brief explanation. Various notes and details regarding milestones can be listed under the timeline, but the timeline is not meant to exactly mirror your other management resources. Plans, reports of progress, detailed next steps, and documentation regarding requirements are contained in, and managed by, your other tools.

REMEMBER ~

Too often improvements are introduced, but are unwittingly applied on top of bad habits or practices that stubbornly remain – often unbeknownst to management. We need to fully understand today's lay of the land. Changes to burdens of security, changes to management of content, changes in the speed of markets, changes to the array of technology and its support, changing demands and expectations of consumers - *and continual, accelerating change in these regards* - means that projects will take on new requirements for proactivity, efficiency and success. Organizations, even small ones, will have an increase in concurrent projects, and in dependencies between projects. There will be a narrower and narrower tolerance for errors or sloppiness.

An organization should always be in a good position to serve any project well: by maintaining a position of change-readiness; by knowing where it is; by knowing where it's going; and by knowing how to get there. Within projects, remember to expose and accurately identify needs, to define a solid project to deliver on needs, to develop sanction and sponsors for the project's protection and sale, to select a proper project manager, and to coordinate and manage through a special project team. The team may be comprised of BIT, or a part of BIT – you may be able to manage some projects as a part of BIT's agenda. But the spirit and ethic of the BIT team must apply to projects and all challenges.

All organizations should task any PM to bring fresh insights and necessary leverage to all areas of a project's management. If you are the PM, you know what to do.

8

FALSE SOLUTIONS - AND HOW TO AVOID THEM

But in our enthusiasm, we could not resist a radical overhaul of the system, in which all of its major weaknesses have been exposed, analyzed, and replaced with new weaknesses.

Bruce Leverett - "Register Allocation in Optimizing Compilers"

We've talked a bit about wasted effort in the Business-Technology Weave. Effort that had no lack of good intentions yet was misdirected and wasteful. We've spoken of feel-good initiatives, and we've reviewed a couple of common mistakes organizations and individuals make in trying to satisfy poorly conceived or false objectives. We've hinted at something that we'll call the "false solution." That's something we'll discuss in detail here – the False Solution. It looks great on the surface, but it's essentially an empty vessel that does not deliver the intended business or technical benefit.

Here, we'll look at a very simple, yet illuminating, example of a false solution. By examining a relatively contained, organizational, risk, we'll be in a position to consider a much more universal scale of risk posed by the false solution later in the book. But at any scale, we need to examine the dangers in mounting false solutions, and how to expose and avoid false solutions before they're mounted. For, false solutions not only fail to deliver, they consume resources and time such that they hold real solutions in abeyance.

We're going to use a Human Resources department in this example. We're not going to pick on HR, or any areas in general – this is just one HR department that serves very well in highlighting the pitfalls of the false solution. Also, the general product software in our example serves many organizations very well, when properly matched to needs and expectations – it just wasn't the appropriate solution in this case. Think about what happened in the "solution" below and apply these considerations to your own initiatives.

A mid-sized organization of several hundred people, XYZ Corporation, dreaded their annual employee appraisal and review process. They used a fairly comprehensive word processing template – a form – with an instruction set from HR on how to use the form. There were also clear expectations for the content that was required for an appropriate appraisal. And, HR made use of reminders through e-mail and staff meetings to bump the process along.

However, the HR department had a difficult time getting managers to start the process on time. This meant that draft appraisals weren't submitted when due. Of course, submission of completed appraisals was not made on time, and there was a further problem in that submissions failed to meet organizational standards for completeness and quality. HR's take on the situation was that many managers "don't know how to write," and stated this many times. Also, HR felt that there was a lack of overall control surrounding the whole process.

AUTOMATION IS GOOD – RIGHT?

HR made a sale to the senior management team; that an "automated" software application for the management and production of employee appraisals was necessary. The software had templates for appraisals that proposed language, based on keyword input. Entire sentences and paragraphs were generated – hence HR's solution for managers who "don't know how to write." The appraisal software generated automatic reminders that went out (through the same e-mail system as before) as ticklers for start of the process, submission of drafts to supervisors, and submission of final appraisals to HR. (The advantage of this auto-reminder capability was largely offset by a pre-existing ability to set up a schedule of reminders. This capacity existed in the organization's native e-mail application; a suggestion to do this did not fit the "sale" and was left unexplored).

The software also had report capability, to track and show status of appraisal drafts, versions, finals, and where in the production process things stood. Reports could be generated by individual, by department, by dates, etc. Hence, HR's solution for tardy start and submission of appraisals – a means of control. Of course the vendor was a major player in this sales dynamic, and found that they had an audience already biased in terms of need, expectations, solution, and delivery. The vendor described a wonderful appraisal cycle whereby managers would enter a few relevant keywords, resulting in whole paragraphs and tracts spilling out, tightly matched to job specifications and individual performance. "Ticklers," that is reminders, would be automatically generated by the system to bump along each draft for approval as the process moved along. Ultimately, a comprehensive batch of final-form appraisals would be submitted to HR on the due date, for rollup and delivery, of all completed, quality-ensured appraisals to senior management.

I.T. WARS

BEWARE THE "SOLUTION" THAT ADDS LAYERS OF EFFORT TO SIMPLE BUSINESS PROCESS

After implementation of the software, training, and completion of the first annual review of staff with the new appraisal system, something interesting was apparent. The appraisal process was no better than before. Appraisals that were supposed to "write themselves" turned out to be shallow, trite, and not particularly representative of the employee or their job. Many managers stated that starting with, and editing, the system-generated material was more difficult than preparing their own fresh draft. In fact, the "don't know how to write" assessment was offset by fully articulated and expressive e-mails on the part of managers.

As far as the adherence to timeliness - for submission of drafts and final appraisals - there was no improvement. It turned out that automated reminders from the appraisal system were viewed no differently than the reminders that had been sent from HR in that past – and through the same e-mail system. The recipient viewed appraisal reminders from any source no differently: They were all essentially "HR." One is as easily ignored, or obeyed, as another. As far as tracking the appraisals, HR now had a new burden they hadn't anticipated – the generation of status reports regarding appraisal production. The reports capability was paired with the expectation they had set with their senior management. Hence the new requirement to produce and speak to these reports in management meetings. Actually, efficiency for all concerned the first year was diminished due to the learning curve, and in everyone's requirement to machinate the process surrounding production of simple text appraisals.

Even worse, the second year's effectiveness was no better. In fact, it seemed to be poorer. Because appraisals were annual, the organization's managers didn't think about the appraisal application for 10 or 11 months. They were rusty each year. Some managers needed refresher training. Everyone stumbled through the application inefficiently until reacquainted with it. Therefore, what was supposed to be a solution was now a contributor to a larger, layered, problem.

How could this have happened? The organization was confused. What happened to their investment? Where was their return? Indeed, there was no positive return – there was a *negative* return. They were now saddled with expensive software, along with the upgrade schedule required by all business software, with the attendant support burden – HelpDesk, backoffice, and annual user refresher training. Where did XYZ Corporation go wrong? Let's examine…

Automating Poor Process is Wasteful

The first red flag should have been the assertion, or assumption, that the managers could not write. The corporation couldn't possibly have hired managers without some kind of writing skills. The matter of poor writing was more a human failing on some part to hold managers *accountable* for their quality of writing. The posit that "managers can't write" should have been rejected outright (perhaps in a BIT team meeting). The focus then should have been to set an expectation, a bar, for managers to clear for the quality of their writing. HR, and anyone supervising a poor writer, should think about this condition as exposing a vulnerability, so as to expose a potential strength. If you want your organization to write well, make that a goal. What could HR's next steps be? Perhaps to sponsor a managers' plan to get necessary people to training. Perhaps to issue, or direct attention to, an organizational style guide. The really important thing: hold people accountable for their writing - rate them on it in their own appraisals. Judge their performance.

Therefore, for XYZ Corporation, there was no *technical* component, *no technical solution*, required for this element of the appraisal problem. It is a problem of discipline and accountability, solved by senior managers, in holding people accountable for the quality of their work. No computer or technical system is going to fix your business culture, or overcome lax attitudes.

There was also the flawed analysis in the matter of automated reminders. No technical assist here helped an adherence to schedule. The only leverage that counts is how the reminders influence the receivers - the managers. Could the appraisal software's e-mail reminders do anything that HR's former e-mail reminders could not? In fact, there was no leverage to be had on the problem. The managers' response to the "new" reminders was the same – to largely ignore or overlook them. HR viewed the automatic send-out of reminders from their own perspective: the efficiency standpoint of the sender (HR), not from a consideration of what the managers would do. Again, getting users to respond to reminders is a matter of discipline and accountability outside of any computer or technical solution.

Real Solutions are Often Hiding in Plain Sight

To drive the point completely home, let's look at the beauty and simplicity of what XYZ Corporation had in place prior to this so-called improvement – this "solution":

They had a very effective word processing template for the employee appraisals. It contained all of the major areas for evaluation of employees. There was a very effective instruction set that had been constructed and improved upon over time. Also, most managers had a ready history for position objectives and employee performance. It was already online as a reference – readily available in past year's appraisals. Reusing and repurposing this information should be a routine part of XYZ Corporation's effective leverage of business content. Consider: Even for new employees (without a performance history), there still exists the position description and objectives from the former incumbent's appraisals, as an assist to new employees appraisals. For brand new positions, neither system offered much assist – new positions require, and deserve, a fresh document set all around.

During XYZ's appraisal season, expectations for completion of drafts, and submission dates for completed appraisals, were well articulated and communicated via *existing* tools – namely, the e-mail system, all-staff meetings, and bulletin boards – things which were still employed, by the way, with the implementation of the "automated" system.

OUT WITH THE NEW, IN WITH THE OLD

Well, what ultimately happened? XYZ Corporation eventually threw out the new system, and went back to the old. Eventually, a fresh set of eyes looked at the appraisal process and saw an opportunity for cost cutting. The vendor and their associated product were simply removed from the environment – saving training costs, upgrade costs, support costs, and eliminating wasted time. Managers were held accountable by their supervisors for timely and correct submission of appraisals, and those supervisors were held accountable, and so on up the line. In other words, this corporation put the push where it belonged – in the general areas of discipline and accountability.

Here too is an important understanding: IT people often don't want to appear as a block to initiatives, and can remain mum on ideas that they see as unwise. Business must recognize this and foster an open dialog on needs and solutions in sponsoring a civil debate on what is best for the organization all around. Again, a BIT properly defined is a great forum. Leaders' responsibility - Business and IT - will be to weigh what they hear during feedback in making decisions. At the same time, IT must maintain solid credibility so that their counsel on the business end of solutions is weighed and considered with proper focus by Business.

One important concept that IT can expose is what the false solution does to economy of scale. Any time you remove specific business from common resources and supports, you chip away at an economy of scale. At the same time, when you institute a specialized resource, asset, application, platform, etc., you now build a new area of overhead. Be very wary in these circumstances. Before you bring in the "new," examine the "old" and its supposed deficiencies very carefully.

Keep in mind that the phenomenon of the False Solution is very real. You may have experienced it in full, or perhaps to some lesser degree. Consider that often times you may achieve a strange parity: a "solution" that works, but is no more efficient or enabling than what preceded it. In those circumstances you live with the squander of resources in simply delivering something different. The organization may yet suffer a poor return going forward, as stakeholders in a new system make erroneous or wasted effort in trying to squeeze out advantages that are simply not there. In all cases, remember the adage to measure twice, cut once. Take very careful measure of needs, solutions, and vendors so as to create proper definitions and deliveries.

Let's next examine the XYZ case to see where people frequently go wrong, and the red flags to look for. There are always red flags to indicate that you may be embarking on a False Solution:

Misunderstanding of "Where We Are": Here, several "where we are" factors were missed. No destination can be reached if you don't understand the point from which you're trying to progress. Here, the point of origin was thought to be one of missing automation, a lack of tools, a lack of enablement. There actually were inadequacies, as there generally are when seeking solutions. However, they were misidentified. This led to false statements of need, a misidentification of requirements, and misdirected actions. XYZ arrived at a destination that did not serve them.

There wasn't a simple lack of automation or tools for their appraisal process. In actuality, there was a quite robust set of general automation and tools – with a wonderfully low overhead of maintenance. The organization just had to *use* these resources, and within the discipline that is required of any effort (business or otherwise, technically assisted or otherwise). The point of origin here, the organization's "Where We Are," was the lack of priority, discipline and accountability. The inadequacies were in the organization's failure to state clear expectations for fulfillment of the appraisal process, and the application of discipline and accountability in order to secure the managers' serious attention and fulfillment of their appraisal delivery. Understanding this point of origin would have yielded a completely different path; a route to a real solution of the appraisal problem. For example, any manager's late submission of an appraisal could yield a mention on *their* appraisal, with corresponding rating impact. Another part of the path would be the setting of the organization's importance on the appraisals: What can be more important than placing, developing, and promoting people in creating the best organization possible?

Erroneous assumptions: HR assumed that the problem with appraisal production was located in a lack of management tools, poor writing skills on the part of managers, and lack of "automated" control for the process. However the actual problem was ineffective use of the existing tools, failure to set clear expectations, and failure to fully explore and use existing means of automation. The erroneous assumptions reinforced an unwillingness to set the simple discipline in prioritizing the appraisals.

False characterizations: HR, a support department with customers, had a very negative view of those customers – a red flag in itself. The erroneous assumption that "The managers don't know how to write" led to a false characterization. Rather than challenging this characterization, other leaders in the decision-making arena allowed this to become a false support to the false solution.

This characterization of managers surely did not "move business forward" in any meaningful way. Surely someone should have popped up to say "Our managers can write – certainly the personnel that *I've* hired can write - let's not mischaracterize or trivialize the real problem." Further, someone could have pointed out that the bulk of most appraisals change very little from year-to-year. They usually are completed by simply updating and making relevant each past year's appraisal, by accommodating specific goals and accomplishments – unless there is a huge variance in someone's behavior, assignments, or performance - or in cases where there is a new position or new hire. This was a point best made by Business, but IT can make it too in a properly positioned BIT forum.

Remember, IT can be loathe in some circumstances to discount what will be IT supported "solutions." This is where we'll reinforce the necessity for Business members to acclimate themselves to the Business-Technology Weave. In this case, everyone involved should have been asking the question: "Does this move business forward?" In other words: "How does characterizing our managers as having an inability to write move business forward?" The answer (It doesn't) would indicate that this characterization, being an untrue statement, did nothing to move business forward, and would require all involved to *continue their seek* in properly defining the problem.

This concept is very important in that it reinforces the necessity for proper identification of problems, which helps to locate where problems actually live.

Even if writing ability is contributing to the larger problem here (either by individual or group) the solution to this sub-problem is obvious: a writing class, or a supervisor telling someone to take greater care and effort with their writing. (We should note that dumbing down a process to overcome deficiencies in people is inefficient; you help convey those deficiencies to other areas of effort. Fixing deficiencies at their source leverages people's abilities/attitudes across the entirety of their contribution to the organization).

Exaggerated claims: In this case, the vendor painted a rosy picture of assisted appraisal production – making the appraisals easy to write, easy to track, and easy to submit on time. But "easy" can be a relative term. For an organization employing thousands of people, perhaps with complicated rating chains, the vendor's software did probably make things easier. But for XYZ Corporation, the burden to the users in machinating the process was greater than simply focusing effort to produce the appraisals. Any claim must be thoroughly vetted. XYZ Corporation should have visited a reference site or two, of similar organizational size, and evaluated the fit of the appraisal system to the business of those like organizations. Here, a technical BIT member, and a Business one, should have paired to make these visits. They could then report back to the BIT team.

Unsurveyed reality: Someone with authority should have examined the real issues. The ultimate issue was late appraisals. Where in the process did the lag begin to occur? Was there a bottleneck in one specific part of the process, or did each step seem to be taking more time than that which was allotted? Were expectations being properly transmitted by the authority (HR) in charge of the process? Was there enough direction? We're the expectations fair – that is, was enough time allotted for each step of the process? We're there any consequences to those who failed to meet expectations in this process?

Remember that any process that cuts across the entire organization (like employee appraisals) merits reinforcement from the top. The CEO, President, Executive Director, etc., merely needs to put the *umph* under the process. The importance should have been conveyed to the executive team, who underscore this requirement and oversight on down the line. No system is automatic, and again, *people* are our greatest challenge – so XYZ merely needs to state expectations and set discipline and accountability.

Lack of objective reporting: Problems must be stated objectively and from a business point of view. For example, one business point of view here could be that late submission of appraisals creates a problem in payroll for dispensation of end-of-year bonuses. Another could be that late submission pushes the administration of the appraisals into HR's benefits review cycle. The objective report of the problem would indicate that despite the use of forms, a clearly defined instruction set, and a generous schedule with reminders, managers were still late in their production of appraisals. Here senior management could then help to expose other managers to the consequences of late submissions, and the impact to HR's overall efficiency.

We can see that at XYZ Corporation, the real problem was that the process wasn't garnering the proper respect. XYZ Corp. finally found where their real problem lived: Managers didn't take the appraisals requirement seriously. In their view the appraisals were an *interruption* to their business, not a *part* of it. Remember that anything deemed important enough to have a schedule for compliance must be understood to be a *part* of business, not an *interruption* to business. HR ultimately got senior management to reinforce the activity's importance.

Failure to test: Before mounting any solution or project, you must do a proof of concept. XYZ Corporation did not test the appraisal software. HR did try, at IT's instigation, to get a test group of managers to use the software. They were asked to input job elements, key words, some standards, and to produce some appraisals. However, no manager delivered on this. This was not surprising – the managers didn't take real appraisals seriously, so "fake" ones were out of the question.

Members of the HR department were the only users that tried the software on a test basis – but did this have any chance of yielding a fair evaluation? Consider: HR produced their department's appraisals on time - HR had no problem utilizing the "old system" – it was the rest of the organization that was having difficulty complying with the requirements for submission. Therefore, HR's analysis and evaluation of the software *means nothing other than vetting the software for further test by the organization*. Because HR was pushing the software, and because HR had no issue as a department with submitting appraisals in the first place, HR is not an objective reporter in this case. They essentially have a conflict of interest.

So XYZ was still left with no proof of concept. This was a huge red flag pointing to a couple of problems that should have been readily seen. IT's responsibility in this arena is to articulate the importance of a test for proof of concept, and to facilitate that test by installing the software at the desktop. IT can partner with HR in defining who the testers (users) would be, and in setting up a schedule for completion of the test by users. But the test's results, and their interpretation, should happen in BIT.

Qualifying the Organization - Again

What is HR's responsibility here? It is up to HR to sell this solution, and sell it they did. However, the organization did not qualify in their ability to judge or assess the software. The organization was an easy "sell," and bought to easily. XYZ needed to establish a BIT forum with savvy business and technical leaders. These leaders could then make sharp assessment of HR and the vendor's sale of the appraisal software. This forum too would have significant insight to the true source of the appraisal problem. (It's very likely that any organization with a solid BIT forum wouldn't have an appraisal problem in the first place).

In the circumstances of the qualified organization, HR has a true sale to make: that is, they must transact with the other business elements, and IT, in bringing opinions together to form the consensus that this is the real solution. In the former case, HR made a sale to an unqualified group – always easy, seldom right.

In this case, when the qualified organization takes measure of the software's suitability from the managers' standpoint (not HR's), it can arrive at a correct decision. In a later chapter we'll discuss "in front of the screen" responsibilities and "behind the screen" responsibilities, whereby it becomes easy to distinguish who has what responsibilities in any thread of the business-technology weave. But for now, realize that HR knows their business better than any other department. Apart from IT's contribution to understanding such things as ease-of-use, supportability, and even in helping to identify various applications for comparison, it is HR's sale to make. It must be done on a thoroughly tested and vetted basis, and it must be sold to a qualified buyer.

The False Solution Writ Large

There are a couple recent examples (of many, many to choose from) that highlight the peril of the False Solution. In addition to highlighting the peril inherent in a false solution, each example provides a specific insight. Let's consider that FBI Virtual Case File (VCF) tracking system and its ultimate failure in a little more detail.

The VCF was intended to automate a largely paper-based system of case files involving potential terrorists, targets, and allied information. Former 9/11 Commissioner Tim Roemer has characterized the FBI's recent case management as "index cards" and "typewriters." Clearly it is difficult to share and leverage intelligence in such an environment. The FBI had a true need to implement a modern system that would allow agents and intelligence analysts to share information in the successful resolution of investigative work. The overall goal of automation was a bona-fide need – the FBI had been criticized post-9/11 for "not connecting the dots" in time to prevent the attacks (essentially, they had an inability to manage and leverage dispersed information content).

Despite the necessary goal of automating the means by which to facilitate workflow, search on information, manage cases, and provide reports, the FBI somehow managed to maneuver this project to a complete stall, and turned it into the ultimate throw away. For, while VCF was deemed "critical" to the war on terror, after four years and almost $300 million the FBI ended up with 700,000 lines of bug-ridden code. The system was so dysfunctional and far-removed from business requirements that it was scrapped. VCF has been replaced with a new project, Sentinel, which will attempt to fill the void of automated case management.

CONSEQUENCE

The U.S. Department of Justice's Inspector General, Glenn A. Fine, released an audit that cited factors that contributed to the VCF's failure. Some of them are: poorly defined and evolving requirements; overly ambitious schedules; and lack of a plan to guide hardware purchases, network deployments, and software development for the bureau. One could well ask: What served as their BIT team, or did they even have something for that role? It is actually quite easy to understand the FBI's failure here: ever more effort was expended on going back and fixing things versus effort for moving forward. They lacked an understood point of origin, crafted a false route, and never reached their destination.

The specific insight afforded here is this: Once you find yourself going back to fix things, then going back again - and again and again – you cannot, and never will, make forward progress. The FBI could not have understood their "Where We Are" point of origin. They crafted a false route, and their "Where We're Going" destination did not reflect a true solution to a business case. This happened because of a failure to understand and expose requirements. Theirs was a failure to set expectations in a language common to all necessary parties, in mounting a successful, properly defined, project.

Let's learn something else here: What differentiates VCF as a false solution vs. a poorly managed project? VCF was in fact both, but here's another important lesson. If we take the Department of Justice at their word, we know that VCF had poorly defined (and evolving) requirements. There's no way to match solutions to poorly defined requirements – that is fundamental. And, these poorly defined requirements were moving (evolving) – everything is changing. So, any solutions that were being worked and attempted had to be divided from what was actually required: hence they were false.

We know too that there were overly ambitious schedules. Schedules themselves are solutions; solving requirements for delivery of resources, for getting people together, for achieving consensus and progress, and for delivering solutions according to expectations. An unrealistic schedule represents one that can't be adhered to, and therefore is a false solution in and of itself. Think of it this way: Building an overly ambitious schedule is no different from relying on a calendar with 35 days per month. Neither reflects the reality that will ultimately compel you to fail.

What is the lesson? Divides spawn divides. False solutions present themselves at all levels of the organization, within all strata and disciplines of a project, and often times small, not easily determined, falsities aggregate and contribute to the ultimate, overarching False Solution.

The conclusion for the FBI is that four years after terrorists crashed jetliners into the World Trade Center and the Pentagon, the FBI still does not have software for "connecting any new dots," and won't for *years* to come. That is the U.S. Justice Department's conclusion. (And a very sobering one indeed to our necessity for the proper weave of business and technology at all levels).

A CLUE: FALSE SOLUTIONS CAN HAVE FALSE PROJECTS

The failure of VCF has been called the most highly publicized software failure in history, but it's not only the Federal Government that suffers from false solutions - and the resulting divide between critical requirements and delivery on these requirements. Washington, D.C. recently "paused" a project involving a mobile computer system for their fire department. The District lost between $4 million and $6 million during the course of a year and a half's mismanagement. Part of the project's confusion lay in the fact that there was a period where the fire department and the city's Office of the Chief Technology Officer could not agree on who was in control of the budget, and ultimately, who controlled the project. That represents a fundamental misunderstanding, and a pretty big divide.

The specific insight in this last case is to recognize that there is no such thing as a "paused project." Once large-scale activity is halted, it ceases to be a project by any reasonable definition. Once you stop work, you lose your timeline, all milestones, control of budget, and your lock on resources. Evaporating too are expectations, definitions, and your anticipated implementation. You've lost control of the solution to all of the issues, challenges and problems the project was meant to address. And remember – the so-called "paused project" is berthed in a larger environment that does not pause *its* change. There is no such thing as a pause within a managed, true, project. Once a project stalls, you have a strong clue that you may be trying to shoehorn a False Solution.

We don't mean to pick on government here – we mean to help government – and you. There are large-scale business and systems failures in private and public organizations large and small, and these failures are avoidable: True solutions match fully exposed, and fully understood, hard business requirements.

REMEMBER ~

Your Business-Technology Weave must execute proper exposure of need, proper planning, and carefully managed adjustments and delivery. Properly executed projects, no matter how large, develop a self-reinforcing energy that lets all participants know they are progressing down the right path. These participants have set their sanctions, set their sponsors. They have aligned their resources. All sides have exposed and agreed to expectations, are meeting true requirements, and are doing so with appropriately sized solutions. Properly mounted projects are not constant pain, constant confusion, and constant rehash of issues that were supposedly decided at the outset of the project. This is a crucial understanding for your BIT team, and any specific project management teams. All levels of leadership and control in your organization should know what to do, *and what to look out for and correct*, at the outset of solutions and projects.

Nothing – no person, no organization – stands still. We're always moving. Make sure you're moving *forward*. A commonality between the FBI, the DC fire department, and XYZ Corporation was that they found themselves moving backward - at considerable expense. Hopefully they are now moving forward.

9

BUSINESS AND IT: WHO DOES WHAT, WHY, AND WHEN?

It's been said that understanding what things are <u>like</u>... is a large step toward understanding what things <u>are</u>.

In many business-technology endeavors there blooms a confusion as to who should do what. This is especially true when going down a new and unfamiliar path. Business frequently thinks that anything involving a technical support structure means that most of the responsibility and activity belongs in the IT department. IT frequently thinks that Business should be responsible for some things which in fact are better reserved for IT's exercise and judgment. We know there is a mutual dependency, but when are lines appropriate and where do we draw them? What answers does the Weave yield?

Let's look at a couple examples that will highlight some areas, then discuss a simple way to illuminate any area for solution. You will be able to employ this model to answer your own questions in cases where you're proceeding onto unfamiliar ground, and unsure as to where to place specific activity and responsibility. You can also look at your existing placements of effort, and in many cases make better assignments in cases where certain efforts have been poorly positioned.

THE FILING CABINET ANALOGY

Your office is cluttered – you have documents all over the place. The paperless office of the future has not yet arrived, will never arrive, and your hardcopy papers are necessary, important, and accumulating. You must get them filed for safekeeping, and you require ready reference of the content. You call up your supply department and order a filing cabinet. A few days later, a supply clerk rolls your cabinet in, asking where you would like it.

As the clerk wheels his empty dolly toward your door, you say, "Wait! You're not finished." Bewildered, the clerk asks you what you mean. You politely gesture to all the stacks of paper on your desk, your table, your office floor. You tell him that he needs to label the drawers. He needs to create tabs for various subjects, projects and tasks. He needs to alphabetize and categorize your paper documentation and file it in the appropriate place in the new cabinet.

What is wrong here? This: you, the recipient of the filing cabinet, expect the supply clerk to do your filing – which is not the supply clerk's job. The supply clerk has delivered a system for filing – the *recipient* must file, or delegate that to relevant department staff. But realize too: The cabinet's recipient must not only use the "system," the recipient must do some configuring and setup of that system. After all, it is the recipient who best understands the business requirement of that system (the labeling, categorization, etc. that is necessary).

Now, we know that no one would ask the supply clerk to do that filing – or configuring - yet IT finds itself in that very position as it delivers its "filing cabinets."

DETERMINE THE "WHY" FOR WHO DOES WHAT

Remember our discussion about finance codes for the Expositions department? This example was provided earlier to show a project manager's ownership of the codes creation as an *issue* (in the project management context). That is, the PM's job was to bump along the Expositions Director's (or delegate's) creation of the codes - an important task supporting a project (the implementation of a new association management system). The Expositions department was the task's owner. The action of creating the codes was that department's responsibility, with a shared component: creating them in compliance with the Finance department's oversight of all finance codes. Let's revisit this situation for the perspective it can yield here – the "why" of the task's ownership by the Expositions department.

Part of the lag in the code creation was the Expositions Director's insistence that this was IT's responsibility. However, IT is not the generator of the codes. Nor does IT maintain them – or use them. The syntax and format of the codes is defined largely by Finance. Further, the Expo Department is intimately familiar with their own financial tracking needs. They know how many codes and definitions are needed in the conduct of their business. They also know the character and number of codes that exist in the old AMS - for various conference booths, hotel rooms, services, etc. Having IT survey a business situation that Expositions is responsible for is not a correct placement of effort or responsibility.

IT effort in this regard would mean: IT must perform the administrative drill of creating the codes for approval by Expositions. This would engender a review, any necessary adjustments, and resubmittals with another Expo review. This would be followed by IT's arrangement for review with Finance. This is inefficient: Expo can drive and complete this process, in its entirety, in less time. Otherwise, it takes IT people away from doing the things that *only* IT can do. It engages them on a largely administrative task that should be assigned within the Expo department. Expo should not require IT to maintain their finance codes any more than IT can expect Expo to maintain IT's finance codes.

Once Expositions creates their codes as tasked, they must let the project manager know they're ready. The PM can schedule a sit down with Finance for review of the codes. Once Finances approves them, the PM (or a delegate) can train Expo on how to enter the codes into the AMS. The Expo department should have the system authority to maintain their codes in the AMS so as to match their business authority.

Ask yourself here: who is responsible for knowing Exposition's codes in order to exercise Exposition's business? It is within that party, or group, where action must transpire. Today's employment of "systems" or technology is not an excuse to defer ability, responsibility, or activity. In any circumstance, an oversight authority from Business or Technology can simply ask: who is the relevant party that knows, or should know, the business of what is under consideration? That party must be empowered in every possible sense so as to match activity to the root of knowledge. It's efficient.

In short: IT delivers the system - Business must utilize the system.

EMPOWER BUSINESS; FREE IT

In the case of the Expositions' department, IT delivered a business module requiring new finance codes. It was up to Expositions to then take action – the act of "filing" in this case was the act of creating the codes, coordinating their approval with finance, and inputting and administering the codes – these were all Business requirements.

How many IT departments are producing reports from end-user software that should be produced by someone in the business element? How many IT departments are orienting incoming hires for entrenched business software – the specific use of which is better explained by someone that is in the business department making the hire? How many IT departments are breaking out, coding and tracking mobile connectivity charges for business? Aren't those an administrative duty better performed by someone in Finance or the actual departments?

In other words, look for situations where "filing cabinets" have been delivered, but where the duty of "filing" is not being effectively picked up out in the business arena. Making effective use of technology is a profit-enhancing lever, and the user community needs to "file" effectively. Do what is necessary: deliver training, place the expectation, and *let* Business set up and run their "filing cabinets." This frees IT to fulfill its obligations in other rapidly expanding arenas – Security, to name one. Content Management to name another. Planning and fulfillment on future, accelerating, business and technical requirements to name more. Let's look at one additional example on the Business side of the equation before we look at some IT challenges.

A BUSINESS DEFICIT

Recently, a business director approached to introduce himself. After his name, his very first words were "I'm 'computer-illiterate'." He went on to explain that he would be IT's "best customer" because he required frequent help. He joked of being proud on mornings when he could just remember how to turn his computer on. He had a smile on his face, and he most likely thought that his confessed ignorance would be seen as a friendly sign. But, it was very dismaying – as his "illiteracy" turned out to be true.

He was also positioned critically; his department relied on external technical subscription services and critical agreements with solutions partners in forwarding the organization's business. Working with this person, although nice enough, presented difficulties. So, how is it that, in this new millennium, a person of otherwise high standing still has a comfort level in divulging ignorance regarding technical matters? This is an extreme limitation for any organization, regarding any job or position.

Thought of another way: Suppose you approach your CFO – you're new to the organization. You're a department head, a business leader, someone who is expected to set an example – a manager, director, or even a VP. You smile and make a confession: "I sure hope I don't have to prepare or balance any budgets around here – I'm 'financially-illiterate!' In fact, I can't even balance my own checkbook! Numbers just aren't my thing."

Every organization's managers are required to maintain budgets and to know how to manage them. Presumably they are hired with some basic skills: knowing how to add and subtract, and having some common understandings of basic budgets and the required accounting principles. Just because a staff member doesn't work in Finance & Accounting doesn't mean they'll never have to perform some nuts and bolts finance and accounting. Likewise, it is not too much to expect that managers and users have some basic computer skills.

That expectation is quickly morphing into the outright need that these people understand and promote their own use of technology in its relation to the business. After all, most people who enter an organization that has a Business-Technology Weave are the sort of people who have computers at home, or have used them in school. No one is allowed to get away with so-called computer-illiteracy any more, or even a stagnant appreciation of technology. Your organizational culture must evolve to one whereby users and managers are imaginative thinkers when it comes to using and growing the organization's use of technology. They should employ the same imagination and judgment when partnering on the use and plan of technology that they use when partnering with Finance on the organization's budget.

AN IT DEFICIT

Let's look at a common mistake on IT's part. How many organizations have a requirement for centralized data, yet have full knowledge that users - the business community - are storing data on local (c:) computer drives, or even portable media? Even the most sophisticated organizations, and the most tightly controlled environments, have this condition. This goes on even in organizations where it violates a document retention and content management policy – policies that are often imposed by outside regulatory agencies, or client bodies. Yet, if business members and leaders insist that it's a necessary "work-around," IT goes along. This can be a major mistake on IT's part. Let's leave the document retention/content management considerations aside for the moment, as they are rather heavy and are dealt with in another chapter. Let's look at the situation from a simple backup and recovery standpoint.

IT's position in any organization should be that all data is secure: accessible according to authorization; safely and securely maintained in the technical environment; recoverable in the case of loss in the production environment through any reason. Too often, users are responsible for backing up their own local drives. This is wrong. If there is genuine business data that is not coming under the umbrella of IT's backup domain, that is a wrong situation and you cannot profess to have complete security. You are at risk. You can hash out in the BIT forum as to how to expose peripheral data, and how to manage it, secure it and back it up – at a minimum you must document exceptions to policy and put them on record. Many important caches and swaths of data have been lost by organizations because the central, qualified, authority for the safekeeping of data (IT) was unaware of it. There was no central authority guaranteeing its safekeeping under these circumstances.

Let's look at one more area where IT is frequently remiss. Increasingly, organizations are responsible for anything and everything that happens within. We see where large judgments have been made in favor of employee plaintiffs who had complaints regarding offense and damages over electronic content containing porn, offensive jokes, illegal advocacy, and other inappropriate content. This is content that has long been defined as this kind of liability by courts. Remember too that just because some content may be legal in the broader sense, it can still violate your organization's best interest. Should your organization's data be subpoenaed, you wouldn't want negative characterizations of business partners or critical evaluations of members made public, for example. Most organizations have policies to guard against inappropriate use of business resources and to explain the consequences of harboring improper content, but many don't adequately reinforce the policy. Further, it's apparent that a lot of IT departments haven't picked up their responsibility, or perceived their own liability, in this area.

Let's be clear: One thing you don't want to have happen is that something blows up into an embarrassing exposure, with people asking how "IT" could have let inappropriate content broach your business-technology environment. For it is IT that implements spam-guards, monitors storage, and has the means (even if only under special permission by Business) to do a comprehensive review of data. The mechanics of, and the burden in, running a "clean" environment is IT's. While it is true that Business must cooperate and contribute to a clean environment, and that this is reinforced by policies both Business (HR) and IT - no business person has the time or ability to look across the board at data and content on a regular basis. No business person is tasked to have knowledge superior to IT's regarding best practice protections and best software solutions. This is a "behind the screen" faculty. If you're an IT staff member, and your IT department is not comfortable in answering to your organization's content, you need to get this into the BIT agenda quickly.

UNCOVERING THE "WHYS": PUTTING ACTIVITY WHERE IT BELONGS

Essentially, we're trying to position activity according to efficiency: to the arena that is best suited to a particular action by virtue of knowledge, resource, and responsibility. This facilitates better business. In parsing the Business-Technology Weave we find that most of what occurs at the users' desktops is in the domain of business: things such as the utilization of your core business software applications: proprietary mission-critical software such as an AMS, a customer-centric management system, sales and inventory, and so on. There too is the use of shelf applications (word processing, spreadsheets, presentation graphics, e-mail, etc.) and likely some specialty applications used by everyone (such as content management). The organization also has specialty applications used by the few (such as payroll, HR applications, laboratory analysis packages, statistical analysis, graphic arts, etc.). From the context of the Weave, we can think of the main business domain as "the front of the screen." This is the utility and potential of the power to be had on the front side of the computer screen at the desktop, as exercised by users.

Those things that happen "behind the screen" (from the users' perspective) are in the IT domain: In no particular order: Internet connectivity, security, server and workstation maintenance, installation/maintenance of software, backup and recovery of data, contracts, service level agreements, and so on and so forth.

Earlier, in determining where activity belonged, we asked: "Who is the relevant party that knows, or should know, 'the business' of what is under consideration?" We can now further sharpen our appreciation to who does what and why by asking that identified-party a question. We can help them understand where the burden of activity truly lies: "Does this happen on the 'front side' or 'back side' of the screen?" Let's apply this question to two items we just discussed: *backup of data* and *department orientation*.

Backup of data: Backups happen on the back side of the screen – that is, backup of data should be done by IT and it should be transparent to the user. You could make the argument that someone dragging and dropping files to a CD for backup is employing a "front screen" process – true. But this is not a backup *scheme* appropriate to a comprehensive security of business. A backup scheme in the Business-Technology Weave context is an automated routine that does not rely on any single individual's memory or action to achieve or regularize it. Also, IT has the discipline and fallbacks to ensure coverage of backups. IT ensures they're running each night, and checks content of the backups. No real backup routine or scheme in a business environment should be in one specific user's hands. You can make exceptions at your peril or convenience – but true data security relies on a backup that is a "back of the screen" process. Therefore, it is an IT activity.

Department orientation: Here we're referring to a narrow slice of orientation – not a general IT orientation, or the overall HR orientation that a new hire goes through upon inprocessing – but rather the hiring department's orientation of the new hire. If IT is orienting the new hire to the specifics of your department's use of software applications, as frequently happens, ask yourself "why?" Your department's use of software is a "front of the screen" endeavor. The organization has people in each department who are much more familiar with that department's procedures and rules for use. Have one of the business staff in the department provide this orientation. An orientation of sorts will happen anyway, in effect, through the new hire's questions of your other staff. Avoid duplication of effort by positing the activity of familiarization in the business department. Use of business applications is "front side of the screen."

When

Things never remain static. If you are not planning the action, driving the action, managing the action – taking action – you are still moving. The stream of time and surrounding change is impacting you whether you paddle and steer or not. As your competitors progress, as your business tools fall out-of-date or become less than optimal, as your organization falls behind on evolving best-practice – you will in fact be moving backward - by a comparative default. Make sure you're moving forward. The *whens* of action should become evident by virtue of the forward-looking postures we've described for individual and organization through discussion in the BIT forum, and the delivery of prudent action to the matrix of Five-Year, One-Year, and Individual Action Plans.

A huge assist to moving forward effectively in technology's support to business is to identify actions that can be turned into routines, and to put them on schedules: a leveraging of "whens." Business should facilitate thorough understanding of the organization's business burdens through exposures: the annual calendar of events, any regularized absences of key personnel, business cycles, predictable tax on resources, etc.

IT should strive to optimize schedules, in sympathy to the business: workstation upgrade and deployment; fileserver review and update; infrastructure review and update; documentation review and update – get these things identified and slotted to a particular quarter of the year. Even if exigencies change your priorities, you can easily swap one thing from one quarter with something from another quarter. You'll still have a balance on your routine and your resources, and you'll still have everything identified – things are less likely to fall off the table.

The proper schedule of "whens" will yield an efficient cycle. The more comprehensive your cycle, the more time you will have for special projects. You will move forward in the best posture for controlling outcomes. If you wait to do something until you are forced to take action, you may move forward, but you'll do so at greater expense – in terms of money, effort and efficiency. You'll find yourself lurching from one area of problems to another. Therefore, find the "sweet spot" for action in all of your routines, in accordance with the organization's events, distribution of resources, and cycles of business.

10

MANAGING PEOPLE IN THE WEAVE
- THE CHALLENGE TO IT

People are funnier than anybody.

Spike Jones

People are our biggest challenge, as we know. In this chapter, let's help everyone - Business and IT alike - understand the special nature of the IT challenge when managing people. Not just IT's management of "IT people," but the effective management of IT's relationship to everyone around them. In a chapter following, we'll look at the special challenge from a Business perspective. For now, let's talk about the IT leader's challenge - be that person a vice president, chief technology officer, chief information officer, director, helpdesk manager, network manager with administrators, etc. – any IT leader will benefit from this discussion. Just as importantly, each Business person will benefit from the awareness we establish here.

Earlier we talked about the proper management of those around you to achieve ultimate success. Let's look at that in detail. Here, we're going to propose that IT manages three classes of people - of equal contribution, of equal importance: Those people they work *on*, those they work *with*, and those they work *for*. Classifying people this way will yield some interesting relationships. We'll also talk about a power-prism – a device we can look through and rotate. The prism will have facets that expose how different issues and circumstances appear to change the class for any given individual - by exposing the dynamic of their power, or lack thereof, in each of those circumstances. In the continuum of change, this prism is a powerful device. The resulting awareness (that regardless of an individual's formal standing, circumstances can cause the individual to shift class on an informal basis) will allow us to recognize a person's behavior, reasons for it, and any negative influence on engagement.

Behaviors can be influenced by feelings of fear, vulnerability, or power, for example. If we can recognize these feelings and their cause, we can adjust our treatment of persons for ultimate outcomes. Too, we can assess ourselves for these shifts and protect ourselves from imprudent behavior or action.

Recognition of these shifts can be a powerful tool in managing your relationships in the change continuum of the Business-Technology Weave. First, let's classify people for you, the IT manager, so as to match their formal standing in the organization's hierarchy:

A VIEW TO MANAGING THOSE AROUND YOU

Those you work on: The first group is those people in the IT department reporting to you, an IT leader. This is the group of people that you formally manage, appraise, mentor, coach, reward, and discipline. This group also includes vendors and contractors, for while they don't report directly to you as their employer, they are subordinate to you. They do report to you within the scope of a project or service agreement. You indeed rate their work as feedback to their employer, and you even hire and fire these people for and from whatever endeavor they are supporting. From here on, let's indicate this group as WorkOns.

Those you work with: The second group is IT's fellow managers and business staff – co-workers with whom IT has no direct formal control from a management standpoint. In keeping with our syntax, these folks are WorkWiths.

Those you work for: The third group is those people who occupy hierarchy in the organization above IT; those who directly and indirectly manage IT. These are IT's direct supervision, the governance team, senior managers, boards, and any other authorities with influence. Hereafter referred to as WorkFors.

A QUICK CONSIDERATION OF CLASS

Remember that, from IT's vantage, there will be circumstances whereby individuals will informally occupy a different class at times. For example, I was once tasked to provide someone to our company president for computer training. He wanted to "get more out of his PC." In this circumstance the president became a WorkOn for IT (because we worked on him, by training him to standards we set), as well as remaining our WorkFor (in that we still worked for him in the larger sense).

Because all training requires challenge, we had to be aware of our limitations in challenging him– because of his primary occupancy in our WorkFor class. Remember too that people in positions of power frequently feel vulnerable when they confess an ignorance or need. Being mindful of these things in this circumstance, whereby the trainer has knowledge (and therefore a small power advantage) over the president, allows us to be mindful of special sensibilities and discretions.

In the next chapter, we'll employ the power prism whereby we'll view the circumstances and shifts that bring individuals into other classes. We'll see how this understanding is necessary for a true optimization of relationships and performance. These shifts are ongoing in the change continuum - and their influence and required management is continual.

Identifying and Managing WorkOns, WorkWiths, and WorkFors

Let's first thoroughly understand each class and define the people who have primary, or usual, occupancy in the class. Within each class, we'll examine the how and why of managing these people within the Weave.

WorkOns: These are the IT leader's direct reports. The people you hire, fire, manage, rate, and hopefully mentor and coach. Managing people in the technology field can be an especially challenging undertaking. Effective IT management here requires three very important things:

1) *Special disciplines and accountabilities* for IT staff. That is, adherence to best practices and standards of performance, with exposure to staff for the measures and verifications of those;

2) *Ability and judgment* on the IT leadership's part to guide people to standards. This guidance is achieved through proper accounting and recognition; and

3) *Control and Power* on IT's part, through sanction by Business, to dispense rewards, guidance, and discipline – in accordance with numbers 1) and 2) above. These are dispensed according to the means necessary in order to lead, sustain, and hold accountable those people that IT manages – in bringing best support and service to Business.

Let's look at each of these in-turn.

1) *Special Disciplines and Accountabilities*: Here we mean, as determined by the IT leader, clearly defined procedures for IT operations, clear expectations regarding tasks and projects, and a quality-of-service bar that IT personnel clear as they deliver service and solutions to Business. As opposed to the common interpretation, "discipline" here is first defined as the understandings, reinforcements, and structured resources necessary for delivery of success. There too is the discipline of accountability – people are called to account by virtue, first, of the very jobs they hold. IT has the organization's business in the palm of its hand. Secondarily, it will include the coaching, guidance, and any necessary reprimand in bringing negative performance or behavior into alignment with standards.

For the IT leader, this means making sure your WorkOns, the IT staff, know what is required to meet your standards, in meeting the organization's standards – and beyond. When you think about it: Exceeding standards is a routine necessity in delivering on business needs in the continuum of change.

To the business leader (here, any influencer outside of IT), that means giving IT the space to set and hold people to standards – so that IT can give you what you need. For example, let's look at ownership of tasks. The network manager is responsible for data backups. What does that actually mean? It means he or she is responsible for: the execution of the backups (making sure they're performed); checking the backups (to insure the appropriate data is being backed up, and is recoverable); and maintaining the backup routine (makes changes to the backup scheme as necessary – to accommodate new servers, drives, or applications, for example). This person also makes arrangement for coverage of backups in his or her absence. In addition, she or he must proactively inform the supervisor about any deviation from normal backup procedure. This person not only owns all of these allied responsibilities for backups, but must have a native understanding for the comprehensibility of all IT tasks and standards. They also understand why such adherence to standards is imperative.

If a night's backup fails, the network manager let's the supervisor know – *on an immediate basis.* A failure or delay in performing a task in another department may be transparent to the department or organization as someone catches up. But in most IT endeavors, there are too many interdependencies not to keep everyone apprised. For example, within IT, a night's failed backup may mean that a software module cannot be dropped into production until a manual backup of the live environment is made. Or, a contractor or vendor may be scheduled to connect from their remote location and place modified files in an area of your environment - overwriting the previous versions – thinking that should any problems arise, they can be reversed by recovery from your prior evening's backup. The IT supervisor will know every consequence for a failed backup in the current environment, or will know those people to poll to discuss potential liabilities. The supervisor will make or delegate the necessary communications within and outside the department regarding situations such as this. What you *don't* want to have, from both the Business and IT perspective, are employees who don't bother to communicate problems or statuses because appropriate expectations were never allowed to be set.

Moreover, beware the deferred consequence for substandard performance on anyone's part. It will set the overall bar for all IT staff; it will lower your quality of service; it will impact your security, and it will eventually harm business. A poorly run IT department also has wide ramifications for the organization. Poorly maintained standards in the safeguard of an incredibly important asset (information), and poor internal service to business, generally points to a comprehensive failure at the top. This failure can be indicative of an overall problem in the organization's management.

Make your IT department the bellwether of excellence – *allow* it to be. It will speak to everyone who visits, interviews, and transacts with your organization.

2) *Ability and Judgment*: The IT leader must have an ability to, once again, get everyone to their best game. In short, any manager will do three basic things:

    a) They will mentor/coach their staff,

    b) They will make reward, and

    c) When necessary they will make discipline (discipline includes setting structures, providing reinforcements, and the providing for punishment when necessary).

What does this mean in the Weave, and specifically to the IT leader?

Mentoring and Coaching Staff: When the IT leader mentors and coaches staff, she will of course lead by example: She will engage in civil discourse; she will deliver quality in any endeavor; she will make good attendance; she will *support business*. In the special discipline and accountability inherent to IT, the IT leader will keep her staff informed, as she expects to *be* informed.

The IT leader also must own up to mistakes or problems incurred through her own actions, just as she expects her staff to do. Much risk and wasted effort can be incurred in an IT environment without timely and trusted communication. An ability to lead by quality example is very important.

Making Reward: A little trickier is the ability to make appropriate reward. The IT leader must balance recognition to individual staff through careful measure, and must balance recognition across the department so as not to appear to favor some staff at the expense of others. At the same time, recognition has to be meaningful. It must assist the proper promotion, reward, and encouragement to those who deserve it most – which happens to serve the organization's best interest, too.

When discussing awards and incentives, we're referring to everything from promotion, raises, bonuses, change in workspace, etc. – to those smaller, but very important, things such as verbal praise, recognition in meetings, compensatory time, early afternoons, etc.

REWARD AND RECOGNITION: AN EMPHASIS ON THE FUTURE

Within each staff member is a potential. Meeting the special requirements of the organization should also mean the satisfaction of individual potential. The requirements of the individual are to improve in the current environment; to improve as the environment changes; and to improve their ability to help *plan and change* that environment. Respectively, you want your IT staff delivering better service now; you want their capabilities to expand as your Business-Technology Weave changes (becoming ever more sophisticated; they become more sophisticated too); and, you want each employee offering their suggestions for the betterment of their respective areas.

You want them to help bring that betterment to fruition. This leads to better overall IT endeavors, maneuvers you successfully into the future, and provides better support to business. Let's call all of this The Edge. We've heard of the leading edge, the cutting edge, and the bleeding edge: Here, we're going to define our Edge as a *responsible forward posture* - whereby we have our plans clearly defined (Five Year, One Year, Individual Action, detailed projects, etc.), sanctioned by Business and IT, and properly balanced according to schedules, resources, and surroundings. (We'll revisit The Edge in *Security*).

Let's speak to staff's maintenance of The Edge. Because the present has a natural advantage in terms of everyone's attention, we want to skew the reward system a bit toward those things that successfully plot the future. This emphasis helps to draw staff's attention to futures planning. The IT leader should not be the only one in the IT department (or the organization) casting about for better use of application software, for better PC workstations, for better backup solutions, for better service contracts, for better business support ideas, for better return on investment. Therefore, the leader should task each person in respective areas to come up with ideas for plug-in to the 5-Year Plan. Too, any idea for betterment of the "present" is a near-term future idea. Build the "ideas" requirement into formal job-supports (job descriptions, documentation, performance appraisals, etc.). Emphasize futures planning on the agenda of the Individual Action Plan preparations and meetings.

Everything, and Everyone, has an Edge

For the IT staff, sustaining the Weave doesn't mean parking oneself in the present until something bumps one along. Each person must be proactive, and you must be casting your gaze to the horizon. Everyone helps plan the future – management, programmers, network managers, database managers, helpdesk technicians, operators, administrators, etc. The future also includes a personal Edge for each staff person. They must be growing, accumulating new knowledge, and sharpening their skills through a proactive identification of whatever is necessary. Much of their Edge is maintained by use of online documentation, self-training, and free educational seminars. Staff should join and attend relevant groups – often sponsored by vendors and applications providers.

This requires solid encouragement. So, for the IT leader, you create and sustain this mindset through measured reward – and you weight the distribution of your stock of rewards to the end of the scale where improvements are happening. In the technology part of the weave, we're not going to reward people for merely doing their job in a competent or even excellent manner. That's what one brings to the daily grind to satisfy a baseline requirement: incentivizing that will be handled through praise. Rather, we're going to reward according to vision, vision-translation, and implementation. This way, we drive the better-business goal of expansion of the possible. We promote continuous improvement.

The Future weighs heavily in your organization's favor once your organization knows how to surf that continuous wave. You're either on top of it, or it's on top of you. When you're on top, you'll know how to look for and recognize the breaks, the paths of least resistance, the favorable timings - in pointing your organization's comprehensive Edge. This allows you to stay ahead of your competitors, to leverage your resources and staff, to maximize profit, and to better your delivery of services. Remember – you master the Future, so that the Future serves you. The Future serves you in offering better business services, better methodologies, better software, better hardware, reduced prices, new and better vendors, new and better IT practices, etc. – *but only if you're looking for them, can recognize them, and can capitalize on them.* In alliance with your organization's various plan systems and change qualifications, you must have a system that recognizes people for their contribution to your organization's status as an effective Business-Technology Weave.

This is why you should set up a reward system that fosters a climate where people will be on the lookout for better, less expensive, and more productive ways to do things. In essence, we will school thought and activity for contribution to betterment, through reward and recognition.

A BALANCE

We don't mean to discount the present – today's business is no less important than the future. What do we do for people who are sustaining the day-to-day? How do balance recognition for daily support? Further, can we reward them according to the futures-bias standard?

We can always reward strong support and quality of service on any kind of daily deliverables. The occasional "spot" award is appropriate. Year-end bonuses are routine in many environments. We can take care of recognition. But how do we spur a forward-thinking posture in a position that seems locked in the present? Can we skew our rewards and recognition toward an emphasis on the future in all positions? We sure can.

Let's use as an example here what some in Business or IT may feel is a difficult application of this principle – reward and recognition to those who are not in the mainstream of planning and change management. Let's use a technician in the HelpDesk support arena to show how we can position that person for seeking improvement of the environment, and betterment of self. At the same time, the position maintains full support to the day-to-day requirements.

Consider that on most days, your technician arrives at work knowing what he needs to do. He's got some holdover items from the previous day and he'll answer the support queue in support of today's items – someone's PC keeps crashing, someone needs help printing something, someone requires an install of something. This is the primacy of this person's world – it keeps his focus narrow and in the present – which is necessary for daily support. But in his down time, which always exists, he can be exploring ways to reduce workstation cost. He can look for vendors with better prices on peripherals. He can inventory equipment to ensure resources are properly distributed. He can take advantage of technical forums and free online tutorials to advance his job proficiency – *and must*. Praise his day-to-day support, but reward him for the fruit his forward posture yields: price breaks he engineered for the new PCs; new job knowledge enabling faster disposition of service packs, etc. Get an awareness and a lean toward the future going.

Let's now look up the line - through programmers, project managers, network folks, directors - in helping to bring an appropriate balance of awareness between the near/short term burden and the long term forecasting and planning. We go all the way up to your IT lead – CTO, CIO, VP, and so on. That person's rewards and incentives are also weighted toward the planning and realization of the Future. And by realization of the Future, we mean a rightsized future. One where your spending is appropriate to the necessities, and further, makes allowance for the *future's* future: ongoing functionalities, scalability for growth, longevities in the marketplace, etc. Make sure you've identified the correct requirements: solid, not false, solutions. Solid infrastructure. Appropriate hires - etc. This method of reward and incentive reinforces commitment and quality in crafting the Five-Year Plan, the One-Year Plan, and the Individual Action Plans.

Now let's take a look at one more IT position to expand our appreciation for how rewards can serve the Edge. How would this principle translate in channeling a programmer's awareness? Easy, right? Programmers are always making improvements. Many of them will be assigned projects. Projects bear on the future. But let's consider something: Even the most comprehensive changes – large scale projects with organization-wide impact – become someone's routine for the day once the project is approved and mounted. We're not saying that there is not reason to reward someone at the end of a long project. However, our whole thrust has been to look for imaginative ideas for leveragability. A project itself is about change, so we should seek something original within it that could serve the organization beyond the project's delivery. Here, look for something clever within the project.

For example, on one particular project, a programmer who was project managing came up with a little report sheet that was required to be filled out each week by staff members. These staff members were testing a new business software module for their department. It wasn't the idea of a report so much, but rather its design, ease of use, and the users' willingness to fill it out that made it important. The programmer made the sale. The report was a form that solicited and collected what the staff person liked and didn't like in the new module – and it required suggestions for improvement. This did several things. It collected many good ideas for improvement to the module. It helped point out areas where the software was not efficient. And, it helped identify adjustments to more effectively support business flow.

One very important thing was that the report took the staff's ability to merely complain off the table. It engaged them, and if they didn't take advantage of the report, and partner in crafting the customization of "their" module, the peril was theirs. Further, the report's consolidated user concerns served as a learning tool. For example, some staff members were asking for so many automatic pop-ups and reminders for data-entry fields, that to implement them all would have served a diminishing return. It highlighted an example of the false-solution: If you "dummy proof" something too much, you inhibit the efficiency of the majority of people who know how to do their job. So the report collected and vetted requirements, and exposed learning opportunities for staff, in serving to help implement a properly fitted business module.

There are many feedback requirements and tools on any project, but this report was particularly well crafted, and its importance was well explained by the programmer in the BIT sessions. Its design and her leadership facilitated the steady flow of positive feedback for betterment to the project. But further - this little tool was employed in other projects large and small. This good idea, within this programmer's project, not only helped to pilot her project, but served other concurrent and future projects managed by all. The organization repurposed it, and leveraged it. So that aspect was recognized and emphasized in her reward, and within the organization.

MAINTAINING MORALE

Keep in mind that, as the IT leader, you possess some powerful, positive, motivators that require little or no outside coordination. Give a hard worker Friday afternoon off – but do it spontaneously. The spontaneity of the gesture is a feel-good-multiplier – that is, staff members who suddenly find themselves leaving at noon on a nice Friday afternoon feel very good indeed.

For the business leader, give your IT lead the freedom and flexibility to dispense these kinds of benefits. Be on the lookout for crimps to the IT leader's effective management of morale, motivation, and confidence. Consider this example, and look for, and fix, similar circumstances: there are organizational environments where the cycle of work requires some departments to put in extremely long hours for weeks at a time. The organization cannot possibly grant compensatory time to make up for those hours, and therefore any comptime at all, for anyone, is often frowned upon in these environments. However, those specific departments are bonused very handsomely for that extra work – bonuses that IT and other departments are often not eligible for. Therefore, Business leaders must give managers in various departments the freedom and flexibility to manage their staff according to conditions within the scope of *their* work, and according to rewards that must be at *their* disposal.

Your IT department is going to have crunch times, emergencies, and exigencies which – if handled right – will be transparent to you, the business person. IT staff may find themselves working all night – sometimes as scheduled, and other times at a moment's notice. You're going to want IT leaders with the ability and judgment to know when to grant extras to staff, in the right measure.

There's also something curious in some environments: the caution against praising staff in certain circumstances. Many senior managers view praise as a zero-sum game: If someone is praised, it will somehow be diluted if someone else receives mention. Or, it will make someone feel slighted. Praise need only be accurate, meaningful, and occasional. Don't over-praise things that are routine.

Beyond praise, you must recognize accomplishment within the daily grind. Shoot out the occasional e-mail to thank a staff member for something – anything. Not as a direct response to a task completion. Wait a day, a week, then send a correspondence: "Frank, I wanted to tell you how much I appreciated your work with the Claims department last week. Several people have approached me to tell me what a great job you did." Also recognize people in the weekly IT staff meeting. Make the recognition matter-of-fact but appreciative. "Carla, great job getting those new PCs to Government Affairs." Start any meeting with a positive comment about someone's performance – and rotate those to whom you compliment. Don't make anything up, but hopefully each of your staff is doing something that you can profile in a positive way.

Rewards aside, look at those individuals who are expanding their potential, particularly on their own initiative. Recognize those who are pushing their small envelope in an effective manner. Who is feeding the five-year plan with good ideas? Who is bringing suggestions to the table? Some suggestions may not be implemented or practical at the moment, but praise this kind of thinking – it will pay off. Recognize those who are delivering excellent service and support, and who seek better ways to deliver. Remember that praise, when written, will serve you in supporting recommendation for reward through bonus or spot awards. It will also serve as documentation when the time comes for employee appraisal.

Making Discipline: Beyond the discipline of channeled energy, support structures such as job definitions, normal job expectations, etc., there is the discipline of correction. Generally, discipline is necessary to closing some divide between necessary performance and expected behavior - and the actual level of performance or behavior that is contributing to the failure in fulfilling necessities and expectations.

An especially astute judgment is required for imposing discipline. When, what kind, and how much? Discipline has many diverse forms: It can be the assignment of extra work to catch up; it can be extra training, whether formal, or self-train, in order to rise to standards; it can be an acknowledgment of a leader's authority; it can be an assignment to bring order to someone's tasks or work environment. Short of punishment, discipline should start as firm guidance so as to define expectations, and provide reinforcements to, a rise in standards of performance and behavior. In the IT realm of the Business-Technology Weave, a sincere effort toward improvement has to be immediate.

There also comes a time when certain staff members will require punishment. When a staff member is under-performing, not coming in on time, missing too many days of work, making too many "mistakes," being insubordinate – it is time to act. Again, any manager should already be familiar with the progressive path of counseling and discipline. We'll revisit that in a moment, and apply it to IT's special considerations. Problems regarding behavior and performance cannot be allowed to jeopardize business productivity and security of business assets. Those things cannot be put at risk under any circumstance.

DETERMINING DISCIPLINE'S SIZE AND TARGET

Lets first say that in cases warranting immediate termination (destruction of company property, physical violence, threats, illegal activity, etc.) not a lot of guidance is necessary here. Your human resources department is going to turn the wheel in those circumstances. We're talking about a person's behavior or performance that, until we know better, appears salvageable, and we expect best outcome. Here, too, HR is going to play a central and very important role.

When discussing poor IT performance in the context of the Business-Technology Weave, realize that we face a very quick slope. You must judge an individual's suitability to the *safety* of the IT department – and hence to the safety and security of your business. You must make a quick, but accurate and supportable, assessment of the individual's prognosis. Much of our action here as IT and Business leaders will depend on the individual's history and the severity of the problem.

Let's first talk about a solid staff member who suddenly exhibits a slide in performance. When a well-rounded staff member suddenly becomes a discipline or performance problem, look for an underlying large event. This person may be experiencing something outside of work that would temporarily derail the best of us. In *all* such cases of discipline, we are attempting to bring the employee back to productivity and job satisfaction. Divorce, custody battles, financial problems, health problems, any problems with family members, can distract the best employees and lead to a performance deficit. As managers of people, we need to bring help to these people – insofar as there is traction. That is, the person has to be *helpable*. For these kinds of "outside" problems, the human resources department is going to be the arbiter for action.

In cases where there is not an outside event, there may be an internal situation where the employee feels job stress through the sense of a loss of control. Ensure the employee has all of the tools and resources at their disposal to get the job done. Evaluate any recent changes in the structure of their job. Look for a specific assignment that coincides with the problem. Someone who gave every appearance of being able to step up into new responsibilities may have in fact oversold himself or herself, and you may have allowed yourself to be sold. At this point, it's up to you as to whether you can help the employee rise to the challenge, or if you need to scale the employee back to where they were. In the IT world, there's really only one direction. That is to grow with new responsibility, and to take on new knowledge and practices. For someone who cannot keep up, you need to begin the formulation of a plan to put that person into a routine position that does not experience much change (unlikely in IT), or make plans to grow your department without that person.

In cases where an individual simply fails to rise to expected and defined standards in the course of poor performance or behavior, the progression to termination must be swift, while remaining within the scope of appropriate evaluation and escalation of action. IT is particularly vulnerable to staff members who harbor grudges, surly attitudes, and damaging intentions. They can harm your IT endeavors, and therefore they can harm your business.

Discipline in Service to Security

For IT, we're going to follow a basic model that is supported by any Human Resources Department – and you must always be within your organization's guidance regarding disciplinary procedures. To HR and other influencers, we must advise that IT be allowed to employ the "full letter of the law" when imposing discipline. Do not allow under-performing or under-qualified employees to tie your IT department down. It is risky to business, it is expensive, and it gets harder to fix as time goes by.

Here's a progression that does one of two things: helps the deserving employee come back on balance (appropriate performance, productivity and job satisfaction) or brings the employee to *your* decision points in progressive action:

a) Verbal counseling: Exposes the employee to his or her failings. Helps the supervisor determine the source of problems. Sets expectations for the resolution of problems. A partnering commitment is made to support the employee with appropriate tools, resources, and guidance. An expectation is set for signs of immediate improvement, and any elements that are dependent on time are defined with a schedule. Here the leader should be timely enough in catching a deficiency such that consequences are not a large part of the discussion. The focus should be on improvement and advantages in making that happen as fast as possible.

The employee either responds in positive fashion – or –

b) Further verbal counseling is delivered, it is written for the record and filed, there is a reinforcement of expectations, consequences are defined. Consequences can include the jeopardizing of formal appraisal ratings, a diminishment in a person's reputation, negative impact to the department, perils to business, and possible removal of duties and authorities.

Failure to improve -

c) Counseling is escalated to HR, a formal noting of the continuation of the problem, updated expectations for immediate improvement, escalation of consequences, up to and including termination.

Failure to improve -

d) Termination.

In IT, you face a very quick slope, whereby you must judge an individual's suitability to the safety of the department. Once a *progressive* disciplinary process is started, it must proceed on a progressive pace so as to quickly determine whether the individual can rise to standards, or if necessary, to remove the individual from the environment before this person puts business at risk. This is extremely important for Business to understand.

In setting expectations for improvement, the person within the discipline not only must perform the raw mechanics required of the job - they must bring the appropriate attitude to the process. They need to be expressing their desire for a positive outcome, and committing to the requirements for what's necessary to put them back in a best-standing with the organization. This is necessary to prevent a loss of confidence in them by the organization.

3) *Control and Power*: Here is where IT needs to know "where it is" in regards to its sanction. Know the extent of your control. In cases where some element of IT fails to account, appropriate and measured discipline must be imposed, and IT management must have the power to bring appropriate disciplinary measures. The organization serves itself well when it ensures it has someone willing to run IT according to real-world expectations and outcomes.

This is where IT seeks an understanding from Business in this part of the Weave. Issues of discipline and accountability within IT may look harsh to an outside business person. But the stakes within accelerative change, and shifting burdens, means that IT leadership must be free to apply the full measure of appropriate power and judgment in achieving security and support to business.

Effective IT management for WorkOns rests on standards of performance that are clearly defined and clearly exposed. Employees must perform according to those standards and be measured against them. Employees have to be held to these measures for appropriate reward, or when necessary, discipline. Managers must set clear expectations, provide examples, and place the emphasis on excellence. Poor performance must be dealt with quickly, fairly, and effectively.

IT's Unique WorkOn Burden

While all managers and departments have a performance burden, IT is in a unique position: that's because from Business' perspective, no single department approaches IT's unique position in mitigating risk to business. Conversely, no other entity is in IT's position to bring harm the organization, be it through negligence or willful disregard, in such an *immediate manner*.

A network that is down means that staff goes to about 5% of normal productivity. An Internet outage means that you lose a large part of your effectiveness in communicating with your outside business interests. A poorly maintained core business management system puts data in jeopardy, and means that you alienate customers through poor service. Improperly negotiated service contracts and service level agreements means that your organization is wasting money and not maintaining appropriate coverage –putting you in the zone of unacceptable risk.

Consider your other departments: no accounting mistake, however embarrassing, is likely to halt operations on any given day. No marketing campaign, no matter how poorly mounted, is likely to halt the conduct of business dead in its tracks. No Human Resources action can crash business in a moment. *No other department can muck up business operations faster or more comprehensively than your IT department.*

For Business leaders: understand that now, more than ever, your IT leadership must "work on" this class of people in a first-rate manner.

WORKWITHS: We all "work with" everyone – whether we're considering subordinates, supervision, or those in lateral positions to us. But in our WorkWith class here, we're speaking of people who are primarily lateral to IT – the swath of other managers and leaders in the organization with whom you routinely deal.

In order to bring a sharper focus, let's start our discussion of WorkWith people by discussing other managers in the business environment. That is, for the IT leader, this is the group of people with whom you have a rough power equivalent. Think of it from the BIT perspective – to include any regularized group or ad hoc people with whom you plot business support and solutions. Here you have the best dynamic for negotiation, and greatest opportunity for brainstorming and planning. Here you have the best sales environment. Comparatively speaking, much less so will things be dictated to you, say, than when working with your WorkFor group. Conversely, less so will you be dispensing instruction and rote, as when working with the WorkOn group.

THREE KINDS OF WORKWITHS

You will find three kinds of people in the WorkWith group. (Indeed this next examination of people in the Weave can be applied with equal vigor to WorkOns, WorkWiths, and WorkFors. But first, apply the following understandings to our WorkWith group, as it is critical to planning and maintaining the Weave. There is also the most significant representation for all three sub-types within the WorkWiths).

The three kinds of WorkWiths are:

1) Those who like technology, embrace it and look for ways to leverage it. These people partner well with IT. They go out of their way to cultivate good

relations with the IT staff. They appear happy, well adjusted, participatory, and understand technology quite well – therefore, they use technology very well. They are generally pleasurable to work with for these reasons. We'll call these folks *TechnoShines*.

2) There is then that kind of person who is ambivalent about technology. The "just show me what to do" types. Give them a computer, keep it running, and you won't hear too much from them. They go with the flow. They "find" that there's a change coming, and roll with it. We can think of them as having a sort of benign "whatever" attitude, and they deal with whatever comes down the pike. These folks can't be counted on for any groundbreaking suggestions, but they are generally positive – at their worst they won't actively inhibit progress. As they find that they're in a Business-Technology Weave, they can be counted on to do what is necessary. These people are *TechnoFinds*.

3) The third kind of person is someone who seems unable to appreciate technology. They may view it as a necessary evil – and worse for them, it is constantly evolving. I hesitate to use the word techno-phobe here, although there are those. But most of the people we're considering in this category are able to use technology, and many very effectively. We know that within the Weave they pose a problem because they generally don't treat IT matters well, and they don't treat the people in IT very well. Whether through extreme criticism or negative attitude, they bind things up. They are, therefore, *TechnoBinds*.

Having defined these folks, let's examine them closer. It should be easy to slot the WorkWiths in your organization into one of these three groups. Recognizing them and their corresponding behavior helps to work with them more effectively.

TechnoShines, TechnoFinds, and TechnoBinds in Detail

The TechnoShine: The TechnoShine is a satisfying, even fun, person to work with. Don't underestimate the power of fun. People are going to be a whole lot more creative, resistant to negative effects of stress, and much more productive if they feel they're having fun and working with fun people. This person is always looking for the better way, and is enthusiastic regarding improvements – thus they bring enthusiasm and energy to change. They work well with others, in and out of their department, and this carries over into their appreciation for what others do. So how do we manage this WorkWith person? What is the leverage in maximizing this person's potential, contribution, and influence?

This person is an obvious candidate for the BIT team. They will not only represent their department well, but they'll have an overall appreciation for the organization's business. This kind of person tends to build time in an organization. They're well connected politically. They don't job hop. They have important institutional knowledge. They give credit where credit is due. They will make suggestions regarding best-practice with appreciation for how it will affect, and enhance, other departments. In fact, they make suggestions regarding other departments in a way that is not intrusive, but helpful and acceptable. They also accept suggestions and criticisms very well.

In addition to soliciting this kind of person's participation on the BIT team, you can employ them to serve as a liaison. Often they'll become an informal liaison between their department and IT anyway. However, the IT leader should push this kind of arrangement. During large-scale implementations, someone in each business department needs to take the lead anyway in collecting business requirements and helping to translate those into effective solutions. No less important, the TechnoShine can help buffer IT from some of the more difficult people in their area. TechnoShines by nature are informal sponsors for initiatives, and IT in general, by virtue of their positivity.

TechnoShines are necessary to BIT endeavors. However, don't load the BIT team with TechnoShines to the exclusion of other valuable people who may not rise to this level. You will have to have representation by virtue of position and influence, as well as ability.

The TechnoFind: The TechnoFind is a person who adjusts to the temperature around them. They "find" that technology is permeating everything. It is an increasing influence on the part of their daily lives, both in the professional environment and the personal arena. They adjust.

TecnoFinds do what is *necessary*. They don't like sticking their necks out. Therefore they don't make waves – which in itself can be valued in many circumstances. They're safe and practical people – they avoid risk. So, how can we leverage this kind of person? Should we merely be satisfied that they, at least, won't muck things up?

Actually, this kind of person is very useful. TechnoFinds tend to be very honest about system performances and deliverables. They are not idle complainers, therefore a criticism usually has value. Nor do they inflate technology's contribution. They don't seek to hang every bell and whistle on a system to the point of a diminished return. Theirs is usually a very balanced, informed opinion. They want to know how to get their job done – they're not fooled by the sizzle and want the steak. Most of the people in any organization will be TechnoFinds – therefore, you must satisfy this important majority. This person is invaluable for feedback – *how's the new software performing? How is your remote-access working? Are you satisfied with HelpDesk support?* Whereas TechnoFinds will likely make up the majority of an organization's staff, surveying them and exercising improvements in service to them is a winning combination.

But don't look to this kind of person for a leadership role. You don't want to select this person to oversee their department's implementation of a business software application module, for example – unless there is no other choice. This person may or may not be a good choice for participation on the BIT team. Remember, the BIT team's seats are valuable. The people who occupy them should be those who are informed enough to contribute, who desire to contribute, and who have the institutional knowledge and the good judgment to occupy one of these important seats. A TechoFind person simply may not qualify.

However, in an instance where you must have a department's representation on BIT, and the department is populated by TechnoFinds, you must choose the best person by virtue of position and influence. Too, a TechnoFind may outclass certain TechnoShines by virtue of deep business-knowledge and sheer know-how in other areas. Choose that person who best meets the diverse qualifications necessary for moving business forward.

We can't afford to imply here that TechnoFinds are unlikely to make a contribution or deliver anything of value in contributing to the Weave's momentum. For example, solicit this person's contribution when conducting requirements-analysis. For the reasons stated above, this person will know the practical side for getting work done, and will be very matter of fact about what a new system needs to do. They'll have high expectations in meeting and beating what the old system did, as you can usually rely on them for the pragmatic view.

The TechnoBind: Uh-oh. The time has come to discuss that kind of person that we'd all rather avoid, but that we must, alas, deal with. We must try to discuss TechnoBinds in keeping with the overall positive tone of our discussions, but there are some simple realities that we need to examine if we hope to overcome the obstacles that TechnoBinds can impose. Let's define the TechnoBind in plain language – then we'll discuss methods to blunt their influence, and where possible to neutralize them. We'll also note that TechnoBinds are frequently correct, and can contribute on occasion. However, it is necessary here to recognize their contribution to inefficiency. We'll need to know how to identify them, and how to best handle them.

TechnoBinds can be very negative people – and frequently are complainers. Therefore, when they're in a Business-Technology Weave, IT represents a fat target. So, too, does work in general. Because TechnoBinds aren't interested in acclimating and moving forward at an efficient pace, they contribute to their own, self-reinforcing, "complaint-ready" environment. Be aware that TechnoBinds are a counter-productive influence on everything they come into contact with: their department, group projects, other's attitudes, and so on. They may not drive things backward, necessarily, but they create enough of a drag on events that they s-l-o-w things significantly, if not carefully managed.

THE TECHNOBIND'S VIEW OF "PROBLEMS"

The TechnoBind finds fault where none exists. The TechnoBind exaggerates problems where they do exist. The TechnoBind usually does not offer solutions – in instances where they do, they pose impractical, self-serving *false-solutions*. The TechnoBind thrives on *division*, seeks to *create divides*, and then works to *widen divides*. The failure frequently lies in the TechnoBinds own sense of inadequacy. In other words: Don't look at (judge) me – look at (judge) *this – isn't it terrible*? It is the deflection of attention away from them. Understanding their motivation helps to vet and identify the value of their input (or lack thereof).

So, what do we do with TechnoBinds? With each parry and thrust, whether in one-on-one conversation, whether in a meeting, whether in an e-mail, etc., you must treat each complaint, suggestion, or critique from a position of practicality: your attitude, your answer, your action, *must move business forward*. The appearance to the TechnoBind, and to observers around you, is such that the TechnoBind is treated no differently than anyone else. You do, however, mitigate risk for any negative consequence, and you briskly evaluate their "contribution," and as necessary move through or past them. You do this by thanking them for their input, and by turning obligation back to them. You do not carry their problem in your pocket – you put the problem in *their* pocket.

What do we mean by this? Here are some actual exchanges with TechnoBinds to illustrate:

TechnoBind: "Can't we have more pop-up reminders on our member data-entry screen? My staff is saving member information without filling all of the fields. We paid all of this money for the new system, and it doesn't even make sure we're collecting all of the member information. Why can't we dummy-proof it?"

Answer: "Thanks for bringing that to our attention. As you know, we've implemented a fair number of pop-up reminders to critical data fields. Our budget limits customizations such as more pop-up screens, and we need to reserve money for increased functionality within the application. The good news is that our vendor says that dummy-proofing offers a false sense of security, and can never compete with conscientious data entry. So, they advise against more pop-ups, and I agree."

"I suggest some user-training sessions within your department to make sure the data-entry personnel 1) understand their obligation to input accurate records, 2) transfer member information from hardcopy to the system accurately and comprehensively, and 3) solicit any missing information from the member by phone or e-mail when necessary, so as to complete the record."

Note that this places the obligation (the "moving business forward" action) where it belongs. The TechnoBind's staff is performing sloppy work – no IT system can overcome that – that is, not without a lot of expense and effort that would burden the wrong areas, and create diminishing returns.

We can note here that relying on dummy-proofing creates a lax environment whereby data-entry personnel become groomed to assume that any field without a pop-up can be ignored as "not very important." Further, this laxity, when not handled here, is free to breathe and grow into other areas. Placing the load where it belongs helps to keep the TechnoBind in a practical mode. Let's face it – data-entry should be a *simple, routine* endeavor. Dummy-proofing implies that this TechnoBind has dummies in their department. Unlikely, unless this TechnoBind is utilizing poor hiring and vetting practices – and that's a different problem. *Don't carry the TechnoBind's problems in your pocket.*

For the IT leader, WorkWiths are an important group – understand them thoroughly. Your understanding of, and relationships within, this group may well be the largest contributor to mounting and maintaining a true Business-Technology Weave in your organization.

WorkFors: These are the folks who "work on" *you* - the IT leader – and include any entity or individual who has sway over IT-business matters. These are your direct supervision, senior management, your governance committee members, your board, and other senior players who have influence. It also includes clients, members, and customers. For your organization, it may include regulatory bodies or government agencies. But the steadiest and most influential WorkFor interactions will be with those superiors in the organization itself.

For the IT leader, you must embrace the fact that many, if not most, of these people are not particularly interested in information technology. Even when they are, they don't have time for a lot of details. They are not oriented to details – at least situationally. They don't have time for details – they have people working for them that attend to those. You for instance.

WorkFors are big-picture players, and are focused on results. They'll want to hear about solutions, not problems. They want to hear about progress. They want to hear about productivity and efficiency. They want to hear about *success*. Keep in mind that anyone you speak to in this group, no matter how highly placed, has to report to someone too. Their burden for delivering success is likely greater than yours.

In order for you to succeed, you must align your resources and methods so that you deliver consistent success to this group. If you're escalating problems to the WorkFors, you have not done your job effectively at the WorkWith and WorkOn levels. You have not established your sanctions, sponsorships, and you likely have failed to make the sale. Perhaps you've exceeded the limits of your lead. It's important to remember this: If you start to sense yourself as tipping toward a problem-reporting stance when engaging with the WorkFors, as opposed to a success-reporting and summary style of communication, you must make immediate adjustments. A qualified exception is your interaction with your direct supervision. Here, you'll iron out problems and strategies. But even here, you must present solutions – you must have a positive answer for moving business forward.

As you may suspect, TechnoShines can be rare in this group. There is an overwhelming majority of TechoFinds here, and a very small proportion of TechnoBinds. The heavy proportion of TechnoFinds in this group works to an IT leader's advantage here, and also to any Business manager when interacting and discussing the Weave. That's because WorkFors rely on your knowledge and the strength of your position to pilot the organization into the future. Once you've established a sound reputation with this group based on solid performance and trust, you should find very rewarding relationships here.

It should be a rare situation where you go to this group to lobby for relief – but if you feel you must, or if you have a special relationship at this level whereby someone specifically wants to be kept apprised in a more detailed fashion than is usual, you must yet remember your audience. Keep things very focused, very positive (even when reporting problems), and make certain you pose valid solutions to problems in a positive way. Your reputation should be such that you are seen as the facilitator to progress. Nothing is personal, everything is business. *Nothing is personal, everything is business*. It matters not how some others engage – this is your engagement, and this will be your reputation's enhancement of your credibility. Those that facilitate progress will ultimately cook to the top, regardless of temporary setbacks or small, inconsequential battles lost. Keep that larger picture in mind when talking to the big-picture people.

Let's next examine the Power Prism – after which we'll examine aspects of Business' special position for managing in the Weave.

11

THE POWER PRISM

The point of power is always in the present moment.

Louise L. Hay

As we consider our WorkOns, WorkWiths, and WorkFors, there will be situations where people take on some responsibilities, characteristics, and behaviors usually associated with occupancy in one of the other groups. Certain behaviors are not only adopted, but they distort: someone may take on additional responsibility and become overbearing, or they may suffer a lack of confidence. We must be aware of situational changes and the feelings they engender in people. This way, we can adjust our own behavior in managing our relationship with them. In other words, we have to maintain that constant of pulling their best game in contributing to maximum success. Also, it's our obligation to support them effectively – particularly during change. We need to be a little sensitive during these times – fortunately, a little sensitivity goes a long way.

Your organization, and specific environment, will have many situations that will influence power in many ways. Change brings about general unfamiliarity. In the case of changing business practices, new business competition, new products, new services, new support applications, new computers – whatever is happening - there is an environment, a continuum, where some are assuming power, and some may be losing it.

It can be helpful, and downright important, to view matters through a Power Prism: that is, to view each situation and circumstance as a matter of who may gain, and who may lose – or who simply harbors those perceptions. Power is often deception, illusion - or delusion - as the case may be.

We'll examine all groups, but we'll start with the WorkOn group. They are a frequent recipient of major change. These folks generally have the least to do with planning change – their power is limited. True, their opinions are solicited, and they provide basic facts during analysis of requirements, but this follows on to the big decision to make a change. The WorkOns are not the big decision makers, and they can feel "put upon."

Occasionally, however, we see a person from the WorkOn group shift when they are asked to step up within a project and represent their department, or when taking on a leadership role in an endeavor that is parallel to their main job efforts. Perhaps a temporary increase in responsibility is even a test; an evaluation of promotion potential. Let's look at a couple of examples and how to manage the shifts.

A WORKON TEMPORARILY SHIFTS TO GREATER RESPONSIBILITY

Frequently a WorkOn person assumes oversight duties, a measure of power, during the implementation phase of a project. Perhaps this person is asked to coordinate internal department meetings regarding the collection of requirements for new software, or to meet with people to design new reports. Perhaps the compelling reason that this person is selected for this is because he has the time to do this – he may never have done anything like this before. Here you have to ensure that this person doesn't become too overbearing. A person in this situation can overcompensate for a lack of experience by exhibiting a blustery over confidence. Or, this person may feel slightly intoxicated with their newfound authority. They can't help but being "green," – they have no prior scale against which to measure effort and delivery. Your responsibility is to mentor and coach them, and as importantly to help the WorkOn balance and adjust their attitude to the new role.

Occasionally an opportunity comes along for a WorkOn person to assume a higher profile in the organization at large. Unlike an actual promotion, whereby a WorkOn might become a WorkWith (with formal power over others), what we're talking about here is a situation. Perhaps it's an additional-duty type of condition, or a nuance to their position. One that now requires a perspective and judgment that the bulk of their job usually does not require or demand. That is, where the duty involves an increase in responsibility, and within that, a certain authority.

A good example would be the assignment of a WorkOn to payroll clerk, or perhaps payroll manager. This person is no longer buried in the Finance department, but is seen by the entire organization as someone who manages a process. That process stripes across the entire organization. Someone stepping into this role for the first time may be prone to panic a little if timesheets are not submitted in a timely fashion. They may go a little heavy-handed in their communications to get the timesheets in. We can see that this person often needs a little coaching to keep things in perspective, and in the proper escalation for problems concerning submittals. Conversely, the new payroll person may be a little shy about communicating expectations for timely submittals. They may lack the confidence to institute a system to help ensure timely submittals. So, the power-prism in this regard is showing us that there is a *situational* change in how people behave, as they remain in their primary group - in this case, the WorkOn group.

A good example for the IT leader regarding WorkOns is the assignment of new responsibility to someone who has, until now, been totally task-oriented. Perhaps one of your new HelpDesk technicians is assigned to manage the rollout of new PCs. This is a nice step up in responsibility, and who knows the PC population and the attendant user population better than a HelpDesk technician? This person should have the inside knowledge as to who needs the latest, most powerful machines, how the departments should be prioritized, and what a reasonable rate for the rollouts is. It is not unusual for the task-oriented person to become nervous about larger endeavors that have a multiplicity of details. At the same time, you should try to prepare the WorkOn for elements of their new work that may not be apparent to WorkOns in general.

In this case, departments may suddenly clamor and compete for prioritized standing in the PC rollout, individual users generally clamor for early issuance of a new PC, late-changing department schedules can upset the rollout plan, and so on. In these cases, the WorkOn's fresh responsibilities, and these related exigencies, can be viewed as a huge spike on the problem chart. The WorkOn feels a loss of control. However, the manager's steady guidance should lead this person to a calm attitude and a balance of perspective in managing these sorts of things. They come to be seen as routine in a real world environment.

Generally speaking, when rotating the power prism with a WorkOn in view, the behavioral change usually involves anxiety regarding an increase to responsibility – they are operating in a WorkWith realm. They've been chosen to assume a managerial role in that they have to lead activity – as opposed to operating in their usual reactive, or parallel, mode. Help this person - a sort of hybrid WorkOn/WorkWith - to a good understanding of their new role. Point them to the tools at their disposal for achieving results, *and* show them their sanctions, their sponsorships, and the limits of their lead.

THE WORKWITH: SQUEEZED IN THE MIDDLE

The WorkWith group helps to select and plan the future courses of business. Many WorkWiths will be on the BIT team. Here there can be a compounding of risk for change in behavior. This is because, as with WorkOns, WorkWiths are required to assume greater responsibilities within the scope of their present responsibilities – but the compounding factor is that they also have to manage and direct change. This group is especially active in the preservation of order amid change, and the preservation of change amid order. In planning and managing change, those involved have to stick their necks out. Simultaneously, they have to cover the bases. WorkWiths have to deal with consequences and are on the hook to *report* what's going on and why. They have to answer for things.

Too, the WorkWiths are likely in the middle – situated between the WorkOns and the WorkFors. I would guess the vast majority of people reading this book are WorkWiths. There is a special challenge to this group, because they're not only communicating within the Weave – speaking with special care to Business and Technology – but they also have to communicate up and down the organizational hierarchy. Theirs is a special balance. For IT, let's examine how this person may appear to you when changing groups.

Essentially, any WorkWith shifts and becomes someone you WorkFor when you're dealing with him or her as a customer (as does anyone, in any group, for that matter). Whether you're updating the WorkWith's department's PCs, implementing new software solutions, or addressing general support concerns, you're working for this person and you have to provide service to their satisfaction. In these cases, the WorkWith/WorkFor can become demanding, even unreasonable, as the power tilts their way. They have to "get the job done," and you have to "deliver." In this case, it helps to understand the pressures a particular WorkWith may be under. (On the other hand, there may be no particular pressure, and the WorkWith may simply be a difficult person – perhaps a TechnoBind – and it is very important to understand if this is the case too).

Let's examine a case of legitimate pressure – deadlines imperiled by a software change, for example. We can certainly understand the WorkWith's behavior due to risk and consequence that he or she may face. The Power Prism indicates that this person feels a lack of control – a definite situation of no power. When anyone feels that they have lost the power to influence outcomes, there is a factor of stress engendered by a helpless feeling. If not managed, this can lead to despondency or abusive behavior. It's easy in these circumstances for the WorkWith to overcompensate by wielding whatever power they can, in any direction they can. Here the course of action is to assure the WorkWith that all care and speed will be employed so as not to hinder the business at hand. Negotiations with the holders of deadlines may be possible. At worst, the software change is bumped back, outside the time of greatest risk to the WorkWith's own deliverables and commitments.

In the case of the WorkWith who is simply unreasonable, we have at least identified this person's status. We can judge what they say knowing they may be prone to exaggerate, or may be a less than objective reporter of actual status. How to handle? We have to do our due diligence in assuring this person that the situation is under control. We must also take extra precaution to document expectations, commitments, and progress. Ensure that everyone around a difficult WorkWith, including you, knows "where we are" – that is, hold everyone accountable and leave no wiggle room for misunderstanding. By all means, hold the WorkWith accountable, and get them to commit.

WHEN A WORKWITH REQUIRES A WORKON APPROACH

Consider an organization where a WorkWith completely folded in the face of a very important implementation. The business software module for her department had an expectation for completion according to a very important schedule – in light of an important business cycle. There was an appropriate lead-time, leaving room for testing prior to the required cycle of business in the Fall of the year.

The WorkWith dragged her feet during every phase of the project and was completely unreliable. She expressed a lack of confidence in the software – however, it was apparent that she lacked confidence in herself, and in her ability to adjust to the change. Indeed her own staff was very positive about the new software. She was a true TechnoBind. Only through bi-weekly meetings, closely communicated expectations, steady pressure from above, and employment of strict accountabilities was the organization able to mount the solution in time. The BIT team had to constantly reinforce this person's confidence, constantly remind this person regarding deliverables, and constantly enforce deadlines for user testing and reportage.

BIT, and the vendor, found themselves in a position of constantly reselling the idea of the solution. Because the WorkWith's implementation was a component of the larger organization-wide solution, and not hers to accept or reject, and because she failed to engage on a WorkWith basis, the team's treatment of her had to be adjusted. In this case, think of this person as a WorkWith/WorkOn. You have to work on them, albeit subtly, in order to keep them honest and on track. In this case, the WorkWith/WorkOn felt a loss of power, a loss control. True, it didn't have to be that way – she should have taken control and taken initiative. She should have participated in crafting the path to a successful implementation. She did not, and instead chose to be obstinate. In fact, it was her intention to drag the project to the point where she could conduct that Fall's business cycle with the old software application.

When you run into a situation such as this, do whatever it takes to hold this person's feet to the fire. Obviously failure should not be an option in a circumstance such as this, so to the Business leader and IT leader alike: define this person's responsibilities, get measures on the table, enforce milestones and deadlines (with only the normal accommodations for slippage), and hold this person accountable for their department's performance in contributing to progress. *Everyone will have to present a united front on this.* If you do this, you'll find that the most obstinate person will yield to the realities this imposes.

WORKFORS IN THE PRISM

The group that feels the least impact, comparatively, is the WorkFor group. There are some exceptions we'll talk about - but the people for whom you work are buffered by change to a large degree, and, if your organization has strong leaders, their power and confidence should be intact. They have WorkOns and WorkWiths at their disposal: their staff, the organization's staff, as well as the Business and IT leaders, to plan, manage, and implement change. Because of their position, they float above most power concerns – at least those concerns relative to the bulk of WorkWiths and WorkOns.

WorkFors have people serving digestible reports and information to them, in keeping them apprised of the larger facts. This makes whatever changes that are happening in the Business-Technology Weave relatively transparent and unaffecting to them. That is how we want it to be.

However, there are exceptions. In the face of new regulatory requirements, and the emerging risks for the senior executive class in the face of evolving liabilities and standards of accountability, WorkWiths may find themselves working closely with WorkFors in the development of certain protections. Whether that means boosting their ability to perform self-serve analysis of data, or plotting the course of major component systems, such as content management or other data security measures, the WorkFors may feel an unfamiliar dynamic as they gain new footing.

Comprehensive change such as new core business application systems will obviously have the WorkFors' interest. They'll be involved to a degree and will make time to be informed. There is a growing class of senior executive who wants ready access to information "at will." There are also very senior people who are now getting aggressive about their general PC knowledge, both from a hardware and software standpoint. And because these folks are leaders in very senior positions, they don't exactly relish situations where they are largely ignorant. Their schedules and constraints don't lend themselves to long periods of training.

The Emperor Has Clothes

Remember that many people wear their authority and position like a cloak (in all groups). If you whisk it off of them, they're going to feel a cold breeze of vulnerability - and they can become defensive very quickly. People in these circumstances may even move into an offensive mode that yields risk to outcomes. In the case of the WorkFors, you have a delicate balance when the power prism rotates.

Discretion and Sensitivity

When staff provided user training to the president of the organization, he wanted the training to be conducted discreetly. Also, he didn't want the trainer to talk about his lack of knowledge, or his ability to learn. He was, as he expressed it, "not a computer person." He obviously felt uncomfortable. He wanted to manage his e-mail better. He wanted to be able to format documents without asking his administrative assistant for constant help, he wanted to know more about spreadsheets. In this situation, the president became a WorkOn relative to IT. The HelpDesk technician that was selected for the job became a WorkFor relative to him – that is, the president was working for IT, to standards of training that we would set, with objectives to be reached in accordance to our scale.

He worked within our lesson plan. Each week we reviewed with him his prior week's training. We had to satisfy ourselves that he had learned what he needed to learn, and had retained it, before proceeding to the next lesson. Overall, we had to test him and bring his knowledge to a satisfactory standard, and had to do it tactfully.

This is perhaps at once a most basic yet dramatic example that can be imparted, but it serves an important point: many people are uncomfortable with technology, and even more uncomfortable when they feel they're in danger of being exposed for a lack of knowledge or skill. The IT leader and staff must show themselves to be very supportive, and if you create a comfortable zone for your senior people to come to you with discretion, where they are able to receive the answers they need, and can understand the answers, you'll do very well. For the Business leader, your presentation of business-technology issues to your WorkFors should be presented according to those same criteria.

Lest you think this example slight, or not particularly noteworthy, consider this: there are now outside companies that cater to senior executives - coming onsite to train them discreetly in their offices. This way, the senior executive does not expose his or her needs, and any self-perceived shortcomings, to the inside staff. This is certainly a desire to hide vulnerability, and a lack of power, and to preserve an image of power while gaining power.

THE PRISM'S VIEW TO SOME SITUATIONS

We can't chronicle all situations concerning all shifts here. It's enough, and it's best, to show a general way whereby we can recognize what's happening. It is up to you to make recognitions and to make adjustments in ensuring maximum success. Simply put, these shifts always involve *change* and *people*. Pretty basic, and yet it's amazing how many people fail to take these shifts into account. So, *observe how change affects people*. Here are some basic situations as further examples. Just remember to adjust your sensitivity and style accordingly: generally you'll be ratcheting up your discretion, tact and diplomacy, within a firm, sustained, push to goal. Where appropriate, be respectful, deferential, and helpful.

Role Reversals: Think of the reverse dynamic involving the HelpDesk person (a WorkOn) training the president (a WorkFor). In this new dynamic, the HelpDesk person became a WorkFor (the president was working for him), and the president became a WorkOn (he was being worked on by the HelpDesk person). Also, any situation where you're giving advice to anyone senior to yourself. A good example of a role reversal is when you have to admonish someone in a lateral or senior position to you. Now, for the IT leader, you may not use an admonishing tone, but you have to make a point nonetheless. For example, sometimes WorkWiths and WorkFors will download unauthorized software, or even purchase it and distribute it within a department. The responsibilities of your position shows you to be in charge of this arena, but the Power Prism shows that you don't really have the same weight to employ as you would if you were addressing a WorkOn. Use the sensitivities we discussed while you show these folks the perils of employing unauthorized software. Go further in showing the liability to the organization, and to yourself if you failed to exercise your duty.

Advice: The IT leader is always advising. The Business leader advises too. In these cases where these individuals advise up the line, to a WorkFor, you are now the expert. The WorkFor is deferring to you, his or her WorkOn. Therefore, recognize that when these people solicit your advice, they've already given you a power token. You don't have to demand it, or assume it through an overbearing voice (which usually makes one sound insecure). There is no need to over leverage the discussion through too much detail, or inflation of a subject's merit. Again, you and your words have been granted the moment's weight to stand toe-to-toe in this elevated discussion – maintain equilibrium.

Loss of Power: If someone is demoted, or perhaps has a specific oversight function removed from him or her for any reason, they may feel they've lost some of their WorkWith or WorkFor status. In this case, the person may overcompensate through challenge of others. They may feel a misplaced need to challenge agreements, authority, or ideas, etc. If you can, let them wind out whatever their contribution to discussion, and keep things on the "moving business forward" plain.

Temporary gain in power, or perceived power: Watch for the changes when someone is assigned a premium project and is suddenly "in charge." A simple example: an administrative assistant is newly promoted to fill the executive secretary position – she or he may suddenly exhibit the same dictatorial style as the executive director. You can project this example to the obvious situations - be aware.

New power: Promotions with increase in responsibility and power may cause the incumbent to feel a need to validate themselves, or just to test and exercise their new power. They may feel a need to do things, sometimes prudent, sometimes not, to justify their new promotion or responsibility.

REMEMBER ~

Any time you see someone behaving in a manner that is not consistent with their usual disposition, look for a shift in circumstances that places them in a role more specific to one or the other group – or just causes in them a need to revalidate their usual status. They may seem agitated, nervous, overly concerned about minor things, unconfident, overconfident, overbearing, etc. If they're thrown into a role by a specific circumstance, or if they assume a new position entirely, this removes their comfort for a time. They're somewhat uncertain of the rules regarding behavior, or unaware of a changed behavior.

Also, be aware of these things when you do your own promoting, demoting, and assignments. And, it won't hurt to remember a little of this as *you* move within the organization and your own circumstances…

Keep your Power Prism handy.

12

MANAGING PEOPLE IN THE WEAVE, PART II - THE CHALLENGE TO BUSINESS

The eye sees what it brings the power to see.

Thomas Carlyle

For Business, your IT department represents a *fulcrum* and a *lever*. The fulcrum is your computing platform, your business software, your data integrity, your infrastructure, your connectivities, the quality of your IT staff – in other words - the entirety of your business and technical support elements. The lever is how effectively you use this structure in supporting and advancing business. Now that you've emplaced sound, aligned systems, can you use them? How effective is your use in generating and accumulating sound data for decision-making? Have you developed a ready ability to mine, deliver, and interpret data; to secure data; to make data accessible and digestible? How solid is your fulcrum (equipment and application systems' alignment to business) and lever (your full employment of systems) in supporting a *Business-Intelligence* environment?

In order to achieve and maintain a full effectiveness, an IT department needs to be fully functional: that means effectively supporting the current environment, handling the unexpected efficiently, and guiding the organization into the future. It does not mean carrying incompetent people, lowering or ignoring standards, or putting up with bad behavior. It cannot mean poor customer service, lowered quality of service, diminished expectations, and risk to effective use, or security, of data. The right people are essential for success. In this chapter, we'll focus on these essentials for an understanding by Business – but we'll be speaking to IT along the way here too.

We know it is important to attract and retain the best people by effective use of the incentives and rewards at your disposal. At the same time, you must hold under-performing people accountable and use effective documentation and discipline to bring these employees back up to standards – or – to remove them from your environment through dismissal. But because dismissals are expensive, time consuming, and not without certain perils, we can see that getting this aspect of the Business-Technology Weave right is of prime interest to Business.

As a business person, you must fully understand the risk in carrying incapable, even culpable, people, and the danger in allowing these persons to remain outside of discipline. At the same time, we must maximize our fit of good people and positions to the organization. To paraphrase from earlier: We can have the best people in the world, but if they're in poorly defined jobs, or the wrong jobs, we have the bottom-line equivalent of the wrong people. In these regards, you must understand your duties to the Weave - in serving it, and in allowing it to serve you.

POSITIONING JOBS – POSITIONING PEOPLE

Part of employing the right people means *employing people the right way*. If you make ineffective use of staff, the perception will be that you don't have the right people in the job. The appearance and result to business will be the same.

Each person is really many people, with a variety of talents, potentials, and desires. You must grow each person in the right direction – the direction that serves the job position, the department, and business the best. It also helps if all of that is somewhere in the vicinity of that person's skills and aptitudes, and where that person would like to go. Therefore, it is essential that you start with, and structure correctly, your job positions. This ensures that you attract people on the right basis, and make appropriate hires for valid positions at the outset.

Fulfilling the requirement to structure positions and populate a department with the right people will also assist us greatly in making the most of what you have. We all have a limit on the size of our staff, and many have a requirement to reduce their staff. We also know that entirely new disciplines, requiring new levels of technology support, are coming along fast. Therefore, it is very important to get this right.

AN ACCRUAL OF RETURNS

The information technology field requires properly defined positions in order to create criteria for disciplines, best practices within those disciplines, and the appropriate selection and grooming of people to serve those disciplines. (So too do business positions, etc.). Your organization requires properly defined positions in order to reflect the *IT field*, so as to have success in building and populating your *IT department*. This understanding of the field, and the avoidance to violating certain well established practices, will contribute to an effective and efficient IT endeavor in your organization. By extension, that will contribute to effective and efficient business. In this regard you achieve an important return by structuring your IT department according to standard field positions and definitions.

The things you rely on for support, from equipment to personnel, will plug in with a much closer initial fit when you "go to market," if you align to market. At the same time, you gain leverage as the collective community of business and support services makes advances to established practices and as they advance the quality of support. You achieve an accrual of return (the opposite of diminishing return): you essentially gain a no-cost partnership with the rest of the world

Avoid any temptation to create job descriptions, or to assign job duties, based on personalities - or the fact that a person in a certain position *can* do something. Determine if that position *should* be doing that thing. Many organizations make critical, yet simple, mistakes that set their IT structure on a bad footing. Some of the inefficiencies engendered go on for years…until someone savvy enough, talented enough, and courageous enough, comes along to pull things apart and restructure. And let's face it, savvy, talented, and courageous people don't come along often enough. In fact, that's part of the reason for the understandings were going to build here. If you're structuring a position by throwing more and more requirements to a superstar, your "good horse," or just someone acquiescent and capable - and formalizing that person's position description over time that way, you're going to be in for a hurting if and when that person leaves.

The "Plug-and-Play" of Positions

Don't misunderstand this next part, but you want your staffing structure in IT to be as much "plug and play" as you can have it. We're not equating human beings to hardware here, but if a network manager leaves, you want the hole that's left to match as much as possible a person that you can readily find to fill it. You want to be able to go out and find a solid, reliable, network person on the open market to manage your network – not a hybrid player to match a departure who was managing the network, performing database maintenance, serving the HelpDesk, and coding software. Sometimes entire teams and departments coalesce around such a person.

If you craft a position and person in violation of a field's best structures and practices, you won't find another person to replace the one that you custom crafted. Remember too that the custom crafting (or perhaps just an unmanaged drift in the accumulation of skills and duties) happened over many months and perhaps years. Now you have a hole without the luxury of months and years to fill it.

In these circumstances, if you find someone close, they're not likely to accept your weird position – think about it: they're a close match, *and* they are on the market, probably in an attempt to leave just such a situation. Conversely, sometimes a person such as this isn't aware that the source of their present dissatisfaction is that they're in a difficult straddle. They may come to you and your position that is the same difficult straddle. This will not serve them or you well.

You don't want to be making hires on that basis. And yet - some do, and *know* they do. They hope that once someone is in the door, they'll stick. That somehow things will work out. They'll get a couple years out of a hire and, these days, who can ask for more than that anyway?

Frankensteins – Expensive to Maintain, Hard to Dismantle

Many of us have seen situations where a person of considerable general competence accumulates duties – like a magnet, they attract responsibilities that in some cases go far afield from that which they're supposed to be doing. Why does this occur? It is often expedient – and perhaps even necessary in an environment where other people are not held to appropriate standards of performance. Many times conscientious people volunteer to get the job done – whether it's in their sphere or not – and deliver on whatever the task, whatever the assignment.

Neither Business nor IT should skew work that way. Don't build up a position as a reaction to negatives – and inadvertently create a hybrid that is difficult to maintain in the longer term. A "Frankenstein" job position. A position cobbled together from many parts (disciplines, requirements and exigencies) without regard to best practice, known IT definitions, or long-term consequence. Many times Business goes right along – that is, HR does not dictate the adherence to appropriate definitions and distribution of duties. Nor does IT's ultimate boss do this. Frankly, often times no one knows any better – or the organization deliberately ignores deviations in trying to soothe the pain of the moment.

This is a looming problem in many Business-Technology Weaves. When good people tire of covering other people's bases, they'll seek greener pastures where they can concentrate on an appropriate contribution within a functional team.

Today's Expediency – Tomorrow's Emergency

There are also organizations that create hybrid, Frankenstein, positions in order to keep their staff small. The problem that arises is that, as the particular disciplines' sophistications increase within the umbrella of the Frankenstein position, more and more time to manage those disparate disciplines is required. It becomes difficult to train up for the changes. It's one thing to track the requirements and attend a schedule of training in remaining current in a particular discipline: its quite another challenge to remain current in a variety of disciplines – too often training is ignored or missed due to the requirement to cover the supported environment.

Consider too that when this person is removed from the environment for one area of training, you are removing your support to the broader range of disciplines supported by that position. This is inefficient. You may put the entire gamut of disciplines at some measure of risk (whether this person is absent through training, or other loss). Not everyone has to be a specialist, and there are always degrees of exception to everything, but if you have extremely disparate disciplines under one job position, they will become increasingly difficult to straddle, the job will become increasingly difficult to do, increasingly difficult to populate, and there will be increasing difficulty in maintaining currency.

Where possible, as work increases in your IT department, or as certain disciplines start to require more time, you're better off creating a new, entry level position and hiring a relatively junior member to populate it. Step that person up over time as the position demands an increase in capability and responsibility. Alternatively, you can hire up slightly when there is turnover, and boost the position description to reflect new realities.

Track Emerging Practices and New Areas of Support

Ignoring increasing burdens or emerging priorities is not wise – whatever else may be hindering action. If you lack budget, approval, and your own authority to build a new position, you can still plan the position and have it ready to go. If you believe in a new position, and believe in a necessary redistribution of work based on changing conditions, you can still create and assemble your supporting documentation.

If you're right, the issue will force itself sooner or later. Without preparation, you may make mistakes when the time and authority to act does come. Waiting until you absolutely have to break off work to a new position means that you'll be standing at the base of a cliff. You won't have the gentle progression of planning as you track the practices and requirements of new areas.

IT should look at the long-range business plan, the projections of growth, and general changing methods regarding the exercise of business in order to assess their own staffing requirements. This should be marked and tracked within the Five-Year Plan. As any new positions begin to manifest and focus, IT should build position descriptions, budgets, and justifications for them. This prevents being caught flat-footed.

A new position may become necessary through an increasing volume of existing work, or the requirement to perform a new kind of work. In either case strong consideration should be given toward emplacing the new position before a critical need develops. Where possible, activate a position for new work ahead of the curve. This way, you can have the concurrent grooming of an incumbent along with the settling of that position as it breaks-in to business.

Waiting means that you may hire and size a position to cover requirements not fully understood. You'll be scrambling to define the position, the salary, and the kind of person you want for it, while needs are crashing down on top of you. You'll have no direct familiarity with the market for such a person. Business won't know how it needs to be supported, HR won't quite know how to hire for the position, and IT will be struggling to define it based on an amalgam of surveys of peers and associates. This, plus you'll be reaping the results of running lean for too long: impacts of bad morale and negative consequences to staff and business are quite possible – frequently there is turnover and the loss of good people.

A Simple Assessment to Setting Structure

Let's discuss some specifics in determining whether your IT structure is optimal, and if not, how to get it on the right footing. Essentially, you should be able to perform a review according to the simple model below. You can extend and apply this view to your own organization's IT structure. Look for any misplaced work, gaps, uneven distribution of load, and general inefficiencies.

- ♦ Assess current positions by relevancy and number.

- Match your positions to standard field definitions.
- Eliminate, add, combine, or separate positions as necessary.
- Adjust individual positions as necessary.
- Redistribute work as necessary.
- Ensure a balanced load.

Let's take a more detailed look at each of these:

Assessing current positions by relevancy and number: Positions should be surveyed against organizational needs, and against the positions' standings against standard field definitions.

You, or someone prior, may have apportioned specific duties and loads based on something other than an optimal structure for your particular organization. Often times the reasons for distributions of effort no longer apply – if they ever really did. It's important to fix any imbalances and inequities. The problems can sneak up on an organization over time. Not only do the internal requirements change: the IT field itself evolves around you. Coming will be new scales of computer hardware and architecture, supporting ever more powerful software applications. These supports are not only enabling, they establish dependency and vulnerability, and therefore burdens of support. Too, other equipment or products may reduce or otherwise shift burdens.

As the climate of business changes, your organization's burden in meeting outside expectations can change radically. Your environment will need new scales of skill, talent, and imagination in maintaining your environment. There will be an immediacy that makes new demands of Business - and thus Business' demands of Technology. We've mentioned the Five-Year Plan in these regards - it should have a template item regarding your evolving burden and type of work, and its influence on your positions and support posture. You'll then have a proactive collection of salient facts, coming into sharper relief as the years click forward, and you'll be less reactive and far better situated to make necessary job and position changes.

Match your positions to standard IT definitions: Try to keep your position descriptions within the bounds of accepted IT standard job definitions. This creates efficiencies in managing and supporting your IT environment *and* business environment. It also lends to efficiencies in managing the structures of jobs themselves, and the people in them. You have ready reference on the Internet to a variety of job descriptions for known job categories, and these can serve as your templates as you fine-tune your own internal job descriptions. You'll also have ready access to the standards to which these jobs should be performed – and, you'll have matching professional training resources for when you need to send people to training. Too, it becomes easier to replace people as they exit the organization, or move up. Interviewing candidates for positions is far easier when your positions adhere to known, industry, standards. Staffing is a smooth, efficient, process. Again - *That which can be routine, must be made routine*.

The positions should fit together like puzzle pieces to create a seamless structure of support to the Business environment. Over time, you may start to experience gaps between the pieces (the positions); that's when you determine the correct course of action to close the gaps (to cover the new area[s] of support): either through assignment of the work to an existing position, creation of a new position, or the determination that the work belongs in the Business sphere.

Add, eliminate, combine, or separate positions/duties as necessary. Take a careful look at each position in IT. Compare the described duties within each position with standard job definitions. Many of us have seen network managers who were performing programming on behalf of programmers, seen HelpDesk technicians tuning databases, seen programmers performing HelpDesk calls – not as an overlapping backup between positions, but as a matter of routine.

A lot of times this happens because individuals within the user body start to develop favorites – people whom they prefer for support. This favoring is independent of what a support person is supposed to be doing in the larger sense, and may mean that this support person has to dig for details or knowledge that are already known by the appropriate support person. It's tempting to go to your favorite IT person with every request, whether that person is the primary responder for the type of assistance you're seeking or not. This can exert a slow gravitational pull, whereby everyone in IT begins to assume a "jack of all trades, master of none" kind of posture.

Business leaders should ensure that calls for help by staff are made through the appropriate avenue. They should call a HelpDesk number, as opposed to specific individuals, and the HelpDesk can dispatch targeted help, or escalate the issue as necessary. The IT leader has to fully explain the process to Business, and the IT leader has to enforce the discipline necessary to ensure an efficient use of support resources.

At the same time, work may be flowing against the grain of your position definitions for very valid reasons. Work may actually be settling into a *correct* alignment, but across the lines of poorly crafted positions (even departments on occasion). You may very well determine that the manner and flow of work needs to be codified as it is, with new position descriptions that reflect the correct order of things as they already informally stand. As necessary, get the primary responsibilities where they belong, and defined correctly so as to manage, acknowledge and reward people correctly. This will become increasingly important as each job position takes on new responsibilities within its specific scope: planning the future of the position, seeking better cost efficiency, contributing to security, and so on.

There does need to be an effective overlap of some knowledge for purposes of coverage. It's up to the IT department to manage requests and overall support so as to leverage the skills, time, and resources to maximum effect.

Adjust individual positions as necessary: Relocating duties to where they belong, as opposed to where they may have drifted, can be a sensitive proposition. Some people may feel they have custody of a particular area. They may feel a loss in prestige or power if a responsibility is taken away from them. View the situation through the Power Prism. Assure each person that the motivator for change is strictly business, and that a realignment of duties and responsibilities is an acknowledgment to the reality of new responsibilities that are anticipated as the Weave evolves and grows – responsibilities that will be apportioned in accordance with best practices. Let them know that the restructure is required so as to make everyone as comfortable as possible in the ever-changing business-technology arena.

Redistribute work as necessary: Here you may have occasion to revisit the assignment of responsibilities between similar, or like, positions. If you have a programming staff, you can look to strengthen your programming front by assessing who is best positioned to do certain things. You may find that people have informally discussed trading certain roles. Either someone has a better aptitude for certain work, or perhaps a different attitude regarding it. There's nothing wrong with this, and you can encourage staff to discuss and seek ways better leverage the department.

Sometimes work redistribution is based on other things, no less practical: For example, Technician A may have started some nighttime education – a change in schedule that may make Technician B better suited to working a little later and handling the latter part of your HelpDesk's onsite hours. This is the redistribution of a class of work amongst people of like qualification. The important thing is to be flexible and imaginative – seek ways to leverage any contingency for the betterment of business – and people.

Ensure a balanced load: Again, be mindful of the load between like positions. We're all aware of individuals who take on more and more work, because they like to be busy, or in many cases because they don't know how to say "no." When it comes time to formally posit some additional work with such a person, it turns out they're ready to pop. Watch out for the conscientious, courteous, and capable employee to whom people turn for best results. Inculcate the values of customer service, quality of service, and *results* across your staff so as to create a natural plane supporting the balance of work. You can't have your eyes on the details of balance all the time – so affect those things that will aid in balancing things naturally.

Remember ~

Over time, everyone involved needs to work to ensure you have the necessary positions in your IT department, to ensure that positions are properly defined, and to ensure the correct breakout of duties and responsibilities. The "everyone" that we speak of here is a weave of: IT, IT's sponsors, HR, and the demands of business - therefore a variety of Business people to varying degrees.

Remember, attracting and retaining good people is smart business. Aid this attraction and retention by balancing work effectively while placing the work in the appropriate place. Be aware that each person who comes to the organization came out of a system where they were educated according to a certain discipline. They gravitated toward a discipline that they were attracted to for one reason or another. They have an expectation to work in that certain arena: primarily within the work that interests them, the work they've been trained to do, and the kind of work they're *good* at.

Remember too that you gain a no-cost partnership with the rest of the world by structuring your IT department according to standard IT field definitions, and by following best practices. Avoid the Frankenstein, hybrid, positions and players. Also, never forget that having a properly structured and balanced IT department speaks well of your department and your organization to outsiders – increasingly, the organization that gets IT right is perceived as having business right.

13

IGNORANCE -
A POSTURE BUSINESS CAN NO LONGER AFFORD

…It is worse still to be ignorant of your ignorance.

Saint Jerome

In many IT folks' view, one of the most puzzling phenomenas in the Business-Technology Weave is the sustained posture of ignorance to technology by some in Business. Conversely, many business staff regard their IT folks as aloof, uncaring, or simply too overburdened to provide an appropriate level of support. In some cases they may even be perceived as under-qualified – true or not. Let's examine things from the Business side first.

Business needs to demystify the technology they own. Therefore, we need to make a sale to our top-most management, and it is this: Business leaders and staff must now have enough real knowledge to contribute in crafting the Business-Technology Weave – *through a Business-driven IT strategy.* We must explain to top management the necessities so that you'll have this top management sponsoring and sanctioning this obligation for Business – they must *endorse and enforce* a savvy business-technology culture.

Business leaders at all levels of the organization often don't know what their obligation is in this modern business-technology arena. Some who do understand it none-the-less deliberately avoid engaging themselves for various reasons. For example, only 2 in 5 business responders believe that their data management strategies have board approval. Only just over half believe that senior management of their company places sufficient importance on data management. *Insufficient importance* placed on data management. Data is our business intelligence. This posture of avoidance will get people in deep trouble as time goes by, and indeed is creating trouble for many organizations today.

WHAT "BUSINESS" DOESN'T KNOW *CAN* HURT IT

If you compromise the integrity of your data, you quickly compromise your business' integrity – something to keep in mind because your number one asset is your reputation. Some like to tell us that people are their most important asset. This sounds good, and we all like to believe it. However, as the old expression goes: The graveyard is full of indispensable people. For the organization, the #1 asset remains its reputation. Consider also that your business-intelligence (data) *is* your business. Lose your data, and you won't know where you are, won't be able to plot where you're going, and indeed won't have anywhere to really go anyway – lose your data and you lose your business.

In addition to postures that can compromise the integrity of data and business, you can compromise your organization's overall security. Security deserves and receives a chapter all its own, but we'll be touching on this important subject here as well. Because of a lack of understanding and engagement on the part of senior business leaders, it is all too often that IT is forced to make an "outsiders" assessment for where levels of business protections should be placed, where emphasis for new initiatives should go, and where precious budget should be directed. This does not serve the organization's business security endeavors well.

TWO BASIC UNDERSTANDINGS FOR THE MODERN ORGANIZATION

Consider that your organization is at tremendous risk for inefficient operation. Any entity in the modern Business-Technology Weave that is not keeping up with new knowledge and emerging concepts in the mutually reinforcing business and technical realm will contribute to an imbalance. All of this helps us to understand two basic things required of Business (and thus for the organization) in the modern Weave:

1) With the increase in sophistication of business information systems, and their comprehensive reach and weave into every corner of your operations, IT needs Business' help more than ever in sizing and fitting support to business. The organization needs an engaged business element that makes a strong, good faith effort to self-motivate in maintaining a base of knowledge. This knowledge includes common information, technical and otherwise, that is necessary for Business to help plan its own support in the Weave through a *Business-driven IT Strategy*. We're not trying to create a duplication of effort and knowledge between IT and

Business, but Business needs a solid qualification upon which to draw so they can pilot the Business-driven IT strategy. As we come to define this posture, we will begin to speak of the *IT Enlightened Organization.*

-And –

2) More and more power, knowledge, and tools are being delivered to the desktop. The assumption by your surrounding industries - that is, training vendors, software developers, value added remarketers, even competitors - is that your user body is going to seize the initiative and make effective use of this "front side of the screen" power. Product developers draw assumptions upon which to scale their products and, increasingly, they assume your users remain informed, educated, and self-motivated. IT needs Business users to actively engage within the zone of desktop power – the zone that has been scaled and marketed specifically for the user class. This frees IT to assume greater and expanded capacities for support to the increasingly sophisticated and time-consuming backoffice support requirements. Also, Business users must realize a full return on investment from this power – that is, the organization must capture the potential and make full use of these tools in making your business run at full efficiency and effectiveness. Users must also understand data, and be able to responsibly use, vet, and manage data. Let's call all of this the *Index of User Awareness.*

THE *IT* ENLIGHTENED ORGANIZATION

In the first case, qualified and engaged elements of the IT Enlightened Organization ensure effective, accurate, and efficient planning in maintaining a proper alignment between support technology and business needs. Successful business-technology alignment requires more than executive level oversight or acknowledgement. Organizations need IT solutions born of an understanding of how technology supports, affects, and enables business-critical services. This must be attacked from both directions. Additionally, organizations need informed managers who can assess the impact of new business plans on IT operations. For all of this, we obviously need IT-savvy Business people, and business-savvy IT people.

When we speak of a self-motivation in maintaining a knowledge-base on Business' part, we don't mean that IT never provides training or education to

Business. Further, we don't mean that Business never needs training from any outside formal institutions. Rather, each of these is central to creating Business' knowledge-base. What we mean is that Business assumes an obligation: it becomes more proactive in soliciting this training, and in knowing enough to contribute to the select and size of the training they need. This contributes to efficiency and management of cost, and compounds in the form of a more intelligent Business contribution. Business also seeks to reinforce training and knowledge by leveraging users of advanced standing to train other users. In addition, Business makes an investment in time – reading articles relevant to business-technology, assessing business through the technology prism, and by perking their ears in an overall culture that is awash in technology.

In an enlightened posture, Business can understand that IT is being challenged in new ways: security demands are zooming; platform and infrastructure are increasingly sophisticated; data must now be viewed and managed not just according to integrity, access, amount, and location, but according to considerations of *content*. Vulnerabilities posed by content materialize as more and more regulatory requirements emerge; as more and more general exposures have evolved to pose legal liabilities; and as more and more avenues into the organization have appeared (e-mail content, internet downloads, etc.).

Associated burdens in managing these concerns have probably not completely identified themselves. These emerging and expanding disciplines - these "back side of the screen" challenges - represent a great test to IT and to the organization. The demands to this back side can be offset to a degree by shifting some, if not much, of the information *services* burden (and hand-hold type of help) out to the Business body of users. This is largely where it belongs anyway. Your organization must bolster the Index of User Awareness: On the "front side" of the screen there is comprehensive documentation, online help, and self-training material in support of the desktop. It is very important for your organization to place the emphasis of efforts in the appropriate arenas. Here, the Business community of users must be self-motivating in making effective use of the technology, services, and knowledge stores at their disposal. Achieving this is a simple enough reinforcement – make it an evaluation area in staff's performance appraisals.

This helps IT step up to the emerging demands of the evolving and new disciplines that serve the ongoing alignment of IT to changing business and technical needs. It also frees IT to plan and manage the process by which effective utilization of tools and resources is achieved. A valid trend has been to get the user body to be as self-standing, self-supporting, and self-motivating as possible, availing themselves of the wealth of help readily available to them outside of IT. The efficient organization most often reserves its engagement of IT for the kind of help *that is only available from IT*. That is, help with broken processes, broken equipment, corrupt data, etc.

For example, coming to IT for help with document formatting, simple report selections, or basic instruction regarding routine use of software applications is going to crash your potential for ultimate efficiency, economy, and return on investment. Continual support to users for basic self-help problems robs them of the incentive to further their knowledge, and robs managers of their ability to hold people accountable to "keeping up." Your user body represents an incredible collective of end-user knowledge – learn how to leverage that among your users. IT then concentrates on its real support nature: technical fixes, fixes to broken applications, restorations of data, alignment of support to business, research on better practice and emerging disciplines, and all of the other longer-term things we've been discussing. If you go against this flow, it will be painful. It's important for the decision makers to understand what constitutes the modern environment and its proper balance; so that they can help plan it, create it, and emplace it – *endorsing it and enforcing it* - for ultimate weave into your organization's culture.

THE INDEX OF USER AWARENESS

The power at the desktop is increasing by leaps and bounds. How do you get your user class to leap and bound in maximizing your return in this arena?

First, let's realize that there's been a definite shift in burden within the realm of the daily business grind. This shift has been happening over the course of years. Twenty or thirty years ago, users would fill out a reports form, or a programming request sheet, for submittal to an information services department in order to receive output: a report, or a change to "the system" for example. Now, users can design and deliver their own reports. In many organizations, authorized users can create such things as their own rapid entry screens specifically tailored to their own job's needs. They can invoke new business rules through simple selects. They can update constants such as pricing, shipping, discounts – and much more.

In other words, users are their *own* information service agents – and in many cases their own system configuration agents. Given the evolution and effectiveness of customizations, online help, training, tutorials, and knowledge – the sheer *power* at the desktop – there is increasing expectation and necessity that users take full advantage of this power. Some organizations leverage this power very effectively. Others cannot seem to harness it. IT must help Business make full use of the lever that this power at the desktop represents. Business must access, use, and benefit from this full desktop potential in achieving the best return on investment for these technologies.

The Era of the "Soft Bed" of Ignorance is Drawing to a Close

Ignorance in this case has been a comfortable bed. Ignorance *can* be bliss – it can also be safety, and it can be a refuge. Until recently it was also relatively harmless. An ignorant posture on the part of any business manager could provide a benefit to them, with little corresponding liability inside or outside the organization. Before we go further, let's mention that this posture is not the norm for every business person. But it is very important that every business person understand that there is a potential, and even a motivator, for this kind of posture in those around you and in those reporting to you. Some may operate on the idea that there is an "ignorance benefit" – it grants deniability in the face of negative or less than optimal outcomes. For these thinkers, whether it be a direct negative business condition (too much bad debt, erroneous sales forecasts, misstatement of earnings), or poor progress regarding support initiatives (implementation of a new business system), it can be very convenient to remain on the periphery of "technical" matters. They can point into a murky sphere in laying blame or fault.

It is a natural fact of human nature to push blame: I didn't receive that report; the reports I received didn't indicate that; my people were operating on different assumptions provided by others… etc., etc., etc. Deniability, finger pointing, redirection of blame is a business – a human - staple. Indeed, many an IT leader has borne the brunt of blame for poor business outcomes. But how can a support element - overseen by Business, reporting to Business, *existing* for Business, *owned by Business* - ever be allowed to wobble out of balance to the degree that business is affected in a negative manner? Fix or discharge the IT element, surely, but fix the Business part of the equation!

There's a maxim: Not all "bad" is discoverable. We could rather say: "not all bad is discoverable *in time*." However, *most* bad is discoverable in time, and eminently more easily handled when you are informed, proactive, and interested in doing the right thing. This is why the condition of ignorance must be reviewed in your organization – from all angles at all levels. In the current and coming demands of the Business-Technology Weave, *ignorance is dangerous*. We will continue to speak of the IT Enlightened Organization.

From the relative comfort of our review here, it's easy to acknowledge that preventing "bad" - inefficiency and harm - is a desired goal of proper business operation (and of course "proper business operation" incorporates IT). And yet, many Business people – senior and middle management (the WorkFors and WorkWiths) - remain ignorant regarding the area of the Weave where technology and business are meshed most closely.

A CLOSE MESH

A *close mesh*: that's a good term to take note of as regards the Weave. It's that place where things "turn" – where the organization has the greatest leverage, the best timing, the most efficiency in doing things that matter. That zone most favorable to putting things right, to choosing the best paths. If yours is an organization that is not IT Enlightened - whether it's through a willful ignorance, or the dim positioning that "you can't know what you don't know" – you cannot have a Business-driven IT strategy. You cannot manage an effective mesh, and therefore you cannot manage your way past danger as you move forward through condition and change (time).

So, the weave of technology and business is an area that Business is now obligated to understand. This millennium and its attendant realities demand that Business pick up this obligation. There is such a tight interweave between the direct business interests and the technology supporting them, we know that for effective planning, and minimization of liability, we need a best mesh that is the ongoing product of the *Business-driven IT strategy*. We need business leaders with some fundamental grasp of technology and its nature to the support of business. In tandem, we need IT leaders with knowledge of business in general, and knowledge of *the* business (the specifics of business that is occurring in your place of employ) in satisfying this same agenda.

Senior-most management is not our target for a detailed knowledge of Business' obligation. We just want senior management's enforcement of an appropriate engagement by general business management in the planning and execution of IT solutions. We want senior management setting the expectation that there will be Business support and an accountability in this endeavor. In other words, IT leadership will negotiate with top management where obligations lie in bringing about the most effective business-technology partnership.

Achieving a Proper Weave in the Close Mesh: Business and IT overlap: they have common interest, discussion and planning. Common resources serve and are used by both Business and IT in crafting the total business support environment. The area of close mesh includes the supervision of IT by Business, or - thought of another way - IT's report to Business. It includes the Business sponsorship of IT - or, IT's sanction by Business. It includes the Business support demands of IT - or, IT's obligation to Business. It includes the Business-driven IT strategy – or, IT's contribution to business futures planning. It involves your BIT team: The close mesh is about IT's WorkFor relationships, and IT's WorkWith relationships. And, *it is about creating a positive correlation between your IT spending and your profitability.*

When we speak of profits here, we refer not only to revenue, but to all positive benefits resulting from better business: increased efficiency is a profit; better staff morale is a profit; increase in quality of service is profit; better products are a profit; happier customers and members are profits. Profiting within the mesh is about forwarding the Business-driven, and Business serving, IT strategy in the best way possible.

To indicate the importance of the fully aware organization's Business-IT relationship, let's look at an operational example and a management example:

OPERATIONS: OPERATING ON CONTENT

Let's take the matter of content and surrounding operations as this example. Content is the nature of your business information, and any other information (non-business) your employees draft, publish, disseminate, download, receive, or otherwise accumulate and propagate - through design or accident. Each electronic document, electronic file, database record, hardcopy paper, posting to a message board is subject to subpoena: your organization has exposure and can face legal liabilities through the disclosure of your content. Not just business content – it has been determined in the courts that if someone in your organization is exposed to offensive material, be it inappropriate advocacy, porn, racially inflammatory material, to cite but some examples, your organization can be liable for damages.

It is an increasing concern because now an organization is responsible for content – all content – electronic and otherwise, business and otherwise, if it is within the figurative four walls of your organization. The organization can even be liable for content that is propagated *outside* of your organization. If you have employees posting and responding on external blogs of questionable repute, and they are using their organizational e-mail addresses, your business can face exposure and liability according to that content too.

Therefore, the organization must know its content, and associated employee activities in dealing with content. It must have the means to review, report, and take action on content. We will talk in detail about content management in a chapter specific to that – content management serves many examples for managing within the Weave. But here we are highlighting the increasing obligation on Business' part to understand, and apply appropriate oversight to, these things. In the realm of content, many organizations are unsure as to how they should operate on content; throwing the issue of content IT's way. Yet IT can't always know content's usefulness or liability to the same degree as the business elements. An organization can create a gross inefficiency here if IT is required to know exactly what Business knows - a duplication of *knowledge*. This causes IT to engage in an "end-use" operator's guise – a poor use of time. IT has to subsequently engage Business to check off on action regarding content (such as deletions, and removals to archive) – which then becomes a duplication of *effort*.

This engagement of Business' time could be spent just as easily by Business taking its own proactive action on content in the first place: an essential Business operation. IT's time is better spent in listening to Business; so as to best fit the content management system to Business' needs, and to maintain its alignment over time. In other words, it will be most effective to the organization for IT to implement and maintain a content management solution, and for Business to operate it. Here again, IT delivers the "filing cabinet"; Business is responsible for making best use of the filing cabinet.

This model – putting content action (operations) in Business' hands - squares nicely with the organization's managers' normal duties regarding supervision of all operations. It is every manager's duty to know what employees are doing – the good and the bad. It is a manager's duty to know what content is being generated or otherwise accumulated by their department. As managers supervise and interact with employees on a daily basis, they are usually the first responders to any negative performance, behavior, or abuse. From the perspective of employees (WorkOns), a similar burden falls on them: their use of technical resources and their treatment of data (content) requires them to be diligent and proactive in maintaining appropriate content. It is only through this understanding (and, abolishment of ignorance) that Business can hope to contribute to an appropriate organizational balance.

These balances, placing efforts where they belong, is an increasing requirement to IT Enlightened business operations.

MANAGEMENT: MANAGING IN THE CLOSE MESH

Let's now look at how to properly manage. Research by the Butler Group has found no relationship between IT spending and profits. Thought of another way, we're missing an opportunity to increase our revenue, to expand our reach, to better serve, to make our customers happier, and to be happier in what we do. The poor relationship between IT spending and profit probably comes as no surprise to professional IT management; they are at the crux of the situation.

IT's view is clear and unfiltered: They see organizations essentially marking time wherever possible – with a sporadic cycle of occasional, convulsive, catch-ups – spending money at the last possible moment, leveraging no advantages, paddling furiously on the back edge of the world's general wave that is progress and change. This situation exists in many organizations because Business often engages IT only when it becomes absolutely necessary. The engagement is often motivated by pain: Changes in operations, changes in market, increased regulations, or other events - which have not only evidenced themselves, but are beginning to bear down in a crush.

The organization is now positioned against influencers that are *already being felt* – as opposed to being in a position to discuss and plan for them in advance. In this case, your Business-strategy will not, and cannot, drive IT strategy. It will *break* IT strategy. This is because much of IT planning goes out the window as IT scrambles to accommodate things either unforeseen, or just unplanned. Often times the scramble is to reconstitute ideas and issues that IT tracked, exposed, and wanted to accommodate, but were discounted or dismissed by Business. Reordering priorities and resources on an emergency basis has a cascading affect – in essence, turning everything into an emergency.

If your Business strategy is not driving your IT strategy, no one can best manage the IT budget or any comprehensive organizational resources. For, it is the organization that must wield IT on its own behalf, apportioning IT's efforts in correct measure. It is the organization, Business, which must position all resources in a planning-mode – as opposed to having them settle into a reactionary mode. The close mesh requires a tight communication between Business and IT for an appropriate planning, selection, sizing, and use of business technologies.

Often times, failure to achieve an effective mesh leads to an unfortunate view by Business: IT is seen as a poorly understood, rather sinister, cost center. Board members and senior executives are left to view IT as a money pit with little positive return in the form of benefits to business. A necessary evil. Here again is the justification for a more technically savvy Business element in the Weave: Business cannot afford to knock on IT's door when changes are imperative, seeking solutions. Business must have IT at the table from the moment a business idea or requirement begins germinating: Business then must engage with IT in the seek and implementation of solutions. This engagement must be on an informed, sustained basis. Your goal should be, and can be, an overall business-technology environment of constant efficiency.

So, the close mesh is where the proper alignment of IT support to Business is achieved and sustained. Likewise, it is where Business strategy gets translated into IT strategy – all through virtue of everything we've been discussing:

a qualified (IT Enlightened) organization; appropriate communication; accurate identification of needs; valid expectations; proper sanctions; sponsorship; knowing where you are, establishing goals, planning a route, and knowing where you're going; a focus on moving business forward. In addition, this area of close mesh is where we have the best view to leveraging our resources such as personnel, time, money, equipment, *knowledge* – in satisfying our better business goal.

It should be clear that the close mesh is not some fixed area, focused meeting, or discreet group of people. The BIT forum is not the close mesh – it is part of it. The close mesh is a *virtual* mesh: an element within every person, project, job, task, effort and goal – the place where each of these strives to achieve the best Business-Technology Weave.

FROM IGNORANCE TO ENLIGHTENMENT – GETTING THERE

Many organizations don't understand the critical balance posed by the appropriate enlightenment and awareness in both management and the general user body. Therefore, these areas of ignorance, these gaps in understanding, and a seeming deliberate avoidance by some in closing these particular divides, must have some murky motivator. There must be something particularly gnarly leading to this state – otherwise it wouldn't exist. Right? Not so - it is easy to understand.

Let's look at Business' obligations in building the IT Enlightened Organization, and the means to eliminate and hold ignorance at bay. After, we'll look at IT's obligation to Business, in helping Business achieve it.

The Obligation of Business in Creating Their IT Enlightened Organization: Business already knows "business." Business understands that it must stay current, evolve, and grow in a business context: business is what Business does. Having said that, let's look in detail at Business' obligations in the area of close mesh for purpose of achieving the IT Enlightened Organization. And, your organization's ability to effect a Business-driven IT strategy. We'll follow this later with IT's obligation – it is incumbent upon IT to help Business build the IT Enlightened Organization. Understanding everyone's obligations in this area of close mesh also helps to better define the area.

First, the area of close mesh requires from Business:

- Placement of the top IT leadership at the highest planning table possible.

- A basic knowledge of informational, technical, and support concepts.
- A basic knowledge of best practices in the IT realm.
- An understanding of risk and its management.
- A commitment to common language and aligned efforts between IT and Business.
- An obligation, acknowledgment, and commitment to bring a certain knowledge-base to the table.

Let's examine each in detail:

Placement of IT Leadership: Business strategy is now completely dependent on IT. Like it or not, acknowledge it or not, manage it or not, it is true – and will remain so. For Business to approach, attack and successfully mount new business, maintain old business, and overcome challenges, it is imperative that Business understand, oversee and control the execution of the large-scale IT strategy. In order to best translate the strategy into accomplishment of real-world objectives, IT leadership must be accessible during discussion of Business-IT strategy. Making IT present at the discussion table is the ultimate in accessibility – so do that.

Once fully present, IT leadership must stand toe-to-toe with your Business leadership. This means that IT must have the same weighted authority as the other strategic partners and leaders. IT's presence engenders the same respect as the other authorities at the table by virtue of IT's full contribution to Business success. IT should be on the same plateau as sales, marketing, governance, etc., at least in terms of participation and counsel. In this strategic circle, no element of the organization can expose an initiative that is divorced from the technical realities. At the same time, IT is able to discuss IT-originated initiatives and their impact on Business. With IT present, you stand the best chance of crafting the best Weave - and in the best (most efficient) way.

This also prevents your organization from treating the management or considerations of technology as an afterthought. IT has been integral to sound business policymaking and planning, but now is acknowledged, treated, and better wielded as such. This prevents other business leaders from viewing technology management as a purely administrative matter, somehow separated from your organization's business and related management. This also creates an arena where Business leaders become individually accountable for the success or failure of technology initiatives in their individual business realm. This is because they are partnered in the planning and execution of this critical technology support. They are the relevant part of the *Business-driven IT strategy* in these cases; they are part of the Business-Technology Weave, *and each represents an element of the Close Mesh.* Business can no longer, either willfully or inadvertently, obscure these roles, engagements, and accountabilities. Therefore, there is no longer any reason, and far fewer means, for hiding behind excuses or within ignorance.

You also help to create an arena where politics is less likely to trump performance. Here we can shine a light so as to define the roles, expectations, and measures for success in a much better fashion.

Basic knowledge of informational, technical, and support concepts: No longer is it practical to begin each Business-IT discussion with a revisit to what should be universal knowledge: certain terms, general issues, and common concepts. We can't afford to craft an alphabet, build a dictionary, and bloom anew the general awarenesses supporting each issue and its path to resolution. We need traction each time we hold a discussion regarding something so tightly interwoven as business and technology. To revisit the BIT team, we want people in the room who can communicate with each other, mark their place, and take up again where they left off in bringing traction to a sustained forward progress.

What does this mean to Business? Those Business people who deal most directly with IT – supervision, sponsors, BIT, people who are directly coupled with IT on a project basis - must bring some fundamental knowledge to the table. If you have IT oversight, you should be at least familiar with general concepts and issues of content, security, databases, business applications, data mining, shelf applications, bandwidth, connectivity, and staffing. This may sound like a lot, but it really isn't – and especially not when IT is reporting to *you*. An afternoon's poking around through reference material readily available on the web will jumpstart anyone's understanding. Business leaders should ask their IT leader for a primer on these areas and any others she or he considers important in their respective organization. Even an hour's time spent in the aggregate on these topics will greatly increase any Business person's comfort level in helping to manage the Business-Technology Weave.

For example, if your department is undergoing a database upgrade or change, know what a database is. Know what *your* database is. If you have a stake in something, be informed about that something. If your organization is about to undergo a large-scale business-technology project, learn something about the general impacts of the specific sort of project that's about to be undertaken. In today's environment, it's unfair and poses a great disadvantage to simply sit back and have IT deliver assessments regarding initiatives, burdens, and liabilities. Business must help plan the load, expectations of effort, estimations for completion. We, all of us, need the experiences, judgments and opinions of a diverse set of people from business and technology alike in crafting the total project environment.

Take the general awareness that we're building here and examine your environment and its Weave – then fulfill the level of obligation you feel appropriate to your situation. By all means, you must adjust your expenditure of effort and accumulation of knowledge. Keep in mind the best balance of effort-and-return in your specific organization, department, project, etc.

A basic knowledge of best practices in the IT realm: This is so important – we could basically state that it's important just to know *general* practices. We can serve up a simple, potent, example of this. It may not match an inefficiency specifically in your organization, but it's meant to highlight the care that must go into Business' appreciation of IT practices in this context. A consultant was approached at an organization by the IT leader with a rather desperate, yet simple, problem. The business manager to whom he reported had decided that the IT leader should know where all HelpDesk personnel were *at any given time*. He was answerable for their whereabouts on a moment's query. Now, the impracticality of this would be apparent to most, except that for him this was building a reality that was bearing down on his efficiency and the efficiency of the IT department.

Most of us would know, but we'll state, that HelpDesk personnel spend much if not most of their time in areas other than the IT department. They answer calls and a queue in servicing requests for help, often times performing that help in the requestor's environment. Along the way, the HelpDesk person is solicited on the fly for help. People stop them in the hallway, in the lunchroom, even in the restroom. They start out with one destination, and end up with many in a chain of destinations. Pinning these people down (having them report their whereabouts while maintaining a status of these whereabouts) is not only impractical, counter-efficient, and counterproductive – it's virtually impossible.

The motivation for the business manager's request was the performance of one specific HelpDesk person: His abuse of the necessary trust extended by organizations for these types of positions. That person was socializing on a steady basis, to the detriment of service and support. But the answer did not lie in creating a burdensome requirement for all personnel - manager and subordinates alike. Rather there were plenty of standards against which to hold the one person accountable: He did not service the organization to an acceptable standard: not in a reasonable number of resolutions to problems, nor in the quality of his service. He did not service to the same effectiveness as the other HelpDesk personnel, which had a negative impact on morale. He created frustration amongst users, and diminished IT's esteem in the organization's eyes.

In this example we hopefully can readily recognize the business-compound to the problem. The best practice in this regard is to hire trusted people for the HelpDesk, expose them to, and manage them according to, standards of practice. When necessary, we would bring under-performers back to standards, or move out any personnel that fail to clear the bar. The Business Manager's mistake was in trying to apply a requirement that might work for one class of employee (one that has a focused, central physical workspace), to a class of employee for which it was utterly ineffective and counterproductive.

For Business, be careful that you don't bring a standard that works in one specific area, or even most areas, to the one area where it may not be applicable. Businesses (and IT) go against general or best practice all the time. (Just consider how many reorganizations and revamping of various procedures you've seen - many of which are reversed, and turned back to something much like those things which preceded the last reorganization).

An understanding of risk, and its management: Webster's has a simple and succinct definition of risk that we'll use here: *Risk* is the possibility of suffering loss. Managing risk yields security. Viewing things from the perspective of ignorance and resultant risk to business brings a powerful motivator for getting Business on board regarding security and all other Business-driven IT strategies.

Security can be defined as the state of being free from unacceptable risk. What constitutes unacceptable risk? It varies from organization to organization. It is relatively easy for IT to define technical, mechanical, and physical risks, and to minimize them through management. Somewhat more difficult for IT is identifying and managing business risk vis-à-vis the finite budget and resource realities everyone faces. Only Business can size and shape "acceptable risk" – if there even is such a thing in your organization. But Business will, or should, for the most part understand best the business-perspective as to where resources should go, in what priority, and in what proportion for the protection of business. For this reason, the blended understanding and management of risk in an environment of dynamic business and technology is essential. In other words, everyone must know what engenders likelihood of risk, what the risk mitigations are, and the cost-benefits for assessment of returns on investment – against those elements of business that most require protection

Remember that business, as much as anything, is about opportunity: to expand, to better serve, to operate more efficiently. IT has opportunities too – to bring about better and more efficient support to business. Opportunity engenders change, and therefore it poses risk: change strives to advance current capabilities, and often is undertaken to achieve something that hasn't been done before. These opportunities for advance cannot be realized without facing risk. It is everyone's job to eliminate risk or at the very least minimize risk to the best degree possible. To meet this obligation, all parties at all levels of the organization must understand their role in managing and mitigating risk. Our later chapter on security will explore risk, its management, and our obligations in detail. For now, its important for Business to understand that there is a new level of obligation in understanding risk, and in helping to manage risk, in helping IT understand Business' priorities of protection.

Commitment to common language and aligned effort between IT and Business: This requires nothing more than an acknowledgement and the practice of a good faith effort to speak in best terms for efficient communication. Best terms are arrived at through common sense. No one should use terms and phrases that they know are unlikely to be understood by one or the other (this does not excuse either from bringing the aforementioned fundamental knowledge to the table, or from evolving their business-technology knowledge). When there is doubt, always use a common language term. This means: avoidance of acronyms, until explained, unless you know them to be generally accepted. Avoidance of slang that may be too specific to your department or field. At the same time, it is perfectly acceptable, indeed desirable, to debut and explain new terms and concepts – for efficiency in future discussions and in advancing knowledge. In all of these regards, speak plainly. People will greatly appreciate it and you'll facilitate the business at hand.

An obligation, acknowledgment, and commitment to bring a certain knowledge-base to the table: Just as the people external to Finance and Accounting in your organization are required to understand budgets and basic accounting principles, as people external to Human Resources must understand concepts and issues regarding the proper management and treatment of people, so too must the class of people external to IT understand these matters of support to business.

As new terms, concepts, and issues are introduced, it is a shared obligation to remember these things. "New" knowledge becomes necessary knowledge as you go forward. Sometimes Business members wave off, or take a concentration break, when hearing what they perceive as technical terms, or "IT stuff." Chances are if you're hearing terms and issues with recurring frequency, you're in the orbit of these things for a reason, and you have an obligation to understand them.

Be sure to think of it this way: In an increasingly technical business world, and increasingly technical *personal* world, there is no such thing as learning too much. Technology will play an increasingly important role to every aspect of business, large and small, and will find its way into every corner of operations.

If you're reading this book, it's likely that technology is burrowing its way further into your personal life too. Your attitude, your level of readiness, your amount of preparation will determine whether this increase feels like an intrusion, or feels like the support and enhancement that it's marketed to be. Be ready to weigh in on business-technology projects. Be qualified to contribute. Be knowledgeable so as to make valid suggestions in helping to ensure the best possible fit to your staff's, your department's, your organization's, business.

Even very basic things benefit when everyone commits to knowledge. For example, if you rely on remote connectivity to connect to the office from home or on trips, you should know how to do some basic troubleshooting on your means of connection. True, IT is there to troubleshoot and is obligated to support you. But 92% of connectivity problems are located at the remote computer (yours). What if you can't reach IT for some reason? Or, what if you have to wait for an answer to a page? Are you comfortable being completely dependent on a resource so far removed? Is that wise, if your trouble is in your local environment and may be solvable *by you* with a little knowledge and prior practice?

Think too about this - in our era of online banking, computerized library check-outs, self-cashiering of groceries, home tax applications, software insurance inventories, home networks, personal broadband, PDAs, wireless devices, iPods, etc., etc. - *any* technical knowledge that you acquire at your place of business can be leveraged in your personal realm (and vice versa) – either directly or in just helping you to maintain your "technical chops."

In each of the cases - creating the IT Enlightened Organization and bolstering the Index of User Awareness - we can facilitate things by documenting the expectations and requirements in a Technology Awareness Policy (TAP). This TAP, and its standing vis-à-vis your overall IT policy, is discussed in further detail shortly.

We've been talking about Business' obligation – but – what is IT's burden in getting Business to what may be new levels in your organization?

THE OBLIGATION OF IT TO BUSINESS IN CREATING THE IT ENLIGHTENED ORGANIZATION

IT's Support Remains Steady: It's important to understand that IT does not divest itself of any duty to support Business in this discussion. A bottom line for IT and Business is that if Business requires support on anything regarding data or technology, IT is obligated to bring whatever support is necessary given the issue. If Business is failing to pick up on an obligation, the short-term concern for IT is to still provide whatever support moves business forward – there is time afterwards for addressing any deficiencies or lack of focus. What we're doing here, however, is sizing some expectations regarding IT's needs from Business in planning modern support, and in enabling full-scale Business-power through best use of those modern support technologies.

We know that your organization must negotiate within, and place a level of awareness and ability, that grants the best return on the effort. But how does IT help to create and sustain an appropriate level of awareness and knowledge on Business' part? How to sell and place that obligation in the modern Weave? Here, IT needs to be the driver in forming the IT Enlightened Organization so that, in-turn, Business is able to mount the Business-driven IT strategy – it's a circle of sorts, and harks back to the mutual dependencies and reinforcements we've talked about since the beginning.

In order to achieve effective awareness, you must set about the matter of educating Business: there is the absolute requirement for getting Business to the proper level of knowledge and participation. That is, helping Business to first "know what they don't know." IT must present to them the things they need to know, and then help Business achieve the knowledge about those things. Once that is done, you must work to put a practice in place so that Business can take a proactive approach in maintaining a steady, current, knowledge-base in the changing Weave. This way, Business doesn't merely rely on the Weave – Business helps to *weave* the Weave. When qualified to do that, you cannot fail to achieve a better alignment and fit between technical supports and the business you conduct.

As in most things, you will drive this formation of the IT Enlightened Organization through a process. Let's define a process in simple detail, and then we'll examine it more closely. In creating and maintaining any awareness, for purpose of a combined effort, you go through a basic process cycle:

- Exposition
- Acknowledgment
- Discussion
- Agreement
- Practice

Let's take a detailed look at these in the context of our current discussion:

Exposition: IT will have to expose Business to the reasons for an appropriate awareness and knowledge regarding IT concepts and practices. Exposing this necessity involves varying degrees of detail depending on your audience.

As you go higher on your management chain, your focus on detail will be softer, and you'll present more of a big-picture kind of assessment. Let's start at the top: At the very top, you'll have a simple (though not necessarily easy) sale to make. We'll talk about this top sale first, because without it, you will have difficulty achieving the aims of bringing a required knowledge-base to Business, and in placing the responsibility of a self-sustaining awareness there.

We seek to make a sale to power: the sanctioning and sponsoring body that has the power and authority to direct subordinate business leaders to an objective. The initial objective here is to work with Business to help craft, agree to, and adhere to a policy. The policy will specify requirements for Business's standard knowledge, or knowledge-base: this knowledge-base is an obligation for Business in your organization in order to ensure an engagement-ready posture. This ready posture is necessary for Business to contribute to the planning and alignment of its own support requirements of technology. This posture also prepares Business to make full use of office technologies at their disposal.

In your organization this authority may be a board, a chief executive, an internal council, a manager in any department - or any combination – it depends on your organization's size and structure, and the reader here should understand to whom they must pitch this sale. It is certainly possible that some areas of the organization may grasp and use these concepts better than others. You should proceed in your craft of the best business-technology alignment that you can, regardless of other's grasp or willingness (within scopes of authority and allowances, of course).

Here we can expose the necessity for Business' awareness to top management with a simple analogy. If you, as a homeowner, call a plumber for repair, you bring some standard knowledge to the table: you know what's wrong: *this* pipe is leaking *here*. You also know something about your plumbing system: it transports water. You know the type of water (drinking, washing, waste). You know how to turn water on, and you know how to turn water off. You know how to control the rate of flow.

So – you know what the system is, and you know how to work the system in order to serve your needs. You have a base of knowledge upon which to draw and with which to contribute. When you call the plumber, you are "Business" with its attendant needs, and the plumber in this case is "IT" – the technical element that will service and support your system. The success of the plumber's support to you will be greatly advantaged if you are knowledgeable enough to accurately point them to the correct need. You, too, will be able to judge service accurately, and if it met all needs. Who is ultimately responsible for the home's plumbing? The homeowner: you must investigate, vet, and hire the plumber.

The more knowledge you have, and the better qualified you are to review and survey the plumbers at your disposal, the better off your home will be.

This analogy can be extended, of course. A homeowner may do his or her own plumbing: this would be analogous to a business element that did some measure of system configuration and maintenance formerly done by IT. These cases are fine, but only by training and qualifying staff to perform these functions.

Make the sale such that top management sanctions and sponsors the requirement that Business maintains a corresponding base of knowledge to know what the organization's systems are, and how to use those systems in satisfying the organization's needs. *Business* is ultimately responsible for the organization and its business – including the drive of IT.

Consider other analogies: your business management is required to know something of finance and accounting, so as to have something to build on when engaging on the specifics of your organization's finance and accounting methods. No manager comes to your organization without some kind of basic budget experience and knowledge, for example. Similarly, your management is expected to know something of general human resource practices, so as to engage effectively in managing people at your specific organization. A base of common knowledge will allow them to engage with the HR department in an efficient manner: *They are already in an engagement-ready posture*.

Once you have exposed the degree of divide between Business and IT in your organization to senior management, and received their acknowledgement and endorsement for defining a Business role in crafting the Business-driven IT strategy, you are ready for the next step: You will present the same sale to those levels of business that function in the Close Mesh. You can do it through the BIT team.

Acknowledgment: If we go back to our plumbing analogy, we know that your best chance for quality service - a fix that fits the problem – and consequently an efficient and effective plumbing system - starts with you, the customer. Why? Because it is you who will select the plumber in the first place, and here's hoping you know how to select a good one - or know where to go to get the help or information to make a good selection. Further, it is your job to direct, assess and evaluate the plumber and the job he or she is doing.

Similarly, a Business person has to engage and contribute to the use, maintenance, and repair of information technologies in a similar fashion. Further, even in a "perfectly" functioning system, Business has to contribute to a progression - by planning and ensuring alignment of support technology to business over the course of time. Our information systems are not static like your home's plumbing system, but are dynamic. Hence, evermore the need for the informed Business manager.

Business remains IT's customer, true, but *Business* is the user, owner, and beneficiary of the overall technology system - not the "plumber" (IT). You simply need to make your WorkWith managers aware that the organization now needs IT Enlightened business leaders, particularly those who manage at the operational level, to help fit IT to Business. Those managers need to bring a basic technology awareness to the table, born of knowledge. Initially their acknowledgement is largely a matter of understanding, or appreciating, their general requirements and roles. This is because the details will become clear through the generation of a policy - a policy they will help to create.

Discussion: Once you have the sanction and support of your top management, and you've exposed the idea of the IT Enlightened Organization to your WorkWiths, you can begin to discuss the details for what will comprise their technology awareness. Your BIT meetings can have an agenda that includes time for defining these requirements. Once these requirements are defined, they will be formalized in the Technology Awareness Policy (TAP). The TAP will also spell out top management's endorsement of the IT Enlightened Organization, and will define common IT knowledge that any Business person, anywhere, would be expected to posses as well as levels of awareness specific to your organization's environment. This policy can then be presented to top management for approval. Once approved, you can do one of two things:

1) Place the TAP into your overall IT Policy. This means that your IT policy (and included TAP) would likely retain whatever title and "market presence" it has in your organization. It might be something like The Widget, Inc. Information Technology Policy.

2) Bring your current IT Policy under your TAP Policy. In this case, the idea of technology awareness is not subsumed in the overall existing policy, but takes preeminence - you then change the title of the premier IT policy document in your organization to, for example, The Widget, Inc. Technology Awareness and Use Policy.

Which is preferable? It depends on your organization and your situation.

Incorporating a TAP into overall IT policy, option 1, is a great idea for organization's that already have a good IT awareness. In this instance, your organization merely needs the formality of expectations to keep current staff on track, and the policy delivers the expectations to new hires so that they know what is expected of them in your IT Enlightened Organization. You may be comfortable with the way your current IT policy fits the organization, and you might not be ready to radically reorder it.

Option 2 is a good one, even a necessary one, for organization's that may feel the need to drive and formalize a culture change. In these circumstances, you don't want to subsume the concepts of a TAP to the existing policy where they might be diluted by a continuity of ignorance. You want to bump the organization out of a rut: you want the element of awareness to dominate.

All policy, IT and otherwise, is about awareness (for purpose of guidance, adherence, compliance, and enforcement) - so it makes perfect sense to lead an IT policy off with the requirements that qualify a person to understand and follow the rest of the policy!

The TAP portion of any policy, be it stand-alone or incorporated, should include those items we discussed above. For Business, think about areas where you felt uncomfortable or lacking when engaging with IT. Not where you felt IT wasn't forthcoming enough, or supportive enough, but rather where everyone seemed to be making a sincere, strong effort, but it was somehow not enough. In that circumstance, Business should do some brainstorming to identify areas where they may have been lacking certain qualifications for engagement. Bring those suspect areas to the table for discussion here.

For example, when detailing *a basic knowledge of informational, technical, and support concepts by Business* within TAP, you should include the expectation that managers be ready to engage in the maintenance of the Business-Technology Weave. They should understand common, across the board support applications. Further, they should understand fundamental concepts of data integrity, reports vetting, and management of content, in their respective departments. The elements of your TAP could include items such as:

- **Managers must maintain their knowledge of the ABC Sales and Inventory Management System (ABC-SIMS) in order to remain current regarding business rules and their reflection in the system. Managers should be ready at all times to engage in the planning and implementation of business-driven changes to the system.**

- ...

- **Managers must ensure that their department maintains integrity of data, produces reports that are accurate, and that their department**

contributes to the appropriate retention and disposal of data in accordance with Widget, Inc.'s Document Retention Program.

The importance of this should be obvious. Those people who are managing business, conducting business, and who are the caretakers of business, must maintain an engagement-ready posture in order to drive the business-driven technology initiatives. Further, for efficiency, managed cost, and ease of operations, you've got to leverage data integrity where data is being created and manipulated. That is achieved by business users. The fine details and associated standards will be contained in job descriptions – here the goal is to deliver the awareness, and to create the expectation and requirement for it. Further, various departments and business managers can create their own internal additions and refinements to the requirements and standards.

Another simple example is that all personnel should have a fundamental grasp of common shelf applications as they exist in your organization. For example:

- **Business users must have a solid grasp of word processing, spreadsheets, and presentation graphics. Users should be positioned to participate in department knowledge-shares, in the organization's Users Group, and in helping to maintain a collective body of end-user knowledge in the use of Widget Inc. systems that they are assigned to know.**

- **...**

In your organization, a discussion within BIT will yield appropriate requirements and levels regarding knowledge of those things we discussed: best practices in the IT realm; an understanding of risk and its management; a commitment to common language and common efforts between IT and Business, and so on. Requirements and rewards will begin to evidence themselves as Business takes ownership of their obligation to bring a base of knowledge to the table. Efficiencies and profits will reinforce Business' self-motivated maintenance of the engagement-ready posture. This chapter is not an attempt to map out an exact TAP - a one-size-fits-all-plan. Rather, these examples are to spur your organization's thinking in these regards. You tweak and tailor these ideas to your organization, department, and even individuals.

In the case of a Technology Awareness and Use Policy, here's something important to keep in mind. While the policy's main awareness purpose is to detail a standard Business knowledge-base (for purpose of a running engagement-ready posture), the policy can also be used to document critical *temporary* requirements in times of large-scale change. These would be longer-term temporary requirements – many months, or even a year or more. These would be placed at the end of the standard knowledge-base. An example of a longer-term temporary requirement would be:

Managers in departments that are participating in the migration from the ABC Sales & Inventory Management System (ABC-SIMS) to the new XYZ Sales & Inventory Management System (XYZ-SIMS) are required to undergo XYZ-SIMS Basic Training. Business leaders and staff must:

- Have a thorough understanding of their assigned area of business.
- Have a thorough understanding of our current inventory management system, ABC-SIMS.
- Attend XYZ-SIMS training as assigned.
- Participate in meetings as required with IT and the vendor in assisting the new XYZ-SIMS' fit to business.
- Perform end-use test as assigned, and provide requested feedback as to quality of data and reports, and regarding the system's accuracy in adhering to Widget Inc.'s business rules and expectations.
- …

When critical temporary requirements arise or drop off, add and remove them from the TAP as necessary.

In your discussions, you can negotiate with Business as regards the kind and level of knowledge required for an effective, collective, team effort. In sizing your organization's awareness, discuss the influence of the following: the measure of, and reliance on, business technologies in the organization; the education and ability of your managers and users; the level of agreement you've achieved from your top management – and therefore their expectations; and the nature and future of your business.

Ultimately, your integrated TAP and IT Policy goes through your organization's review, and then becomes a formal policy. Human Resources needs to be involved in the crafting of this policy, and all levels of management need to incorporate performance ratings for individuals in these regards when appraising employees. The TAP, or extracts from it, can go into your Employee Handbook. It serves as a reference to the organization's expectations for maintaining a robust team in piloting Business-Technology endeavors. It's also a necessary reference for incoming personnel, particularly those in key positions:

their first exposure to high-level detail about your organization's solid management of the Business-Technology Weave.

In your discussions, you should define requirements for WorkWiths and for WorkOns because although requirements for each group will overlap, there will be some differences. In your organization, you may have several strata of people for whom you wish to define requirements. Your meetings will yield some interesting discussions, and your organization will seek its own level of awareness, and related efficiency – hopefully the optimum for each required case.

These are meant to serve as very simple and basic examples. Ultimately, your policy needs to set standards so that Business truly understands mission critical business application softwares: knows how to use them, knows something of the underlying data and business rules that support respective business process, knows how to make full use of all other office technologies, and has sufficient knowledge to make meaningful contributions in the planning of future business-technology alignment. Your policy should spell out expectations and obligations for managers and departments when changes in support technology occur that affect them. You'll use your own imagination and creativity to mold these examples as a best fit to your organization in employing a TAP policy to maximum advantage.

Agreement: Come to an agreement that Business takes a self-motivating posture regarding use of what are *their* business tools. No one has a wall-to-wall understanding of end-use business and shelf applications – not IT, not Business. But everyone has access to support resources for end-use products. Therefore, it is most efficient to draw a direct line between the end-user with the questions, and the *closest* support resource. The closest resource is already at Business' desktops – ready and waiting. IT should provide end-use help only when a business user has made a good-faith effort to answer their own question, and either needs further explanation, or found the help resource to be lacking. But generally when questions arise, it is essential for Business to use online Help, and other vendor supplied documentation. Most business and shelf applications vendors supply CD, DVD, and web-based tutorials for their products. Your business users should be required to take these tutorials. It is really essential for IT to make this sale – you've got to secure this agreement and TAP it.

IT must also secure Business' agreement to participate in the planning of their own training. For example: the online tutorials we just spoke of are frequently released with notices sent to an e-mail list. Have your business users on that notification roster so that they can take the tutorials as released. Business must build and sustain the expectation that users will assume some self-maintenance in their currency with these business tools. Many business application vendors have electronic newsletters with Tips & Tricks for use of their products. Users from a broad spectrum of organizations such as yours contribute the ways and means for achieving results using the same products that you are using.

Your Business users must learn how to access and leverage this collective knowledge. The larger vendors host monthly users meetings for training and the sharing of knowledge. Where they exist, your organization should have a small team from Business and IT attending these on a regular basis. Bring hand-outs back and share relevant material within departments. Highlight important information and put extracts on your IT and Business department bulletin boards. Business should also build an internal user group with IT's help. We'll be talking more about this user group and its structure.

Senior managers should task their managers for a plan: identification of users who need formal training. Who can self-train? Can we benefit from department knowledge-share meetings? Do users simply keep up through their own aptitude, attitude, and proactivity? Disperse the training budget – don't centralize it in IT. Let your departments request and allocate technical training budgets (with the necessary IT help that's required). That way, you can "follow the money" to see which departments require more outside training than others. Of course, you must weight this according to a department's use of and reliance on support technology. But if you notice something fundamental, such as a Finance department that is hiring users and sending some out to spreadsheet training, you have a problem that is pretty obvious (and not all that uncommon).

Senior Managers: ask your managers how much IT time they need to keep their staffs operating effectively. Ask IT to deliver like-information: how much support does each department need? Then evaluate the symmetry, or lack, between the reports. If you seem to be getting fairly accurate information, look to those departments that seem to be more self-standing and self-motivating. Those departments that self-motivate and maintain with more efficiency and to a higher degree can then be solicited to share their ideas and successes with other departments.

Agree that as all look forward, it will be not only with an eye toward better business, but too with an awareness for its attendant technology support. Build the awareness that end-use technology is a *business tool* – owned, used and effectively wielded by Business. In IT's case, it is very easy to support this through the dissemination of short articles in the BIT meetings – articles of interest to your organization's business, from a technology perspective. This sets an example for Business, and they should be making a like contribution. Bring these outside articles to the table to spur discussion within. This helps everyone to stay informed.

You should also have a dedicated bulletin board in your IT area. This board should include an area for information specific to your organization's business and technical environment. Just as importantly, you must have a section that has forward-looking material. In this area, you'll want to post articles that speculate on the future of various technologies, technologies you may or may not presently employ, and even technologies you may *never* employ. You want this to be as much a brainstorming area as anything else - to spark interest and creativity among your business (and IT) staff. Make it informative – and direct people's attention to it. If space permits, other departments should create their own technology awareness boards. *Why not?*

Practice: For Business, there's a big advantage when your organization introduces, defines, establishes and adheres to these requirements. Put them into practice. Weave them into your organization's culture. Craft and publish your Technology Awareness and Use Policy. Get IT at the Business table where business-driven strategies, including IT, are being generated. Get Business at the business-technical planning and implementation table – BIT. Weave the detail of requirements and standards into your job descriptions – that will be accomplished through BIT, with HR's oversight. Help Business to create internal knowledge-share teams, set up an organizational User Group, and help Business avail themselves of self-maintenance materials. Make full use of things such as online Help, web-based tutorials, electronic newsletters, other support media such as vendor-distributed CDs and DVDs. Essentially, you're creating a circle of communication and support.

Remember ~

Business must fully engage when initiatives influence process. Let IT know that you're a team player. Offer to plan things, to test things and offer to provide feedback. Rather than relying on others in the organization to do this, get on this edge yourself. You will then have an influence in the outcomes, and the best opportunity to align new systems to fit your business best.

IT must remember that you'll achieve the greatest measure of success by starting with those things that Business is most *willing* to do: concentrate on achieving the possible. There is always time to expand the possible as the culture and expectations slowly change. If your organization is not currently postured to take every advantage of technology, and if your organization has a relatively ineffective business-driven IT strategy, you must realize that you cannot achieve the IT Enlightened Organization overnight. Select methods that are functional and that will be used. Get agreement and acceptance from all regarding the chosen methods, sustain traction, and use new awareness and practices as a foundation on which to build further awareness and ever better practices. *Expand the possible.*

As you go along keep in mind that in your organization, IT may feel that your policy makes weak requirements of Business – or - Business may feel that your policy shifts too much burden to Business – but at least you will have codified important "where we are" supports. Once the policy exists, it must live, breath, and grow according to what your organization can do, is willing to do, and ultimately *must* do over the course of time. It will help reinforce the "where we're going" for your business-driven IT strategy as it helps maintain Business' qualification when developing any and all plans.

Keep this in mind too: Most people, upon procuring a new phone, home entertainment system, game, etc., will fiddle and fool with it until they master those things necessary to gain acceptable use from the product. In the business environment, this same attitude must apply. This is not to suggest that people exceed their authority, or twist their use of office tools into inappropriate results. But within the realm of acceptable use, they must be willing to be aggressive in maximizing their proficiency in the use of tools and systems.

14

IGNORANCE, PART II – THE IT CONCEIT

Half knowledge is worse than ignorance.

Thomas B. Macaulay

How often has Business delivered a requirement to IT, and after all of the communication, process, oversight and testing, you hear:

This isn't what we _____ (wanted; asked for; saw in the demo…).

How does this happen - over and over again? This is costly, frustrating, and frankly – post-9/11 – dangerous to survival. We can answer the question here by recognizing that each side of the divide frequently harbors a half-knowledge. If Business has a poor understanding of technology, and if IT hasn't an appropriate understanding of the business, you have two sides with half-knowledge. Half-knowledge means that each side has eminent expertise in their own area - they can talk amongst themselves – but they lack the specific understanding necessary to engage and fit to the other. You can't build an optimum team on this basis, and the problem is so obvious and simple that we can only arrive at one conclusion: Many are looking past this issue as it hides in plain sight. Stop looking past it.

It is IT's Obligation to Know What Business Needs: We need to examine how IT contributes to this problem, and what IT can do to rectify things. To fix a problem, we must first understand it. When IT finds itself participating in less than ideal outcomes, IT's posture is frequently that Business "doesn't know what it wants." Here *want* equals *need*, as IT is obligated to qualify wants, and to help translate wants to appropriately sized needs. We just hammered home the concept of Business' obligation in assuming the Business-driven IT strategy – but now what? The next condition should be obvious: Regardless of a "Business" posture, IT needs to be in a fail-safe mode so as to always know what

Business wants, so as to proceed with continuous improvements. Further, IT must do so with sanction, in accurately filling Business' needs. Any time you hear an IT claim that Business doesn't know what it wants, you have an immediate certification: It is certified that *IT doesn't know* what Business wants. Your organization cannot afford an IT endeavor that does not know what Business wants (needs).

Further, as frequently happens in these circumstances, IT should *never* maintain illusions that they know what is "best" for Business. That would be an enormous conceit. Harboring this assumption leads IT to operate without appropriate sanction. As we've mentioned, some in Business are content to let IT lead in this manner – it sustains that posture of ignorance that we talked about and all that goes with it – including deniability in the face of negative outcomes. It is only a matter of time before such a condition catches up with IT, and hence the organization. You are operating in an upside down, dysfunctional, posture if any part of the organization operates on this assumption.

Therefore any time IT has knowledge of a superior Business-IT mesh than the one employed, whether narrow or comprehensive, IT must share this knowledge at the appropriate table. It then becomes a shared knowledge, with an appropriate review and an appropriate potential for sanction, sizing, and implementation.

To emphasize: When we hear "Business doesn't know what it wants," there is one safe assumption we can make: *IT doesn't know what Business wants*. This is true because one or the other applies:

- Business knows what it wants, but what it wants somehow hasn't transmitted to IT.

    –or–

- Business isn't sure what it wants.

Either way, IT is disengaged from operating on valid business goals and strategy due to a posture of ignorance. IT's ignorance may be of its own making, or IT may be forced into ignorance: here, we're not crafting an issue of fault or an exercise to assign blame. This is a problem for the *organization*. So let's be clear: It is IT's burden to facilitate the focus and transmission of the Business wants in either case, because IT serves at the pleasure of Business. In other words, IT must engage effectively for a seamless understanding of, and contribution to, the Business-driven IT strategy.

As we look at the overall support of IT to business, improvements may best be clarified if we consider the bulk of the IT department first; programmers, technicians, analysts, etc. - those people directly servicing the organization's daily and near-term business support. We'll leave discussion of high-level IT leadership for the end of the chapter.

IT IS MORE CHALLENGING FOR IT TO UNDERSTAND BUSINESS ISSUES, THAN FOR BUSINESS TO UNDERSTAND IT ISSUES

Bridging a Divide: Let's examine modern phenomena so that we can fully understand today's IT burden in supporting Business. The statement above is not meant to imply, or assign, a level of difficulty to IT's understanding of business. It should be a straightforward undertaking for IT to understand "the business" of the organization, and to emplace standards to do that. Instead, the statement is simply a *comparison*. It expresses the idea that Business should have a much more natural disposition to the understanding of technical issues, than does IT to business issues. This is the opposite of where things stood a few years ago, and it is not anything self-generated by either Business or IT. To help understand this view, let's consider how this reversal has occurred, and how things stand.

Some years ago, people had no real technical involvement or environment outside of their business or work realm (if any) – not the kind we have today. Dealing with technology, data, or just general equipment, and gaining a practical output from these resources, was a cold-start upon entering the office, the plant, or the field. And, whatever your place of work was, homes and personal lives were not particularly automated. Any home devices representing automation were rudimentary by today's standards.

A Culture Awash in Technology: Today it is a radically different story. Let's consider what is happening with our society in general. Where is the leverage and reinforcement for understanding the other's realm – Business vis-à-vis Technology? With Business. That is, Business should be naturally inclined to understand general technology. Why? Because many technical issues in the workplace have a mirror in your home and personal environment.

Think about the aforementioned online banking, your management of home e-mail, and other applications that you use. Things such as tax preparation or cataloging programs. Those are *your* applications, yielding your fit to business issues. You have a *Personal*-Technology Weave. To reinforce, lets again add: the self-checkout at the library, self-cashiering, software insurance inventories, home networks, personal broadband, PDAs, wireless devices, iPods, cameraphones, etc. You have to learn how to use these items. You have to maintain them – either tweaking them yourself, or procuring repair and fixes. You have to upgrade them, expand their capabilities when desired, or replace them outright when you feel it is to your advantage.

The Personal-Technology Weave, and The Business Pre-Disposition: All of this should predispose a Business-person for acclimation to an organization's business-technical environment. For the audience of this book, the Personal-Technology Weave outside of work largely mimics the Business-Technology Weave at the workplace. For business members, there is an outside (personal) motivator for the acquisition of technical knowledge, and for gaining practical use of technical things. Whether they realize it or not, people's Personal-Technology Weave reinforces the Business-Technology weave.

This happens through people's experience with databases (spreadsheet or other software household inventories, budgets, etc.), mission critical business applications (tax software), data transfers (iPods, MP3 players, cameras, etc.), infrastructure (their home computer setup, DSL, cable-modems, and even networking, etc.), and any number of things that equate. For this reason, most non-IT members of the organization should have a natural bias and favorable disposition toward technology, and a solid general aptitude for its use. Certainly more people will as time goes by.

The Lack of a Similar IT Reinforcement: However, the IT person has no real corresponding bias. True, seasoned IT personnel have been in various business environments, and many of the issues and solutions they've seen will translate and have effectiveness in the next organization. But that's organization-to-organization. There is no real corresponding outside motivation (compared to the one Business has) for the broad IT staff to acquire "business" knowledge. There is no Personal-*Business* Weave that reinforces the organization's business, quite the same way that the Personal-*Technology* Weave mirrors the organization's technical supports.

Now, some may say that any household is a business, and therefore constitutes an outside motivator. You have a budget, you have to plan and forecast things (college tuition, major purchases), you have maintenance, etc. However, the things you do in maintaining your home's business do not really translate to your organization's business. Not with the same effectiveness that the technology in your home translates to the organization's technology.

Remember too that the outside technical reinforcement for a Business person comes not just from the home. It also comes from the library, grocery store, hardware store, etc. Reinforcement comes from anywhere that a business invites or requires the consumer's technical assist. There simply is no outside, corresponding, business reinforcement here: Home Depot does not invite you to help balance their books, staff their phones, conduct an inventory, or to perform any other business function whilst you swim through the increasingly technical outside culture. Outside businesses do, however, invite you to use their computers, scanners, self-checkouts, ATMs, and all manner of technical gadgets and systems.

So, there's not much of a corresponding outside reinforcement, comparatively speaking, providing a natural accumulation of business knowledge by IT. Many an IT department can lag in the upkeep of its knowledge regarding the organization's business methods. IT can become so focused with its technical and process upkeep that it may overlook or pay insufficient attention to evolving business practice. In an environment where Business is piloting a Business-driven IT strategy, this would obviously have a negative impact on efficiency. Therefore recognize that it is in IT's best interest to self-generate a methodology in sustaining a culture for steady accumulation of specific business knowledge and better understanding of general business practice.

When IT is Immersed and Myopic

We know that Business has an obligation to partner on planning of support initiatives, but whether it does that well, poorly, or not at all, IT must be in that posture constantly. Regardless of the business wrapping, anything less than a complete engagement is a conceit that has no place in a professional IT endeavor.

Every Business and IT person I spoke to about this book stirred up an immediate conversation. In the case of IT people, the overwhelming majority of conversations generated an instant blizzard of details. It didn't much matter whether I was talking to a CTO, HelpDesk technician, or anyone else in the hierarchy, the details flew. And, it didn't matter if it was management issues or operational endeavors - I couldn't follow most of these conversations. And I'm "IT." Whether it was abbreviations, acronyms, jargon, junk terms, arcane detail about specific projects - none of it was offered with the perspective of hearing it through *the recipient's* (my) ears.

Because I was a relative stranger in many of these conversations, I have to believe that these IT folks were even worse when dealing with the business people with whom they are familiar. We can base this on the old "Familiarity

Breeds Contempt" view – where contempt indicates less of a sneer than an arrogant, ignorant, posture of assumption – and lack of an appropriate level of care. It was clear that many of the IT people needed an opportunity to vent – something anyone can certainly appreciate. Many wanted an outsider's perspective to some project or situation. Some wanted to contribute ideas to the book. What became clear, however, was that most IT people are immersed in their environments. This immersion happens to the degree that they lose sight of the big picture. Many people seem to be drowning in their particular situations – they are drowning in details - and they're not coming up for air and rejuvenation.

You have to back off and reflect a bit even during the most trying circumstances. We've all been guilty of subsuming ourselves in details: being bashed and bashing back, as we juggled, fought fires, tried to be in two or more places at once – all through the best 20/20 tunnel vision we are afforded given the pressures. The immersion and its affect sneak up on you – the old "a fish doesn't know it's wet" thing. We realize that IT, at all levels, is involved in the detail of making things work. Often it becomes difficult to disengage from the detail in order to talk on a practical level with a "regular" person, or even to have an effective internal dialog with yourself as you make assessments and judgments. For this reason the immersion, and any attendant inability to climb above the fray, will impede decent discussion among *IT members* too. Everyone needs to operate in a regular person mode from time-to-time, to assess those things you're doing from the *listener's* (recipient's, customer's, member's, business person's, fellow IT member's, outsider's...) *point of view*.

Up For Air; Take a Breath; Communicate Effectively: All IT people, even planners and visionaries, need to guard against a rather myopic view. But those most susceptible to this are those people managing projects and providing close-hold support. Especially people such as HelpDesk folks, as they directly interface with Business on a weekly and daily basis. This is somewhat ironic, as these are the very people who need to be able to speak the most plainly to their audience. This is not to say that anyone needs to dumb-down their engagement – you just have to have the sensitivity to assess whether your message, your instruction, your sale – is getting through effectively. You need to assess and adjust accordingly. IT also needs to be able to hear as Business brings their business-driven needs and ideas to the planning and execution tables. This effective Business-IT engagement has always been a necessity, but it is of critical importance as IT pauses to reflect on their requirement for plain speaking.

Too, it is important for IT to size, reveal, and explain detail according to the audience so as not to alienate, or tune out, anyone. We're not talking about abandoning our expectations for a more enlightened IT organization. Let's assume a perfect world: if everyone is fully engaged at their respective level of care in supporting the IT Enlightened Organization, how does IT engage most effectively? In discussing communications here, we can think of the need for detail as being roughly inversely proportional to the level of business management you're engaging. The higher your audience, the bigger the picture you'll present, and the less granular the detail. This should seem obvious to most, but I mention it here because it's so important. There are some simple rules for communication that are perhaps less things *to do*, than things to *avoid*.

Problems should always be resolved at the lowest possible level. In other words, you should never have to bring problems to your senior-most WorkFors – you want to achieve sanction at this level, you want to report success to this level, and you want to make people at this level *look good* (and feel good). As importantly, you want to look good to them. The closest thing to a problem that you should ever bring to these upper levels would be the seek of advice or guidance in nipping something in the bud, or in staving off a potential bad outcome well in advance of a major drain on resources. When engaging the top, you also want to *get in*, communicate the necessities, and *get out* – they're busy. At the same time, IT must have the judgment in making these determinations so as not to screen necessary information from decision makers.

Communication becomes more focused on process and operations – on details - when you engage your WorkWiths and WorkOns. In circumstances where you work on your projects, dispense help, engage vendors, or impact users, you craft the appropriate rules of engagement. Here is where IT needs to perform due diligence in communications with Business. IT can talk about "bouncing" servers (rebooting), "slicing and dicing" data (manipulating, reporting), and hashing projects amongst themselves. But when engaging Business, it's best to stick to concrete, mutually accepted and known terms. Rather than explaining slang or some trendy term of the moment, use the time to explain emerging, industry accepted terms and concepts.

Better language also makes a better impression. IT needs to speak to Business with a sincerity that shows a vested interest in business. IT isn't an appendage that can be swapped among organizations. At the risk of too many metaphors: IT is going to be steeped like a tea bag in any particular organization – why not a hand-in-glove fit? Think about this – IT is there every day of the workweek, and supposedly sized and shaped to be specific to your business. There's no excuse for a bad fit. IT should speak in a business-like way, in a business environment.

Even amongst vendors, resist slang. Sticking to formal definitions reinforces who is in charge (the organization), whose interests are being served (the organization's), and it reduces the opportunity for miscommunication of needs (the organization's). In other words, you set the select of language (business-like), and you therefore control *who is <u>in</u> control – the organization*. Not to say that you can't be personable, have fun, and be friendly. Not to say that vendors can't educate you or advise you – they'd better. But when business is on the table, you want to control the factors of the engagement with vendors. You want to minimize miscommunication, and that is best done on a business plane.

From here, you can pretty much extrapolate an appropriate scale for communications at the bottom, the top and everything in between.

IT Leadership – Speaking to All Levels

What about IT leadership? In smaller organizations, IT leaders often perform at all levels – they may speak to a board member one moment, and visit someone's desktop the next. These folks have a solid knowledge for how a relatively small IT department should run, and how it should support business. This is due to their history of a close proximity to actual operations – technical as well as business. For smaller or mid-size organizations, seek a good technical leader with solid communication and interpersonal skills.

Larger organizations, and any enterprise with more complex governance, regulatory burden, and affiliations, will emphasize a business background. Increasingly, organizations are looking for IT leaders with solid general management skills, placing an emphasis there rather than on narrow technical expertise. Don't cut technical expertise too thin, however. According to IBM's Advanced Business Institute, studies show the two most critical qualifications for CIO's to be the ability to lead, and the ability to apply technology, to meet business needs. That sounds pretty fundamental.

To do this, you must know something about business in general, you must know *the* business in your place of employ, and you must have leadership qualities. Other criteria cited in the study are innovation, interpersonal skills, and technology awareness. Business requires IT visionaries who are qualified in partnering for a shared understanding. This creates the mutually understood and agreed upon foundation for moving forward.

At Any Level, The Weave Requires Understanding of "Both Sides": In the case of the successful lead IT executive, there has to be a credibility with top management. He or she must possess strong leadership and organizational skills. At the same time, however, there must be a solid understanding of technology – how else to qualify in meshing both sides of the Weave? Many tomes argue that successful IT management can be achieved by employing a business professional as CIO, for example. There are many IT lead executives who come to IT "sideways" – from a background with no particular technical experience, exposure, or even prior IT supervision. Their success, as anyone's, varies. But, for the organization that emplaces an IT lead executive from a relatively technology-free background, you need to be certain that this person has done the necessary things on their own to be comfortable with technology. There are many executives who are leading IT because it was thrust upon them by top management. Sometimes these "thrust-upons" are without qualification. This presents its own ignorance.

If you select IT leadership on the wrong basis, you certainly create a diminished capacity for an optimum IT Enlightened Organization. Think about it. If you don't have at least a somewhat technically savvy leader in IT – just where *is* that leader in your organization? Think about this carefully: for every Tonya, Dick and Harry out there administering their own home network, broadband, and home theater setups, you'd better have someone at the IT top that people can look up to. And if another business leader has made it *their* business to get informed, which many are doing, your IT leader can lose credibility in other business members' eyes. Remember, we're building awareness and better ways: get an IT leader who will have credibility with his or her own IT people right down to desktop support, and who will have credibility with everyone else in the room.

What exactly does that last statement mean? Of course it doesn't mean that your CTO, CIO, Director – your IT leader - is capable of pulling desktop support calls, or upgrading infrastructure, or writing code, etc. It just means that everyone who comes into contact with this person comes away with a solid secure feeling – whether Business, IT, outside contractor, Board member, etc. Too, the IT level that is directly under this person is going to understand on very intimate terms just how well this person understands the issues, and will also understand just how "real" this person's experience is – in very short order. That impression is going to filter down throughout the department, and it is likewise going to eventually steep the rest of the organization – *up and down, and wall to wall*. Your IT leader has to have some measure of Tech Cred.

Leadership's "Tech Cred": What is Tech Cred? Let's define it for our purposes here: Tech Cred is credibility with, and the ability to engender respect from, two distinct classes of people: 1) Technical people and 2) People who conduct business with technology.

We can classify technical people as engineers, software developers/ programmers, technicians, project managers, business/systems analysts, and other general people who help translate needs and ideas between Business and Technology. The others are the people using and relying on technology to get the job done. The IT leader also has to have Tech Cred with Business. Business needs to know that they have IT leadership capable of a vanguard posture in bringing the best possible technical, as well as business, contribution to the Business-driven IT strategy in your organization.

Therefore, your IT leader must understand issues from both sides with equal facility, in order to promote the best solutions and to bring the appropriate resources to bear. Further, this person needs to be the premier authority in understanding these two sides. Putting a pure business person in this lead IT position compromises your organization's standing. You may think this kind of IT leader can get all the technical advice and recommendations from a strong #2 in the department – but what if that advice is poor, or ill-informed? How can your lead IT executive vet that information? How can this person *lead*? He or she also needs to be able to stand firm when necessary, and only knowledge will yield that kind of confidence. Having the courage of his or her convictions helps to make the right sales, helps to define a leader, and brings Business fully on board during challenging times.

The IT lead has to set the example. This person also has to assemble and maintain the right team. That team obviously includes extremely technical considerations, and of course the team's mission is to align technology and related support to business. All other things being equal, it can never hurt to have an IT executive with some measure of technical background, but it *can* hinder to have someone without one. The organization holds the dice.

A Trend; A Trap: Don't fall into a trendy temptation to put a technically unaware business person at the head of your IT operations, thinking you'll get "new," "fresh," insights borne of some kind of charmed "lack of prejudice." The thinking here is frequently: "Bob snapped the Marketing department into shape – let's turn him loose on IT. He has no IT background, isn't particularly technical, so he's free of any baggage and won't bring pet assumptions to the process." Let's be blunt: There is no Magic Ignorance.

Your IT lead executive needs to be *IT as well* as Business savvy. This is not to say that there aren't those who are immensely talented in a general way, and that the "technically-unaware" couldn't ramp up for ultimate success. You may have a situation where someone's overall aptitude and character trump all other concerns – and that's fine. But what is important to note here is that your odds are best if you seek to emplace the best possible person who has both tech creds and business creds.

Many organizations emplace a business executive in the relative backwater calm of recent, settled, large-scale change (after resolution of problems). The prior IT executive has departed for any number of reasons, but the point here is that the business executive generally takes a more sympathetic approach to management: softening problems, smoothing relationships, and creating a near-term appearance of improvement. However, any misunderstanding of the environment, and unwitting misrepresentation of reality, will bear on the next large challenge in stunning fashion. Here, the business executive will be underspec'd in important ways, and will not understand unique IT requirements and standards. This executive can damage the IT team in terms of expectations, standards, and performance. Any hires during this period run the risk of being poor, or awful, fits.

Particularly if you're in an organization that is having problems: you don't want to go *against* the odds. If you have IT leadership that is wedded to pet assumptions, or one that is channeling an ineffective groove in your organization, or that simply isn't bearing positive results, your course of action – your solution - is to get an *IT* leadership in place that *knows better* in all areas – not leadership that *knows less*.

Leveraging Knowledge Requires… Knowledge: Leaders must also have the skill to recognize skills in others. The IT field, like any, is rife with people who talk a good game. Some walk like they talk – some don't. The average candidate for your IT department will appear conversant in technical matters, they will profess a belief in quality of service principles, and of course they are brought on board with high expectations. We know that many people fall short of these expectations - in all fields and areas of endeavor. In cases of flat-out bad IT hires, we have an enormous drain on resources. In the IT department, a sub-optimal hire compounds across the organization in a very detrimental way, as IT supports virtually the entire organization and almost every effort within.

We also know how much time and effort it takes to dismiss an employee. Often an employee must be left within a performance arena in order to record and document poor performance. For IT, this is a cruel irony and a ticklish game – trying to maintain security and solid support while leaving job duties in the hands of a poor performer. The associated inefficiencies brought about by increased oversight, double-checking, and counseling are their own drain – in addition to the lack of results. There is also the impact to staff morale. For these reasons, you need an IT leadership that can smoke out the true candidates worthy of hire, investment, and promotion.

These things make it imperative for your IT leader to understand something about most areas of IT technical endeavor. This person does not need to have a deep background in all areas or even specific areas. This person just needs to have a solid understanding of the principles that guide areas, and a good familiarity with the higher-level best practices for managing each area. Much of the vetting of personnel falls to the managers just under the top leadership. Therefore, top leadership needs to qualify in making *those* managers the best possible investment that your organization can make, as those managers groom the rest of the department.

DUTY HAS NO ROOM FOR CONCEIT

It is IT's job to figure out what Business wants and certainly what Business needs – by listening, communicating, digging - by engaging. If IT comes away from the table without all requirements, exposure of needs, and understanding of Business expectations, IT has to go back in and get these things. Sometimes it can be difficult, and it's going to require tact and patience. However, for best success, you have to smash ambiguity. Smash it with a velvet hammer, though. However difficult it may be to pin Business down, it will be far *more* painful in the long run if you don't.

Only a qualified understanding of business will allow IT to partner on the alignment of support to business. Remember that, in addition to IT's place at the planning and execution tables, IT can survey business. Ask Business what it wants! The simple survey will yield needs from the bottom of the organization on up. Depending on your organization's size, you will decide whether to issue a survey on a regularized basis, or to do a survey based on other triggers. It's always wise to survey the organization prior to large-scale change. It's also good to survey where the organization is in terms of level of comfort with business tools, and to assess training needs. IT can then sit down with supervisors and business managers to help plan a department's training strategy.

Realize that if you've established credibility, and achieved sanction in the past, you stand your best chances for success. If you're in a challenging business environment, and you feel there's a gap in understanding on Business' part, with possible negative outcomes to the organization, concentrate on "doing what you can do." Communicate concerns to the appropriate level. Be decent throughout - it's your reputation, your own personal and professional #1 asset – maintain it. If you, as an IT person, hit a wall with a concern, your duty is to carefully go on record with your view of potential negative outcomes. You've done what you can. The point here is that IT must tactfully come back to the table, again and yes again, in the good faith, fully informed, and engagement-ready posture that is imperative in a professional IT team. The exception would be knowledge of illegal or questionable organizational activities – those issues will be discussed later. For now, IT must recognize the duty to align business and technology.

Remember ~

At all levels, it is necessary for IT personnel to possess knowledge for the application of technology to business. This applies to your IT lead executive right down to your HelpDesk technicians. Everyone should have a strong sense of the business at his or her respective level. At the same time, technical awareness should be a given in IT – again, from the lead executive on down. The real strength to be leveraged is your IT staff's ability to clearly express ideas, to listen, to negotiate, to make sound presentations, to emplace technology according to needs, and to remain in a customer-driven mode.

We spoke of improving the standing of IT in your organization. This is largely how to do it. Get an IT leader with technical *and* business qualification. The IT leader's confidence, born of ability, will give the other top executives the confidence to trust IT's assessment and recommendations regarding your business-technology path. This enables IT to carry its weight in organizational decision-making. These other executives come to see top IT management as possessing the same general management skills they do, and the relevant specific skills for IT's own respective area. The IT leader must be conversant in both the business and technical fundamentals of forming a viable strategy in the organization's market. Further, he or she must have a sound basis for translating support strategy to the main business strategy. Hence, the need for their ability to emplace a solid department. This qualified leadership, and example, will set the tone for a better IT endeavor, and for a better organization.

15

THE CRITICIZING OF EXCELLENCE
(HOW TO DISPENSE AND HANDLE CRITICISM)

The absent are never without fault, nor the present without excuse.

Benjamin Franklin

The only way to avoid criticism is to do nothing, say nothing, be nothing.

Truism

Why *The Criticizing of Excellence*? Because that phrase snaps all criticism into an important perspective: Once it's understood that criticism is going to come, regardless of circumstances, we can recognize that fact, accept it, and effectively deal with it. For most of us, dealing with criticism is not the best part of our day - whether dispensing or receiving it. Poorly managed criticism, and critics, can impair business. If not carefully managed, criticism can set up a sort of negative ping-pong exchange of recriminations, attendant "scoresheets," and possible "get even" scenarios. Preventing this sort of atmosphere is far easier than repairing an environment that has been allowed to drift. You don't want personalities clashing. We must not allow problems between powerful people to be woven into your organization's fabric.

Many an organization suffers through the silo-ing of departments and the resultant impairment of communication and efficient business. Working through a minefield of political liabilities is what mucks up many good faith endeavors. But that's largely because most people haven't learned what criticism really is meant to be, and how it is to be used (both in its delivery and in its receipt). When we understand the nature of criticism, we learn to *value* criticism. In learning how to value and use criticism, we need to recognize constructive (or justified, valid) criticism – and destructive (or unjustified, invalid) criticism – and we need to act on criticism to effect the appropriate outcomes.

In Defense of Criticism: Why a whole chapter devoted to criticism? Let's establish a little background: In a field as challenging, dynamic, and high profile as IT, there is much that presents a ripe target for criticism. At the same time, the pressures faced by Business, and their demand for quality support and services, generally means that Business has a fully stocked quiver of critical arrows. Yet, healthy criticism is *necessary* to the Business-Technology Weave. Critical evaluation and communication will be ongoing. This, paired with the challenge in creating, interpreting, and implementing the Business-driven IT strategy, makes it extremely important that we understand criticism and how to wield it. If you're not making effective use of criticism, you not only lose out on the positive lever to be had in progressive business, but you allow the deployment of a negative, depressive lever. Particularly in circumstances where we suffer divides, and have not yet achieved a proper Business-Technology Weave, there is that tendency to mount criticism from a less than fully informed perspective. When we combine that with a natural tendency to bristle at criticism, and mix in the resultant impairments, we find that we have a perfect storm formula for significantly diminished returns.

In those circumstances, we build resentments - we damage relationships between people, departments, and even organizations. We create avoidance to people and issues, *we slow progress, we hamper business*. Repair is costly. So, we have to take special care with criticism and its disposition in all circumstances. When we do, we find that proper criticism and proper reaction to it helps to expose important issues and aids in the resolution of problems. Criticism must always satisfy the "does this move business forward?" question. Therefore, criticism must have a positive motivator, helpfulness in spirit, and a benefit to be had in the form of suggestion and outcome. Again, valid criticism has value – *business value*.

Once we know this, we realize that we need to manage criticism under a dizzying variety of circumstances. It must be managed at all levels of the organization; criticism between individuals, as well as between and within departments. Criticism must be managed between organizations that have relationships: it is dispensed between discreet organizations involved in shared missions and outcomes, for example. Here there is a special risk: poorly managed criticism can severely damage effective cooperation between allied organizations, particularly when it is motivated by protectionism and jealousy. (The special circumstances in these cases are important enough to revisit in chapters *The Success Culture* and *What's At Stake*).

Criticism is delivered to vendors and even, in carefully crafted communication, from vendor to organization. On a more local level, there is a critical need in keeping individuals on balance. Those technical people directly supporting business on a daily basis are in a particular zone: They face business staff who need to accomplish business, often under pressure, and these support people can face a larger proportion of criticism than the average staff. The supported business people in direct contact with their support half are also in a target environment.

The good news is that criticism, large and small, is essentially handled the same way. If we're able to take a dispassionate, objective look at the full range of criticism - from whiny, empty, counterproductive carping - to the valid critiques, suggestions, sound advice, and requirements - we'll be much more adept at recognizing and handling criticism. We can vet criticism: defusing negativity and leveraging the positive to yield better outcomes.

Maintaining a Balance in the Face of Criticism: We need to keep a balance in our reaction to all criticism because there is value even in much criticism that is poorly delivered. There can be merit in critiques that are rude, or even delivered in attack mode. Too, we can recognize criticism at the bottom end of the scale, and dispose of empty criticism through appropriate channels before it spreads and infects other opinions and attitudes to the detriment of the organization. It helps to build an immunity to the negative sort of criticism that, unfortunately, permeates certain endeavors. With experience, knowledge, and well-placed faith in the organization comes a patience that, however unjustified and harmful some criticism may seem, it can be handled and disposed of in a forum sanctioned by the organization. We also need to take a look at the sponsors of different sorts of criticism and learn how best to handle those people. It is always helpful, and in most circumstances downright necessary, to consider the source. Here it is especially important to maintain a balance, as many critics are powerful people.

As we consider the receiving end of criticism, we see that too many of us assume that our efforts should be immune from criticism. In that unbalanced posture, we cannot fail to resent criticism – no matter how on target, and no matter how expertly delivered. Reasons vary, but perhaps it's because we feel we're doing an excellent job: we're putting in extra hours (without being asked!), we're "carrying" our department ("they'd be in big trouble without *me*"), or maybe criticism just catches us on a bad day. Often, we feel that we're doing the best we can in murky circumstances (another reason to get the Weave under control). Therefore, when criticism is directed at some of us, we respond in a negative fashion - with negative outcomes. Responding to criticism with anger, sarcasm or defensiveness is counterproductive. At the same time, it's counterproductive for leaders to allow others to engage in invalid criticisms. If we don't take care, this can become a self-reinforcing cycle; for the individual, and even for the organization. Criticism and its disposition, as much as anything else, influences the organization's culture.

For leaders, criticism can bring a particular kind of pressure. Too much pressure for anyone can lead to an imbalance: the stumble of mistakes that otherwise wouldn't be made. Pressure can yield bad judgments. Managers - Business and Technical alike - should watch for undue sensitivity to criticism; in them and in helping others. Ultimately, everyone needs to inculcate a healthy perspective to criticism – this includes the deliverer and recipient. Balanced people are aware of the appropriate, positive, responses to criticism – again, *valid and otherwise.* This healthy perspective toward criticism, and the appropriate method in delivery, receipt, and disposition, will defuse sensitivities and lead to progress. None of this is to say that we should ignore egregious instances of pure belittlement. Leaders need a balanced, objective, ability to weigh criticism, assign the relevant worth, and dispatch or handle it on that assigned basis.

Cloaked Criticism: As mentioned, there can be validity in criticism that is poorly delivered. This leads us to acknowledge a category of criticism that is generally not addressed in other discussions. It is a category that is especially important to IT and Business, as we cannot afford to miss important requirements and details (regardless of source). Simply: It is either constructive or destructive criticism that has the appearance of the other.

For example, you may receive "constructive" criticism that has you doing busy work at the expense of emerging priorities. The critic may have a good heart, but in this case the criticism will *destruct* our efficiency. Too there is criticism that has the appearance of destructive criticism, but which nonetheless contains merit. In pressure environments, criticism that is often legitimate (therefore valid), gets perceived as *unjustified criticism*: it is criticism that comes to us in anger, or as an attack, and therefore it is poorly expressed. Regardless, the issues may be legitimate. If something is in dire need of attention, we can't afford to miss it just because we don't care for the critic or his delivery.

Therefore, in all cases we need to recognize that criticism isn't always packaged correctly – like anything else, the delivery of criticism won't be perfect. In extreme cases, we could say that criticism is cloaked. Because some "constructive" criticism can yield poor outcomes, and because some "destructive" criticism can have value in part or all of it, we'll discuss how to recognize this cloaked criticism. We can then handle it according to what it truly represents; we pan for the legitimate portions of critical information, and neutralize whatever remains.

Examining Criticism

Now that we've established some general background on criticism, let's take a closer look at the types of criticism, the associated critics, and how we can leverage criticism. Indeed how we *have to* leverage it - for a better Business-Technology Weave.

Here's the order of our discussion:

- Constructive Criticism
    - Motivation
    - Delivering
    - Following Up

    - Receiving
    - Handling
    - Responding

- Destructive Criticism
    - Motivation
    - Guarding against Delivery of Unjustified Criticism (or that perception)

    - Receiving
    - Handling
    - Responding

- Cloaked Criticism: In Between Constructive and Destructive Criticism

    - Receiving
    - Handling
    - Responding

<u>*Constructive Criticism*</u>:   Most people understand the concept of constructive criticism. It comes our way in a formal sense during a performance review, for example. It also comes to us in an ad hoc way from supervisors, peers, etc., in the form of direction, suggestions, and advice. This criticism should mean that the deliverer is coming from a strong position of experience, knowledge and fact. Constructive criticism (or valid; justified criticism) is meant to *help*.

- *Motivation*: People who provide constructive criticism are helpful, and motivated by a sincere desire to expose an issue in order to better its standing. People who take the time to provide this kind of criticism do so under one of two broad conditions: they either provide criticism in a forum specifically designed for the delivery of it (such as a performance rating, formal counseling session, etc.) or within a general circumstance, such as a status meeting, drop-by visit, hallway conversation, etc. All constructive criticism is important, but realize that formal critiques are more than mere motivators - they are requirements. It is within these required sessions that we find the true motivators for criticism – they are specific critiques that have the same basic reasons to generate relevant criticism (and praise) as any other general criticism that comes our way: *exposure of issues and actions for betterment.*

Whether constructive criticism comes in a required forum, or is delivered outside of any strict format, formula or timetable, it is handled with this in common: It needs to be acted upon. This realization allows us to make our discussion of criticism more efficient, because, whether formal or informal, we can now talk about a criticism's motivators from the perspective of an actual driving event or situation. We can examine what causes the critic to specify and focus on a thing in particular. At the same time, we also have to look at the possibility that the critic is motivated by the receipt of his or her own criticism from somewhere.

Understand that regardless of specific situational motivators, all constructive criticism shares a common general motivator: the desire to help – or - *helpfulness*.

- *Delivery*: When criticism is genuinely constructive the deliverer is usually polite, and at least civil.   Because the critic has the relevant experience, knowledge and facts for a given situation, those circumstances yield confidence. The critic is a calm and calming deliverer. The criticism's content is clear, and there's an articulated benefit expressed as an improvement to be had. If criticism is delivered optimally, there is an invitation for open discussion. Ideas can be exchanged, positions explained, and it is here that hidden issues or evolving circumstances can be exposed and examined. The deliverer should have enough knowledge and experience to know that criticism is generally a ticklish business. Sounding too critical can tune the listener out, or worse, cause the listener to become angry or defensive.

When discussing the delivery of constructive criticism, there are two sub types that we should examine in order to effect optimal delivery. One is targeted at process, or activities, external to inherent behavior. We will simply call this *Process-driven Criticism*. The other is targeted at inherent behavior, and things such as issues of character, and lapses in judgment. We will simply call this *Behavior-driven Criticism*. Let's define each of these for this discussion:

1) *Process-driven Criticism*: Process-driven criticism focuses on activities that can be made better. The critic is generally focused on something narrow and discreet, though not always, and enjoys a confidence that, once an issue is exposed, the right people are on hand to make improvements. The criticism is meant to redirect or focus attention and energies. Usually, the recipients of the criticism are not the direct target. They are not deficient in performance – or, if they are, it is not the result of a character issue. They are hard-working, sincere, and qualified. They merely need guidance or input in order to make the required improvement. Criticism in these circumstances can be viewed as a tune-up, or regular maintenance of workplace issues – things external to the core character or behavior of the people.

2) *Behavior-driven criticism*: Behavior-driven criticism is meant to improve an attitude, to eliminate a bad habit, and to bring an individual, team or department back into standards of conduct. Usually it is directly targeted to a person or people. While there can be something narrow and discreet motivating this criticism, it's important to understand that the behavior usually poses a general peril to anything it comes into contact with. In other words, the behavior has broad potential for negative outcomes. In these cases, the issue is such things as rudeness, anger, tardiness, sloppiness, dishonesty – things that reside, or are generated, *within* people.

Of course, better behavior yields better process, and better process can help morale and thus influence behavior. They are reinforcing. Frequently they are blended, and each is meant to contribute to better outcomes. But, there are important differences, and we need to understand the two for optimum delivery of criticism. Let's take a look at delivery of these two:

Delivery of Process-driven criticism: Process-driven criticism is a little easier to deliver than behavior-driven criticism – it tends to be less personal. It is only indirectly linked to behavior or performance. For example, someone can be making the best faith efforts, and doing very sincere and good work overall, but there may be one or a few things that they are doing, simply put, wrong. Or, perhaps they're just doing something the hard way, and therefore they're not being as efficient as they can be. A person, a team, or a department may simply need the guidance that anyone is entitled to in the course of regular management.

When criticism happens between departments, or between disciplines such as Business and IT, there are special sensitivities and vulnerabilities. These apply even between organizations, such as yours and a vendor, or between agencies that have new working relationships. It is especially important to provide critical feedback effectively so as not to injure relationships. Yet in all of these circumstances, friction between parties, or a potential for friction, should not dissuade us from candor, nor from taking appropriate action. It is important to realize that progress requires traction, and traction requires friction. Friction in this case can be thought of as a facilitator of progress – you can risk someone's irritation or initial grumbling, but the objective is to get the issue out in the open, to address it, and to better it. In any case, criticism must be dispatched correctly, and received correctly – therefore, both parties must keep their eyes on the prize: They should be focused on the desired outcome.

When Business criticizes IT, it is important for Business to keep in mind that they hold the real power: IT is there *for* Business, so there should be no reason to be heavy-handed. At the same time, Business requires a certain level of performance from IT; the objective of the criticism, therefore, is to expose IT to a business consequence. There also has to be exposure to the positive business expectations resulting from overcoming or avoiding the consequence.

In addition to showing a benefit to clearing a negative, it is very powerful to show *additional benefits*. Often we think of criticism as purely addressing something negative, therefore it is too often employed to clear negatives without going further. Clearing a negative returns you to a zero point. Rise further on the scale into a positive zone. Seek further positives from the criticism – *they always exist for discovery*. By seeking further positives from criticism, we pull criticism itself UP into a positive tone and posture. Indeed, when providing any kind of criticism, it's helpful to start with a positive facet of the issue, which is a common "trick" – there should always be something positive to find and highlight. But further, bracket the criticism's main point on the back end with additional positives to be had. As an example:

"Bill, the test module of the Exhibit Hall Space Manager was made available right on time – thank you. My staff has given me some positive feedback on it, and the changes we asked for are a real help. Great work. But, there were quite a few changes in the module's screens that we didn't ask for, or expect. The staff felt put upon because they had to stumble through the module. They had to re-familiarize themselves with the flow and process of it before they could get to the evaluation of our business-inspired changes. A lot of the data entry aspects, and the way the screens related to each other, didn't reflect our training, nor the way the prior version of the module was laid out. Can we prevent these unanticipated changes in the future, or, if the vendor or IT has to make changes that aren't at our request for reasons we're not aware of, can we get a heads-up? Some quick familiarization for unanticipated changes will help our staff maintain a better attitude about it. **In addition, it will help us get our required feedback to IT that much faster. It might even help us understand some of your logic behind the unanticipated changes, and we might be able to weigh in with suggestions on that too – we're willing to pitch in any way we can."**

So here we have a problem with staff feeling put upon. They expected positive traction whereby they would receive a familiar test module back, against which their requested changes would readily show. Instead, they got their changes along with other changes to the fundamental product – they found their changes swimming in a sea of larger, unanticipated changes. It should be clear in this circumstance that it was a rather rude realization that the product had changed to the degree that the staff no longer felt familiar with it. Their criticism is justified by the reasons for it. It is highly constructive. The critic starts on a bona-fide positive, then specifies a problem, makes a suggestion to remedy the specific problem, and goes beyond in describing a couple other potential benefits to be had by the proposed remedy.

Remember this too – even if your additional, attempted positives can't be utilized, you've still provided a positive in that your attitude comes through loud and clear: *We're here to help. We're all pulling in the same direction.*

Delivery of Behavior-driven criticism: Whether behavior is deliberately negative or simply wrong because of ignorance, we need to expose the behavior to the individual or team. This also acknowledges the critic's awareness of the situation in the recipient mind. When instigating a change in behavior, we find ourselves in the position of talking to an individual, or team, about performance or conduct that can be interpreted as an overly *personal* criticism. Actually, this criticism *is* rather personal. In terms of the individual, you are criticizing the person's behavior, and that is central to the person. Even a performance review of a team, in a team meeting, can cause members to view criticism on a personal rather than a business basis. It is important to make the delivery so that it is truly received, while at the same time maintaining its focus. In other words, you must make the point without rankling the recipient – otherwise you risk the recipient's erection of a defensive barrier, which inhibits effective communication. How to best achieve this?

Again, it's best to start with a positive. Highlight something that you like about the person's character or recent behavior in handling a situation:

"John, I've received a lot of compliments on your support at the desktop. Accounting was especially happy with how smooth the upgrade to the payroll software went. Several people complimented you – your care and concern insured that they were able to work effectively in processing last week's payroll. I do need to make you aware, however, that just recently several people have complained of a sort of arrogance on your part. Specifically, you've been telling quite a few people lately that you're very busy, and that you'll 'get around to them when you get around to them.' Have you said that to people, and is it possible you've been rude?" [Here, we would pause to confirm whether John felt that this was an accurate assessment of his behavior]. "John, there is no excuse for rudeness in the support arena – ever. Generally speaking, people will engage others based on how they're treated. Working on a friendly basis, no matter how difficult the circumstances, is a heck of a lot better than the alternatives. So, being busy is ok. But failing to provide people a courteous estimation for when you can help them is not. Most will be reasonable if you can at least give them a general indication when you can get around to them. If you're feeling pressure you can also ask the team for help, and you can solicit my help in balancing your load. You need to make an immediate adjustment to your attitude so that you don't create the wrong impression amongst the users. I don't want to see you damage your reputation, as people trust you and generally compliment you. I know the Accounting project went well because you kept everyone informed during delays, and because everyone felt informed they were very pleased with the way that went. You'll find people much more cooperative when you keep them genuinely informed. We all either help or hurt the department as a whole through our attitudes, so let's all give each other a break and put our best face out there. Thanks, John"

Let's note here that we're discussing constructive, justified criticism, so we're stating as a given that John was actually rude, was a normally courteous employee with a history of positive work, and needed exposure to his behavior so that he could take corrective action. (Note: In cases where a productive employee suddenly loses efficiency, or starts to have behavior problems, we definitely want to find the source of the problem. It may even be something outside of the workplace. If someone doesn't respond to constructive criticism, we cross the threshold into formal counseling; here we're focused on how a quality staff best delivers and handles criticism).

Expose Negative Outcomes: When criticizing behavior, it is essential to point out the actual negative outcomes, as well as the inevitable future ones, that are sown by negative behavior. Frequently, an individual is not aware that their behavior is negative, or can be perceived that way. In John's busy state, he probably thinks he is helping himself by letting people know that he is harried and not immediately available (when in actuality he is hurting himself). Also, his communication, as empty as it is, will nonetheless set a flag in his mind; that is, a belief that he set some kind of expectation in the user's mind. *They know not to expect me any time soon.*

What's missing is his appreciation that his communication is coming off as uncivil and unhelpful – which erects a barrier to the transmission of actual information *in either direction*. In his case, no information is following anyway: I'll get around to you when I get around to you. "Great," the user thinks, "I know not to expect you soon – but when *can* I expect you?" No useful expectation is being set in the users' minds.

So, the critic must first expose the present condition of behavior; show the liabilities of the behavior; next describe the corrective behavior; and then discuss the benefits yielded by the amended behavior.

For criticism of behavior or process, constructive criticism should do four essential things:

1) Expose and acknowledge any existing quality in behavior or a process.
2) Make sure to expose and address the real issue.
3) Express exactly what needs to be done to improve the situation - and
4) Provide follow-up.

Following Up: After delivering criticism, you need to do a very important thing: *follow up*. Even if you are made aware of the result of your critique from some other source, it is important to show the recipient of the criticism that it was a professional communication – and therefore, you as the critic need to provide a direct closure. You show that the criticism's motivation was due to a vested care and concern for the issue – not just an opportunity to exert power over someone, or to pick on somebody. The follow-up can happen as an assignment; for a recipient to report to the critic upon completion of something. It can also be a drop-in session on the part of the deliverer.

An Example of Follow-Up: "Debbie, thanks for working to correct those reports for Marketing we spoke about last week. Marketing is very happy now. They can proceed with their sales forecasting." The follow-up helps to certify that we're communicating on a business-basis, not on any kind of personally motivated agenda. It helps the listener's internal voice anchor the context as business: *"That was important; Marketing needs accurate information. I'm glad I was able to tell my supervisor that the marketing reports were corrected and that everything is ok."* It is a further acknowledgement for the criticism's importance, and shows that the critic had weighted that communication with importance.

When the recipient is able to provide a positive answer regarding his or her effort in making an improvement, and in supporting an issue, they get a positive *feeling* in that they:

1) Made an improvement.
2) Met the deliverer's (in this case, the supervisor's) expectations.
3) Met other's (in this case, Marketing's) expectations.
4) Were recognized for their effort.

Proper follow-up acknowledges that responding to criticism with positivity and improvement is necessary and <u>*worth it in this organization*</u>.

Never issue criticism without a follow up. Lack of follow up can undermine authority and respect – respect for the deliverer and respect for the process. The recipient can be left to think that the matter wasn't truly of consequence in the deliverer's eyes, or that the matter isn't an overall priority (which it is, if it merits criticism). Lack of follow up will generally weaken future communications of this nature. It will contribute to a lack of focus and gravity the next time constructive criticism is delivered. Follow-up also provides an important opportunity to praise the recipient's efforts (assuming expectations have been met).

<u>Receiving Constructive Criticism</u>: When we receive criticism, we generally have a sort of internal evaluator – we immediately know if the criticism is warranted, and thus constructive. Call it a gut feeling. Regardless, when receiving criticism you must always ask yourself: Is there merit in any, or all, of this?

Generally speaking, we know criticism is valid if we hear something from more than one person or department; if the originator of the criticism knows a great deal about the subject; and if the originator is known to apply reasonable standards of behavior. The criticism is motivated by a desire to help, and provides solid suggestions or directions for positive change.

When you receive constructive criticism, and the criticism is accurate, the best response is, of course, to agree. You should summarize the criticism so that the deliverer is satisfied that you heard him or her accurately. *Ask questions* as necessary – be certain that you understand the criticism. As necessary, ask the deliverer how they would improve things, or what improvements they need. Thank this person for bringing matters to your attention.

Handling and Responding:
When you are the recipient of constructive criticism, you should:
1) Understand the criticism.
2) Ensure the deliverer knows you understand.
3) Know exactly what needs to be done to improve your work or the situation – in other words, know what is necessary to meet expectations.
4) Arrive at a consensus for a course of action.
5) Thank the deliverer for their direction, suggestion, advice, etc…
6) Make the improvements, fix the problem, change behaviors, etc.
7) Participate in follow-up, or check back with the deliverer to confirm that everything is satisfactory.

In the case of process *or* behavior-driven criticism, we've all been a recipient at some point; whether we're Business or IT, whether we're senior or staff. Remember that everyone deserves to be managed, so in essence, everyone deserves to be criticized. We all need guidance from time-to-time. For the most part, we're making good faith efforts within the scope of our knowledge, time, and other resources – but we can't see and do everything at once. Whether you are on the delivering or receiving end of criticism, always remember that part of supervision is *Super Vision*. The critic has the luxury, generally, of flying above the trees and having time to look at an overall perspective. The deliverer too is generally the person who has the big picture details in advance of everyone else, and can best sense the necessary corrections to course. Comparatively, the recipient of criticism is generally the person down in the trees, handling things on a more granular basis, focusing on things that are directly in front of them. With this perspective in mind, there is no reason for the recipient to take umbrage at properly delivered criticism.

Keeping this perspective in mind helps the critic to make criticism more palatable for the recipient. Criticism becomes less of a see-saw; each party on opposite ends of an issue, one side up, and one necessarily down. Rather, criticism becomes a *lever* that both sides puts their hands on, in order to wield it in the same direction for better outcomes. Criticism becomes a mutually employed tool, exercised with equal effectiveness by both parties.

Criticism should be viewed from all angles as a "win-win-win" undertaking: a win to the critic; a win to those critiqued; and a win to the organization.

<u>Destructive Criticism</u>: Destructive criticism is unjustified, and invalid. It is not helpful. Worse – it is damaging. It's fairly easy to recognize destructive criticism. It is frequently dishonest in its content. The critic may feel that he or she is justified in making the criticism, but because it is negative and inaccurate, there can be no justified purpose to it. We can consider it a dishonest, or dishonorable if you prefer, engagement. Destructive criticism destroys trust in that it sows mistrust. It destroys efficiency because it wastes valuable time.

Destructive criticism frequently originates within the critic, and is usually meant to hide some deficiency with that person. Therefore, destructive criticism's motivation is often to deflect attention from the critic, while attempting to pull something or someone down. This then is an attempt to level, or even to advance, the critic. The model is: "Look at *this* (don't look critically at me or my work) – see how *bad this is*?" (attempting to sustain focus away from them).

The destructive critic is frequently insecure, lacking in ability, or simply lacking in results – we'll get into specific conditions and motivators shortly. But usually, they are desperate that others don't see them for how they're feeling inside. As people generally aren't anxious to face fault within themselves, you can bet that the destructive critic will positively abhor the idea that someone else might scrutinize them, evaluate them, or judge them – and find them lacking. They will do anything to deflect serious attention from their own self-sensed deficiencies and fears. Whereas that is their true priority, there is little rational basis for selecting something deserving of criticism – any handy object, person, or process will do. At the same time, realize that they'll shop around to look for something that can be made to appear legitimate. And again, even if they hit on the happy coincidence of identifying something that truly needs critical attention, their criticism is seldom fully, if at all, constructive because their motivation is really to protect themself.

There too is the destructive criticism that attempts to pull things down, in order to supplant them with something the critic is sponsoring. In this case, the critic cannot emplace their goals through legitimate means, and thus make an attempt to destruct something legitimate in order to usurp it. Our coming discussion of *motivation* should also aid in these circumstances.

Destructive criticism doesn't just hold good things in abeyance – it grows and fosters a negative environment. It creates disengagement between individuals and groups. It creates anger and bad feelings. It lowers morale. It threatens goals and projects. *It impairs business*.

Examples of Destructive Criticism:

A few examples serve us well here. Destructive criticism is frequently general:

"This new marketing initiative is lousy. It will never work…"
"Why?"
"I don't know, nobody understands it…"
"I do. It can seem a little tricky at first. Did you go to the training on the initiative? There's another session next week…"

Here the criticism's generality is actually necessitated by the critic's ignorance. Again, here the destructive criticism is generated by some deficiency in the critic. Even if some of the criticism is on target, the destructive critic can only bring friction to the process; he or she can't bring the other component, the *traction,* necessary for progress, through valid suggestion. Maybe the latest marketing initiative *is* lousy: maybe it doesn't help current customers, can't reach new ones, and its implementation will rob us of precious time for a truly effective marketing initiative - whatever. If you can't specify that and the reasons why, you can't separate your criticism from that which is invalid. Your criticism just takes up air that can be better used by better people with better assessments.

This highlights a most important point: Just because criticism hits the happy coincidence of targeting something that is worthy of critique, that is not a condition that makes it *constructive*. Criticism must deliver self-justifying reasons, such as pointing out specific, actual deficiencies, and some real clues for progress. Beyond friction, criticism must yield traction, and traction must be in the correct direction for progress. (Again, "Does this move business forward?").

When destructive criticism does manage to be specific, it can still be born of ignorance or hostility, and can be incorrect in its assumption. It can therefore offer no real remedy, and it remains destructive. For example: "IT's e-mail cleanup policy only lets us keep 30 days of e-mails. I need stuff around that's older than that. You know, they're always trying to make things easy for themselves instead of thinking about us…"

"Yeah, e-mail does get swept away pretty quickly - but, it's not really IT's policy. IT just follows the organization's overall Document Retention Plan, under which e-mail falls. Look at it this way: I'm glad that I don't have to manage my e-mail under the Document plan – IT does it for me. Maybe you could save important e-mails to the appropriate network folders, where retention would be dictated by content, not the fact that it was an e-mail."

"I hadn't thought of that…"

It is extremely important to manage destructive criticism. What does that mean? It means that it must be defused through appropriate disposition and channels so that it cannot have negative affect on morale or efforts. Destructive criticism can lead to erroneous perceptions: therefore it can have a damaging affect on cooperation, achievement, and *success*.

Success is often times driven more by attitude than anything else. Indeed, attitude frequently makes up for challenges in other areas, such as reduced budgets, shortage of personnel, and tight timelines, etc. Therefore, perception management goes hand-in-hand with the management of destructive criticism. Often times the difference between success and failure is simply the will to succeed. For this reason alone you must handle destructive criticism and the negative attitudes it inevitably fosters and supports. In the Business-Technology Weave, all endeavors require total commitment from all parties. Just as we established an incentive to respond with positivity to constructive criticism (through confirmation; follow-up, and the recognition for improvement), we must put in place a discipline for the disposition of destructive criticism. We will discuss this further in *Handling*, a little later.

In this way, we promote a valid system of criticism, and dismantle the invalid one, and gain control of the organization's culture. We bias the organization for success. Therefore, in managing criticism we find that, over time, we retain and attract like-minded, positive, people. We achieve a collective attitude that reinforces success. When managing criticism, remember that people want a leadership *that can accomplish these things* – and - *they deserve no less*.

- *Motivation*: Destructive criticism frequently originates from feelings of insecurity, perhaps general lack of confidence, or outright fear. When people are discomfited by these feelings, they attack anything that exacerbates these feelings; hence that which is bringing them discomfort. The more powerful the feelings behind destructive criticism, the more difficult it is for the destructive critic to recognize his or her own behavior as being inappropriate. Unfortunately, the behavior is destructive to the organization as well as them.

People can become active with destructive criticism during times of stress and change. A feeling of a loss of control, and a belief that one has lost the ability to influence outcomes, puts one in the greatest stress arena. People feel entitled to complain in these circumstances. (Indeed they may have valid complaints. Here it becomes important to expose issues through *constructive* criticism –they must resist the temptation to steer into destructive criticism). Sometimes being wronged, or harboring that perception, leads to destructive criticism. Here the critic perceives some mistreatment, or being the recipient of unjustified or destructive criticism himself or herself. People will attack the thing that is bringing them discomfort or "injustice."

Recognize too that some people feel that delivery of criticism, of any kind, is a perk of their power. Many people, high and low, complain as a hobby – they just enjoy sniping. (Perhaps we all do, to one degree or another). Powerful people also may criticize things as a way of attempting to position their goals ahead of "competitors" – whether real or imagined.

Also recognize that destructive criticism has to enjoy some kind of bed for it to exist. In other words – destructive criticism requires tolerance. For these reasons, it is important for someone in the destructive critic's realm to rein them in and bring them into balance. In a short while, we will discuss ways to do this, as we handle destructive criticism – the means of handling it also helps to understand motivation to a further degree.

- *Receiving*: It is important to remain calm in the face of destructive criticism. This can be hard to do, because the destructive critic can be ill informed and judgmental. The destructive critic can be jealous, angry, condescending, and frequently given to exaggeration and untruths. Because there is peril in invalid criticism, remaining calm in instances of peril requires emotional maturity, experience, and a trained, practiced response.

It is important for the recipient to be steady, as the destructive critic is unpredictable. The recipient may have the following thoughts: What is the depth of their motivation? What else will they criticize, and how personal will they get? To whom are they expressing the criticism, besides me? If they possess power, to what extent will they use their influence, and what is their ultimate aim?

If you're in the sights of a destructive critic – define them. Understand everything around and within them: their issue, their true motivation, their past history of engagement, and their expectations. The better you identify these things, the better you can report details regarding this critic's engagement. From there, the routine management process in disposing bad behavior can take over. Part of defining the situation is to identify your response to destructive criticism in advance. It will always be constant, steady, and the same – it should follow this model: Your response should be mature, controlled, and directed along lines sanctioned by the organization for the resolution of any complaint or inappropriate behavior.

Don't Hold the Target: Don't encourage the receipt of destructive criticism. Every organization has people who shoot at targets. These shooters are snipers; their targets are people. By their nature they *must* shoot critical arrows. To do this, they cast about for their targets of criticism. Don't hold the target for them!

What does that mean? It means not overreacting to destructive criticism. The critic is looking for a reaction, and achieves a smug satisfaction in making someone jump, become defensive, and in particular take some sort of empty action. Worse, (but "better" for them) they may glean an apology. Do not make empty apologies. Beware the false apology – it can be like catnip to some, and they will manipulate anyone they can into a zone of constant apology. Never apologize for something that you undertook in good faith, and for which no better effort could be made. Make apologies for legitimate errors or difficulties, but do not apologize to appease a destructive critic – you will only be compounding problems your organization may face with destructive criticism. You become further removed from reality-based conditions and relationships in your conduct of good business.

One of the greatest challenges in the Business-Technology Weave is in responding to destructive criticism and in building an appropriate system of disposition for that criticism. When the destructive critic attempts to make you a target, neutralize them by defining them: ask for specifics; solicit suggestions for improvement (putting action items in their court, thereby lowering their perception as having gotten a reaction from you); and when necessary, by making a suggestion that you would like to elevate their concerns to your supervisor for possible engagement with their supervisor.

Remember, we're talking about actual destructive criticism here – so concrete suggestions, and especially the positing of action in their court, usually deflates that critic's motivation for making you a target – now and in the future. Destructive criticism can be defused very effectively by reducing its payout to the critic, and by increasing their cost in mounting it. Remove their "return on investment." They may go elsewhere with their arrows, seeking other targets and hopefully running into the same steady and appropriate response. But regardless, this is how you, the reader, should act when receiving destructive criticism that is aimed directly at you, your associated responsibilities, your department(s), your achievements, etc.

We're now in a good position to take a more detailed look at handling and responding to destructive criticism according to specific motivators:

- *Handling and Responding to Destructive Criticism by Specific Motivators*: Destructive criticism is best handled according to what motivates it. Whereas constructive criticism has a common *general* motivator - Helpfulness – destructive criticism has no real, common, general motivator. The opposite of Helpfulness is Unhelpfulness. Unhelpfulness is not really a motivator here - although I'm sure some readers will beg to differ given their experiences in some environments. But rather, Unhelpfulness is an unfortunate *consequence* of destructive criticism. Further, there is damage.

Handling and Responding to…

...*Ignorance*: People are prone to criticize that which they don't understand. They may not understand how to use something; therefore they can't effectively judge its usefulness – nor get anything productive from it. They may not understand a policy's purpose; they cannot balance the overwhelming good of the policy (the return) against the investment of their effort in complying.

Managers may not understand what motivated a subordinate to take a specific action, and that may engender undue criticism. It is possible too that a person is ignorant about the way they sound to others. If they're *stressed out, and lashing out*, they're entitled to know that their behavior is not acceptable, and how to rectify it. People aren't usually anxious to find fault with themselves, thus the flow is toward the external object: in their mind *it* becomes worthy of criticism – this is their default posture when things aren't working well.

We're all ignorant about something at all times, and we're all in various stages of ignorance when new things stream our way. Ignorance can serve as a positive motivator. When we become aware of ignorance, it should motivate us to become educated, informed, and aware.

Resolving destructive criticism that is motivated by ignorance is a simple course of action: removal of ignorance as a factor through the dispense of knowledge. It is not necessarily *easy*, but whether the situation requires training, an informed visit, or a managed adjustment to behavior, the ignorant critic must be defused by knowledge. Also, we can note here that managing the destructive critic need not always involve an opposing posture on the part of the manager.

Notice that in our e-mail example above, the responder doesn't necessarily disagree with the critic. The responder offers a different perspective to a perceived short shelf-life for e-mails, the reasons for that condition, and the current condition's *benefit* to the critic. (The exposure of the reasons and benefit brings the critic out of his or her ignorance without taking issue with the critic).

    ...Insecurity/Fear: Insecurity and fear merits a serious discussion. These have a powerful influence on so many of life's circumstances and relationships – it stands to reason that business relationships and situations are not immune from these powerful influencers. With this recognition, we know that we have to manage insecurity and fear just like anything else. We can minimize their destructive influence, and we can flip them to drive awareness, caution, and sound judgment. For many destructive critics, whether they're a situational or chronic critic, it is just human nature to assume the worst. Perhaps this is part of a primal survival instinct. All of us take caution in certain circumstances.

However, the insecure destructive critic does not operate rationally, whether based on legitimate or imagined perils. They frequently magnify and exaggerate issues, and often create their own perils. It is when insecurity and fear are the result of irrational thinking, or are simply in the character of the person, that unjustified actions are born. When someone feels fearful or insecure, they don't want others to know that. Therefore, they must deflect attention, if not from themselves, from what they're feeling. So they point to an external.

People feel insecure for a variety of other reasons. We've discussed the importance of managing change. Change is particularly vulnerable to criticism, and change contributes mightily to insecurity and fear. During times of change, people feel a loss of familiarity. Some people deal very well with this, and make the changes necessary within themselves in order to deal with the external change. Others resist change because they may feel that new systems will tax and perhaps exceed their own capacities or resources. For people who resist change, and delay their own adjustment to it, there is a very real situation of being left behind. There is obvious peril in being left behind: People will fear that their job is jeopardized, in that they may no longer be able to perform it. This only compounds their fears.

Managers may feel a loss of control, and a loss of standing with other managers. They will worry that their staff will sense their insecurity. Worse, they will fail to set an appropriate example – they can bias an endeavor for failure. Here we can mention: a person occupying a leadership position is not necessarily a leader. A good sign of such a condition is if the leader is a consistent source of destructive criticism. When mounting change, choose the change-leaders based on their management of past challenges, their management of associated criticism, and their knowledge of practices surrounding constructive criticism.

While events often drive insecurity, it is frequently driven by other people. A new team member, a new manager, a new board, new governance, new working relationships, etc., can instill fear and insecurity. Until the "new" becomes "old," people seem to operate in a relatively negative posture, assuming the worst. We have to guard against these negative assumptions because they can otherwise become a self-fulfilling prophecy.

In a business and technology environment, facing unknowns is *part* of the business. Resolving unknowns - while certainly requiring care and concern – require exploration, confidence, and action. Feeling somewhat insecure or fearful in these situations is natural – but that is not an excuse for mounting destructive criticism – do not employ it yourself, and guard others in your charge from doing this.

For managers who deal with insecurity on the part of another, you enjoy a certain distance from the issue and can hopefully look at it objectively. Help the critic in this circumstance to understand their ability, control, and influence within their state of affairs. Help the person to take positive action on issues causing insecurity. As they gain a sense of proportion and control, their insecurity and fear will dissipate. This helps them to take a positive stance – rather than expending energy toward destructive criticisms. Helping someone to take effective action also lowers his or her level of stress, which we will discuss shortly.

The need for an occasional pep talk is fine, whether you're dispensing one or receiving one. If you are the one feeling insecure about something, instigate a discussion with your manager. Don't criticize that which you don't understand. Managers can help to maintain a positive attitude, and therefore confidence, by keeping their staff informed. Informed staffs feel respected and appreciated. Information heads off erroneous assumptions and dispels rumor. In the case of situational insecurities, explore and expose the destructive critic's fears. Show the destructive critic how to manage fear, by taking control of the situations instilling fear. Remember that anyone can feel insecure at times. Insecurity and fear serve useful purposes in the Weave, as they do in life, but only through their proper management: by making proper assessments of their source, and only by taking effective action.

In cases where someone is, simply put, chronically unconfident, we have to realize that no team can afford to be constantly picking up the attitude of someone who can't pick up their own attitude. It is grossly inefficient. Not only are we burning time as we try to shore up another's confidence, we find that the unconfident member lags in all actions as they attempt to gather the courage to move forward. Rather than leaving them to operate at a level of responsibility for which they are unsuited by disposition, it is better to remove them so that they can seek their own appropriate level. This removes them from conditions that lead them to produce destructive criticism and hopefully delivers them to a more positive match of capability and responsibility.

... *Stress*: We've talked about stress elsewhere, and the importance of managing stress is evident. A detailed analysis of stress is outside our scope here, and many resources exist for evaluating stress, its effects, and the ways of managing it. But we have to look at stress as it relates to many of the other motivators of destructive criticism. Stress contributes to many less than optimal outcomes in the Business-Technology Weave, simply because the Weave is so susceptible. The Weave necessitates the interaction of people from various backgrounds, disciplines, and fields, and runs them through the mill of change. This environment is ripe in supporting two huge conditions for stress:

- ♦ The ever present change dynamic and the associated natural uncertainties born of change, (vis-à-vis stable, relatively known conditions);

- and -

- ♦ Loss of control, or that perception, for assigned outcomes.

We've discussed change to a fair degree, so we can summarily say: Where change is managed appropriately, so too is change-related stress appropriately managed. If you keep people informed, roll out change according to an effective model and plan, assign accountabilities, and make room for adjustment along the way, you should have a condition of managed stress.

But it is the second item in our discussion, loss of control, or even that perception, that creates enormous stress for those people responsible for outcomes. You may think that the loss of control for outcomes happens exclusively during change, but not so. While change certainly presents large responsibilities for large outcomes, there are also more routine outcomes that are none-the-less extremely important. For example, if you're delivering a performance appraisal, and you are not being allowed to rate an individual accurately, you may be forced to retain an under-qualified person in a key position. There can be enormous risk in this, and that risk compounds by stressing the manager, who knows the liabilities in failing to account accurately. It compounds by allowing the under-qualified employee to drive down efficiency, and even perhaps put the organization's business at risk.

Another example where loss of control engenders stress is a budget situation. Consider situations whereby an authority too far removed from cost realities cuts a budget to an unrealistic level. The person responsible for managing the budget and the associated deliverables that that budget supports (products, services, expectations for improvements, etc.) now has the responsibility for deliveries without adequate resources to back those requirements up.

For those who manage or oversee a process, take care not to crimp the process. Don't hurt the associated people who are animating the process, and who are attempting to deliver on expectations. In these examples, a rater was being prevented from documenting a truthful evaluation, and the manager of a budget is given an inadequate amount to finance expected outcomes. These things would certainly create a fertile garden for constructive criticism, but because we're talking destructive criticism, let's assume that those being crimped have had their suggestions, and warnings for liabilities, discounted and ignored – and that *certainly* happens. WorkFors and WorkWiths should watch carefully for constructive criticism and its denied due.

What we now have is a garden for *destructive* criticism – and it will certainly come. Because constructive criticism was denied its due, the criticism that now comes will not have an outward positive focus – it will be generated to balm the spirit of those who feel disempowered and short-suited in resources. Feelings of disempowerment, loss of control, and fear of bad outcomes are very negative feelings, and criticism of outward things and other people becomes *extremely* negative, in order to make the critic feel better in comparison. It is important to see the damaging potential to the organization's morale and business. Therefore, find any areas in your organization, large and small, whereby those who have responsibility are being shorted in the areas of authority, resources, and control – and put an appropriate balance in place.

Managing and mitigating stress can clear up a lot of other things. Reducing stress to manageable levels helps to lower or deny insecurity and fear. Also lower stress by removing doubt - dispense knowledge; keep people informed. That obviously becomes a reinforcement in helping to eliminate ignorance, as both a contributor to stress and to destructive criticism. In reducing stress, make certain that people have the knowledge, resources, and the empowerment so that they feel they have what is necessary to achieve success.

...*Hobbying*: We know this type. Complaining can be fun. Some hobbyists complain with a large measure of humor. Their criticism may not actually be destructive – theirs is a lubricant for getting through challenging situations. But for another kind of hobbyist, complaining about things and propagating destructive criticism is for them a balm that soothes some continuous psychic need deep within themselves – yet is like acid to others, the organization, and goals.

For those who enjoy making criticism just for the sake of making empty criticism, theirs is a practiced art. They've likely been doing it for a long time, and it is a habit they'll never break – and one they'll never be broken of. Recognize this. However, through measured counseling and discipline, you may be able to channel their criticism into relatively benign areas – maybe if they sense enough peril in criticizing superiors, or projects, or policies, they can be made to spend their time criticizing the coffee, the size of their workspace, or the color of the carpeting. Be creative, use your imagination, and put things in their path that will readily soak up their critical energy.

...Protecting: Often times destructive critics feel that they are protecting either themselves or some interest of theirs. Perhaps the upcoming implementation of a new business information system has exposed a more efficient alignment of major business practices. Maybe the Customer Service Center is better allied with the Membership Department, and shouldn't be reporting to the CFO. When people lose chunks of authority and part of their domain, they frequently feel a keen sense of loss. There are many people who react with grace and a sense of what's good for the organization. However, when others lose pieces of authority, they react as though someone took one of their arms at the shoulder – they lose their business perspective and personalize the action. Theirs is righteous indignation, and they attack the thing that they feel has attacked them.

Sometimes too people enjoy the role of "protector." It's one thing to back up staff – which is appropriate – it is another to side with people to the disregard of the ultimate, true, aims of the organization. Protecting the "little people" often does them more harm than good – don't kill people with kindness by buffering them from challenge and change.

There is also the protection of pet projects, or the attempt to position one's own initiatives and ideas at the top - through criticizing and attempting to drive down other's ideas and initiatives, many of which are superior to the critic's.

Destructive criticism arising from protectionism must be removed by counseling the critic about the overall goals of the organization. Reinforce the reasons for change, and selections, and don't hesitate to expose the critic to the consequences for continued, unjustified, and destructive criticism.

...Jealousy: Jealousy is a destructive emotion and a potent source for destructive criticism. When people engage in rivalries, when they are resentful of the success of others, when they covet what others have, they are prone to

criticize others in a negative way. The jealous critic denies this emotion – to themselves and others. No one likes to be seen as jealous; jealousy is a shortcoming born of an extreme desire for something coupled with a lack of knowledge, power, talent, etc. for acquiring that something. No one likes to be perceived as falling short, and no one likes to be seen as going without, therefore jealous people often try to mask their situation with destructive criticism. It is extremely important to note that jealously can be a group-think - involving an entire department or organization.

The jealous critic masks their emotion by again directing attention away from them, and onto a target. This is both for their benefit, and for the attempted manipulation of those around them. Frequently this critic is trying to diminish those around them in a vain attempt to make themselves compare more favorably in a relative sense, or to advance a cause that has failed in legitimate forums.

Some of the sub-motivators within jealousy follow:

Deserving: A person may feel that they deserve something that they're not getting. More money; an office as opposed to a cubical; more respect; more responsibility; better consideration of their ideas and achievements, etc.

Feeling left out: A person may be perfectly deserving, but can be left out in many circumstances. The organization has a limit on a training budget, or available seats, and only a portion of qualified personnel can go, for example.

Overlooked: Particularly in large organizations, or fast moving operations, someone may feel overlooked – and can be.

Coveting: A person may be yearning for something that they cannot reach.

Suspicion: Someone may believe that people or events are conspiring against them.

Resentment: A denial of the critic's inflated value of himself or herself, or a denial of some "deserved" reward or status, can cause the critic to become chronically unhappy.

When jealously motivates criticism, it is usually bitter, and very destructive. The jealous critic must be exposed to realities that will be, to them, harsh. However, the counselor must discipline this critic firmly, as they frequently harbor delusions that they are better, smarter, and more deserving than even their counsel. Expose the jealous critic to blunt realities.

...*Power-Tripping*: People who criticize from a position of power represent a special challenge when their criticism is destructive. Destructive criticism in general has negative influence and impact on any organization, but when powerful people mount it, there is a sort of force-multiplier at work. Destructive criticism gets a boost because powerful people have a large audience, and that audience is comprised of other people with power. They can influence other influencers, thus an organization's culture - its beliefs, its standards, its confidence, its potential, its direction and its level of success.

Also, because they have power, they wield reward and consequence. Sometimes powerful people define multiple organizations. They often times have been around a long time, and they may be far removed from even a rudimentary understanding of technology and its relationship to modern business. They may even have outlived their general usefulness to the organization, but they are so firmly ensconced that there is no possibility of their removal until retirement. Hence, we can have a combination of ignorance and power-trip as a foundation for destructive criticism. This is a very potent mix indeed for a most negative impact on the Business-Technology Weave. Due to their power, these people's criticism can be difficult to swat down. Still, with care we can deal with it.

Why should we bother to deal with it? After all, if a destructive critic wields power, influence, and consequence, aren't we simply creating further peril - to ourselves and to the organization - if we go up against this power? Is it prudent? Is it wise? The short answer is: it is *necessary*. Remember, what we were able to tolerate in years past – what was affordable – is no longer affordable. Certain burdens in maintaining the Weave are going to compound, therefore there are certain impediments that we can simply no longer entertain. Power-trippers who amuse themselves with destructive criticism, who may foster duplication of effort, who enjoy dissent, and who feed on a certain level of disarray, are dinosaurs. Therefore, eliminating the power-tripper's destructive criticism should help remove an informal structure of accommodation.

If people have their hands on policy (strategy, principles, action, direction…), if they control approval processes and measures (gates), and resources (levers), then overcoming destructive criticism takes on a whole new purpose: It must be effectively engaged and countered in order to achieve the best business outcomes. We're not talking about the "best business outcomes under the circumstances." We are speaking here of outcomes that are the best that can be achieved according to our desired, best faith, and *necessary* business goals. Less and less affordable are compromises designed to accommodate difficult people, broken agencies, or some political crippling of the right thing to do.

The whole point of refusing to lower standards, according to conditions we know to be wrong, is to *force a square look at what is hampering ultimate business and/or technology outcomes in order to overcome or prevent deficiency in process, ethics, conduct – and <u>success</u>*. Therefore, we not only seek to sweep destructive criticism away for purpose of making better day-to-day business – but for purpose of ongoing ultimate outcomes.

Accommodations to these sorts of powerful people are always made out of fear, or a belief that there is no relief. That is to say those who want to make, and want to elevate, the best faith efforts have the belief that no one will join them in tackling the problem. So-and-so is too powerful. HR will not join an effort to effect a change. There is no real payoff for taking a difficult position. Worse, there is a negative consequence in speaking a truth, no matter how carefully exposed. If these are the beliefs in your environment, the organization has to inculcate a different set of beliefs by emplacing appropriate values. You must back those values by putting in the appropriate systems of support and paths for resolution: for example, start with accurate and truthful evaluations of people. Once that happens, you remove the unspoken tolerance, or even sanction, for destructive criticism, and less than optimal ways of doing business. These are *not* to be tolerated.

Finally, the most effective way to tackle a power-tripper is to round up other targets of the power-tripper – there will be multiples, and each will already know the others by virtue of shared-supervision, common projects, and interrelated responsibilities and outcomes. This collective has to make a careful overture to the power-tripper's supervisor. Because you will be self-identified as a critic, and because your communication to that supervisor will be criticism, you must be helpful, factual, and balanced – you must deliver constructive criticism of the highest order. This will help to prevent an arena of "he said, she said, you say, they say" type of communication.

You will also request a common meeting of all principals who are directly and tangentially related to the power-tripper's criticism. In this way, any and all targets are able to expose, and dispassionately discuss, issues and problems for identification and agreement on disposition. If you are that supervisor overseeing the power-tripper, you must clear the immediate impediment to good business: vetting criticism and helping to hammer out a path of progress for the team. There must be progress in the relationships, and progress to the normal business at hand. The supervisor must go one-on-one with the power-tripper and expose that person to the inevitable consequences in any continued, negative, behavior.

This advice is not to give the impression of a naïve view; to overlook the difficult circumstances these people pose. We can acknowledge the risky business of tackling this person – from any level.

If you are in the realm of a power-tripping, destructive critic, and you feel powerless, you still must ask: If something doesn't move business forward, why is there a tolerance of it? Realize:

- ♦ The organization takes care of the problem (the good in fixing a problem is self-evident)

- or -

- ♦ The organization doesn't take care of it – for whatever reason. It has now made an important exposure: You collect an important "where we are" piece of knowledge. You are in a position to answer those questions: Is it worth striving for excellence here? Can I be successful here? Can this organization effectively know where we're going - if it won't acknowledge, and fix, "where we're at"?

Taking Control of Destructive Critics: In any of the cases we've mentioned, regardless of specific motivation, if a destructive critic continues in the face of appropriate knowledge, or is a chronic and habitual complainer across the board, the organization has to take the appropriate action: the organization must deem the criticism(s) unjustified, therefore destructive, in the formal sense. After all, anyone who does anything to the detriment of the organization must face a consequence – if there is true interest in stopping the detrimental activity.

It must be explained to the critic that there is detriment not just to the organization, but, if not stopped, *to the critic*. This is handled in the same common-sense fashion that any inappropriate behavior is handled. Generally speaking this would start as a discussion between the critic and the critic's supervisor. Subsequent follow on counseling may be required, and as necessary may be performed in concert with HR. In other words, the unjustified critic can be handled through the normal disciplinary channels, subject to the normal escalations that are employed to control and manage negative behavior and activity.

Remember that the destructive critic is more interested in complaining, and offers nothing of real value in their criticism. Negative, destructive, criticism can crash a project, can deny you your objectives, can damage or break relationships, and will injure business. A fundamental of success is the will to succeed. *Destructive criticism is an attack on your organization's will to succeed.* <u>Manage destructive criticism</u>. Lead. Set an example. Educate. Hold destructive critics accountable, discipline them, and bring them into balance.

CLOAKED CRITICISM

Cloaked criticism appears as its opposite (in terms of the constructive-destructive poles of criticism). In other words, criticism that appears constructive on its face is actually *destructive* (as determined by impacts and results). Criticism that appears destructive has many, or wholly, constructive elements.

We have to effectively determine when criticism is cloaked, and handle it according to what it *actually contains* – or thought of another way – what it actually can *do*, or *yield*. This satisfies not only the effective disposition of criticism, but also serves other important requirements in the Weave that will soon become evident. First, let's create some shorthand for cloaked criticism:

- CAD: Criticism that appears **C**onstructive, but is **A**ctually **D**estructive

- DAC: Criticism that appears **D**estructive, but is **A**ctually **C**onstructive

CAD Criticism: Here criticism that may initially appear constructive to the recipient, and deliverer, is actually detrimental. The criticism is delivered in good faith by a "constructive" critic; it may have a positive motivator, and it is delivered in the spirit of helpfulness. However, it's results that count. Watch for these yields or clues when determining cloaked criticism of this sort:

1) *Busy-Work*: The criticism is delivered in a friendly, helpful manner, but is not particularly specific. It seems to target something that doesn't really require a critique (or prioritizes something at the expense of resources that should be targeting something much more important). The criticism frequently yields busy-work. No real output is to be had that has much practical benefit. Results of the work may be difficult to measure, or results may even be intangible. There will be a detrimental impact to efficiency and morale. In these cases, look for empty burdens that can be "zeroed" – that is, neutralize CAD criticism, and stop doing things that don't contribute to better business and outcomes.

2) *Keeping Staff "on their toes"*: The critic's motivation is to keep people sharp, working hard, and accountable. In this instance, the critic feels he or she is bettering staff performance, and serving the organization well. This person may feel that quality of work and service is not to be had without constant oversight. However, constant checking up, looking over the shoulder; and unremitting suggestions just makes people tense and under-confident. As performance suffers, the CAD critic is compelled to provide more criticism and oversight – and now we're in a destructive

cycle. Compounding all of this, the situation creates a ripe zone for staff's own destructive criticism. Here the critic's motivation is genuinely outward, and he or she feels they are bettering the organization – but they are not.

3) *Power Flex*: Here a power-tripper believes their internal hype, and simply must share their genius on a constant basis. Unlike the "on their toes" critic, theirs is an internal motivation – they enjoy "guru-ing," and need to do that in satisfying their ego. Just the same, they genuinely believe that most people want and benefit from their knowledge, and that people enjoy receiving unremitting guidance. The recipient people perceive (correctly) that power-tripping people expect agreement and acquiescence – therefore they shy away from providing reality-based feedback to the powerful person. This is what inflates the power-tripper over time. They like the sound of own voice, so you'll notice they use a lot of words to say very little. Therefore, when they have a lot to say, it can take an excruciatingly long period of time. They make demands. They like a too-frequent schedule of reporting. Staff end up scrambling to show progress on action items when there hasn't yet been time to achieve anything. People are forced to inflate activity, and make things up to serve the report. All of this serves the CAD critic's sense of importance.

If you are dispensing CAD criticism, you need to stop. If you sense that you may be dispensing criticism from a less than fully informed perspective, you must pause. If you sense that you're mounting criticism simply because it feels good, you must pause - and ask yourself: Is it possible that I am occasionally dispensing CAD criticism? Is it possible that some of my criticism, advice, suggestions, has had a negative impact on efficiency? Have I introduced burdens that have little positive yield? Has my critique and requirements of staff helped or hindered their (our) proper return on efforts?

If you are the recipient of this kind of criticism, you must carefully and cogently rebuff it. Difficult? In many circumstances, yes. Impossible? In many circumstances yes! But, hopefully, not impossible in most circumstances. Most importantly, if you fail to neutralize CAD criticism you will face an increasingly inefficient environment, and an increasing frustration as the Business-Technology Weave's challenges increase. The Weave is fast losing any tolerance for inefficiency. Come back to the critic with the liabilities that will be imposed if you follow their criticism's guidance. Remember that you will be coming to them with *criticism of their criticism*. You must ensure that your criticism is *constructive* from every angle.

So, whether you may be dispensing or receiving CAD criticism, do what is necessary to channel your creativity and that of your staff's into true service to the emerging burdens of the Weave.

DAC Criticism: Much criticism with destructive *appearance* can actually be constructive. The trick in identifying and handling DAC criticism is in how you listen for it, and in how you handle it. For example, someone may be angry, on the attack, and have the appearance of complaining just for the sake of complaining. We can frequently defuse and decode the DAC critic by acknowledging the gaps, the faults, the improvements to be had. Often times valid criticism gets cloaked by a desperate manner simply because the critic has not met with success in getting his or her issues addressed. This leads to a mounting frustration, and stresses the critic to the degree that they lose their ability to manage an effective discourse. Sometimes it robs them of their ability to remain on balance through the course of the daily pressures, and their output may suffer. But if we can ignore for the moment any defect in the critic, any imperfection in the delivery, then we can rake the criticism for two things: a legitimate issue, and an exposure for betterment. Thus, we turn criticism to a positive yield and outcome and, if we're good, *we can turn the critic toward positivity too*.

This sort of criticism requires discussion precisely because it is a major source of problems in many Business-Technology environments. As we've noted, people are our biggest challenge – we're not perfect. Therefore, to expect optimal delivery of criticism, perfect reportage of facts and problems, a perfect illumination of issues, is not only unrealistic – it would be folly to operate on these assumptions. So, we've got to become practiced and efficient at evaluating all criticism in order to vet it, and take action on it. We can't afford to overlook the positive yields from DAC criticism, becuase it is *very* important that we don't miss things as we strive to move business and technical supports forward.

We all know that things are frequently overlooked. People often ask: "How did we miss that?" Or, "Why didn't someone bring this to our attention?" In an upcoming chapter we'll be discussing major initiatives at large organizations that went terribly awry. That only happens when people are overlooking major concerns and issues, which is essentially a failure in communication: You can bet that many missing items were wrapped in DAC criticism – and it's probably a safe assumption that these initiatives and organizations didn't have effective methods of handling criticism in general.

Again earlier, we talked of criticism as "not being justified" just because it hit the happy coincidence of targeting something that needed attention. We said the criticism had to have suggestions for improvement in order to be constructive –

the criticism had to have a *helpfulness*. How then, do we distinguish the type of cloaked criticism that appears destructive, but has some measure of constructive worth (DAC), from general destructive criticism? Here's how: There will always be an attempt, however feeble, inside the cloaked DAC criticism, to point out a specific, legitimate area of concern – and – there will be some kind of expression that can be turned into a suggestion. No matter how defective the critic and their communication, no matter how angry, ignorant, jealous, stressed, etc., they are, no matter how much of a hobbyist, power-tripper, or anything else, something will slip through that we can use.

Look for a complaint of the "why can't we…" variety. Their motivation may be to simply cast some decent condition in a negative light. Yet, this kind of complaint may actually provide clues to an actual path for progression. For example, their "why can't we do this" may not be appropriate, but it may lead you to think "Hmmm… we can't do that, but we can do something else." Also, look for reverse-positives: a "this makes us work harder" sort of phrase, whereby we can flip it around: that is, "If we did that, things would be *easier*." Don't hesitate to put the ball back in the critic's court in these circumstances as well. "Your ideas have a lot of merit. Can you provide some suggestions, further detail, beneficial outcomes, etc., along with your ideas? Maybe you can bring them to next week's staff meeting." In general, consider the target of the DAC critic's criticism, then take any negativity and see if there is an opposite, positive, side. There will lie any clues to be had for betterment, thus qualifying the criticism as DAC, and worthy of further analysis.

In most circumstances, the CAD and DAC critics can be turned around fairly quickly toward a positive posture. In the case of the CAD critic, there is probably a genuine attempt at helpfulness, but the critic is none-the-less steering things the wrong way, or placing the wrong requirements in front of people. Because they have a helpful attitude, they will *want* to know about any liabilities in the criticisms they are dispensing.

In the case of the DAC critic, once you handle the legitimate issues in their criticism, there is usually relief, and a relaxing of their negative posture. Managers must also expose the cloaking critics to standards of effective communication to reduce all misunderstandings. We're all human, and the recipient of criticism, any kind of criticism, must strive to be that constant in the equation that we spoke of earlier, so as to make a valid judgment about delivered criticism. In this way, we can effectively analyze criticism, and recognize cloaked criticism.

I.T. WARS

CRITICISM AND ITS DIVIDING FORCE IN THE ELECTRONIC AGE

Communication has suffered in the electronic age. How can this be so? After all, we've expanded our options for, and the immediacy of, access and communication. Through e-mail; instant messaging; voice-over-IP (VoIP); access to web content; near-instantaneous transmission of large documentation sets; transmission of graphical and motion content; online meetings; online demonstrations, wireless communication, etc. We're communicating more than ever – aren't we?

Perhaps – but maybe we're just communicating more often – not necessarily communicating more information. For Business, we may merely be increasing the raw amount of communication – not necessarily enhancing the informing-content of what we're communicating. It's *useful* communication that counts in the business sense. The irony is that as we've expanded the width and immediacy of access and communication, we have found that we can no longer control *discretion*. To some degree too we've obliterated a natural, built-in, time for reflection and careful crafting of communication that existed with letter writing and hardcopy document preparation. We've enabled the "firing-off" of hasty, poorly constructed e-mails, and other text-enabled messages, which may not accurately convey that which we're trying to express. We open the door for misinterpretation.

In years past we had more face-to-face meetings - we could readily assess an expectation for discretion based on who was in the room. We also had non-verbal cues, and the real-time of collaborative assent, and dissent. Even when we communicated in remote methods, we often had a reasonable control to whom we imparted information. For example, we phoned discreet parties. In cases of documents and letters, we understood that physical recipients could control physical copies. There were no guarantees, of course, but there were many circumstances where we could make reasonable requests and assumptions. These former methods also had built-in time to care and reflect as we crafted those communications.

We now have little or no control on discretion when we communicate electronically. If you send an e-mail to someone, you cannot know to whom he or she will forward that mail. Even if they are the soul of discretion, you cannot know for certain that no one will take advantage of unauthorized access to that e-mail. Instant messages can be intercepted too. Whereas the interception of physical mail or documents often left evidence of such interception, the interception of electronic communication often leaves no easy trail.

Another liability of electronic communication is the sheer volume of it. Ever more sensitive communications are conducted remotely via text. You cannot be certain how a recipient will interpret, or misinterpret, your communication, yet you may not have the luxury of waiting for a face-to-face in today's high-speed world. Recipients may become angry at something they perceive, but which isn't actually "there." Perhaps in your haste you've sent an inelegant, or poorly thought-out communication. Perhaps you even deliberately sent a missive that you immediately regretted sending. Misunderstandings can become, simply, a text-enabled miscommunication due to the lack of time for reflection. The same goes for any other electronic communication. For this reason, some prudent people and organizations are very circumspect in their communications these days, and for good reason. However, this can contribute to the silo-ing of departments, organizations, and activities at the very time we need open cooperation and sharing of information the most.

The effective management and use of criticism is an absolute must within the realm of electronic communication. The reality and perception must be that all communication is being made on a business-forward basis; this lessens the opportunity for misunderstandings and misapplication of suspicion.

Things to Keep in Mind at All Times

When dispensing criticism, make certain that it is accurate. It must come from an informed perspective. Make certain that it is helpful – that it provides suggestion and guidance toward an *actual*, positive, business goal. Keep the feelings of the recipient in mind; if you are a manager making criticism, understand that it is you that holds the power. Therefore, it should not be necessary to amplify or exaggerate your control of others. If a situation merits criticism and guidance, the situation should be able to carry the point – you merely articulate it in steady, reasoned, fashion.

We all know people, people of consequence, who will criticize things no matter what the level of success, the effectiveness of things, or the height of achievements. Therefore, when things go wrong, and they do; when mistakes are made, and they are; when the unforeseen happens, and it does; there is a ready contingent of people who are loaded with an infinite variety of critical comment. It is helpful to remember that many, if not most, of these people criticize everything. Keep criticism in perspective. The most talented people, engaged in the best faith efforts, in support of the most laudable endeavors, are going to suffer criticism. It's the nature of life. In your organization, help to turn criticism into the positive lever it is meant to be.

Keep your complaints private. That is, if you need to do some plain old griping, don't do it publicly, or in an indiscriminate fashion where it could end up being public. This kind of venting can be an important coping mechanism for stress, but do it with a trusted friend, or between yourself and your supervisor in a way that has been shown as being acceptable. If you lose your discretion, and your complaints are made public, you can suffer obvious embarrassment, possible discipline, and other unanticipated repercussions over time. But as importantly, you are now seen as sympathetic ears for other complainers. In fact, going public with complaints exposes you to the "professional complainers" (critics) and marks you as a deliverer of gripes. Those who gripe as a matter of discourse are seen, in turn, as a ready target for gripes. It should be pretty obvious that if you are negative, complaining, and seem overwhelmed, you should expect those kinds of people to be attracted to you. Any others will be compelled to interact with you on this limited basis in order to sustain a relationship, as necessary in affecting their needs. Your attitude and discourse will go steadily down. Avoid complaining. In relation:

Protect yourself: If critics conclude that you are withering away, at best they will feel compelled to water you with advice; at worst they'll be like sharks in a feeding frenzy – with you as the chum. Generally, people will give what you give. Give respect – you'll receive respect. Those who don't operate on this basis are not worth bothering about, except to facilitate their best game as best as you can. You also must report egregious critical behavior when it crosses the threshold where it is becoming a liability to success.

When you know you are right, pay more attention to the flow of encouragers, and less to the critics. Don't feel you have to explain everything to everyone. There may be many critics, but only a few who will know what is best. Eventually your outcomes will be the proof that what you have done is right. There will be those smart enough to be glad that you didn't take their advice, although this is almost *never* acknowledged.

We know that Business and IT drive change. Most initiatives within the Business-Technology Weave are going to generate a certain stress, and stress creates a fertile ground for the generation of criticism. Remember to parse constructive criticism from destructive - watch for cloaked criticism - and turn all criticism toward proper disposition. Generally speaking, criticism is something we have to learn how to handle. Dispensing and responding to criticism effectively does not come naturally. Whether it's a formal rating of our performance, the handling of a legitimate complaint, destructive carping, we require education and practice in making effective dispatch of criticism.

We learn when and how to react; to prevent the unnecessary spread of criticism and any resultant perceptions that do not reflect reality; and to vet good faith criticism as a legitimate engagement to making things better. We want to guard against a festering and spread of any kind of destructive criticism, and we want to guard against spoilage of constructive criticism by doing one of two things: 1) Fixing whatever problem or situation is generating legitimate criticism, and 2) Neutralizing spurious criticism through appropriate action and channels.

Remember ~

When dealing with criticism, your reactions will contribute to your reputation. It won't help matters if you've been steady and mature for years and you fly off the handle today – tend your reputation every day. Remember too that whenever dealing with others - by ones and by groups - their impressions become *your reputation*. Having a solid reputation helps you to survive situational criticism that is unjustified – no matter how expertly delivered, no matter how powerful the critic. One thing sure: you don't want to diminish your chances.

Don't hold the target. Don't inadvertently collude with the sniping critics in your organization. Many people react with an over-sensitivity to critics, and some critics relish this. They like to see people jump at their instigation. Granting a reaction to this kind of critic invites additional critical barbs – you're accommodating them by holding a target in front of yourself! The hobbyists and the power-trippers are constantly scanning for targets. Let them find them elsewhere.

Manage criticism. If you don't, you'll find that criticism impairs you and the organization. You'll waste energy, you won't think as clearly, and you may damage relationships or reputations. Further, you'll help to generate a culture that will inhibit open communication and trust. The capacity to handle criticism and grow from it is a very important aspect of becoming successful. This is true for the individual as well as the organization – and its *culture of success*. Criticism will always, and must, come our way – how we handle criticism is what is important.

16

THE SUCCESS CULTURE

It is no use saying, "We are doing our best." You have got to succeed in doing what is necessary.

Winston Churchill

A Success Culture happens by design, not default. Success starts with a desire, and then a will, to succeed. When the will is strong, either in the individual or organization, there is a *belief* in success – and success will be the outcome. In building a culture of success, it is fundamental to build teams of people who know how to succeed, and thereby organizations that can and will succeed.

We're not talking about success alone – for we can succeed in spite of costly mistakes; we can achieve an ultimate success after many preventable failures; we can often succeed where *dumb luck* plays as big a role as anything else. We can succeed in spite of a poor culture; we can "beat the odds." But the odds catch up with us – and why take chances anyway?

The Business-Technology Weave is dependent on success, and business success depends on *it*. Your organization deserves a proper foundational culture and the right collective attitude to maintain and advance success against the challenges of a changing world. So - we need to succeed on an intelligently designed basis – we must commit to succeeding on the most effective and continuous basis. *We will have a lock on success.*

Define. Or Be Defined: When we commit to success and a culture of success, that doesn't mean we can't have some failures, and that we can't make allowance for mistakes. There is always the unforeseen, and there are always human mistakes to contend with. What we mean here is that we don't tolerate sloppiness, empty excuse, and ineptitude. We tailor and maximize known practices, best practices, and emerging practices, in managing business and its supports. We pair these practices with the kinds of people who have the will to succeed: the strength of character (possession of ethics and sense of responsibility); the care for what's required (knowledge, preparedness, teamwork); and the desire to put forth the effort in doing what's to be done (a willingness to work).

Unless we shape our environment, circumstances will shape it for us. Unless we define our culture, it will be defined for us. Unless we make it our goal to retain positive, qualified people, we will find ourselves retaining lesser qualified, and less positive people. We must plan and carefully maintain the culture as we would anything else, in order to leverage it for best business outcomes. Nothing manages itself and, like people, your culture deserves managing. We must craft the Business-Technology Weave with positivity. The *success culture-positive* is an enormous lever in moving things to successful conclusion – its influence and power cannot be overstated. Why would any organization not bias everything it could toward success?

Most importantly, when you set a bias for success, you have a primed system in place for taking on the emerging burdens, seen and unforeseen, in the Business-Technology Weave. Rather than blinking, stumbling, or choking in the face of some challenge, your organization's wheels go into motion. Whether faced with exciting new challenges, or discovery of bad, you have people, teams, and methods that are identified, in place, and possessed of knowledge and confidence in doing what needs to be done. Further, what's done is done prudently, efficiently, and with accuracy. Getting there always starts with attitude... a "where we are" factor. Where is your organization's attitude?

GROOMED TO ASSUME

We've all seen it: that sardonic view that things won't go well. That something or someone is going to be particularly difficult with this, that, or the other. That we won't have the resources, or cooperation, or permission to do what we have to do. Besides, Murphy's Law is going to hold sway despite anyone's best efforts.

We've exposed destructive criticism and the sap on energy that it entails – so why do so many people have negative assumptions? Why would they waste time and energy on negativity at the expense of rolling up their sleeves and bettering the circumstances? And – does this negativity contribute to less than optimal situations and in the denial of ultimate outcomes?

You bet it does. Negative attitudes don't help. We know how crucial it is to keep things on a positive plane. There is *no business value* in negative attitudes: They don't move business forward. Many people employ negativity as a comfort aid. They need to complain, as they are comfortable complaining – the old "don't look at me, my insecurities, my failings, my lack of control – look at how bad *this* is" method of deflected judgment that we discussed in the previous chapter. They've been permitted to condition themselves, and now employ this manner of engagement.   This is largely because they've been allowed, even encouraged, to do this by people who did not have the courage to lead. They are now *groomed* to behave this way. There are often times an assumption that this negativity is funny, allowed, and safe.   It frequently engenders laughter (support). *Groomed to assume.*

Beware the Discounting of Success: Many times, in meetings for example, we hear a tone that is impairing. How often do we hear sarcasm, defeatism, empty rumination? All too frequently if just one person engages the issues in these manners, it drives the whole meeting down. The meeting's efficiency and productivity has been crippled.

"How are we going to get this done, when we can't even…?" "Why are we doing this, when we should be doing…?" "That department never changes, we're wasting our time counting on them…" Yet, any time people meet regarding sanctioned change, the team has to handle it, and has to get it done. It's time to smack down the negativity. You can handle it by simply, and dispassionately, asking: "Where is the business value in your statement (or position)?" This is a "does this move business forward?" type of question. In other words, we have to drive every engagement and discussion up toward a qualification. The qualification is that they must present a worthiness to our Success Culture's time and attention.

None of this is to discount the value of humor, or to strip the fun out of work. Nor is this to make everyone a Pollyanna – that is, a person who sees everything through rose-colored glasses, with an inability to weigh and judge actual problems. Rather we're talking about that zone where heads are turned to results. If one is going to point out deficiencies and problems, that person or reporting body must meet the clear expectations that people will bring ideas and offers for improvement to the table. They must come ready to move the organization's business forward.

Some environments seem to labor with a discounting of success. Results and achievement are laughed off, or discussions of quality and goals are seen as put-upons. Turnover may be high. Morale is bad. The values are skewed: people take every break they're entitled to, and stretch them. They visit, socialize, and under-produce. Each day they arrive as late as they can, and leave as soon as they can. Often at work here is a lack of pride in a job or the organization itself. There are many influencers in these circumstances. Some organizations are populated by key people who thrive and maintain their position through a certain dysfunction – one that they emplace and support. They do this through expertly managed dissent, duplication of efforts, inexact expectation and direction, and the maintenance of guessing postures for staff. They also support a particularly nasty system of politics which, when it suits their purpose, deflates achievement and inhibits progress. If you're helping to run an organization that doesn't have the right attitudes, it is your obligation to counter this dysfunction. You must do your best to engage the very top in exposing the challenges and solutions to a bad business culture.

If you find yourself in a zone whereby so-called leaders seem to be slowing, or discounting, success, look for the sustaining root. This can be happening due to jealousy, fear, or protectionism, etc. They may feel that their contribution to overall success will ultimately profile an "opponent" in a favorable way – so they withhold or drag their own support to comprehensive missions or goals. There may be enormous ignorance at work in these circumstances – people may not understand the risk to success that these sorts of actions may pose, and the ultimate consequences to success diminished or deferred. Senior-most leaders should watch for these negative activities, seek their motivation, and abolish them.

The Stark Relief of Success: Fortunately, the removal of ignorance leverages itself for real power: Once an organization qualifies itself as an IT Enlightened Organization, it is able to launch a sensible, Business-driven IT strategy. With the attendant disciplines and accountabilities that that entails, your organization's esteem will shoot up – as will its productivity. Also, once you have a solid basis not just for conducting business, but for effectively managing change, and bringing optimum supports to business, you then have confidence in this environment. The systems and supports are reliable, optimized, and tuned.

Against this uniform backdrop, the IT Enlightened Organization has an easier time in identifying spurious arguments, destructive criticism, and bad faith actions. It also gets easier to identify the people who are truly moving business forward, and doing it with the most effectiveness. Think about it: once "good" is in the majority of your organization's activities, you have a stark relief against which "bad" is readily profiled. Hence, bad is more easily identified, exposed, and dispatched. Your rewards system becomes better targeted. Your people are more accurately profiled. You gain efficiency and emplace excellence across the entire organization and throughout all of its layers.

Happily, you go a long way toward establishing a success culture just by clearing negatives, and setting a positive example. Once negative behavior is seen as not being tolerated, people will fill the vacuum with positive suggestion and better attitudes. We've seen many a nice person, with positive disposition, go to work for a bad boss – one who is negative and critical – and we've seen that person adopt their boss's tone and attitude. We've also seen people who are perceived as negative going to work for a good boss, and completely turning their attitude around. This is not to suggest that people are sheep, or without their own spine, but people do what they have to do to get along and survive – it's human nature. Use this nature to create a natural attraction to a success culture.

A success culture is directly related to your whole strategy of how to manage and treat people. Often times in business we feel that we're doing the best we can with the staff we can afford. Too often there is the belief that the best talent is only available to the top dollar. This is not so. The pool of candidates, and their motivations, is *diverse*. There are many, many educated, knowledgeable, and talented people who chased down big paydays, position, and prestige, and still found something lacking. Thus there are plenty of people who want to find an environment that is rewarding and fun (*satisfying*), and who will come to such an environment and *stay*. Here, the stark relief of success will be evident to quality people when they cross your threshold.

For any person in any organization, your position – large or small – is to contribute to the success culture by creating and leveraging all organizational systems and supports toward ultimate positives. Your success culture will yield a culture of desirability. People will want to work in your environment. Better, they will let other people know about that desirability – and exponential attractions will be the natural yield. The organization that knows how to attract and retain quality people never suffers hardship through departures. Quality people within the organization are ready to advance. In those situations where you must go outside, your reputation helps you to quickly assemble a quality pool of candidates, leaving you that much more time for scheduling and analysis of each candidate.

CREATING THE SUCCESS CULTURE – GROOMED TO <u>KNOW</u>

How do we create this culture, and this sort of organization? First, we must maximize and make fully understandable these existing fundamentals in your organization:

- Mission
- Values
- Beliefs
- Standards.

It is not our intent here to create a business plan, to write sample mission statements, or to provide a primer about values, etc. Your organization, and the reader, understands these things and their importance in defining and sustaining the organization and its conduct of business. Rather, it is our duty here to re-examine the obvious – what reflection is there in these areas regarding *success*? For, in looking at the loose standards of some of those around us, in looking at the mistake-prone organizations, or the hierarchies with their ethically challenged reputations, we realize that we have to make a conscious decision to be different.

Those others certainly have missions, values, beliefs, and standards. But if they see value in cutting corners, if they have a belief that inflating profits will yield positive business outcomes, if their standards are ill-defined or deliberately loose, there is no service to the mission. There is no true accommodation for the idea of success. Sustained, long-term success (the only kind that really counts) is achieved by being honest and in matching actions to realities. The success culture starts with this honesty, which inspires trust, cooperation, and good faith activity. We therefore need to groom (mentor, coach, train) so that no one has to *assume* anything regarding the culture – they will *know*. As things stand now, how many people can you scratch in your organization – querying them on matters of business culture – to yield a response with some semblance of: "We have a culture of success"? Try it. If your leadership is not biasing the organization for success – what *is* it doing?

Further, our stated mission, values, beliefs and standards will ensure that, if and when a gray area leads someone to wonder what a standard is, or be left to ponder what they might get away with, we have in place a culture that will groom them to know that excellence is the bar. That the job, large or small, is to be done *right*. They will disabuse themselves - and they will dissuade others - of any notion of entertaining an impropriety. This is where you achieve true strength: *From the bottom up* as individuals self-regulate; *from the top down* as example-setting, ethical leaders manage, mentor and train; and *across* the organization – or across organizations - as departments and agencies engage in good faith activity by virtue of solid reputations and trust. Let's look at some supports to this:

SUPPORTING SUCCESS: MISSION; VALUES; BELIEFS; STANDARDS

Mission: The idea of a mission would seem to be pretty obvious. However, if you ask people on a random basis to articulate their organization's mission, you may be surprised at the result. There will be a degree of struggle in expressing the mission with accuracy. Forget about any degree of comprehensiveness. Even Business people can have trouble – but for support elements such as IT, there may be many people who fail to understand, or even care about, the overarching business mission.

Every organization has a mission, and every reader's organization has a mission statement. The mission provides the answer as to why the organization is here. An organization's stated mission should include primary products and services, your service model (such as the importance of excellence, creativity, results, *success*, etc.), and markets. Everyone in an organization should know what the organization's mission is, understand it, and support it. Remember that the mission statement is a ready handle in defining who you are – after the organization's name, it is often the first exposure someone has to anything about your organization. It communicates essential information to people, beginning with the people right in the organization – *the employees*. It is the definition of your organization seen by clients, customers, members, prospects, potential employees, vendors, contractors, business partners, and any other interested party.

Further, each department, group, or project should also have a defined mission and statement. Each individual has a mission – and an allied statement in some form or another in their job or position description. People should certainly be able to articulate and understand their job mission according to their job description. They should be able to do this better than anyone else (with the possible exception of the supervising authority). It is very important to note that all elements of an organization must understand their missions in the context of the larger business mission. Understanding the ultimate overarching mission, and a department's, project's, person's fit into it, helps to elevate activity. Products, services, deliverables, etc. assume a greater quality as people vet what they are doing against the ultimate business aim. When the real goals of the organization are firmly in mind, and respected, it helps to remove a sort of ticket-punch, near-sighted mentality.

All missions have this in common: they define doings by people, in offerance to other people, according to some philosophy and standard. Any mission, whether the organization's or the individual's, has success at its core. So too should the mission statement. This doesn't mean crafting obvious declarations, but, think about what constitutes success and its supports: relevance; knowledge; quality; timeliness; accuracy, friendliness; principles, etc. Weave these concepts into your statement, and subsequently position them in your organization's culture by reinforcing missions, jobs, and associated statements. In other words: maintain awareness and focus by requiring people to know what they're doing and why! This doesn't mean that people merely understand the activity that is front of their face – it means understanding what their actions do in support of the overall mission, whatever your larger business aims may be. Also, be able to answer the questions that your customers, members, constituents, vendors, etc. will have when accessing your mission statement – it should convey a posture for success. By extension, does your staff create a comfort and faith in your ability to deliver success?

In our Business-Technology Weave, we know that all missions, regardless where they reside (individual missions by job; project missions; department missions) are in support of a larger mission – the mission of the main business purpose. IT must understand its own mission's fit to the overarching business mission. This can be stated simply if you wish: "IT's mission is to deliver, support and improve appropriate information technology, and to facilitate its effective use, in contributing to the improvement and support of XYZ Corporation's stated mission." For brevity, it is enough that IT's mission statement points to the organization's statement. You don't want to require unpacking of each individual mission from a larger business statement. At the same time, you must require employees, for their true notion of success, to understand the organization's mission. People need to understand what their position is supporting at the end of that pipe where goods and services are being dispensed.

Focusing on the Real Objective: For example, if we're in an office with a network, it is not enough for a network manager to "keep the network running" as an understanding of his or her mission. Although, realistically, we know that's what is in that person's mind from day-to-day. Still, why keep the network running (besides maintaining employment)? Well, the real objective is "to ensure optimal network service in sustaining daily business operations, while bringing continuous improvement to office technologies. This support enables business planners and staff as they deliver better goods, services and value to customers in accordance with XYZ Corporation's stated mission."

This helps a person to understand that it's not enough to deliver – a deliverable has to be used effectively in the larger context of what we're really doing. Whether you write individual mission statements that spell this out or not, you have to ensure that people understand their ultimate purpose in the organization. Generally, this pulls self-discipline and accountability up, and helps to ensure that every endeavor fulfills its ultimate objective – making delivery to Business so that Business can make delivery. We'll make a good example of this in the next section, when we pair values with mission:

Values: A value is a belief, a principle, a quality, or a philosophy that has meaning and *worth* to the organization. It also must have meaning and worth to the individual. It is important to note that any organization will have formally defined values – but it will also have informal values.

In recent surveys of business, the identification and implementation of values has been cited as the one of the greatest keys in the success of those organizations that thrive. Values lead to direct action, quality of action, and appropriate treatment of people. When looking at most successful organizations, we find that values are directly linked to their success. For example, Sears places a high value on customer trust – in the 19th Century, customers in rural areas enjoyed a money-back guarantee on any returned product. Can you imagine the comfort that that sort of trust engendered when ordering from a remote organization through a catalog?

The Marriott's value of standardization enabled it to efficiently duplicate its standard model hotel all across the country. People on the road experienced a welcome familiarity.

Coca-Cola's value of their customers' opinion and satisfaction allowed it to quickly recover from the wrong turn that New Coke represented.

Your organization has a set of values in place – make certain that those values are effective, known, and understood. The trick is not merely in having values: the trick is to make certain they expand and occupy every corner and crevice of your operations, your supports, your management, your products, and your services. In the case of our Weave, we can see that business values occupy the upper, overarching agenda. IT values need to support and help fulfill business objectives. One of the most obvious values today is the sustaining of continuous improvement. Generally, the identification of an important value leads to discovery, and discussion, of other supporting values: innovation, reliability, trust, confidence, truthfulness, and so forth. At the same time, a discussion of values needs to identify gaps, or divides, between stated organizational values, and the full employ of those values in leveraging them to the ultimate mission. A simple example of a gap, or divide, and its closure will serve well here to illustrate fulfillment of an ultimate business value (and also of an ultimate mission):

Meaningful Values: An organization had a very basic, yet critical, problem in that business travelers had repeated difficulty accessing the organization's network from remote locations. There was no failure in equipment – but there was a failing on the part of IT to familiarize the traveler with the proper steps for connecting to the network. There was also a failure to arm the traveler with some basic troubleshooting procedures to handle common problems on the road.

These problems involved various hotels and their available connectivity measures such as phone lines, Wi-Fi setups, and access methods. The IT HelpDesk was dutifully handing out laptops to business travelers. The laptops were tested, and their setups verified as working by IT. The HelpDesk technicians were accounting for the status of laptops by virtue of a sign-out/sign-in sheet. Busy business travelers were picking up laptops at the last moment and heading to their business destination. This HelpDesk felt that value was achieved: means to access the network has been delivered. *Laptop signed out and accounted for.* Mission accomplished.

But there was a problem – business travelers were not familiar with the means of access. They frequently had trouble purchasing Wi-Fi time, or achieving dial-up from various countries, or utilizing their credit cards during access attempts. The IT HelpDesk would laboriously resolve these problems by phone: a frustrating, patience-challenging, practice – and one that was wasting precious time that was supposed to be dedicated to the conduct of business. An important value to business was not being delivered in anything resembling an effective fashion. The real value in dispensing laptops to Business is provision of a *quick, easy, and effective means of accessing the organization's business-intelligence content for the ready performance of work.* Handing off a laptop without insuring the recipient knows how to access the network from a remote location means completely overlooking the business objective. It means a diminishment of the overarching value to business for possessing the laptop.

Here, the only way value is achieved is by keeping the overarching *business* concern in mind – a real mission. The mission here is to enable work and productivity from the remote-location, not merely for Business and IT to respectively sign out and check out the laptop . This *must* be understood by IT, as they are the business enabler here. In other words, IT shouldn't place any particular *value* in checking a virtual box: *laptop delivered*. IT's value and mission here is to *enable business productivity*.

Business value was ultimately achieved by imposing a requirement, to IT and Business: each traveler had to sit down for a familiarization and troubleshooting session – Wi-Fi-ing and dialing in to the network *before* departure, for verification that the traveler could actually access and perform work. Further, this familiarization was offered and strongly recommended prior to each and every trip, because most business travelers needed a refresher. (Also, things change).

This enabling value is not only a benchmark value internal to IT – it is a delivered value that IT provides to business. Business will *value* this enabling of productivity. This highlights an important concept of values: Values guide, values support, and values deliver. Values help to drive reality more ways than one, and the right values drive your reality into the zone of success. Also note a cascading affect here: Values directly support the quality and success of your missions, and the ultimate business mission.

Beliefs: Beliefs support values. If your organization wants to value excellence, for example, people need to believe that excellence is worth striving for, is recognized, and is rewarded. Further, it will be believed that excellence is appreciated by the customer, client, member, etc. Vendors will acclimate quickly to your culture of excellence, and they will partner according to their natural sense of your expectation for excellence. Beliefs yield confidence and trust (desirable values in and of themselves). When people believe that others engage in good faith, and that the organization itself behaves in, and supports, good faith, we build value. We begin to build a collective mental acceptance of truths, and conviction in them. Again, think about defining your culture through mission, values, beliefs and standards: don't let it default to something you don't want. Beliefs directly support your mission.

An important belief is that an organization is a team, rather than a collected set of competing silos; each complete with their own selfish agendas, competition for resources, negative belief-set, and poor expectations of the other silos. By extension, allied organizations that have been tasked with a common mission must acquire the belief that they are a team in order to be at their united best. Consider what your organization believes – truly believes. Is your organization's belief-set acceptable to you? Consider the beliefs that you would like to instill in your organization, and the reality necessary to emplace and sustain those beliefs.

Believing in Beliefs: Beliefs must be supported by reality. Just as values can be meaningless if not energized for optimizing your culture (and outcomes), beliefs are meaningless if they have no real reflection in your culture either. That is, you can't ask someone to believe in something that the organization does not support - or <u>value</u> – itself. Further, the organization must make it <u>evident</u> that it holds and believes in that value. For example, if the organization calls for a value in "trust," but past action, history, and bad faith action do not support this call, the organization will not enjoy trust as one of its active values. People will not believe in it.

Talk, as ever, is cheap. Rather, to further this example, the organization has to bring accountability and discipline to those who have broken trust, and conversely, must support and reward those who maintain trust. Then, and only then, *trust will be an organizational value*. Recognize that people believe according to what they see, hear, and experience. People then act according to *their* beliefs – not someone other's. In order to effect best actions on the part of people - in support of success - we need to emplace a collective belief in quality values. Leadership can help people experience the positive measures of a success culture, and must strive to reinforce positive beliefs and values through organizational reality.

As we've stated before, success is largely achieved through a will to succeed. When you have the will, you have a *belief* that you will succeed. This belief in success cannot be overstated or over emphasized. Your organization's belief in its success yields commitment to success: from individual to group to department. This yielding to success means that everyone will seek the levers that activate success: not just focus, dedication, hard work, and other values – but the more difficult things - the removal of political impairments; the redistribution and share of resources; the jettison of protectionism and jealousies. When the stakes are high enough, and *understood* (and success is indeed a very high stake), the sheer necessity of success will yield some amazing accommodations.

Remember that in order to support a solid set of values, we need to believe in them. Our belief in them is supported by the reality of things around us, as evidenced by our success culture. Finally, as we'll see next, you must have people believing in *standards*, in order for success to be real, meaningful, and achievable.

Standards: A standard is a requirement, a level, or a degree of something. Standards define and guide conduct. They set benchmarks in the performance of systems and people. They help to provide comparisons and measures in order to evaluate levels of things that lead to success. Standards help to measure success itself.

Harboring a respect for standards is a value. You value a degree, or level, of performance from employees – and from yourself. You must meet and hopefully exceed a standard in order to certify the value of that performance. Overall, your organization has a requirement of conduct – the level of conduct you require is a standard. We manage and perform according to standards.

Standards should be a clear expression of our expectations: We should know how our organization expects us to behave and interact with each other. We should know how to resolve conflict. We should have standards that support growth and progression for the right people. Proper standards help us to leverage "human capital" to competitive advantage.

Standards also help us to establish commonly accepted guides to productivity and quality. A review of standard best practices in any field of endeavor will present essential standards for success. A success culture both yields, and depends on, productivity. Efficient and effective (quality) production of anything represents success: whether it is production of new designs, production of output goods, producing better service, producing more satisfied customers, producing more accurate performance appraisals - these all represent *success*.

In-turn, success (successful productivity) yields pride in the organization, pride in what you do, confidence in a job well done, and it yields a positive model for future success. Consider the business traveler's laptop as an example: the true standard is not to issue the laptop in a timely fashion (important enough, but easily done), it is not to vet the laptop as functional (also important), *but rather the standard is to meet the business traveler's need to access the organization's network in order to successfully accomplish online work*. If you meet the *true* standard, the others are *met*. The ultimate standard pulls everything else *up*. This is why you have to solidify in your mind, and the minds of your staff, the ultimate, true standards to be met (and as necessary, exceeded) in each task, project, and endeavor.

The identification of ultimate business standards does not mean that you don't need checklists or interim qualifiers/standards. Indeed true standards support and lead to the establishment of those things: "Hmm, if BusTraveler 'A' has ultimate need to work from City 'Z', I need to test a laptop, issue it, and certify that BusTraveler 'A' knows how to use it." Recognize here that standards beget success.

All of these things in your success culture help you develop a winning people strategy – which in turn helps your organization develop an overall competitive advantage.

THE EXCUSE FACTORY

The opposite of a Success Culture is not necessarily an *Unsuccess* Culture. We're all largely in organizations that are succeeding somehow, moving forward in time, achieving results with some measure of control. The opposite of the Success Culture is really "The Excuse Factory" – it's where the default attitude is one of negative griping and excuse making, instead of a managed and properly reinforced attitude of positivity, contribution, and forward momentum.

There can be swirls of both cultures, and everything in between, throughout the organization, throughout projects, and throughout planning, etc. But time spent in the Excuse Factory is time spent away from the job… in fact, people who inhabit the Excuse Factory are AWOL. Excuses presented without ideas, gripes presented without solutions, engagements that do not move business forward, are empty time. We can still recognize that everyone needs to gripe once in awhile. But let people complain about the coffee, the weather, even about the size of their desks or cubicles. But so far as tasks and projects are concerned, the energy should be directed toward positive results.

Again, we're not trying to produce Pollyannas, but prudent people and culture so as to support efficiency and effectiveness. As you work to emplace a Success Culture, realize that this culture becomes easier to achieve, and easier to maintain, as you reach a tipping point – that is, as more and more people "get it." They will be less prone to make excuses, as their attention and time is taken up by the seek of solutions. As more and more people operate according to the ethics of success, your culture begins to reinforce and attract all of the elements for success: best personnel, best behavior, best practices, best vendors, and best results.

REMEMBER ~

A Success Culture is managed. Success starts with a desire, and then a will, to succeed – supported by appropriate missions, values, beliefs and standards. It is the organization that must show itself as being committed to success. No one can be expected to believe in something that the organization doesn't *evidence* itself as believing in. Therefore, the organization must close any divides between diminished expectations for success, and success itself.

The organization must formally recognize success with real encouragement, reward, and promotion. The organization, from the top on down, must identify and communicate its commitment to the values, beliefs, and standards that it holds as being necessary to best outcomes. Too, those things and people that inhibit success must be managed and corrected – or removed.

The expectation of success is self-reinforcing. Create the culture that ennobles and enhances your mission. People, within and with-out the organization, will know that excellence is the bar. People will self-regulate in concert with your organization's guides and practices. Thus, in rare instances where activity or expectations are cloudy, people will *presume* excellence as the bar, based on the entirety of your success culture's known expectations.

17

CONTENT:
LEVERAGING INFORMATION; LIMITING LIABILITY; MANAGING DOCUMENTS AND THEIR RETENTION

The next best thing to knowing something is to know where to find it.

Samuel Johnson

What you need is what you get.

Maxim

[Note: Content Management is an evolving discipline, and its necessity is impacting more and more organizations - large, medium, and small. If you have no experience with content management, have struggled with its understanding, or are having difficulty with a management system now, re-read and review this chapter as necessary].

Business success requires the ability to develop, acquire, secure, make effective use of, and dispose of, information - *content*. Content is simply the information that your business *contains*, or harbors. To start with, there are two basic categories of content: business content and non-business content. Within those are two subcategories: appropriate, and not appropriate. It's quite simple.

Most business content is appropriate, so long as it has value and relevancy. Appropriate content is that information which is necessary in the pursuit and support of your business. Non-business content is those things that aren't of direct necessity to business. Much non-business content is tolerated, and some is even essential: as a normal lubrication in your staffs' managing of important personal affairs, and in the support of general employee morale. In either main category of content, business or non, we'll see that inappropriate content can exist, and can pose extreme liabilities. We'll define inappropriate content shortly. We'll see too that there are even emerging perils to the efficient use of appropriate content.

In this chapter, we will *identify* content. We'll explore its relationship to successful business, understand how to maximize use of content as a leveraged asset, define and minimize liability posed by all content, and learn the importance for disposing of content that has lost its value. Once we have a good understanding to all of content management's implications, we'll examine ways to put a system of content management in place. Different organizations will need systems of differing sizes and sophistication. Therefore, a part of our discussion of systems will include your identification of a solutions partner – a vendor – and appropriate product.

However, long before we get to the "system," we must have a thorough understanding of what content is, what a policy of content management really constitutes, and what the solution really entails:

THE "SOLUTION" MUST SOLVE

IT and Business have to keep something simple in mind. Remember that a policy, associated process, and support system must represent a *solution*: everything must leverage as being helpful to Business. This is a solution – not an empty burden. Here, as anywhere, we cannot afford the false solution.

This solution must:

1) Identify and leverage existing, new, and accumulated content for maximum business use and success.

2) Minimize liabilities involving: inefficient access and loss of business content; the unwanted accumulation of outdated content; the distribution of conflicting content; cost of storage; damage posed by unnecessary discovery and exposure; the unwanted accumulation of non-business and inappropriate content; and burgeoning overhead in meeting necessary regulatory requirements.

3) Enable our ability to audit and report on content in an uncomplicated, fast, and effective way (in direct support to 1 and 2 above).

This will be a pairing of Business-driven policy and process with an appropriate technical solution - a further weave of business and technology. We build a sound policy, we define our process, including the right-sized technical support, we train staff, and we manage content. When we complete a people, policy and process model, we *control* content by virtue of knowledgeable people, supported by a defined policy, supported by a sound process.

... So – how do we get there? Like most things, the devil is in the details:

A DIVIDE THAT WILL GROW

Management of content is already well underway in some organizations – with varying degrees of success. But for most others it is a looming imperative. If you do not have a method for determining and using your information effectively throughout the organization, you will grow an ever-widening divide between your <u>needs</u> and your <u>reality</u>. That is, between the sheer necessity for effective use/leverage of business information - and the conditions of inefficiency and diminished returns that accrue with the accumulated glut of unmanaged information. You must avoid or close that divide now. Here's why:

Business is faced with an explosion: it is the exponential growth of content. But what exactly is "content"? It is any information that your business holds, whether known or unknown, and whether asset or liability. Whatever electronic information resides in your business systems, on your network, on workstations, in your e-mail system, on backup tapes, on all those scattered discs – is content. It also includes whatever information exists in the form of hardcopy – printed reports output, written notes, mail you've accumulated, etc. – things existing in filing cabinets, bookshelves, and piled on desks. Whether electronic or hardcopy, content can exist as text, artwork, photos, presentations, etc. Really anything in your enterprise containing information of any sort, business and *non-business* related - is content. That menu from the corner deli is content, and if it's in someone's desk drawer, it is part of *your organization's* content: your organization contains it. The importance of that realization will be made evident, but for now it is imperative that we understand that the organization is *liable for all content it harbors*. This is whether it's harbored by design, or by accident. This understanding will be necessary as we talk about specific liabilities imposed by certain content.

Also realize that there is content that can be "tied" to your organization, but which appears "outside." Employee-generated material appearing on blogs, disseminated through e-mail, and even instant messaging (IMs) is unregulated in many organizations - and poses risk. Therefore, think: *What's being done in the name of your domain*?

DAVID SCOTT

Content: A Basic Understanding of Need

Content management can be illuminated further in very practical terms. Some will remember the old WYSIWYG (Wiz-ee-wig) acronym: *What You See Is What You Get*. WYSIWYG came about around the time of Windows-based applications, as they replaced DOS-based applications. At that time, a graphical user interface replaced a text interface. Software applications delivered to the screen the exact font, formatting, colors, and images that would be produced when you printed your work. Before WYSIWYG, what you saw on the screen was an approximation of your output – the screen showed, primarily, uniform text. Fonts, sizes, graphics, and colors were represented by codes and symbols – you couldn't confirm what you were getting until you printed, and often what you got was wrong.

Obviously "getting what is wrong" is inefficient, counterproductive, and frustrating. This is no less true in the realm of content, and the stakes are high. Today's challenge isn't aesthetic correctness; it's content correctness. Getting what you need. Content management can be thought of as WYNIWYG (Win-ee-wig): What You Need Is What You Get. And just as importantly, what you *don't* need is what you *get rid of*.

The growth in content is paired with an increasingly important requirement. Whereas data management, or information management, was once viewed primarily as a concern regarding simple access, delivery, storage, and space - this data is now understood to have value beyond its face and local residency. It often has continued value beyond any immediate need, and becomes a leveraged asset across the organization as we develop, share, combine and repurpose content. Data's content can also pose a potential liability – to the organization and to those with whom we do business. Content's liability depends on its nature and, further, its exposure.

For these reasons there is a whole new realm of standards, within an already established (yet evolving) discipline, in basing the management of information according to content. This isn't something that's never been done before: electronic information on any computer network is managed to some degree according to content. Things are filed in specific folders, according to subject matter. Permissions are granted to users based on their need and the data's nature and sensitivity, and so on. Hardcopy information too is filed, often locked in filing cabinets; access granted according to the content and who is authorized to access it. Your HR department's hardcopy files, for example.

A Missing Accountability: But until fairly recently, most organizations had no comprehensive view of their content – those paper and electronic files that comprised the whole of their information. It's true that IT had a certain handle on information - regarding disk space utilization, allocation of storage to users, and administering of electronic security. Too, departments, various bridging teams, and ad hoc groups would have some measure of knowledge regarding their specific content's information. But no central authority knew, indeed no one could know, what exactly was on the organization's computers or in its files in any comprehensive manner.

There was simply no practice, discipline and allied system for the central control of, knowledge of, and reporting for, content. *An absence of accountability.*

GETTING IT; USING IT; RE-USING IT; AND GETTING RID OF IT

Beyond mere accountability, however, the modern and evolving discipline of managed content is more sophisticated and powerful than anything previously established. We make content searchable and relevant to people in powerful new ways, in support of projects and disciplines within the organization. We find supporting and illuminating relationships between existing content that were previously hidden because there was no way to find or readily expose these relationships. We see new clues regarding markets, customers, products, services, trends, activities, and *risks*. As importantly, when new content is developed, we automate the assignment of key information fields to it so as to make this new content a part of our leveraged information assets. Instead of being buried under an explosion of content, we explode content to splay its purpose, relevancy and value. We then snap content together with other content to form a completed picture.

Imagine this: a scrambled jigsaw puzzle where the pieces reside in various departments, in various physical locations – perhaps all around the world – with individuals and groups working the various pieces in some measure of ignorance for the efforts and work of others. We now connect all the pieces with an interwoven thread. The thread guards against loss, and identifies puzzle pieces as relating to each other, among other things. On demand, an authority pulls a master thread, and all the pieces come together to form as *complete* a picture as the moment allows: not part of a picture, not a picture with missing pieces, not a picture that requires recreation of missing parts that had already been created – but a 100% collection of parts with corresponding context and fit to the other parts.

That is a large part of what content management delivers to business. It can be the assembly of information regarding something in process, such as status that reflects the true moment of progress. Or, it could be the review of completed project materials and all related effort. It can be a search for relevant supporting content when mounting a new initiative. Or, it can just be general research within your assets.

What's important to recognize is that you get the complete, best, picture of the situation according to all assets, according to the moment. When we achieve this system of confidence and control, we gain enormous efficiency and leverage by reusing, re-purposing, and assembling content by optimizing its formerly hidden business value.

Reducing Exposure – Minimizing Liability: We're also talking about a comprehensive process that can give a central authority a ready report, at any time, on *all* content in your organization, according to any criteria by which they query: What is its subject matter? Who created it; who has it; who's been using it? What is its useful life? How does it relate to and support other content? Which members, customers, staff, projects, products, services, regulations, agencies, etc. does this content pertains to? Where are versions of similar content residing? Which version is current?

Accumulation of content contributes to inefficiency. Multiple versions and drafts of documents can exist in all sorts of locations. As things get passed around within the organization, and saved in various user and departmental folders, you build all sorts of redundant, near-redundant, and ultimately erroneous data. There may be content that was created by persons who have left the organization - there may be no one who can readily answer whether the content is correct. Outdated content, or content whose value is murky, should be weighed against some standard in order to determine its disposability.

Content management goes beyond eliminating glut, and yields the possible exposures (liabilities) that certain content may represent. For example, your organization may have all manner of outdated business policies, stored in various departments, which may be based on expired outside law and regulation. You wouldn't want anyone taking action within such policy that no longer applies. How can you be sure that everyone is operating on the most recent issue of organizational policies? Another example may be emerging client relationships: relationships to you, and their relationships to other agencies. How do you best disseminate breaking information throughout the organization? How do you ensure it's received? How do you ensure it supplants the old? How do you remove the old?

Policy: Content Management vs. Acceptable Use: Sooner or later, every organization is going to have some measure of policy for content's management, and that measure will likely increase as time goes by. It is important to note here what a Content Management policy is, and what it is not.

It is for leveraging content, exposing and reducing specific liabilities, and for taking action on content in an administrative sense – reporting on, archiving, and destroying. It is not the central policy regarding expectations of appropriate use, and regarding actions taken in circumstances of willful abuse of content. Content management measures certainly do help to identify and expose abuse; however, the definitions of abuse, and measures regarding them, will be contained in the organization's Acceptable Use Policy.

Jumping ahead slightly, this Acceptable Use Policy details appropriate use of *all* business resources, tools, and assets - including information. Your content management policy can point to the Acceptable Use Policy (or contain extracts from it) regarding things such as the improper access, accumulation, dissemination, removal, and destruction of information. But again, content management helps us to identify and leverage content toward a positive purpose; helps to limit liability and exposure; and to take administrative action on content. [We will discuss the Acceptable Use Policy in the *Security* chapter – if your organization is lacking such a policy, or needs a better one, you may wish to quickly skip ahead, for clarity, and return here].

Pairing Process and Policy: Any policy simply formalizes and documents the understanding of needs, shows the value to be had, and details the mandatory course and standards of actions - the process - in satisfying those needs and requirements. However, many processes find their way into practice without a formal policy. Either they don't require much formal documentation and standards, or they stagger along without them. But, that *cannot* be the case with content management. There really is no middle ground with content: you either know what you have, or you don't. You're either actively managing your data environment - culling bad and leveraging good – or you're not.

Without a policy, your means of reporting on content will be less than comprehensive. Therefore, we must develop a specific Content Management Policy that concentrates on three basic things:

- ♦ Category of content (identifying it according to taxonomy [subject matter]). This categorization leads to our leverage of content;

- ♦ Retention of content: Retaining content for a period of time as defined by its category, against a prepared schedule for the retention/disposition of the various categories of content within compliance of laws and any other regulations. This allows us to ensure that content remains reportable, known, and available during its useful life; and

- ♦ Disposing of it in an efficient manner (removing it from the active business environment at the end of its life, either through deletion or archiving). This allows us to remove content from the active environment, and helps to prevent the glut and liability of unmanaged information.

In this manner we help to secure content through its lifecycle. In defining the terms of content management, we'll see that *retention* drives the policy.

Retention: Retention is the expected length of time that a piece of content will be in your active business environment. Retention helps to drive the efficiency that content management delivers. It sets the periods and dates whereby you can remove data from the active business environment, generally through deletion. A retention policy is part of your overall content management policy, and ensures that all business records are retained for a period of time that will reasonably assure the availability of those records when needed. Also, certain fundamental, vital, records are identified and appropriately safeguarded – their retention period is "permanent."

Due to growth in business content and increasingly stringent compliance requirements, Business must recognize that we can't keep everything forever – much content steadily loses value, ultimately having little or no value. Here we must recognize that over the course of time, any record that is not required to be maintained for legal or business reasons should be destroyed (or at the very least, removed from the active business environment, by virtue of some kind of archiving). This removal is necessary to reduce the high cost of storing, indexing, and handling the vast amount of documents and paper that otherwise accumulate. The retention part of content management ensures the minimization of storage and maintenance costs. It also helps to increase the efficiency in finding documents, and is an overall lever in building a tight, solid, fit of content to your business-intelligence needs. It becomes much easier to repurpose and combine data that is reinforcing to the projects and initiatives that business pursues.

So, how long do we retain specific information against the measure of time? For that, we refer to a retention schedule. Retention schedules indicate every major category of information the organization has, and the schedule for disposition – such as destruction, or archiving. For our early understanding now, appreciate that once the schedule exists, we remove specific content according to that defined schedule of retention.

For example, you may have royalty records, within a comprehensive category. Your portion of the retention policy, and your chosen, defined, retention period for such records, may look something like this:

VII. Copyrights, Patents, Royalties, Licenses, Trademarks, Intellectual Property Rights, General Business Relation Agreements:

- …
- Royalty records: Life of the patent or trademark, plus 5 years.
- …

Conversely, there are categories of documents that you would never archive or destroy. The retention policy accommodates these too – in fact, it protects them. For example, general corporate records specific to the creation of an organization, and detailing its constitution, partnerships, and qualifications to do business, etc. would be indicated as being "Permanent."

Another example common to all organizations would be your handling of various personnel records. Your organization may choose to destroy performance appraisals five years after an individual's departure, for example. Regardless of commonalities, a retention schedule acts on categories of content that the organization defines – the organization is serving itself. It sets retention according to its need, and in compliance with all Federal and State laws, and any other applicable regulations.

Further, our retention schedule can help clean up hardcopy content. We can help to eliminate the divide of electronic content from its hardcopy counterparts through an understanding of taxonomy (subject matter) – for purpose of categorization. We can then set an associated schedule for the management of retention according to the *content* of documents and records – regardless of physical form or media type. (This also leverages content's use, removing liabilities of its form and even physical location).

A table of taxonomies will help your organization and its members to define types of content for categorization. Your retention schedule then defines the term for which you keep various kinds of content (according to category) – starting from an individual piece of content's original creation date.

THE RETENTION SCHEDULE

Once an organization's documents are categorized, their content's retention is managed on a schedule. The schedule simply lists various categories of content based on taxonomy, each category's retention period, and action taken on that content after the retention period expires. Only your organization can capture the comprehensive categories of documents relevant to your business. We cannot craft generic retention, and content management, policies here. Therefore, purely as an aid to understanding, let's show some broad examples.

An organization should have a schedule for its "defining" documents; things such as records of incorporation, charters, business agreements, etc. These things are permanent. Other permanent items may include meeting minutes of board committees, minutes of evidentiary actions and consents, and records of settlements and releases, for example.

Beyond foundational documents, there will usually be a general schedule for organization-wide content types – things that any department grapples with (such as working papers, minutes to meetings, confidentiality agreements, personnel records, etc.).

In addition to this, each department will have its own schedule for content that is specific to that department (a Marketing department, for example, would produce a retention schedule for things such as marketing plans, sales reports, forecasts, etc.).

Taking Action on Content: Each department's schedule rolls up to the organization's main retention policy. As time goes by, reports are run on a routine basis – usually monthly, and usually by a person in the form of a content/records manager. The reports identify that month's actionable content, in various categories. Action is driven according to content's age from date of creation, and its having reached the end of the retention period. After review by appropriate authorities, the content is either archived or destroyed according to instruction in the Schedule.

Many templates for schedules of content management are available on the web. Organizations with their own legal resources will generate a good part of their retention schedules and content management policies there. Here it is important to understand the concepts so that you can begin to plan your system, and deliver proper expectations when evaluating vendors and implementing a solution.

A Retention Review: Retention drives a large part of your Content Management policy. All content should have a retention period based on categories of subject material (taxonomy); it is the categories that yield the length of the retention period based on business value of that particular category of content. A retention period can be extremely short, extremely long, and anything in between, from months to years. For example, meeting notes' retention period can be extremely short: the schedule can dictate that once formal meeting minutes are produced, the notes are to be immediately destroyed. At the other end of the scale are things such as records of incorporation or organization, partnership and membership agreements, etc. These would be permanent. Other content can have a conditional retention period: you may choose to retain employee attendance records for a period of four years after the end of employment, for example.

Retention must comply with any laws governing content, and any other regulations. Also, your organization will be legally obligated to retain all content relevant to pending or reasonably anticipated litigation, investigations and administrative proceedings. Here, we cannot and do not want to be seen as advocating a system for obfuscating truth or sheltering an organization from consequence to actions of bad faith or bad business. However, in an age of many frivolous lawsuits, we can see value in reviewing content for potential liability on a proactive basis. We must recognize the importance in moving and removing dead-value content from our active environment.

We must maintain an efficient, relevant, *useful*, bank of content, and that is a laudable goal and achievement. In fact, archiving and destructing content on a disciplined retention schedule has become a duty within the true Business-Technology Weave, and is a crucial process in our overall management of content.

CONTENT: BUSINESS ENLIGHTENMENT, AND KNOWING WHERE WE ARE

We must realize that managing your organization's content requires a strong, steady commitment on Business' part, and it must in fact be *Business' lead* in getting this off the ground. There must be understanding and sanction from the top. There must be enterprise-wide sponsorship. There must be a strong business presence in the BIT meetings. In specific project management meetings, there must be a solid, knowledgeable business representative for each phase of the project's implementation. In this regard, and most others, IT will help design and will deliver the crank that turns and satisfies the process – but Business must define the *business requirements and expectations* of the crank. The *business process* that the crank will turn must *first* be identified.

These needs of the business are based on its size, nature, number of locations, volume of content, regulatory requirements, risk management, protection against liabilities, employee oversight, and anything else the business requires of content management. Don't make the mistake that so many other organizations make, on so many other initiatives: do not try to make this an IT-driven initiative: Business cannot drop content management on IT and say "take care of us." This must be Business-driven. It is, after all, business-content that will be managed according to internal and external requirements and standards best known by Business.

Remember that IT can, and should, do research and make suggestions. But remember too that IT's primary purpose is to align a right-sized solution to the policy and process defined by, and required by, Business. When we make projects such as Content Management, and the creation of associated policies, *Business-driven*, we guarantee *Business* sanction, *Business* sponsorship, and full *Business* participation and commitment. IT's participation in these regards is already guaranteed by its report to, and subordinate status to, Business. For Business and IT: Make sure that these understandings are "Where You Are."

THE PROLIFERATION OF UNSTRUCTURED DATA

We know that business success will increasingly depend on the most efficient use of its information assets. These assets must be centrally managed for security purposes, and for quick dissemination to where they're needed. To do this, we need a special structure around data – *all data* - to manage it. But in the vast majority of organizations, information is scattered throughout a variety of resources and vessels. There is no cohesive, managed plan of access according to actual work, leverage, or liability to be had by the content of the individual information asset. The data is unstructured – that is, there is no ready "handle" by which to identify data according to its relevancy, its level of importance, or its possible liability.

We have things locked up on servers, workstations, filed in various cabinets, and piled on desks. Content is parsed, fragmented, dispersed, etc., between electronic documents, e-mail, images, and hardcopy – all being managed, if at all, within discreet silos of various systems. Under these circumstances, the content is not only difficult to leverage – it is difficult to ensure that the most current version of information is shared across the organization. It is even difficult to guarantee that the organization's various disciplines are presenting compatible information to the outside. Yet, The Gartner Group reports that 80% of all information generated by business today consists of *unstructured data*.

Compounding this situation is the estimate that the average employee spends 50% of his or her time looking for things.

What exactly is unstructured data? Unstructured data is anything that lies outside of a centrally managed, and accessible, "repository." (A repository can have special meaning, and we'll revisit it shortly). Unstructured data is generally in the form of documents, spreadsheets, presentations, e-mails, and any other electronic form for which no automated central control can be exercised.

A piece of unstructured electronic content (such as a document) does not represent a "record." It does not belong to a community of other records, sharing similar structure and collective maintenance, through a common base of data: a database. Therefore, it's not that we're refusing to leverage these unstructured items (through the lever of common, related, or timely content) it's that we've never *had* that lever with this unstructured material.

Unstructured data also exists in the form of hardcopy data. When hardcopy has no centrally managed measures for leveraging content, we know that reinforcing subject matter can be scattered throughout all manner of departments and disciplines; residing in filing cabinets, on shelves, on desktops and in desk drawers. Frequently it's stacked on the floor, or hidden away in boxes. Industry analysts estimate that Fortune 500 companies lose $12 billion each year because they cannot manage and take full advantage of unstructured content.

Regardless of your size – if you don't know something exists, *you can't use it*; if you can't find it, *you can't use it*; if you've lost it, *you must recreate it*; and if it takes time to find it, you've *lessened your efficiency in using it.* This kind of inefficiency and duplicated effort is plain unaffordable.

Unstructured Data's Other Liability: Consider too that it is impossible for a central authority to state with ringing certainty that your organization is not harboring inappropriate content. Are you certain that employees aren't downloading obscene or illegal material? Can you certify that people aren't passing around defamatory information through e-mail? Can you be certain that employees are not using company e-mail accounts to post to Internet sites and blogs (web logs, message boards) that support positions or advocacy that is contrary to your organization's positions? Can you be certain that employees aren't using these same company accounts as reference when ordering products and services of questionable repute? All of these things leave an audit trail, outside the scope of your control in the absence of content management. These things can impact your organization's good name and can bring harm to your business.

What about hardcopy and portable media? How can you know that laxity and carelessness aren't contributing to loss of this material? Anyone can print out sensitive information, or download it to portable disc, take it to an offsite meeting, and leave it behind. How do you know whether staff is complying with your Acceptable Use Policy for this content and associated resources? Without some kind of structure for review and report on data, you can be certain of nothing. This is the gross inefficiency and liability that springs from unstructured data, the associated lack of control, and the uncertainties it brings. Uncertainties will be increasingly unaffordable to business, as we shall see in upcoming chapters.

Structured Data is "Unstructured" Relative to the Enterprise: Within the emerging necessities for leverage of content, and management of liability, we have to recognize something else. Not only is unstructured data outside of a central control. Even structured data, such as records in databases, and e-mail within systems, is not within a central control. The records are not leveraged across and with the full enterprise of information. This is because structured data is only actionable within its own native (structuring) application; database records within the database application, and e-mail records within the e-mail system, as but two examples.

Any of your other disparate systems of managed data, such as the accounting system, core-business management systems, claims systems, HR systems, and so on, suffer the segregation from other systems' data and content. This segregation of data is normally an asset: it is necessary for data and system integrity. But from the content management perspective, it's a liability. Therefore, absent a true content management system, structured data has no central control when viewed in the totality of the organization's enterprise-wide content. Much of this content can be ancillary and extremely important in the context of certain necessary views where comprehensibility is essential. This ancillary content can be other structured content, silo'd in its own application's control, or it can be relevant unstructured data.

For example, records within core business applications, such as customer or member records, are only searchable, retrievable and reportable through those native applications. That is, each customer record exists within the control of an application system, and can contribute to report information when combined with data *from other customer records, from within that same application.*

Suppose you wanted all the information, as of a certain date, that your organization harbors for a client - EFG Corporation. Perhaps upcoming litigation is driving your concern. You want all statuses regarding EFG from your main client business application; all relevant e-mails from respective employees and client contacts; all policies referencing EFG; all letters and correspondence; and location of all hardcopy reports and products regarding

EFG Corporation. Without an independent system that manages all content, you cannot automate a comprehensive, enterprise-wide search of electronic content by criteria. Too, without the electronic cataloging of hardcopy, you cannot query content's physical location in support of this current need.

Assembling a comprehensive report in this regard would involve searching for data within many controlling systems, manual assembly of some data, and some kind of tedious collation from the many disassociated parts. Here, your best option is to produce reports from the disparate systems, and then tediously assemble and format information.

And – you'd have no real way of knowing if you had captured all relevant content. So, in the context of "full asset leverage and liability management," even structured data is "unstructured." If you are interested in, and need, true content management, you must structure all of your data for dictate by an overarching system in order to achieve ready action and oversight.

Business users today need a means by which they can approve and review content during its creation and use, regardless of format, regardless of its location. They must be able to search for and quickly find content. They must access the most current versions of various content. They need to be able to repurpose and share content (as opposed to reinventing the wheel). They must have confidence that when seeking content, they are finding all relevant, authorized content. And, they must identify and dispose of content at the end of its useful life.

QUALIFYING TO IDENTIFY A SOLUTIONS PARTNER

Delivering content management to the organization requires an outside solutions partner – a vendor. The vendor will supply and help to fit their content management product – a system - to the organization's needs. It is important, therefore, that your organization understands the nature of your content, the business processes that rely on this content, and the products, services, and positions that your content supports. Come to agreements regarding content in your BIT meetings, select a content/project manager, and project management team.

Have the project manager research content management in order to qualify their understanding of it. The PM should task other project members for the gain of necessary knowledge too. Here, Business leaders should avail themselves of all material at their disposal – content management is detailed very nicely on the web. Outside training classes are available too. Thus qualify the organization to solicit vendor presentations as potential fits to your content management needs.

Just as there is no "magic ignorance," there are no magic vendors. Don't expect to have vendors come in to educate you from a cold-start regarding content management. Do some research, understand your needs thoroughly, review this chapter as necessary, and be an informed player. It is ok and necessary to query vendors and to learn from them – but you must be able to judge any vendor's veracity, capacity, and true value. To do that, you need some solid base knowledge – and you need to fully understand what you expect from the vendor in vetting them against, and in fulfilling, your needs.

CONTENT'S COMPONENT PARTS

Let's now understand content's form in regards to some component parts. We're not yet talking about categorization of content according to subject (taxonomy). First, we're going to identify *formats* of content so as to enrich our collective view. In other words, these are the many file types that subject matter can be spread across.

Some vendors may refer to a slightly different set of definitions for various content, but most vendors will be close to these identifications:

- Electronic documents
- Database records
- Web content
- Other digital assets, such as native-file:
  - Photos
  - Artwork
  - Audio
  - Video
- Hardcopy assets.

Your organization may also have its own idea for how it would like to identify groups of content. You may yet have a large stock of microfiche, for example. Further, your organization will have its own priorities and weights of importance regarding management of certain content. That is, the content type that is most worthy of tight control. A media company would place a high importance on tracking digital assets such as photos, images, streaming video, and artwork for example, while a law firm would be interested in tracking case files, status of litigation, and other documentation.

What's important is that you understand your content, your needs, and how well various vendors' solutions will mesh with those needs. In this way, you can select the best vendor for purpose of gaining a full solutions partner. Let's provide a definition and discussion of each of these content areas:

Electronic Documents: The term "document" was originally used to describe a file created by a word processor, such as MS-Word, or WordPerfect. However, the line between files produced by word processing and other applications has become blurred: A word processing application can be used to produce graphics, and a graphics application can produce words. Therefore, for purpose of this discussion, we'll define an electronic document as any file, produced by an application, that is not controlled by a database, and which relies on text to establish its context and meaning. Most organizations today (with their associated policies), and vendors, (with their associated content management applications), will define documents that way. These would include the following files: documents (such as those produced by word-processing), spreadsheets, presentations, and other text files. Note that a spreadsheet is a database (each row a record, and each column a field of data within the records) – but most spreadsheets are not themselves a record within a larger database – that is, there is no application providing control and whereabouts of spreadsheets. Spreadsheets are "documents" in the context of content management. Too, note that a presentation can be made up primarily of pictures (slides with photos, for example). However, these overall presentation files will not have context without the text of captions, and there are usually interim slides which may be all text. In these regards, presentations too are considered documents. Documents almost always represent *unstructured* data.

It is sometimes easier to understand what a document (or, unstructured data) is, once we understand what a record (or, structured data) is:

Records: Records are files that share common characteristics and *structure*. They reside in a database, and that database generally shares the record files' information through use of an associated business application. The business application may be effecting the intelligent use of data from a variety of related, or relational, databases - all under the purview of that particular business application. From the user's view, all maintenance and activity in using these records, and their content, is achieved through the business application.

Records are structured data, in that their form is dictated by a record template of defined fields for specific types of information. The records are centrally managed through the application. Through this control, the data these records harbor is reportable and deliverable within a specific context. That context is the finite content that the business application, associated databases, and associated records, contain. In other words, the application cannot deliver that which it does not harbor or control.

Think about a customer management system – it will have any number of reports that can be run for output: things like total orders per customer, outstanding invoices, customer demographics, etc. However, from the perspective of content management, the data is not structured for ready use with other data that exists outside of that specific database system (that other data can be unstructured documents, or other records with their own separate structure and context). There is no ability to leverage a more comprehensive report that takes full advantage of *all* of your organization's information assets.

For example, you may wish a report that uncovers *all* content in your organization according to a defined period of inactivity for clients: your ultimate aim may be to archive all of that data relevant to these "dead" clients. It would be nice to pull-the-string in collecting a comprehensive report of all documents, records, web references, e-mails, hardcopy content location, and any other digital assets regarding these clients, and to simultaneously create an action-window through which we can make ultimate disposition of this latent data in one powerful, swift, movement.

Another example would be an agency that is tasked to provide content to another allied agency, according to a criteria in support of a combined mission. It would be very important to fulfill that criteria in the most comprehensive manner, and provide *all* relevant content. We can't allow systems' inhibitions to dictate content's availability. We must make *the content's nature and the call for that content* the priority in delivering total quality of information.

Not all vendors and solutions can yet accommodate the myriad forms of structured data – however, the day will come when structured data of any sort will be able to be a part of your comprehensive content management solution. (As necessary, bookmark this idea somewhere on your 5-year plan).

Web Content: Web content is material that is meant for access via the Internet. It poses an interesting challenge. Web content must be managed in the usual fashion of "full asset leverage and liability management" of course. Much web content is posted for easy access by the organization's own employees, but largely web content exists for people outside of your organization: members, customers, clients, prospects, partnering agencies, etc. It must therefore be current, accurate, and potent.

But unlike other content, web content has a unique consideration. Web content can have a built-in inefficiency: the content's creator is frequently not the one who makes delivery of it to the ultimate destination. To understand this, consider other content: e-mail is dispatched to its destination by *you*, the writer of that content. Documents (word processing, spreadsheets, etc.) are created by you, and can be stored and disseminated to a destination very easily by *you*. Data entry personnel enter records *directly* into their destination - a business system.

However, if you are not managing your web content effectively, the content creator/authority *cannot* put that content to its destination: *the website*. The creator must hand it to a web developer. Part of web content management, therefore, is to go beyond leveraging and accounting for data. It is also a means to enable content creators and authorities to post content directly to the web. This eliminates the involvement of a developer and thus creates a cost benefit and an efficiency.

Digital Assets, other: Other digital assets that your organization may posses are largely graphics files in their native format (such as JPGs, MP3s, etc., before incorporation to a document). They can be artwork, photos, video files, audio files, etc. You may also consider throwing other assets into this category, such as portable content: removable hard drives, flash memory, floppy discs, tapes, PDAs, CD-ROM and DVD discs, etc.

Hardcopy: Hardcopy is physical material, such as reports output, printed e-mails, regular mail, accumulated material from other sources, etc. For our definition here, it can be helpful to think of hardcopy material as ready-read. That is, you don't need a collaborative system to expose hardcopy's content (the way you need a word-processor application to read an electronic document, or a drive to read a disc). Hardcopy content is independent - you just pick it up and access (read) it.

THE CONTENT MANAGER

We've established background regarding content management. Let's introduce one more important thing: a *content manager* in the form of a qualified person. Increasingly, Content Managers (or if you prefer, Records Managers) are operating within a certified discipline. Most if not all of the standards regarding the general duties of a content/records manager are detailed on the web. Organizations that are about to embark on a full-scale content management solution and system should hire or delegate a content/records manager at the outset of the project. This person also is a logical choice for this project's selection as project manager. As with all projects, make this selection carefully:

It is this person who will drive the organization's qualification for selection, implementation, and use of a system.

GETTING TO THE "SYSTEM" OF CONTENT MANAGEMENT

Instituting management of content where there has been no real management is a daunting challenge to most. There are so many forms of content, in so many differing structures, in so many different places, within the authority of so many different individuals and departments: Yet, if we can understand one area, we can understand them all. The principles are the same.

Let's gain an understanding for the management of unstructured electronic *document* content first (your word-processing documents, spreadsheets, presentations, and any other unmanaged electronic, unstructured, data). This is an area that most organizations tackle first – and, an area that is frequently most in need of control. We can say that unstructured electronic documents take this priority because, conversely, structured (database related) content is at least managed to the degree of their native applications.

We can also afford to prioritize electronic documents over hardcopy assets in most cases. This is because there is a comparative advantage regarding hardcopy content: ordinarily, it at least exists where you can see it. Because hardcopy content is physical, you have a better chance of at least sensing where common subject matter exists. We can point to a file cabinet and declare: "Those are accounting records." And, "There are more accounting records over there in those cabinets." It is more difficult to do the equivalent with electronic data.

Our understanding of the methods employed for unstructured electronic documents - and lessons learned - then position the organization to effectively take on other areas of content, in-turn.

Electronic Document Management – A System of Control: Think of content management as an establishment of control over data by *enriching it*. We enrich data by assigning information tags to individual electronic content – to individual files. These tags mark the file according to what it contains – that is, according to its content. Once tagged and so marked, an associated application system can grab and assemble that data with other data. This enables and simplifies our research of data; and enables our ability to report on data for administrative purposes. This tagging (enriching) of data is effected through the assignment of metadata to the individual document files.

Metadata has been described simply as *data about data*. This is a great definition for our purposes. Metadata tags are based on the subject matter and other general attributes of the specific document's content, and can include such information as:

- Document Title
- Category (or Categories; based on Taxonomy)
- Author
- Abstract or summary info
- Access (permissions)
- Usage history
- Keywords (dates, places, individuals, etc.)
- High-value concepts
- Disposition date (archive or destruct triggers)

The real power comes when metadata is automatically applied to documents, records, web content, and other digital assets according to a schema, or template. Various templates contain prepared metadata for each condition of content in your organization, according to policy. These prepared templates are then assigned to electronic workspace folders – much like those folders that are already in your network environment.

When you create content, and file it in a relevant folder based on content's subject matter, the metadata is *automatically* applied to that document. A dialog box with default descriptive (enriching) information tags pops up. The document's creator accepts the metadata as is, or can manually edit specific fields of metadata. Once accepted, the metadata is tagged to that document, and it becomes *managed content*. When we query data based on content-criteria that is available through this metadata, we receive all relevant documents which satisfy our query - in a *fast and comprehensive way*. The structure that supports the linkage of metadata templates to folders, and which supports all other action and reporting utilities within the managing of content, is a data *Repository*.

The Repository: The Repository is a component part of the vendor-delivered, overall content management solution. User action is taken on data through their normal native applications – a word-processing application in the case of a word-processing document, for example – but with the added benefit of the Repository's control and enhancements to data (such as the metadata tagging). Further, an allied Content Management software application accesses the Repository to perform content management and administrative functions - such as finding, reporting on, and taking disposition on content.

Various vendors may have differing names for it, but essentially a Repository is a vessel for data. As desired, it can mimic your current network structure of folders and permissions. This way, it will present a familiarity to users as they negotiate for files, and save new files. In this regard, the Repository is relatively transparent – but it brings with it several very important utilities. The Repository represents the achievement of a specialized, central, storehouse of data. It not only will have a similar structure of filing as a network hierarchy, the Repository will facilitate *proper* filing and control of new content as it gets created, according to subject matter. It manages data's security. It maintains and facilitates reportage and action on data so as to enable oversight. It does this in a very efficient way, removing this burden from the content's creator and the organization at large. The Repository is the key by which content can be found, accessed, used, repurposed, reported on, and actioned for administrative oversight.

THE LIFE OF A MANAGED DOCUMENT

Essentially, the life of a document and its associated control would go something like this:

Creation: Staff creates new content, perhaps a new word-processing document. This new content may be generated as entirely new material, or it could be content that is being repurposed and built upon (edited and added to) from existing content.

Filing (Storing): The new content is filed, as a file's creator would normally generate and store documents (File, Save, or Save As…, etc.). The Repository will take action based on the file's destination folder; based on the creator's choice of folder according to subject matter, and the content's relation to other like-content.

Categorizing (Taxonomy): Storage is also the means by which content is categorized; by virtue of the folder in which content is stored by the creator. Folders within the Repository will be dedicated to specific categories of content. Depending on your desire, the content management system can also suggest storage and categorization based on its inspection of the document's contents at the time of its creation, and subsequent comparison of key content to an organizational taxonomy table.

Metadata (Tagging): The content's location and categorization also lead to the assignment of key metadata. The document's metadata is assigned by virtue of a metadata template that is associated to each content area (folder). This way, each template's information is leveraged for the tagging of all like-content in a specific folder. The system can also extract specific keywords from documents for inclusion to the metadata, and can generate an abstract or summary.

Delivering/Sharing: Content is now delivered when users query for various categories of content, on keywords, and concepts. Collection and reference of data is now as comprehensive as possible. (You can even have your content/records manager query on content that has specific areas of metadata that are *unpopulated* [unfilled/missing] - for purpose of generating reports concerning these documents. The reports can then be delivered to various content authorities for completing the assignment of metadata to this content).

Re-using and Repurposing: Now that content is locatable, identifiable, accessible and readily understood, it is easily employed for reuse. With proper authority and access, departments can glean knowledge, formatting, and process from other department's content. Further, content can be repurposed: it can be modified and incorporated to new content.

Review and Reporting: Content now is available for review by any appropriate authority. Reports can be run to review all documentation generated in a given day for a specific client, for example. You can view who produced the most effort – who is doing the bulk of the real work?
  This is also where you take action on content in accordance with a retention plan. Disposition dates of documents provide the yield for a monthly report. The report can indicate all documents subject to archive, and subject to destruction (pending review by the appropriate authority, of course). This report can also expose those documents that must have their disposition date adjusted – this can be due to reasons of regenerated business, inquiry, subpoena, discovery, etc.

Action: Once content ages to the point where it is no longer being accessed (easily determined by reports), and is unlikely to provide further, or timely, business value, it can be archived or destroyed.

  - *Archiving*: Archiving the information means that you remove it from your active business environment, and store it somewhere else – perhaps with a vendor who maintains your offsite backups, or in an offsite warehouse where your organization makes other storage of items. Archived material can be compressed and stored on high-density (high capacity) storage media, such as DVDs and CD-ROMs.

This material is cataloged, and can always be referenced if the organization needs to go back to it. It can even be reintroduced to your active business environment if the need arises – nothing is lost. The purpose in archiving is to prevent the active business environment from becoming overrun with useless data. Taken to its logical extreme, if you don't manage the removal of relatively useless data, it will eventually outweigh your useful data.

- *Destruction*: Business material that becomes completely obsolete, as determined by Business, and technical documentation as determined by IT, should be destroyed. Anything that serves no further purpose to the organization should be destroyed.

A Practical Example: Let's provide a quick practical example in the life of a document: let's say that the organization has a current project; Project LMN, and associated content. The project's scope or domain could be anything: a marketing initiative, it could be legal representation of a client, it could be a new software solution and its implementation.

Project LMN documents reside in a specific *Project LMN Folder* - that folder would have an associated metadata-template for the management of this project's content. Also, the main folder would have attendant subfolders, such as an LMN Budget folder for specific budget info and docs regarding the project. Of course, specific subfolders to the main project folder would have their own metadata templates too. Subfolder-templates can inherit the main folders metadata if you like. However, many subfolders will require at least some unique metadata information. For example, it's likely that budget material associated with the project has a specific authority for access and edit; so, a budget subfolder within the main project folder would have a metadata template that differs, and it will tag budget information with different metadata. Of course, authorized content creators and users within any folder can edit and tweak metadata to reflect the desire for control and disposition of that particular content.

Creation of new LMN content, such as a document, would bring up a dialog box requiring a destination folder – once identified, that folder's default metadata would fill this new document's specific metadata template. This would tag the document based on its content, and its match to taxonomies used in the organization. Thus, when we create and file content in a specific folder, it gets tagged with appropriate metadata based on the folder's template. In this manner, controlling elements that are common to *all* Project LMN material are applied to content: Such things as its category (Project LMN), its life, its disposition instructions at the end of that life, its securities and permissions, among other things.

In addition, other specific tags relevant to the document itself are made. The contents can be surveyed by the system in order to automatically generate very specific metadata that is relevant only to that individual document - extracting keywords such as author, names, places, dates and other key information. The system extracts these things based on built-in pattern recognition. These keywords can be gleaned based on a predetermined list provided by the vendor's application, and by your own internal table of keywords - you can build your own custom pattern recognitions.

This document could also inhabit multiple categories: for example, its metadata could indicate that it is a general budget document, *and* contains specific Project LMN budget components. The document would have a disposition date for archive or destruction, in accordance with the project's standing in your retention plan, and as necessary, within compliance for any of the other categories.

The creating user would either accept the metadata, or edit it – as authorized. All new content that is generated and saved within the Project LMN area of the Repository will automatically assume the appropriate metadata for the management of that content. Now the document is enriched according to attributes and keywords associated with that document – things your users can identify and use when searching for LMN content. This way, authorized users can search, browse, and aggregate critical content regardless where the content is stored.

Let's say a creator generates a document regarding the project, but chooses to store that document in their User folder. This is ok, because the document's overall subject matter (Project LMN) will still allow appropriate categorization, and subsequent associated default metadata. The system will still review the document's content in order to generate the other specific metadata. In fact, a likely scenario would be one whereby an authority would arrange for a Project LMN subfolder within all User folders for those staff associated with the project – using the same default metadata template for the main Project LMN Folder. Therefore as you go along, all Project LMN documents will be traceable, retrievable, and actionable no matter where they reside – in user folders, central project folders, or even e-mail, if desired, and no matter what the form of the document: wordprocessing, spreadsheet, presentation, or e-mail.

We've now enabled a powerful way to identify the Project LMN files, and anyone associated with the project can search for them, and if authorized, access and use them. When we capture content, we can: develop; manage; review;

approve; archive; check-in/check-out; maintain version control; perform full-text and metadata search; optimize team communication; automate routing requirements; and deliver notification of status changes and new documents. We can provide specific information and the surrounding context needed to optimize work within the project team. We add value by exposing such related material as additional documents, tasks, calendar items, and team e-mail. Our intellectual capital is in a secure, centralized repository. All project matter is centralized and accessible.

This material can also be copied and repurposed within other projects and initiatives when it has relevant content. Too, when Project LMN is long completed and done, and its material no longer of any practical use in the active environment, this content can be fully identified and acted upon for ultimate disposition.

Existing Content

What about an organization's existing content? How does the huge amount of existing material get tagged with relevant metadata? You may be thinking that this is an exhaustive, manual task invoking massive effort. Not so. First, let's review how we achieve an enormous economy of scale in regard to our efforts here. Keep in mind that formerly unstructured data becomes structured by virtue of its residency in the Repository. The real power of the Repository is its content locations (folders) and associated metadata templates that are built and assigned to these folders. We also establish taxonomies for the organization, and build reference tables, which help categorize content according to subject matter. All of this helps to automate the assignment of specific metadata to existing electronic content.

The Repository Does the Work: Here, the system has the means to review the content, and gleans relevant, specific metadata. Therefore, we expend effort *once* in creating a structure and control for the enrichment of content. Upon implementation of a Repository, your organization and your vendor import your existing data into it, according to a map that sends your data to the right folders based on content. Once your information has been moved into the Repository, it is already tagged with metadata, and is now immediately manageable in a powerful new way. Your existing data becomes true content within a managed system upon this importation.

In terms of user data and User folders, simply require that everyone in the organization have a similar structure of subfolders within their User folders. There will be variance by department, but everyone in the organization should have core User subfolders for budget documents, personnel documents, performance documents, committee work, and so on. Set metadata templates for these, and import the users' data. Specific departments' members will have unique follow-on structures within their User folders: for example, IT staff will have subfolders that differ from users in Accounting, and so on. Here, the individual departments and users will create their own metadata templates for these areas (within the guides of the policy, and according to individual department schedules of retention - subject to review and approval).

The Rest of It: We haven't forgotten about your other content: images, structured (database) records, hardcopy, etc. This information requires enriching metadata and the actionable, reportable, system of oversight too. Some organizations choose to scan hardcopy as images into an electronic system. Some just create managing electronic records regarding hardcopy's location, and associated key metadata. With the knowledge we've gained through our exposure to electronic document control, you can scale and apply those principles to your other content, in accordance with your assessment of needs.

The important thing for every organization is to determine where the bulk of the burden is: what sort of content represents the *majority* of your content, and what sort of content harbors the most purpose, and conversely, the most liability? Then work to create the appropriate business processes that support effective content management, and find the vendor/product that suits your situation the best. We will discuss vendors shortly.

Remember this: The organization achieves enormous efficiency and power by employing a content solution that can *automatically categorize* documents based on keywords, phrases, and other contextual cues. When you have a solution that can do this, metadata *too* is automatically generated based upon this categorization and tagged to the content. The system can also further associate metadata based on references within tables that you create. Each piece of content has then assumed a small enriching set of data (metadata) that can be exploited by a content management application, for gain. The power of this is becoming apparent to more organizations, and more and more are tapping into the true power of their content assets.

CONTENT'S LIABILITIES: MANAGING THE DARK SIDE

It's becoming increasingly apparent that unmanaged content yields inefficiency and waste. This includes storage costs; the cost to efficiency when trying to locate, repurpose and assemble data; the outright loss of data; and the expenditure of effort when trying to "clean up" content absent a cohesive, comprehensive system.

There too is a dark side of content: inappropriate and even illegal content – things such as porn, copyrighted music and video, unlicensed software, games, advocacy material that goes against law or your corporate policy, etc. We'll revisit the nature of inappropriate content in additional detail during *Security*, but whether your organization is laboring under an explosion of content or not, there is that crucial necessity to know *what* you harbor at all times. Through this, you can mitigate risk and harm posed by outdated, inappropriate, and even illegal, material.

The Floodgate: Are You Recognizing it? Are You Regulating It? The past decade or so of ready data exchange afforded by e-mail and the Internet has opened a floodgate. There is now a wide conduit of flowing information going in and out of your organization. In the course of each day, whatever is going out, and whatever is coming in, is not readily observable by any comprehensive Business oversight. It's not even readily observable by IT – no one has time to watch and report on a steady stream of data. For this reason, it's important for any organization to make periodic survey and report on content. Understand that a survey of content is not the only oversight being applied. A variety of systems such as firewalls, virus screens, a solid Acceptable Use policy, and staff training all contribute to the safe accumulation, and the safeguarding, of content. But in the context of Content Management and our use of it against the "dark side," we need the comprehensive ability to know what content we have, we need to be able to report on it, and we need to be able to take appropriate action on it – in an effective and efficient manner.

Business Content and its Exposures: Your content represents potential exposure to clients, customers, members, yourself, and anyone else upon whom you build information. Your organization accumulates sensitive information about your constituents. Legal firms have long recognized the need to manage content. In the easiest example to understand, let's consider old, outdated, no longer useful information on your computer network. This information takes up unnecessary storage space. While it's true that electronic storage is inexpensive these days, it does take up space nonetheless, and just creates more junk information through which to wade when you're trying to find something useful.

This junk information also extends the time of backups, and adds difficulty in mounting recoveries to content when necessary. It can add to insurance costs. Destruction of this data, or moving it to an archive, removes it from your active environment and helps to keep your overall operations smooth and efficient.

Also, in the case of destruction, you bring the added benefit of peace of mind to the situation as you no longer have to worry about damaging information that may reside in content that is plain obsolete from a business perspective.

Your content also represents exposure to your own organization's good reputation. If your outdated data is subpoenaed in action against a client, customer, member or other (your organization itself?), your standing in your particular business world is going to suffer. You must guard your reputation through responsible management of content. It's an obvious win to eliminate as much obsolete content as you can – in compliance with all law and regulation. This is not to advocate the destruction of material that requires keeping.

Let's next talk about some simple categories of content liability:

APPROPRIATE BUSINESS CONTENT THAT IS BEING MISUSED, ABUSED, OR INAPPROPRIATELY EXPOSED

Abuse or misuse of content can be many things: it can be the making of unauthorized electronic copies, the storage of which happens in multiple folders, generating subsequent confusion over which version of content is authorized, correct, and current. It can be the erroneous or malicious destruction or corruption of data. It can be unauthorized or accidental dissemination of content, either within the organization, or transmitted or carried outside of the organization. For this reason, many systems of content management have "check in/check out" features. That is, you must request content by filling in a template that collects and logs information: who you are, your use for the material, the date you're checking it out, and your anticipated date of "return" of the material (that is, when you'll save any revisions). The system may enforce a required date for finish with the material, as desired. Creating a log of who has what, for what purpose, and for how long is a very powerful way to ensure appropriate use of content and business resources, and to expose abuse.

Also protecting against misuse, abuse and inappropriate exposure of data is such things as version control, notification of status changes, and notification of new content – all of these things report statuses to identified individuals (such as a content/records manager), and add to the knowledge for what is happening with critical content.

Business Content that is No Longer Needed: Accumulating information that is unmanaged eventually reaches a tipping point. It starts to impact our effective use of practical data. How many organizations have junk-data? Most. If you've experienced reports that contain erroneous data and conclusions, if you've wondered which copy of policy is current and in effect, if you've received complaints from customers about receipt of multiple copies of the same mail – if your employees are burning time in dealing with these kinds of things - you need to manage your content.

You also face mounting costs – some of which may be seemingly small and incremental, but they will begin to add up. Things such as storage costs, backup media, time spent searching through a vast volume of content (an increasing percentage will be wasted search time), and most importantly, issuing corrections and fixing problems that arise from the dissemination of erroneous content. Consider this liability: does your organization issue instruction, statement, policy, position, agreement, provision, etc. to anyone? In these regards you need a high degree of certainty and accuracy.

If your organization is harboring content that no longer has business value of any kind, yet which can represent liability and harm through exposure, you must get a handle on it and eliminate it. Here we must emphasize that this action will be taken within applicable law, regulation, and in the absence of any anticipated *pending* outside requirement to hold this data. Absent those, you owe your fellow business travelers the courtesy of proper risk management in these regards. Exposure of data can be injurious. Obsolete data *must go* – and in as timely a fashion as possible.

Once you establish a managed system for identification, use, and action on content, you can remove identified content in a timely way. We can't keep everything around forever, and we shouldn't allow indiscriminate, occasional lurches into clean up efforts. This will yield mistakes, and often puts people in the posture: "when in doubt, throw it out." Your business content assets deserve a managed, disciplined, and accountable approach.

Archiving and Destructing: Once we archive things, we have the advantage that they're still stored somewhere outside of our effective, efficient, active environment, and are therefore retrievable if we ever need them for the occasional or unanticipated reference. When we destroy content, we have reports on file that indicate when specific content was removed, and why.

NON-BUSINESS CONTENT

Non-Business Content that is Benign: Every organization contains content that has little to nothing to do with business. Personal e-mail, voicemail, calendar entries and correspondence are generally tolerated at most, if not all, organizations. People also have download-information from the Internet on their workstations and in network folders: information about hobbies; news articles; how-to information, etc.

They also harbor non-business hardcopy material: catalogs, books, travel information, and so on. What's important regarding this benign information, particularly when it regards any reliance on business systems and resources, is an ability to identify it, to ensure that it is free of harm, and to make sure employees are aware of the limits to which business resources can support personal information and endeavors. This content too should be disposed of when employees are no longer in need of it.

Non-Business Content that is Harmful: Courts have ruled that an organization is liable for damages to individuals who are exposed to harmful content. This is whether the content is sanctioned by, owned by, known by, or tolerated by the organization – or not. For example, someone sued a company because that individual happened to pass a co-worker's PC, on which was displayed pornography. The exposed employee successfully argued that their resultant belief was one of a hostile workplace to a specified gender. There are more details to the story, but the bottom line for our purposes is clear: In this case, the company had a written policy expressly prohibiting the download, storage, and viewing of inappropriate content – including pornography. The company also had robust policies against all manner of harassment.

These did not matter because the organization was judged to have a disregard for a comprehensive knowledge of the content that it harbored, and therefore a lack of care concerning the risk and damage that certain harmful content could present.

Your organization too is responsible for whatever content it harbors. For example, if someone is downloading copyright material for which your organization *has* no rights, it is the organization that can be made to pay for violating copyright laws. Regardless of your policy and your ignorance for the content that you harbor, it will not excuse nor protect your organization from the damages it can suffer. Likewise, if your organization is operating unlicensed software that employees are downloading in violation of your organization's policies, your organization can be made to pay.

People have been known to disseminate defamatory information about organizations, clients and members within and with-out the organization – through e-mail, through message boards, on blogs (web logs) – even on personal websites. Your organization can suffer severe economic damage, and damage to reputation, under these conditions. People have also used their corporate e-mail addresses and identifications to post opinions on publicly accessed forums; opinions that are in opposition to organizational policy. Further, even postings of inconsequential content represent peril if they are made on forums that in and of themselves are off-limits due to other considerations. Any content that can be tied to your organization can pose an extreme liability. In today's environment there is no excuse that suffices when it comes to embarrassing or damaging consequences as the result of inappropriate content.

There too is the simple problem of unauthorized software that competes with or occludes your approved business software's objectives. Employees may be downloading freeware or shareware – there is no outside liability from a licensing standpoint in those regards. But if they are employing databases and data-sets that are external to approved repositories of data, they're not only setting a structure for possible duplication of content, it's unlikely that they're adhering to your organization's standards for integrity, backup, and protection of data. There is also no oversight to evaluate the accuracy of this content, nor to manage it according to policy. In these regards, they are violating a policy of Acceptable Use – as regards both content and business resources.

SIZING THE SOLUTION

By now you should know whether a comprehensive management of content is for you. We're speaking primarily to Business here, as it is the business' needs that drive the requirement for content management. The implementation of content management will be a Business-driven initiative.

If, on the other hand, it is IT that is first aware of gross inefficiencies posed by problems of access, integrity, disposition, or anything else regarding content, certainly IT should make Business aware of potential advantages and rewards to be had in managing the organization's content. However, no matter how debuted for discussion, it will remain a Business-driven fulfillment.

Where the Challenge Lies: If your organization chooses to go forward, your biggest challenge should be the selection of a vendor. We can state that as the main challenge because your organization should now be in a good position to qualify needs and objectives, and to give rise to the other elements of any project, based on this understanding from our prior discussions:

- ♦ Based on a solid understanding of where it is, the organization can identify needs and objectives appropriately in order to define true solutions with strategic value and appropriate returns.
- ♦ Based on a solid understanding of where the organization needs to go, the sale can be made: elements of Business sell themselves on valid needs;

sell senior-most management; and ultimately will sell the rest of the organization.
- IT is sold on the idea, in that they have participated in the appropriate planning circles; have contributed to the identification of needs; and to the identification of appropriate solutions.
- The organization understands the "getting there": the importance of sanction, and establishment of an organization-wide sponsor with authority.
- Your BIT team should be well defined by now and meeting regularly; it is positioned to accept its role in large-scale projects.
- The organization is knowledgeable in selecting project leaders and in constructing project teams.
- The organization understands the importance of group/department owners and their role in supporting a project.
- The organization understands the importance of having a well-defined business process in each area.
- The organization understands the importance of change management, and the basic model for grooming the organization's stance for change:
  - Announce the upcoming change
  - Train for the change
  - Implement the change
  - Support the change

Your organization should now have a solid representation by, or sponsorship of, IT at the highest planning table regarding business initiatives and direction. From this, authorized IT and Business members can carry appropriate information regarding requirements to the BIT meeting.

The BIT meeting will have a riding agenda item concerning content management (and any current large-scale project), with ongoing and evolving specifics. The Business and Technical representatives in this meeting will include the constant attendees – that is, formal BIT team members from management that have influence and interest in the organization's direction – as well as the project manager and any associated/necessary members of the project management team. It will also include the occasioned, specific, group and department owners of designated responsibilities – those people who are responsible for meeting the objectives of the project at the *level of conduct*: out in the business arena. (That is, the people who will ensure that a content management system is utilized properly, and that users will use and administer content within the dictates of the content management policy and solution).

The BIT team will craft requirements documentation for delivery to vendors, who will be invited to compete for the opportunity to become a *solutions-partner* in the delivery of the content management solution.

BIT should also ensure that:

- The organization-wide sponsor of this Business-driven initiative is the one to announce content management's upcoming implementation, the reasons for the implementation, and the expectations and requirements of staff.
- Business elements and areas have well-defined business processes, and where necessary, will sharpen their definition of processes.
- The project manager(s) will meet with business managers, and associated departments, to meet the expectations of business-fit between application and process.
- Business and IT evaluates vendors together: their products, their service standards; where possible their reference sites; and their potential fit to the required solution.

Fulfilling the Challenge: Selecting a Vendor as a True Solutions Partner

These days, many technology vendors strive to be all things to all organizations. They may not only offer solutions to a variety of needs, they likely have different solutions, or scales of solutions, to each specific need. This is to be expected. But these vendors also have radically different and competing approaches to these specific business needs. Who is right? Who is right for *your* organization? Instituting a poor fit regarding content management, or worse, implementing a "false solution" would be debilitating. We need to strip away marketing hype, in order to expose basic truths.

In the early stages, many vendors obfuscate your needs – not necessarily deliberately, but you'll be asking for advice and receiving advice. This advice from vendors will be generated after they pull your needs through their own filters. They'll have their own assumptions and blinders, perhaps miscasting your needs against another customer's that they worked with. Remember to define the actual needs of your business, with accuracy. You must leverage a *comprehensive* understanding of your needs. Your organization may *seem* similar to another – to them. But remember: this is the first time they've seen an organization *exactly* like yours. You must hold them accountable to the value to be had in that condition – and to the standard that your environment is new to them.

You must run their advice and products over your own *thorough* understanding of your needs as best as you possibly can. Keep in mind: Only those people of the organization can readily understand what is necessary for business – the vendor has to survey for it.

This need evidences itself best if you consider the alternative: The alternative is to vet their advice and products against a foggy, poor, or ill defined, understanding of your own needs. This also puts the vendor in a position where they may inadvertently oversell or misapply aspects of their solution. They must first have a solid understanding of your process and needs.

Don't be like some organizations that look for the magic bullet, the magic vendor, some magic revelation - for salvation. Don't rely on that. In getting the best vendor, (to revisit a prior discussion) remember to *qualify* your organization for change.

Getting the Best Vendor Means Evaluating the Best Vendors: Your chances for finding the optimal solutions partner are greatly increased by bringing in the best possible vendors to compete for your business. Identifying potential products and vendors for any project should be routine. You have a wealth of leads. First and foremost, consult with your other solutions partners: IT can describe the needs to their current support vendors, such as network support and disaster recovery partners. Ask them who they use; ask them who their other clients use. Business can ask their outside associates and supports how they handle their content. In other words, consult those with whom you have an association, a relationship, and a trust.

Most organizations will generate a request for proposal (RFP), which details your needs and specifically what you're looking for. It is prudent to phone-screen vendors, through a general description of your RFP and associated requirements. Vendors who express interest, and who interest you, should sign a confidentiality agreement as necessary. The organization should screen as many vendors as seem qualified, and evaluate them against the standards of your requirements.

Review their websites – not just for the obvious content, such as the business partners, mission, products, services, clients, history, etc. – but also for other important things. Websites are revelatory: Is it easy to find what you're looking for? Is the material understandable? Do they provide material for the Business audience, as well as the IT audience? How are they handling their own content? The answers to these questions go a long way toward answering how the vendor will interact with you.

How does the aesthetics of their site strike you? Do they have any online demos or animations of their products? Do *they* capture the best use of the technology at-hand? You can get a real indication here as to how well they'll be able to mesh your needs and process with their technology. As necessary, have them e-mail additional material you feel you need in order to understand their business posture, their products, services, and potential ability to fit your requirements.

The "Difficult" Easy Decision: Bring a number of qualifying vendors through your phone screen into the organization – generally three is the minimum. Additional vendors can be invited in depending on how the initial three perform. When selecting vendors, you want a real decision. There is nothing wrong with discovering that there is a vendor that is heads and shoulders above all others in suiting your needs. That can be dangerous, however. You may be basing your decision on warm feelings that have little to do with the vendor's ability to really match your needs, to suit your style, and to provide a solution that will pay off year in and year out.

Too, it can mean that you haven't brought in the right vendors – you have to have a group of vendors that meet some initial qualification for a look-see. If you've got a "winner" because the other vendors are extremely poor, it may be that someone didn't do the job in staffing vendors for a valid competition. Just be very careful in the case of the "easy" decision that presents itself early on. Consider: the easy decision short-circuits further analysis of vendors in general, and also the specific vendor in question.

Conversely, it is certainly reassuring for the organization when it has a difficult decision between two or more vendors; you feel that the evaluation team did their job, and if you're on that team, you feel well satisfied that you've discovered worthy vendors through due diligence. But there is something else that emerges: in parsing out the best vendor, within a true competition, a selection team has to go deeper and farther into each vendor's posture and offerings. You take a more thorough look. You become imaginative, and examine things you may never have thought about before – perhaps that no one has thought about before. Suddenly, you'll have a Eureka moment, and a vendor will emerge that will evidence itself as *the one*. The decision suddenly becomes clear – and perhaps in retrospect, easy.

Satisfying the "Difficult" Easy Decision: What happens if the first vendor you call is "perfect"? Obviously, if you discover an initial great-looking potential vendor, you cannot relax your standard. Here you must resist the temptation to loosen standards – to just toss in two more – in satisfying a requirement to survey three vendors. This brings the temptation to invite a couple more vendors on what we'll call the "Google" qualification. In this circumstance, we believe we hit on a winner early, and think: "Hey, we'll just Google two more 'content management' vendors, have 'em in and out, and be done with our selection."

Don't be in such a rush to get things moving that you step off a cliff. Don't even be satisfied with two attractive vendors, and get lazy and throw in a mediocre looking vendor as a third "consideration" either. Scramble if you must to identify strong players. Make it so that your decision is *difficult* during the selection process. This forces everyone into a hard-look posture. The hard-look posture is exactly what you want and require during a comprehensive evaluation process.

Evaluating a vendor not only means qualifying their business as a reliable, solid endeavor in general, but also that they have products and solutions that are worthy of your consideration and time. Therefore, looking at what they have to offer should aid the organization in its own understanding of the overall project's fulfillment. Once you have some measure of vendors who look favorable, invite them in for a demonstration of their product(s). Here it is important for the vendor to do some measure of configuration so as to fit their product to your requirements. You should evaluate them on this, too. They should be exposing their product's specific solution to your specific requirements – that is to say, their demo should be *customized* in some measure so as to be relevant to your business. If anyone shows up with a canned presentation that is devoid of specifics to your process, it is evidence that they have discounted your carefully prepared requirements document. Thank them and dismiss them.

Once you have vendors of merit involved and competing for your business, you should make demonstration copies of their application available. Have designated business test users, and create a survey. Where possible, put actual business content into the system and practice with it. Solicit feedback from these test users. Visit the vendor sites. Solicit references from the vendors – talk to the references, and where possible, visit the references and evaluate how they are using the systems and how well these systems fit their business. When you make these visits and evaluations, be sure to include technical and business representatives.

In the case of content management, various vendors will have systems that bias their treatment toward certain kinds of content. You should match the system that is biased most effectively toward your primary content (while still being reasonably effective for all content), whether that's graphics, or text, or images, or web, etc. Require each vendor to speak to their particular strengths (and their weaknesses) regarding your electronic unstructured data, your structured (database) data, your hardcopy data, and any other specific content that you have - by type, volume, location, purpose, etc., and your expectations regarding the share, dissemination, and administration of this content.

When evaluating software, consider who your users are, and how they work. What is their technical level, and their comfort with existing applications? How well do they handle the current workflow? What level of training will they need? These will be major factors in the success or failure of a new system.

THE SYSTEM YOU WANT, VS. THE SYSTEM YOU NEED, VS. THE SYSTEM YOU GET

When the organization has done its job correctly in evaluating needs and vendors (and associated systems), you are able to select a system that meets three important, overarching, criteria. These criteria need to overlay and match as exactly as possible. You get the system you want, which matches the system you need, which matches the system you get. Consider: if you haven't defined "where you are," the system you want may not be what you need. Consider: if you haven't forced a hard decision to the easy one, through competition amongst truly qualified vendors, the solution you need may not match the one you get.

Where possible, try to leverage a system that enables quick user adoption, with little to no training. Desktop productivity tools that are intuitive and user-friendly contribute to a lower cost of implementation and a quick return on investment. So-called best-of-breed solutions may be beyond your organization's budget, and even beyond the capacity of your staff to use. But also, they may just be more bang than you need. Thus, as you look for intuitive interfaces and ease-of-use capability, avoid as you can process and workflow re-engineering, large training efforts, and the potential for a general lack of adoption.

This is not to say that a system that requires training is less desirable. Just bear in mind that whatever effort of training is involved, it must have a payoff in the form of a return. Keep in mind that whatever training effort your present staff goes through, there will be an ongoing, corresponding training burden imposed on new, incoming staff.

The System Serves You – You Don't Serve It: In most cases, try to avoid applications that will dictate your workflow – hopefully the organization has achieved an effective and efficient workflow by its own design, and is looking to automate and enhance it. So, efficiencies should come from automating proven workflow. Also, you want the application to be flexible as time goes by: changes in business may benefit from a reordering of workflow – therefore you don't want an application "solution" locking you into a rigid accommodation to *it*.

We must ensure that the application serves you, and guard against you serving it. Of course, you don't want to cement poor workflow by designing an automated system that rigidly enforces that sort of inefficiency. The consideration and planning that goes into a new business information system provides a good juncture to take a careful look at what you're doing, why you're doing it, and how you're doing it. If you know where you are, know where you're going, and are planning appropriate routes to destinations – you're well qualified.

Remember ~

Keep in mind the goals of managing content: One is to get the right information, in the right format, to the right place, at the right time. Content management not only improves upon your present condition, but also creates new channels of communication and collaboration, and exposes all of your organization's content assets. Powerful combinations of content will always be greater than the sum of the parts. The organization that can most quickly and efficiently organize, distribute and reuse its valuable content assets will outperform its competition, will reduce overhead, and will improve its speed to market. Therefore, it will improve the quality of delivery for products and services. Your organization will eliminate bottlenecks and increase efficiency, and thereby improve productivity.

Another goal is to save time and money by improving productivity of employees by automating the tasks of organizing information. You can maximize your return on investment by making content available across multiple business initiatives, and can cross-reference it for cross-sell and up-sell merchandizing. Unlock hidden assets by exposing content for reuse and repurposing. End the cost of recreating content for a particular need, audience, location, media, distribution device, etc. – or simply because you lost it. Accelerate the development of new initiatives by more effective use of existing content. You can protect brands, stated missions, positions, and levels of service; through consistent naming, descriptions, definitions, and categorization of all enterprise products and services. Enable better business decisions by accessing and understanding all relevant asset information for fully informed decisions.

Another major goal is to limit liability posed by unnecessary accumulation of content, loss of content, use of outdated content, and inappropriately exposed content. All content represents potential harm: You have appropriate business content that can be injurious to a client, customer, member or business partnership if exposed in the wrong manner. You have content that can harm your business itself. Most content is material that was generated or accumulated in good faith in the legitimate conduct of business – but even this content can, and likely will, steadily lose value over time as it ages.

Recognize too that almost every organization has other content that is simply inappropriate material. It has been created, downloaded, disseminated or otherwise inappropriately gathered and distributed by your employees. You must identify and eliminate this material on an intelligent and ongoing basis.

Once we intelligently manage business information according to content, we can accurately represent the organization to others as being a safe, and safeguarding, entity in the realm of our business-intelligence. And, we show that our business-intelligence is wielded in optimum fashion for them – on behalf of our members, clients, constituents, etc. – and on behalf of the organization's own staff. We deliver confidence and success in this area as in all others.

18

SECURITY:
MANAGING PROTECTION, RELIABILITY, RISK...
AND RECOVERY

Chance is a word devoid of sense; nothing can exist without a cause.

Voltaire

Security is safety from harm and freedom from unacceptable risk. Managing security represents an ongoing protection, and the exclusion of negative consequence that can arise from risk. This is achieved through responsible precaution, planning, policy, and practice. As we manage our security, we find that we have to actively survey for areas of risk, or chance, in order to identify them. Further, we have to reevaluate known risk on a recurring basis, as these so-called knowns undergo change.

We also have to identify completely new risks, as they will certainly come in the face of the change continuum. We must expose any chance that something undesirable could happen, and take action. As Voltaire states above, nothing can exist without a cause, therefore risk and its potential yields are identifiable - <u>if</u> we survey for things that can cause us harm.

Our unqualified success in this sphere is required – and possible. Even natural disasters and deliberate human harm, which are not particularly predictable, can be accommodated – and indeed must be accommodated in some manner of policy and plan – to the degree that you can ensure recovery and business continuity in the face of such disaster. At the same time, we can't forget routine security and its proper maintenance.

When we talk about security, we must realize that all reasonable, proactive, measures must be identified and taken to secure business: Users have accounts that grant them appropriate access to systems and data; content is managed according to confidentialities, exposures and liabilities; equipment, platform, infrastructure, and supplies are safeguarded; assets are inventoried and protected; technical procedures and business processes are documented; appropriate backup and recovery methods and strategies are in place; personnel are cross-trained; recovery partners are engaged and service level agreements are in place, suitably sized, and understood...

Further – we need to build an awareness, and a knowledge base, regarding security. In this manner beliefs, values, and standards are incorporated into organizational policy. Security is reinforced within job descriptions and performance evaluations so as to adhere to proper accountabilities, and to maintain appropriate discipline. In other words, we have a *mission* of security, with a solid, documented understanding for what constitutes secure daily business even within the routine. In this way, everyone understands his or her role within, and support to, the security mission.

SECURITY: A DEADLY SERIOUS BUSINESS

Later in this chapter, and specifically in *What's At Stake*, we will examine the organization's security stake in its "security wrap." That is, the organization's reliance on, vulnerabilities within, and obligation to, a larger surrounding public good (think of a business in News Orleans).

First, let's understand the local scope of organizational security – it is quite enough to get our attention. Security is increasingly serious because there is a nexus that is heavy in terms of your business survival. This nexus is brought about by:

- *A Shift of Foundation*: There is the business shift of foundation to electronic enablement and support; this is a large dependency. Any dependency creates a matching vulnerability.

- *An Expansion of Access*: There is expansion of access to this foundation: to those known to you; to those unknown to you. In expanding access to those who advance your business, you expand the potential to those who would bring you harm.

- *An Expanding Risk of Harm*: There is therefore an expanding risk of harm (natural and intentional).

Here again, as we go through our security discussion, we must make a thorough exposure of bad, in order to avoid the appliqué of good on top of it.

SECURITY IN AN IMPERFECT WORLD

Security isn't just an abeyance of harm: In an imperfect world, we suffer harm of varying degrees on occasion. Therefore security must mean that we mitigate risk of harm, and even eliminate risk where possible. At the same time, we must ensure that we can recover, and recover *quickly*, from harm that comes our way due to circumstances beyond our direct control. We must plan for contingencies such as catastrophic equipment failure, natural disasters, simple human error, and deliberate acts of sabotage or terror that are not directly foreseen.

The prudent organization surveys its environment for risk. The survey will expose areas over which we can assume complete control, and it will also yield potential causes for harm that we can only mitigate. Too, we'll become more deeply aware of outside risk; that is, to the larger surrounding public good. Large-scale harm to the public infrastructure can present great risk to the organization's path, and even its existence. We will explore those risks shortly, and related activities for participation. An organization can make a meaningful contribution to a society's wellness in terms of security, and in bettering its own security standing. After all – the organization has a stake in this.

Our survey leads us to identify and agree to a likelihood of events, and to rank associated risk accordingly so that we can apportion critical resources in the most effective manner. This manner must support elimination or mitigation of risk on an intelligent, real-world basis. Various organizations will have their own special security needs based on mission, size, location(s), content, native risks, available resources, and other factors. For example: Your survey may yield a need for offsite reservation of space, equipment, and content to accommodate even the ultimate risk – total loss of a business location. Other organizations may not be able to afford that, or may decide that their risk for suffering total loss of business premises is very low.

Any organization should seek assistance from experts in necessary fields as they size and suit their security policies and plans to their own specific needs. Yet, we all understand most of what security represents, and every organization needs to do fundamental things – and needs to do them well on a continuing, and evolving, basis.

RISK – UNMANAGED POSSIBILITIES BECOME PROBABILITIES

Risk itself is the possibility of suffering a negative yield from harm, loss, or danger. Risk is also represented by factors. Identifying and eliminating, or minimizing, factors of risk in your organization is a necessity. But further, you need a system firmly in place to constantly seek and identify new, or evolving, factors of risk. As any Business-Technology Weave evolves, it becomes ever more complex and ever more comprehensive to the core of your ability to conduct business – therefore we find that possibilities of risk become *probabilities for harm* in the absence of management. As to those conditions that are external to us, largely beyond our control, we must recognize, rank, and make contingency planning so as to best direct our limited resources to a solid recovery posture. In managing risk, it is helpful to start with an absolute, and adjust from there:

Managing to Zero Risk: What does "managing to zero risk" mean? Can you achieve zero risk? Is this worth striving for? Frankly, there can be no zero risk in an imperfect world. However, this is the initial target so as not to prejudice risk's evaluation. This is your target in all endeavors as you conduct business – you must strive to manage to zero risk. Yes, the attendant realities will present themselves in short order: budget constrictions; time constraints; and forced reliance on outside elements over which you have no control.

Particularly for IT, striving for zero risk doesn't mean that you'll achieve it in every circumstance. You may not have the budget to protect things to the ultimate degree. You can only expose the risks and liabilities under these circumstances, make Business aware, and employ the most affordable and efficient system of risk management that you are able to. However, anything short of "zero risk" as your guiding standard and principle does two things: you set a bias for diminished expectations before other risk-influencing factors even come into play (such as budget, resources, and contingency planning). And - you cripple yourself at the starting gate.

So, do not limit your thinking right out of the gate: you must brainstorm and be as creative as possible in mounting solid security. The zero risk concept helps to prevent a reliance on too much conventional thinking.

Business can define and handle its own risks in the business arena – but further, in the context of the Weave, Business should not face risk from its own support structure. Therefore, in the IT Enlightened Organization, it is Business and the Business-driven IT strategy that sets and manages risk according to standards, resources, and dispensations set and granted by - Business. At the same time, IT cannot be paralyzed by Business constrictions or unwillingness to engage. IT must fully expose facets of issues and all risk, so that Business can make informed decisions.

"Zero Risk" Does Not Mean "No Risk": No one can afford to be maneuvered into a posture whereby prudent situations of managed risk are never undertaken. The granting of assumable risk is routine in the necessary order of progressive business. This zero risk concept is not intended to turn everyone into frozen cowards. Rather, it is a bias of view, in order to open a vision toward those ideas that drive risk *down* to the furthest practicable degree. It is Business' and IT's job to reduce, minimize, and eliminate risk to the best degree possible, and to do that with best-knowledge, best-practice, and best-effort.

We can realize that in establishing a zero-risk-mindset in those charged, we create a bias in their mind to *get there* if at all possible, and we create fertile ground to craft "new possibles." Keeping the concept of zero risk uppermost in mind also sets a natural bias toward *prevention* – something we'll talk much more about in *What's At Stake*. A lot more creativity and imagination will be employed within this mindset as the organization strives to make the most of what it has - in driving risk down as far as it can possibly go given your particular resources and concerns.

The zero-risk mindset also provides an energizing force: you can never achieve it, yet still strive for it - so, you create a dynamic where security and risk are constantly being managed on a progressive basis. In today's world, security and risk management must progress on a continuous, rapid and agile basis.

SECURITY STARTS WITH AWARENESS

As in most successful things regarding our Weave, the best security starts with a top-level awareness. Senior management must be aware of risks and consequences, and must sanction a security awareness that permeates the entire organization. When we consider what's at stake, we realize that security really cannot be overemphasized. It's true that security's emphasis can be costly, but really only if it is poorly managed. The organization has to seek ways of prioritizing and sizing security according to its risks, levels of exposures, and the consequence to be had. It's just another area to achieve the best return on investment, and therefore your best security posture.

Another aspect to awareness is this: That the employment of true, declarative, and understood assessments of situations creates real awareness. As an example: In this book, we will not refer to "lessons learned from Hurricane Katrina." We will refer to lessons learned from "Post-Katrina New Orleans," or even just "New Orleans." Let's understand this for a full awareness:

- Hurricanes happen often. Several times a year. We name them.
- Entire American cities are not often lost.

In fact, New Orleans is the only one in recent memory. Emphasizing this particular disaster as "New Orleans" is a recognition, an awareness, and an acknowledgement that a comparatively modest amount of hurricane's damage was compounded in extraordinary fashion by human failure.

Our motivation is not the assignation of blame. Our motivation is our service and obligation to reality and awareness – our only true hope in bettering our outcomes of the future.

The Ultimate Security Failure; a Failure of Awareness: Let's further consider the disaster and preventable tragedy of New Orleans for an important lesson and example. [Before going further, this book makes no criticism of the responders on the ground. Their dedication and efforts are an inspiration. But, it is fair to make justified and valid criticism of the response planners, and also criticism of a failure to prepare].

If we, for the moment, disregard all aspects of disaster recovery in this case, and imagine a perfectly executed, coordinated, comprehensive response to the loss of New Orleans, we still must know that *prevention would have been supremely better*. We must all consider the knowns in this situation, and we can do it in an objective fashion: Why were plans of evacuation being tested in the years prior; why were assets being pre-positioned for a disaster; why were experts running computer simulations of category three, four, and five hurricanes against New Orleans for knowledge of outcomes? The answer is that these things were being done because people at the Federal, State, and local city level knew that a massively destructive hurricane *would come*. There were also enough people in positions of power and influence who understood that the levees in New Orleans were inadequate to the challenge of nature.

However, lack of awareness in this case was myriad. The populace was otherwise engaged in their day-to-day existence. Politicians, community leaders, business people, and others, probably had moments of concern, but largely relegated these to the "we have to do something someday" category of "priority." As we will see, there's awareness, and there's *awareness*.

In essence: People knew the cause of a coming disaster, understood the impact to be had, and failed to prevent that which was preventable. In this case, *chance* truly is a word devoid of meaning. We had the knowns necessary to understand what would cause a disaster – and we knew it was only a mater of time before it came. However, levees that were known to be under-specified were not strengthened. The people of New Orleans were forced to assume an unacceptable risk: either through selective ignorance, inertia, political impairment, or other things.

Achievement of True Awareness Makes the "Easy Sell": The "sell" here should have been an easy one, in order to successfully build the prevention to this disaster: Those with influence needed only to expose the relatively low short-term cost of prevention - against the walloping near-future cost - in terms of lives, fiscal resources, and total, comprehensive, disaster. To put New Orleans into proper disaster awareness perspective, let's pretend for the moment that no one died (death being the supreme tragedy). It will cost over $400 billion to reconstitute New Orleans. The levees could have been strengthened for perhaps $30 billion – over time. Was there no one who could sell the wisdom of timely action? (Or perhaps there was no true BIT – the sales-ready environment that specifically tunes its ears for prudence and appropriate planning? We will come back to that).

Now we add in the loss of life, the loss of property, the environmental catastrophe, and what should be the shame and embarrassment of losing an entire American city – and we have a head-snap realization: Prevention reigns supreme. Prevention is a value – it should not be compromised. Prevention is a zero risk type of goal – it should have an attendant mission. *Prevention is an awareness*. Prevention must also be the standard - with attendant planning for contingency if something happens in spite of the best prevention posture we can manage.

Once we understand awareness and prevention, we understand that there is no acceptable political, fiscal, or ethical answer imaginable for a poor security posture. For New Orleans, people were concentrating on *response*, and not *prevention*. And they didn't even get the response part right. The only real thing lacking was leadership's true awareness – therefore there was lack of a proper Weave between the *business* of what should have been done, and the alignment and deploy of people and *technology* to do it.

PREVENTION: A MISSION, A VALUE, A BELIEF: A STANDARD

New Orleans serves as example to situations large and small. When you sit down at your planning table, consider your vulnerabilities and consider "problem managing" as *preventing* problems, first and foremost. Do not make the mistake that many do, which is to list potential problems, their outcomes and what to do in response - while overlooking the first rule of problem management: prevention.

Let's look to another area for a simple example: you manage a budget to remain sound. Budget management is not the identification of what to do once you're bankrupt. Likewise, problem management must be viewed as managing to sustain a problem-free environment. At the same time, prudence dictates that you craft the plan for contingencies if the unforeseen happens – the *truly* unforeseen.

Who held "prevention" as a value, given New Orleans' known vulnerabilities? Who mounted a mission to secure New Orleans? Who upgraded the levees to a standard of prevention? Given the outcome, *no one in positions of influence did*. True planning would have involved a clear, concise articulation of the risk, likelihood, impact, and the range of hurricanes' impact to the city. True awareness would have sold the plan and execution of a proper securing of life and city.

Awareness and Prevention: Learning from Others: Not long ago, the FBI was attacked, and they were shut down electronically for three hours. Some feel that this a condition of "…well, if the FBI can't get it right, what can we do?" To the contrary, what happens to other people, other organizations, other environments, is simply added weight to your organization's awareness for the necessity in mounting effective security. Too, your Business and IT leaders must review these outside mishaps in order to add to your own collective body of knowledge regarding risks and exposures - so as to acknowledge them, and to size and rank them as appropriate within your own security standing. This sort of activity has to become a part of your organization's routine. Your security team should ask the following questions, and determine the answers:

"What happened at the FBI?"
"Could it happen here?"

If "No," a report should be made to the supervising authority showing the protections and accommodations for prevention of the condition.

If "Yes," likelihood of a similar security breach must be evaluated and accommodated according to risk, resources, and direction from the supervising authority. Senior management along with IT should actively survey other high-profile security mishaps and weigh them against your organization – this will help to illuminate like-vulnerabilities where they exist. In other words, profit from others mistakes - rather than running the risk of making them independently through ignorance. Security should be discussed, planned, and reviewed in the BIT meetings. Review of outside events helps to position security on a path of constant improvement and evolution in your organization.

Without proactive identification and action, the shifting and evolving factors of risk will present themselves to you when it is too late – as harm. We only have to look to 9/11 as a model example for what happens in the realm of security when risk is not properly surveyed, weighed, scaled, exposed, shared, and acted upon. Therefore, within the Business-Technology Weave and all that yours supports, actively survey for risk within, but learn from outside examples too.

Re-weigh and re-scale the range of risk. Mount the awarenesses, resources and the plan to execute the fix on the prioritized conditions before bad happens. Your survey and exposure of risk should be on a regularized agenda within BIT meetings. In this manner you'll have many perspectives, the most comprehensive view to emergences, and less chance for overlooking something. You'll also be discussing security within a very potent team.

RISK ON A LOCAL SCALE

A recent SANS (System Administration, Networking and Security) Institute survey shows that a high percentage of *security people* lack the necessary knowledge to understand *technology and security principles* in order to do their jobs effectively. Consider that carefully.

Management must cope with this. Top-most management must foster the creation of a security-savvy organization; from the top down, the bottom up, and across the board. If your organization has a dedicated security officer, you hopefully have a robust security policy, adherence to it, and its manifest in a secure environment. Yet, if security personnel themselves are lacking as the SANS Institute indicates, what is the answer? For the modern organization, the answer lies in sound security policies, plans, schedules of review, and robust training and awareness programs for all personnel. In the smart organization, security awareness is part of new-hire orientation, and periodic refresher training for all staff.

Security: Again, People are Our Greatest Challenge: We need this awareness and training because, with or without a dedicated security officer, there is a shared condition in all organizations: people still, and will likely always, represent the greatest security vulnerability. Many of the largest security violations involve in-house people. For example, a global-bank employee was bribed to give documentation and information necessary for making funds transfers, allowing unauthorized access with the expected results. In another case, a New Jersey engineering firm fired an IT staff member who retained his access to their system. He is alleged to have taken action that destroyed intellectual property that cost that firm nearly $11 million.

Even when harm originates from outside, it can be possible and necessary to ascribe responsibility for security blunders to in-house personnel. This is obvious when they have not done due diligence in protecting from those out-of-house attacks. The denial-of-service attacks of 2000, which affected Yahoo, ebay, and others (including security apparatuses thought to be "unbreakable"), are alleged to have cost those companies $1.2 billion. If your organization suffers similar harm from a lapse in security that has been experienced, chronicled, and solved by others for your ready review –where does the fault lie? The fault (defect) lies within your organization. The other fault (the assignation of responsibility) will also have to be made… internally.

Don't Blame the Rain if You Get Wet: To really understand this, think of a hole in a roof. If the rain comes in and wets contents, do you fault the rain? The defect lies in the roof, and the fault (lack of awareness and action) falls on those who did not recognize the risk of rain, and the security problem of the hole.

So, the responsibility falls on those who then did not repair the roof and secure the house in a timely manner. Your organization must understand today's "rain" in a comprehensive fashion in order to set true security for your organization.

MOUNTING SECURITY: THREE BASICS

If security awareness is not now a top priority in your organization, you must make it one starting now. A solid system in support of security is driven by three general things:

1) *Internal Conditions*: We have to manage our ever-present condition of internal change, which brings new factors of risk into our environment; the organization may choose to explore new lines of business; new products; new markets, etc., which require new internal systems of support. Also, our own people represent the greatest vulnerability; an active program of awareness and security training is paramount within your larger security program.

2) *External Conditions*: Changing external conditions regarding the normal evolution of business and other events forces new systems of business and technology upon us (which accelerates our first condition above) – we have no choice but to keep up.

The organization may forge new relationships, or be directed to do so, in alliance with a common cause. Your security then is only as good as those allied agencies' security: You may be forced to a new level of recovery ability, or may need to spend additional time in allied security planning.

There are also other external conditions – various threats are on the increase. Viruses, hacks, spyware, etc. expose our business and our technology to ever-present danger. We also face the external threat posed by things that are beyond our immediate control. We must make allowance for everything from a simple loss of power, to larger-scale threats like natural disasters - flooding, earthquakes, or fire. We also face a threat from man-made catastrophes up to and including terrorist attack. Whether natural or man, disasters can yield temporary loss of access to buildings; temporary loss of primary data and associated platforms; and even permanent loss of current, primary business premises and all associated contents.

Keep in mind that while you can control your internal program of awareness and evolving security measures, any organization is dependent on the community of all other organizations to do their part.

3) *Priorities*: Last but certainly not least is an intelligent prioritization in managing areas of risk. Various risk orders itself according to likelihoods. These likelihoods, as ranked according to what's most liable to happen, represent an unevenly distributed weight and range of consequence from the business perspective – the only perspective that counts. (Again, "business" being that which you do in support of your desired outcomes. If you can't "do," you're out of business).

Managing According to the Weight and Range of Influences: It is up to us to interpret risk accurately in order to match our priorities, attention, and resources accordingly. This way we efficiently manage the most secure environment we possibly can, within finite resources, in order to maintain an effective ability to "do."

Our management of risk should be driven by weight and range. For our purposes, *weight* is the heft of the influence that a bad outcome can have, whether that influence is in a narrow area or over a broad area – the area can be one of operations, opinion, confidence, etc. *Range* is the extent of a bad outcome's weight – the influence may be local or global, or anything in between.

As a simple example, an outcome can influence the desktop. The weight of the outcome can be small or large. One application corrupting is a smaller weight than having the entire PC corrupted and inoperable. In terms of *range*, an outcome can influence one desktop, or the whole company - *every* desktop – whether the weight is small or large (one application corrupted, or entire PCs, respectively). Weight and range can influence each other.

Weights and Their Range of Influence Change with Time: As a simple example, let's consider the small organization of perhaps twenty people - of perhaps twenty years ago. Most of these small organizations had a very small computer network, if they had one at all. Occasionally the network went down during business hours through some mishap or failure. For these small organizations of the time, much business was still conducted offline, with forms and various hardcopy making up the bulk of content and its associated storage. There was either no outside connectivity, or very little in the form of some rudimentary dial-in and access – usually restricted to an extreme few. Sometimes only a fraction of the staff even had workstations. Hard to imagine now, but network reliability was a relatively low priority (compared to today) for these small organizations – hence there were no redundancies and no real consequences to down time. Network "crashes," or even maintenance during the day, did not carry the weight (influence) or range (extent) that a network outage causes in even a small organization today.

Over time, computer networks began to be the large focus of even small business infrastructure. Today, network outages can no longer be tolerated. An outage's influence now carries much more *weight* – halting most business within the organization. Also, due to things like 24-7 business operations and e-Commerce, outages represent a much larger *range* of influence: if your customers, members, allied agencies, etc., experience the same inconvenience that the organization's own staff person does, you have a very uncomfortable situation influencing a much larger population.

How many organizations grew during this period, in the size of their business and in the size of their support systems, and how many effectively reevaluated their risk according to weights and range of influence? How many acted to stay ahead of their changing dynamics of risk, and managed their security effectively? Was it done on a cost effective basis? Was there a genuine return on investment – that is, were risks prioritized appropriately so as not to direct resources to a falsely perceived risk at the expense of an actual risk?

We can project the small organization's model of advance and evolution of risk to any size endeavor or organization. Thus, any conversation regarding change, new solutions, re-ordering of business process, evolving influencers, acceptance of new missions, etc., requires an evaluation of risk and security.

A Larger Example: Let's consider a big example: The FBI operates a Terrorist Screening Center, which maintains a constantly updated "watch list" of people who are suspected of being terrorists, or associates of terrorists. Until June of 2005, the FBI's Terrorist Screening Center did not share its data with the U.S.

State Department. Therefore, the U.S. State Department's Office of Passport Services was issuing passports to people regardless of their possible relationship to terrorism.

Incredibly, almost 4 years after 9-11, this was not being done despite an existing model – one posed by the department's check of all passport applicants against a database that contained other fugitives and deadbeat parents.

Because of this the State Department's Office of Passport Services did not always know that some of the people applying for passports were already-identified and known terrorists. Therefore, America was actually issuing passports to terrorists in some cases. This represents a failure of awareness, a failure to leverage existing content (the knowledge it grants, in addition to the action it should inspire), and a failure of people to identify, and secure themselves from, *risk*. If the necessary agencies were merely to survey the risk involved regarding hidden content, and the risk in not making effective use of this data, these agencies would work in mutual alliance to uncover and share this data. However, it requires awareness.

Here, someone should be surveying for risk according to weight and range – which as regards terrorism are off the scale in any interpretation regarding consequence. Any agency, whether local, regional, or National, should survey its assets to determine who should be authorized to co-leverage those assets, and go about the necessary project of determining permissions and appropriate sharing and leveraging of those assets. That needs to happen on a comprehensive, proactive (not catch-up), basis now.

Defining "The Possible": Short of natural disasters, whose impact we must work through, it is possible to thwart harm (including large-scale terror); everyone, regardless of your business, must get through that gate first. Thwarting harm before it manifests itself is possible. Even allowing for human mistakes and political impediments, which are inevitable, we can safeguard and secure anything we set our mind to. It is a matter of belief and appropriate action.

Think of *the will to do that which will be done*; the question: *"does this move business forward?"*; and *the Success Culture*. Think back to mission, beliefs, values, and standards. Once we make it our mission to be secure, and believe that we can succeed, we make security an essential, non-negotiable value, and we bring standards to be met in order to achieve security. We can, and should, weave those essentials into anything regarding the Business-Technology Weave. Any organization, and on any level within, must simply make security a prioritized part of the daily business. Through system protections, user education, defined policy, survey and action, we can weave a tight fabric of security for an environment on any scale.

AREAS OF SECURITY

When we think of security within the Business-Technology Weave, we concern ourselves with securing the following things – that is, we cannot risk harm to:

- Business process
- Systems reliability (including solid postures for recovery from harm, as well as recovery from disasters)
- Confidentiality of data
- Integrity of data
- Asset Protection

Business process is the comprehensive operations you perform each day in fulfilling your objectives. Further, when we process business, we're not just talking about immediate deliverables, such as delivery of products or services to customers, for example. We're including the process of development for our progression into the future. We include all things that enable our courses of action; the things that protect our route; and the tools that contribute to our method for reaching all objectives.

Systems reliability: Systems need to be online and fully functional 100% of the time. Increasingly, systems maintenance means that you must have redundant systems of support - parallel support platforms in place while something is being worked on – so as to make maintenance totally transparent to Business. Even the smallest organizations are supporting remote users, home users, and people doing work in off-hours. Increasingly, the organization can ill-afford to put people off-line.

For example, studies have shown that the sudden inability to access a computer network puts people at about 5% of their normal capacity to produce. At the same time, any down-time concerning systems (such as scheduled maintenance) has to be kept to an absolute minimum, as people are now apt to work, or are required to work, during any manner of off-hours. With international concerns, systems are supporting users during the course of a "business day" that literally winds its way around the clock.

Confidentiality of data refers to the discretion and privacy of information. Individuals should only have access to information for which they have a "need to know." That is, they should have a justifiable business reason for the knowledge and use that the access to data grants. They may also require other credentials – for example, special training, or having committed themselves to a formal confidentiality agreement. Confidentiality also represents the protection of member, customer, client, etc., information from interests who do not merit access. Too, it involves issues of intellectual property such as copyrights, trade secrets, and business methods. Content Management and Acceptable Use provide a good method of establishing and maintaining a comprehensive confidentiality.

Integrity of data is its accuracy and relevancy. Data's accuracy and relevancy is supported by human and non-human systems of support. For a human example, it is important for data-entry personnel to accurately transfer information from hardcopy and other sources when keying, translating, or converting data. At the same time, non-human systems must be tuned to responsibly act on data. For example, accounting systems perform a myriad of calculations in the course of a day, and the resultant bottom lines must be accurate to a standard of exactness.

Asset Protection: Anything contributing to the forward momentum of the organization is an asset, but those things most squarely in the scope of security include:

- Computer hardware, platform, infrastructure, and peripheral equipment; related operating systems; utilities; and documentation
- Communications equipment
- Business and IT applications, and related documentation
- Information, data (content)
- Premises (physical location)
- Supplies

THE ACCEPTABLE USE POLICY

When we look at the above areas of security, we realize something: everything, again, starts with people. Every person represents a potential security liability to the organization. The organization needs to ensure that people respect and protect business resources, that people use them appropriately without exposing them to harm, and that people understand the consequences - to the organization and to themselves - for inappropriate use. Because of this, we cannot afford ignorance on anyone's part regarding appropriate security measures, and simple, appropriate use, of business resources. In these regards, we find that we need a policy.

The Acceptable Use Policy: Acceptable use is the assurance that resources such as business tools, systems, and data are used for the purpose for which they are intended, with attendant care and appropriate safeguards. Your organization should have a specified Acceptable Use Policy. The employment of such a policy ensures that staff are trained and knowledgeable regarding acceptable use, are exposed to clear expectations for appropriate use, and helps the organization ensure proper use of time and resources.

A solid Acceptable Use Policy and adherence to it is your pre-emptive, "front end" guard against abuse. It manifests itself as a proactive security awareness that weaves itself into every activity. It is for the prevention of harm, as leveraged through every individual in the organization. Without such a policy, and associated monitoring and action, you are at tremendous risk.

If staff is employing random, unsanctioned applications, tools, and utilities, they can cause system conflicts and corruption. Unapproved software cannot be allowed to manifest itself in your organization, and you will want to identify it before it can weave its way into significant business "support." (If something is that good, it should be exposed in the BIT forum for discussion and possible official inclusion to the array of business-supports in your organization. This way, it becomes known, is integrated properly with other systems of support, and gets on IT's schedule for upgrades and maintenance).

Too, we've discussed the vast exposure that the organization has due to the tremendous amount of content that is going back and forth between it and outside entities. Without a firm sense of acceptable use, your staff *will* visit sites of questionable repute – this will in-turn create an exposure for unauthorized access to your business systems. Because of the explosion of things like blogs (web logs), chat rings, online gaming sites, IMs, iPods, other portable media, etc., everyone from senior staff and general users, to contract employees and temporary hires, are accessing content at a high volume. In many cases they are bringing some of this content into your organization – and taking some *out*.

Beyond that, there is the sort of content that is not even intentionally invited: cookies, cache, spyware, adware, viruses, and other malicious software (malware), such as tracking and data-mining items. Malware is any **mal**icious soft**ware** that is invited into, or that sneaks into, your environment and presents either risk or harm. These are technically "content" – they become part of that which your organization *contains*. These things can be deposited throughout the organization if you are not actively surveying your systems for them, and if you are not actively guarding against them. They, in-turn, pose great harm to your appropriate content. Your data can be stolen, corrupted, or destroyed. Identities can be stolen: an individual's, even the organization's.

Think about this too: beyond the internal staff (upon whom your organization has some measure of control) you are acquiring content from outside people. Often it is unsolicited. We'll talk more about this later, but the understanding here is that your organization can be, and likely is, accruing information from people whose judgment and character you know nothing about. By that reasoning, we can see that *your organization* can represent a threat to those with whom *you* do business – if you are not maintaining a thorough front-end guard that is augmented by Acceptable Use.

Recognize another risk to content: that of unauthorized removal. Even credentialed people, with appropriate access to data, must not move or copy data to unsecured locations – for example, unauthorized, unsecured, home computing equipment. Once secured content is taken from your organization's safeguards and protections, to an unauthorized outside location, anything can happen to it. Unsecured data can be stolen from the remote location. As bad, it can be manipulated and returned to your organization, creating unknown liabilities. Copied data that is removed for "update" at a remote location to be returned later can pose extreme problems: legitimate, internal, updates to content are in peril. When the copied data is returned and inserted back into your environment, the internal updates are overwritten – and lost.

Acceptable Use's Influence on the Nature of Content: We spoke briefly about the concept of acceptable use in the chapter Content. Your Acceptable Use policy should warn against, and indicate consequence for, creation and accumulation of content that is injurious and harmful - to include:

- *Characterizations* that are inappropriate, false, defamatory, injurious, etc., to clients, co-workers, competition, partnerships, etc.
- *Jokes* of similar nature.
- *Advocacy* that is contrary to your organization's positions; any advocacy that is not in the nature of one's job; other things such as illegal advocacy, or statement of opinions or support to controversial positions that have nothing to do with your business.
- *E-mail*: misuse such as a large volume of personal e-mailing; receipt and distribution of material having inappropriate content, etc.
- *Instant Messaging* (IMs): IMs can open security holes to your environment. Further, unless your organization has granted permission

and set associated security for legitimate business IMing, your staff is wasting time while posing this security threat. Any chat-enabling software, or instant communication through web browsers or portals, should be discouraged, unless specifically mounted according to business need and oversight.

- *Downloads*: Staff should not be downloading material into the environment, unless directed to do so, or unless they posses specific authority according to the definition of their job or position. Downloads frequently deposit uninvited stealthware, in addition to delivering unauthorized applications and content.
- *Data Transfers* can happen independent of downloads from the Internet. Staff should not be transferring data from personal items, such as iPods, cameras, flash memory, drives, or other portable media to their workstations (and vice versa). Much material contained on personal storage devices is unlicensed, and in violation of appropriate copyrights. And, as you may suspect, much of it poses the risk of malware transference to your business systems. Also, staff should not carry data *out* of the work environment on these personal devices.
- *Postings*: All staff should be aware that posts, even "anonymous" ones, are frequently tracked according to IP address. Regardless of firewalls, IP translators, service provider protections, etc., domains *can* be traced – so employees must be made aware that they cannot use organization resources in ways that can expose the organization, and its reputation, to any kind of harm.

An effective Acceptable Use Policy will be a living document, sizing and adjusting its scope for various changes to business and environment. Also, differing organizations will have differing needs regarding acceptable use coverage – but most will need to cover certain common basics. Any Acceptable Use policy needs to make clear that business resources are to be used for business purposes - *with very few exceptions*. Usually, personal use on a limited basis during non-working hours (including lunch breaks) is acceptable if it does not interfere with use for business operations and would not be considered professionally inappropriate. It is also recognized that people need to communicate on a limited basis during business hours to their spouse, doctor, babysitter, plumber, etc. in order to effectively conduct routine personal matters, and that business systems such as e-mail and phone are used for this.

Monitoring Acceptable Use: Any use of business resources that violates federal, state, local laws, regulations or organizational policy must be prohibited. Also, guard against use that may violate new or emerging internal policies, such as content management. Your organization may or may not choose to monitor employee use of resources on a comprehensive and continuous basis. However, the organization can and should monitor an individual's use of resources to search for evidence of any suspected misconduct or wrongdoing, or pursuant to a court order or applicable laws. Also, periodic monitoring of all resources is routine, to ensure proper business and technology alignment. Your Acceptable Use Policy should make your users aware of this condition.

Make clear that accessing resources, such as a network, associated hardware, software, and data – in addition to other things such as the Internet - without proper authorization is prohibited. In addition, any computers that are offsite, such as laptops on loan and any other portable or wireless devices, are to be used only by authorized staff, and cannot be shared or further loaned to other individuals. Use of your organization's resources by non-employees is prohibited without express authorization from the proper authority. It is a good idea to scan any portable hardware upon return for content liabilities (malware and inappropriate content). Make this monitoring known to the organization, and that this occurs upon return-receipt of the equipment.

Further Leveraging of Acceptable Use to Security: In the course of crafting your Acceptable Use policy, don't be afraid to state the "obvious." While you don't want to go overboard and create an inefficient document that is overburdened with mundane, common-sense items, you should consider weighted and scaled risks as you consider items for inclusion to the policy. Below are some areas to think about, to define, and to make clear within the organization's expectations of acceptable use:

User Accounts: Access to your data, your content, your business intelligence, is controlled by user names and passwords. Maintenance of these is the responsibility of the IT department, but Business can always make a request to force any degree of password changes – as necessary for Business' sense of security. For that matter, the securing of accounts can include the disablement or deletion of any user's or group of users' accounts as necessary, and as authorized by the proper authority. Any action designed to compromise user names and passwords must be prohibited. This includes sharing passwords, and logging in as someone other than self.

Internet Use: As should be obvious, access to the Internet is intended for business purposes only. However, most organizations understand and make allowance for a limited personal use, such as e-mailing a friend or looking up directions to a location. This use should be occasional and limited to non-work hours or break periods. Many organizations track the sites that are accessed, and build logs. Random or periodic review of these logs will show any abuse. They also serve as documentation when disciplining someone in order to bring them back into compliance with policy. You can block access to sites according to keyword content, or even specific blockage of certain sites by name, URL, or IP address – your acceptable use policy should state that blocking and monitoring is being done.

Physical Premises: You should indicate that access to the computer room where main computers and servers are housed is normally limited to the IT staff. While this should seem an obvious prohibition, many an organization is unaware that often times average users feel they can drift in and out of the computer room based on some friendship, or "special relationship," with an IT member. This is unwise. For example, a very high profile organization maintained an unusual, limited-access, workstation within their computer room, which contained a very specialized application requiring special permission for access. Over time, a summer intern was granted permission to enter the computer room to use this workstation and its specialized application. By the next summer, the workstation had been removed over the course of changing requirements. In its place stood a fileserver – a piece of equipment that was central to daily business operations. The intern returned for the next summer's work. She saw that the computer room's door was propped open, and sat at the fileserver. She began pointing, clicking, and typing her way around, attempting to find last summer's application there. Fortunately, the IT member who had propped the door open returned and was able to show her where the workstation had been moved to, out in the user arena.

Here, of course, the door should never have been propped open, the computer room should never have been left unattended in this manner, and users, much less interns, should never have been permitted to work in the computer room. But realize that this is how easily, and innocently, security can be breached. When determining your organization's security in any quarter, do not let the sinister and dire blind you to the necessity of guarding against simple ignorance and misplaced innocence. Expressly state that the computer room is off limits, and handle any unusual access on an exception-to-policy basis. (Exceptions could include vendors, contractors, a highly *qualified* user on a narrow and limited basis, escorted visitors, etc.). Firmly state that any action designed to gain unauthorized access to the computer room is prohibited.

Destruction: In keeping with our theme of the "obvious," mention that destructing, defacing, or tampering with the organization's resources is prohibited. As to destruction and defacement; these are obvious prohibitions and can be handled in accordance with a broader organizational policy. Here, you can point to that.

Impacting: State that any intentional action designed to tie up network or other shared computer resources is prohibited. Further, state that there is also consequence from inadvertent negative impacts to computer processing and bandwidth utilization, when it is shown that those impacts were originated by things such as large-scale downloads of unauthorized, non-business material, or through the introduction of malware.

Tampering: Here we're referring to people's tweaking and tinkering – oftentimes the motivation is to make something "better," maybe through the download of software, a utility, or perhaps someone is "tuning" their PC. However, action of this sort, independent of sanction by IT and Business oversight, is prohibited.

This provides a broad protection, and helps the organization take action on people who profess ignorance when you discover that they've tweaked and "enhanced" their company-owned resources – in defiance of the better knowledge you know them to posses. You create an important condition: Here it is not necessary for the organization to define tampering to the nth degree. Any organization member should be oriented such that when there is a doubt in their mind regarding the change to, or use of, any organization property or asset, they should forgo any action and *ask* somebody in authority before proceeding. Simple enough.

However, we should mention that other forms of tampering do not have positive motivations. Unlike the condition above where there is an attempt to make something better (at least in the tamperer's eyes), here there is an attempt to defeat a broad protection in order to satisfy the selfish, generally non-business, interest of the tamperer. Perhaps there is an attempt to access controlled content, or they may try to streamline and speed the boot up of their PC by removing virus protections, as examples. Further, the tamperer knows that what they are doing is wrong.

People may attempt to circumvent a firewall's block of certain sites. They may attempt to e-mail offending jokes, and thereby try to defeat the blocking of certain words and phrases – things that your organization is taking great pains not to associate with. Users constantly receive phone calls: "…did you get my e-mail? You didn't? I sent you the funniest joke, attachment, picture,…," etc. If your user didn't receive it, there is frequently an attempt to force its delivery. Your user may take receipt of it in an internet-based e-mail account, for example – one that is lacking your organization's protections.

Once that joke, attachment, picture, etc. is in that user's workstation environment (thus your *organization's* environment), it's "game over." Now, whatever harm that may be contained (after all, it was blocked by your systems for a reason) is loose inside your domain. Your user(s) can forward it around to their heart's content – unless they are trained and warned specifically not to do these kinds of things.

Be certain that users understand that anti-virus software and any other protections must be operational on all computers; disabling or working around protections is prohibited. Your organization may be employing software firewalls and other protections on distributed laptops and devices. When on the road, there can be enormous temptation to defeat these, and to use the distributed device for personal reasons. Therefore, make certain that this part of the policy is well defined and well understood.

A View of Hardware and Software Inside Acceptable Use: In addition to protecting your organization's content and ensuring its acceptable use, and quite beyond tampering and tweaking of software and hardware, you must make something thoroughly understood.

Your approved set of software application solutions must be defined for protection, as well as their associated operating systems. It should be usual policy that installing or modifying software on any network server or desktop computer is not permitted by anyone except members of the IT staff. Again, exceptions to policy can be made. For example, during heavy implementations, it is possible to train LeadUsers in departments to assist with troubleshooting and necessary modification and fit of programs. However, exceptions should always be presented as such, and should not lead to expectations that future prior approvals are no longer necessary.

Personal software must not be introduced to the IT environment without prior approval of the appropriate Business supervisor, and only after a review for compatibility by the IT department. Generally speaking, personal software doesn't have much place in most modern business-technology environments. However, occasionally it can be beneficial. For example, someone may have a certain kind of PDA (personal data assistant) that they prefer, that the organization does not usually support. You may decide that it makes sense to approve the installation of the transfer/link software to support that PDA. Just be certain that users aren't procuring business PDAs and other devices on their own, in the absence of Business and IT review for efficiency and expense. IT must have the opportunity to judge compatibilities, and further may be able to suggest use of already existing, approved, solutions. No one should be introducing anything to your environment without specific approval from a valid authority.

All software must be properly documented and maintained (licensed, patched, upgraded, reviewed for security, etc.). To this end, the IT department will maintain all software licenses and will perform periodic audits of software on all computers. Be certain that your users understand this. Users must not perform installs of even sanctioned business products, for example "as a favor," to co-workers. Only IT, or approved delegates, are to do this. They should understand that violating any software licensing agreement or copyright, or copying and distributing copyrighted computer software, data or reports without proper recorded authorization, puts the organization at risk – therefore they put themselves at risk.

Further, in the absence of copyrights or other controls, the same standards apply. For example, your organization may contain freeware or shareware – and copyrights or legalities may not be an issue. However, system compatibilities, and who does what with what software, *is* an issue. Therefore, regardless of specific rights, users should not acquire, disseminate or share software unless engaged on a project and granted those permissions.

It is also important that your organization's hardware and infrastructure resources not be tampered with, and augmentation of hardware cannot be tolerated. Sometimes users are tempted to procure their own PC enhancements, and add them to their company workstations. All computer hardware and software must be acquired through the IT department to ensure compatibility of all components of the IT environment.

Any awareness of abuse is to be reported. Anything that puts the organization and its security in jeopardy is to be reported. Failure to report abuse, as known, should be disciplined to the same degree as those performing the actual abuse.

Examples of Unacceptable Use

It is important to give examples of unacceptable use within the policy. It gives users a further sense of what is allowed and disallowed. Also, violations of acceptable use are more easily dispatched when you can categorize them with a defined example of unacceptable use. However, your policy should make clear that these examples are not exclusive to other instances of abuse that are clearly within the spirit and letter of the policy.

<u>Use of Unauthorized Software</u>: Unauthorized software includes, but is not limited to: games; music and video players; instant messaging (IM) or chat agents; and personal software. Unauthorized software can be the source of viruses, may conflict with your organization's hardware and software, and may compromise the security of your resources and data. Unauthorized software may also deliver inappropriate content, whether solicited or not, and can introduce

spyware and other stealth survey software that can report information about the organization to outside entities. It can even report information about an individual user, without their knowledge. Other malware, such as viruses or hack-enabling portals, can be introduced.

Beyond the introduction of malware, unauthorized software takes up computer storage space, places undocumented demands on processing power, and can utilize large amounts of bandwidth - slowing access to the Internet. Unauthorized software also may not be properly licensed and its use can place the organization at risk for penalties from the associated licensing authority.

Another category of unauthorized software is that which is being used for legitimate business purposes, but the software itself is *unapproved*. While the intent may be laudable, the same risk for introduction of viruses, system conflicts, and improper licensing apply. If anyone feels a need to modify their suite of supported office technologies, they should speak with their supervisor. That supervisor will forward a request with justification to the IT department. IT can then evaluate the justification and speak as necessary with senior management regarding requested changes, or open a discussion in the BIT forum.

Abuse of User Accounts: Users must not share their user account information with anyone. Once account information is shared, regardless of the trustworthiness of the other person, exclusive control and security of the account has been removed from that user – another user's knowledge of the account information compromises that exclusivity. Users must not grant co-workers access to their accounts, they must not share their password, and they should not remain logged into their computer when leaving it unattended – particularly when leaving at night. Obviously sharing user account information with friends or family members is a big factor of risk. Yet that happens – people take laptops home, access their organization's network, and then let their children or spouse use the computer. Remote access to your organization's network and other business resources is not to be granted to any unauthorized user.

Abuse of Storage: Storing, or retaining, data (content) of any kind beyond the defined retention period for that data must be prohibited if you expect your content management system to have any meaning. When necessary, appropriate authorities can reclassify data and put it within the control of a different retention period – but this cannot be done outside of the system of control. For example, there may be a strong need to retain specific content that has changed its nature by virtue of a new context or shift in circumstances. Here, the Acceptable Use policy can point to the organization's *Content Management Policy & Program* for complete guidance regarding retention and disposition of data.

Also, it is important to provide specific warning here to the download of inappropriate material, particularly extremely large files that can take over large amounts of storage before IT has an opportunity to notice, mitigate, and correct the impact. If users have storage limits (as they should), they may overrun their allotted network space, inhibiting storage of legitimate work in progress. If they are downloading to their PC, they may crash it or corrupt its operation. If they are downloading to an area on a network server, they may slow network performance.

Frequently users download inappropriate files to the "wrong" folder (here any folder would be wrong, but we mean to a folder other than one they intended). When the user subsequently cannot relocate the file – what do they do? They download it again. Meanwhile, the original copy isn't even known to the offending user. It remains as a hidden liability of inappropriate content. It's of particular importance to emphasize avoidance for abuse of storage because of the very large video and graphics files that exist today. Remember that relative to users' home resources, your organization's resources may represent an enormous temptation. For those places with robust resources, the user sees "unlimited" storage, and extremely high transfer speeds due to your high bandwidth. Therefore, you invite abuse if you do not manage your expectations for compliance in this area.

<u>Abuse of the Internet:</u>   Abuse of the Internet includes the inappropriate use of e-mail, instant messaging, Internet browsing, posting to sites, and the downloading of unauthorized software or content. Think of anything that can cause poor reflection on, or outright damage to, your organization by exposing its domain, its content, and its security in an adverse way to *the whole world*.

1) <u>E-mail</u>: Personal use of e-mail often takes the form of jokes and other personal messages that may be considered harassing or offensive to recipients. These messages frequently contain attachments that take up considerable storage space on an e-mail server. Also, e-mail attachments are the prime source of computer viruses. You cannot forget that inappropriate e-mails can make you the target of spam – unwanted junk mail. Not only can you open yourself up to uninvited e-mail, but you could make your organization's entire domain (your registered presence on the Internet) susceptible to spam – not a good thing.

You can limit your organization's exposure to jokes and inappropriate e-mail by telling your employees to let their associates know that you don't wish to receive jokes, and particularly, questionable content. Far from seeming prudish, there is a growing awareness that many firms monitor e-mail transmission at the server, and screen to block content according to various words and phrases. These blocked messages then inhabit a secure area, where IT and others as necessary can review and forward them if they are found to be legitimate business messages. At the same time, inappropriate content is deleted, or dealt with on any behavioral basis if it appears the content was invited, or was the result of willing exchanges. Certainly friends are not willing to put each other at risk of harm in their respective workplaces. Even if no active monitoring goes on, you want to encourage employees to let associates know that yours is a business system of e-mail, and to save jokes, videos, and any non-business-related, personal type content for that person's personal e-mail account – *accessed strictly from home, and exclusively by home resources.*

If your users receive inappropriate e-mail content, they must know not to forward these types of e-mails – they should be reported. If e-mail spam shows up, or any e-mail from a sender that is not recognized – they must notify IT. Remember too that sender addresses can be "spoofed." That is, you may receive an e-mail that appears to be (but is not) from someone you recognize – the e-mail itself makes little sense: it is not business related, and the communication is outside of the "senders" character. It will frequently contain an attachment with instructions to open it, or to look at it. In these cases, staff must NOT OPEN the attachment. Again, they must be directed to notify the IT department.

2) <u>Instant Messaging</u>: Instant Messaging (IMs), chat agents, Internet Relay Chat (IRC), web-enabled chat, and similar real-time communication agents cannot be installed and used if you are to maintain a secured environment. It is important that each member of your organization understand that every instant messaging session opens a portal into your business-technology environment. This portal can be used maliciously by hackers, distributors of viruses, and those who would introduce spyware and other malware. This entry to your systems can result in identity theft – of an individual, or even the organization's identity assets.

Certainly any organizational necessity or desirability for instant communication on a text basis can be approved and installed with all necessary protections, training, and appropriate conditions of use. This way it is controlled and managed. Do not let users fire up their own ad hoc communications – which generally are time wasters and not related to business.

3) <u>Browsing</u>: Internet browsing is frequently used for personal entertainment and personal business. Merely browsing the Internet is not normally a problem unless inappropriate areas such as pornographic sites or sites advocating illegal, or questionable, activity are accessed. A good rule of thumb is: If you're looking at something on the internet that would create discomfort at an all-staff meeting, you're probably looking at something inappropriate for the office. Again, not to harp on this, but just recognize that browsing non-business sites increases your risk for malware of all types.

4) <u>Downloading</u>: Download of "outside" content is a business necessity. Virtually no one is operating on an isolated platform these days – not even a sole-proprietor. Therefore the downloading of content must be controlled. Ensure that your organization limits downloads to legitimate business content. You may have authorized users gathering content from a site such as Lexus-Nexus. People may be downloading articles from other approved subscriber sites for breaking news that is specific to your industry or interest. Other organizations may gather content that is scientific, political, or of general research interest in nature.

Here there must be a thorough understanding of acceptable downloads and their use. Malware can be introduced this way. Inappropriate material takes up storage space and may use processing and bandwidth resources. Your organization must ensure that people are not downloading software or content that has not been previously approved by the appropriate Business authority, and through proper review by the IT department.

5) <u>Data Transfers</u>: No one should ever remove content from an organization, or carry content offsite on portable media, without authorization. Extraordinary amounts of data can fit on portable elements such as drives, flash memory devices, PDAs, laptops, etc. Also, with broadband capabilities, users can access the organization's content remotely, from home for example, and transfer large amounts of data. It is of critical importance that the organization make known its definition and policy of "portable content," and all other transference of content, and emplace the controls and oversight necessary in securing content in every possible way.

<u>Remote computing</u>: Most organizations will be accessed via electronic means by a variety of people; staff, vendors, contractors, and other outside individuals (such as when teams bridge organizations, etc). Basically, anyone with need and authorization. The trick is to limit access to authorized individuals; to limit use

of that access to legitimate purpose and efficient utilization; and to thwart intrusion and delivery of harm to systems and content.

Staff and others must use remote capabilities with the same understanding regarding acceptable use that applies to the internal use of business systems and resources. This means that an authorized user protects his or her network account. Family members, friends, and associates are not to use your organization's offsite resources for access (desktops, laptops, wireless devices, etc.) to the business platform. Further, family members, etc., are not to use their *own* devices to log onto your organization's network.

Authorized remote users must maintain their standards: Just as in-house rules apply regarding accounts and access, remote access has the same rules regarding inappropriate sites and content. Authorized users, whether remote or local, must guard content and the organization's reputation to the same degree no matter where they are – no matter "when" they are.

Further, aside from unacceptable use considerations, most organizations have a limited number of licenses and connections for remote-access. Personal use and abuse further limits the availability of remote access to legitimate others, and inhibits their use of systems for business purposes.

Security Awareness is Top-Down, Bottom-Up, and Across

Security is not something to be put off, or relegated to an anemic checklist that exists purely as a feel-good or "CYA" item. Regardless of your organization's exposure or size, security has to have teeth. It needs to be tested. Put people, all people, on account for security, and rate them according to the job they do. We said earlier that appropriate awareness starts at the top-most level. It also needs to be bottom-up, as every single individual has a security awareness. Too, as people report breaches up the line. It needs to be across the organization, as all strata mount the appropriate awareness, take appropriate action, and exercise appropriate caution.

Security need not be heavy-handed; it need not instill fear. People should understand that a human mistake in the pursuit of good-faith business activity is not going to get them terminated. At the same time, repeated mistakes in the face of proper training and knowledge has to be addressed. People are entitled to know beforehand what constitutes a security breach, and how security breaches are to be handled. For these reasons, you need an open, virtual forum where people feel comfortable raising security questions and concerns. Whether at an all-staff meeting, with a supervisor, or a peer-to-peer discussion of concerns, people have to engage.

For any organization, a Security Suggestion e-mail box for review by a designated security officer is a good idea. Large and small organizations should make everyone a Security Officer by virtue of training, and awareness of the organization's policies. Everyone should be aware of what constitutes risk to the organization. Everyone should know where to report security breaches, lapses, observed risk, and yes, their own mistakes. All of this aids in your evolving security efforts.

Disaster

Disaster is the ultimate threat to security. From the organizational view, disaster is a comprehensive catch-all category. For most organizations, so-called "disaster recovery" encompasses everything from corrupted data to central hardware failures, to loss of utility (such as power). And, the bulk of attention, time, and resource go toward those things. They should, because within "disaster" those are the most likely things to happen – that is where the likelihood of bad events congregates in the real world of most organizations.

Still, in these same organizations, contingency is made for bigger disasters – largely on a fantasy basis. Organizations don't call it that, but we have to acknowledge something: It's not particularly pleasant to discuss floods, fires, terror attacks, etc. And, there is a dire need for the belief that these things will not happen. There's generally a lot of humor surrounding discussion of enormously harmful events. These larger disasters are difficult to size for; nor is it possible to wave a wand, procure unlimited resources, and thus buffer the organization from any event, to the ultimate degree of protection.

For your organization, you probably struggle with two central questions: Where to start? Where to end? Let's consider where we are, and where we want to be.

Relax – It's Only Disaster: Let's begin with a conversational approach to disaster planning, and recovery. We'll get around to various choices, and activities later: The reader can choose, size, and implement ideas that best suit their organization.

There are many, many variables involved in disaster planning – it is helpful to begin with a relaxed approach. (The relaxed approach is not to be confused with a posture of procrastination). Because a relaxed posture is in diametric opposition to thoughts of disaster, this approach is pretty much overlooked. However, discussion of disaster with attendant feelings of doom, or discomfort, or an overage of giggly gallows sorts of humor, will inhibit the free flow of real thought, engagement, and discussion. When discussing disaster, it is helpful to remember that control is the goal. Feelings of control lower stress, and empower your ability to plan.

As we discuss disaster, we'll keep prevention uppermost in mind. Too, we'll look at harming events and circumstances, such that you can consider their possible impact to business. From there, you can size and apportion your critical resources against threats and risks – as ranked against prioritized business processes.

A Rough Order of Discussion

- Gaining Control
- New Thinking for Disaster Recovery
- Prevention as a Mission, Belief, Value and Standard
- Contingency for Harm and Recovery
- Policy and Planning
- Assessing Threats and Risks
- Setting Priorities
- Apportioning Resources
- Ranking and Documenting Key Business Areas
- Harming Events and Circumstances
- Impacts to Business Areas
- Key Considerations of Impact
- Plan Fundamentals
  - Complete Loss of Premises
    - Loss of Entire Geographic Region
    - Loss of Limited, Specific, Business Location
  - Temporary Loss of Premises
- Comfort and Confidence
- Getting There

You've noticed that catastrophic loss, such as a complete loss of business premises, is at the bottom of our discussion. This is to first allow us an understanding of all incremental considerations that bear in the most usual circumstances.

The most commonly occurring events within the scope of disaster control involve such things as equipment failure of central business processing hardware; large-scale corruptions to data; perhaps loss of critical online transacting for a period.

It is logical to think through these increments first as they are 1) more likely to happen, and 2) are necessary for documentation and control in support to large-scale business recoveries and moves.

Having said that, we'll get around later to a common discussion regarding large-scale losses – such as premises or regions. We can use our treatment of that as a mental exercise – helping to sharpen our awareness and critical thinking postures for all manner of disaster, however you choose to scale your preparedness.

GAINING CONTROL

NATURAL VS. DELIBERATE HARM

Let's note here that for the *average* organization (an important distinction), terror attack manifests itself much as a natural disaster. From that perspective, it is largely unforeseen, and can have severe consequences. However, we cannot view terror attack that way when discussing organizations that have the mission, the obligation, and the comprehensive influence to mitigate terror risks. They have a consequent responsibility to abolish potentials of harm through the elimination of poorly managed, or even unmanaged, risk. That discussion will be mounted in *What's At Stake*, and for them, prevention will be their watchword. Contributions to their mission by the local organizations of any area will also be discussed at length in that chapter, as the local organization is a stakeholder in the larger Public security.

For the remaining majority of organizations, the case of natural disasters and unforeseeable terror events (or acts of sabotage, and other human harm such as mistakes) require that we secure ourselves against risk through disaster recovery planning. Further, we also have many obligations of prevention within the local scope of control – and our standards of prevention wherever possible must be well marked. For us, disasters can range from loss or corruption of data, damage to assets, and large-scale damage to business through such things floods, fire, earthquakes, power outages – perhaps even chemical, nuclear, and biological attack.

Too often, when "policy'ing and planning" these things, there is a mentality of "Something is happening," – or has happened - and "Now what do we do?" A true consideration of disaster is not reactionary. It is a proactive posture to prevent harm through identification of threat, risk, and reasonable action regarding risks. Further, it provides the guide to side-step harm when circumstances beyond our control manifest themselves. It also prepositions resources and defines our actions so that we can recover from short-term harm (indeed it helps to ensure that any harm *is* short-term) when there is no avoidance of a disastrous event's harm.

Disaster Recovery vs. *Disaster Awareness, Preparedness, and Recovery (DAPR)*

Organizations, vendors, and practices have created a ready handle for recovery from disastrous harm - *Disaster Recovery* – with the attendant disaster recovery plan. The venerable Disaster Recovery Plan is meant to secure business, and business-continuity, in the face of disaster. However, security is ill-served by this handle, and so too are many of the plans (and associated realities) that fall under it. "Recovery" is reactive, when we should have a plan that includes prevention of disaster. Some measure of prevention is within our internal control, and some lies within a planned agility in sidestepping much of outside disaster's influence. And, we strive to make disaster "transparent" to those whom we serve.

Too, mere "disaster recovery" is often given short shrift in terms of attention, resources, and any sort of test or proof of concept. Many people, particularly Business people, are left to assume their disaster recovery efforts are in place, and will work, when in fact there is no reliable evidence to support this assumption:

"Can you recover from disaster?"
"I guess so – we have a disaster recovery plan."

Many don't really know, because there's never been an event to recover *from*. But they have a plan. (Place a check in that box. Sleep well).

Absent are identified, known, and agreed upon *missions, beliefs, values, standards*, and <u>tests</u>. Here, again, we're building awareness.

- *Mission* will be defined by your requirements for prevention, recovery, subsequent assignments, and exercises. The mission will be associated with a policy, and the policy's manifestation is achieved through a plan.

- *Beliefs* include "prevention" as a standard; the understanding of prevention's true value; those things that need protection according to assessed risk and available resources; and your confidence and control.
- *Values* support your beliefs – those things valued as necessary for sustenance of business. Values will help establish that which is protected to the best point of prevention from harm. There are also those valued business elements that determine the order of recoveries according to priority.
- *Standards* establish the degrees, or levels, to which your protection is certified, in supporting preventions. Too, when recovery from damage is made, standards establish a period of time for how quickly full recovery is expected or necessary. Standards can define increments of recovery, and they support the prioritization of the valued business elements through ranking of them.
- *Tests* will be those simulations of harm that you employ to expose your level of success in preventions, recoveries, restorations, and the employment of identified alternative resources.

You must satisfy yourself (believe) that you can meet your organization's identified values and standards of business continuity in the face of disaster. These things are necessary in order to provide some assurance that the best efforts have been made according to acceptable risks and available resources.

When we arrive at that place, we find that what we really have is a policy, plan, posture – a mission - for:

DAPR

When we talk about *Disaster Awareness, Preparedness, and Recovery,* we stand a better chance for securing business in the real world. Just as we established a real, defined, handle for the loss of an American city (the "New Orleans" disaster, as opposed to "Katrina") we must associate a reality-based handle to disaster, and all business/technical considerations that go with it. The leverage to understanding and compliance is essential:

DAPR forces, not a different question but, a set of questions:

> "Are we prepared for disaster?"
> "I guess so – we have a disaster recovery plan."
> "Do you have an updated awareness for potential disasters?"

"Well, let's see – I guess we should list them."
"Now that you have an awareness, are you prepared?"
"No. We've added some events, and we have a better understanding of others."
"Are we properly prepared to prevent certain outcomes?"
"Prevention? I thought this was recovery…?"
"Can you prevent harm where appropriate? Further, can you truly *recover* from disasters - have you tested your preparedness?"
"Well, we'll have to develop some tests, and then conduct them…"

As usual, we can leverage understanding in a powerful way when we set simple and accurate identifiers right up front. DAPR helps us to better know "where we are." Disaster's potential is a part of where we are, and we need an awareness of our surroundings as a part of that. Preparedness is a route to a destination – a journey – a "how do we get there" factor. It leads us to the "where we're going" zones of prevention and recovery.

Awareness is required before you can achieve preparedness, and preparedness is necessary for requirements supporting prevention and recovery. Can you see the "where are we," "how do we get there," and "where are we going" elements of the previous statement?

We then require the satisfaction of a test to indicate your level of success in arriving at a state of prevention or recovery – and in arriving at a properly sized DAPR position for any moment in time.

Who Drives DAPR? One Guess… Particularly for Business, it is inadvisable to rely on a simple conversation with IT regarding this area. This is not to put down anyone's IT endeavors, or disaster recovery efforts. This is simply because IT may feel that they've done the best they can regarding security of business in this regard, based on the resources they've been able to lobby for (including Business' attention). It also includes IT's belief (whether erroneous or actual) that they've met the Business expectation, and mounted the best mission. But here again there is an ignorance in many organizations. Business may like the numb comfort they often have in this area: Walking away with a simple "Yes, we're covered" allows Business to go back to the core business focus of the day.

There is also a certain denial at work in many organizations, or a simple pushing aside of DAPR: "We'll get to that next quarter, next year, soon," etc. – or – "our vendor handles that." But like all things in the Business-Technology Weave, the IT Enlightened Organization makes disaster awareness, preparedness, and recovery a *Business*-driven initiative too. Who owns business-continuity? IT? No. After all, it's Business' continuity. Further, IT can only establish DAPR according to its allowance, safe-channel and lead - from Business' sanction and support. When IT fulfills a Business expectation, Business has to make sure its own expectation is sized and filled appropriately.

To Business: You own it. It is your business that will suffer from a state of non-recovery. You must oversee DAPR, its maintenance, its evolution, its testing, and you must believe that you can rely on it to your satisfaction, values, and standards. IT will serve, participate, suggest, focus, and implement the mechanics of preventions and recoveries. IT will lead when that lead is designated by Business – but policy and planning must be driven by Business.

Understanding the Elements of DAPR: Because prevention of, and recovery from, harm is so central to security, let's take a closer look at some of the fundamentals:

Awareness: Awareness starts with the board or governing body's commitment to establish and maintain a Disaster Awareness, Preparedness, and Recovery (DAPR) policy and planning process. From here, all management and staff are made aware of their requirements. Everyone has a duty to conduct business in the best possible way, in the most secure fashion, in compliance with all policies and protections. Prevention of harm begins with awareness.

If harm comes, everyone has a duty in ensuring the ability to recover from it. It requires planning at every level in order to ensure that essential business of the organization is able to continue in the face of adverse events and circumstances.

Important projects like DAPR planning have to be approved and sanctioned at the highest level in order to secure the required level of commitment and resources throughout the organization. The sale for DAPR planning should be easy to make in today's environment – for reasons we've touched on. Primary is one of business' most important foundations, which we touched on earlier:

 - *An Awareness Regarding the Business Foundation*: Business has shifted from a mostly linear, non-abstract system of paper, filing cabinets, adding machines, and largely non-intermediary systems of support - to a virtual, almost abstract environment. It is now one of electronic bits and bytes, accessible only through the intermediary of computer systems, allied applications, and associated availability. Further, there has been a steady expansion of this foundation. Growth of wide area networks, their ties to the internet, their ties to other business locations, and remote access that ties in home computing and all manner of other access, has exploded the vulnerabilities to be managed. Thus, through the corresponding expansion of access to this foundation – there has been expansion of exposure and expanded risk of harm.

Remember that we are talking about a *foundation* to business here – not some enhancement, appendage, or luxury. This is a foundational underpinning that you cannot allow to be knocked out from under – otherwise your business crashes, and you cannot "do."

Harm to this foundation can be unintentionally sourced: things such as earthquakes, power failures, weather damage, etc. Short of nature, harm can arise from simple human mistakes or oversights: someone can corrupt the content of a database by transferring the wrong information into it. Someone may accidentally delete or move (lose) entire structures of data, break important links, and throw crucial parts of business offline.

Harm from human interaction can also be intentional: things such as acts of sabotage from within or with-out, or terror attack. We'll take a closer look at a number of specific risks when we discuss *Threats*. For now, awareness starts with a true appreciation for the vulnerability to this foundation, the sheer weight and range of disruption to business should this foundation be removed for any period, and the absolute necessity in securing it to the best possible degree.

Preparedness: Preparedness should first and foremost be seen as a posture of prevention from harm. Preparedness next defines action and resources in the event of harm. Preparedness begins with its contribution to policy, such that our awareness gets translated into a plan and an outcome. The plan can then be effected to meet the policy's stated objectives.

You can combine your policy and plan: *The XYZ Corporation's Disaster Awareness, Preparedness & Recovery Policy and Plan*. In fact, your policy will not completely take shape without the plan – they are reinforcing, particularly as they develop. But a firm sense of policy must precede the plan; so as to identify your organization's concept of DAPR, and the basic principles and levels of prevention and recovery expected (you must know the "where you are" of expectations before you can plan to your "where you're going" destination of deliverables).

The policy states the *mission* – the detail you deem essential in explaining your organization's critical business functions, the expectations for preventions, the required recovery protocols for disastrous harm, and responsibilities. Further, it should expose the beliefs, values, and standards for these essential business functions and their dependencies, or supports.

Because resources are not unlimited, the organization must arrive at agreement for what constitutes the greatest risks, the likelihood of events, and the impact of those events on various ranked business elements. Once your organization has agreement among various lines of business, practices, departments, agencies, etc., you have common *beliefs* in what merits protection – *values* – and can proceed with the plan for protection and recovery of those things. We can note here that you may not achieve total agreement, but in that case the belief will at least be acknowledgment of, and agreement to, compromises made, and actions resulting.

Once things have been prioritized, you can set various *standards* for prevention and recovery: the planning of the what, when, how, and where. When you've established the mission, beliefs, values, and standards through policy, and made the plan for meeting the policy's objectives, we define the tests that we'll employ to validate our recovery plan.

Recovery: Unlike other Business and IT objectives, your disaster recovery posture is usually never fully realized, and never fully known. That is to say, your ability to recover from disaster does not usually evidence itself (hopefully) in a real-world manifestation. Conversely, almost anything else you do is reflected back to you in the form of real-world success and feedback. For example, if you launch a new product, it either succeeds in the marketplace, or it doesn't. You may have tested it beforehand through survey or some small market, but you *will* have the ultimate arbiter of the real marketplace as your final ringing authority; it will either deem your product some measure of success, or deem it a failure. You won't have to wonder.

Disaster recovery is something we hope never to "test" in the real world. Of course, right up front we know that we don't want to experience disaster – that's obvious. But secondarily, if there is a disaster, we don't want our recovery efforts to be the first test. A test implies an unknown – will we pass or fail the test? That is the test's purpose – to eliminate that unknown by exposing a true level of knowledge and ability.

Therefore, we want to test beforehand, and on some regularized basis, so as to expose points of failure, and areas where we can improve. As our environment changes, our disaster recovery testing continually exposes and helps us to eliminate unknowns – divides between our ever-new requirements, and standards for prevention and recoveries. This way, we can reasonably expect a yield of *success* when following our plan, in meeting our policy's requirements when we have to deliver on a real-world test.

As best we can make it, recovery from disaster needs to be efficient, effective, predictable – and safe.

DAPR is Never Finished: Security must be made a routine part of the day. A good way to handle DAPR is to have delegates, such as members of the BIT team or their assignations, participate in the creation, maintenance, and evolution of your policies and plans in this area, and in the testing of the deliverables necessary for continuity of business. Further, this team should deliver a regularized report to senior management regarding the organization's security posture against evolving conditions of risk.

Any denial is extremely risky as the destination is always moving further out: you accrue new systems, exposures, and risks – the world turns – and challenges to the organization mount. You continue to drive toward the evolving destination in fulfilling the best state of preparedness you can – regardless of limits. Prevention is possible only through exposure and mitigation of risk. Recovery is possible only for having prepared for a recovery.

If and when your organization has a robust DAPR plan, still realize that there is always room for improvement, and that meeting essential DAPR requirements is a moving target. If your organization has no DAPR plan, or has one that is outdated, incomplete, or merely represents a feel-good placeholder, Business and IT need to begin an immediate address of the problem. Getting a basic plan in place is akin to acquiring your wind, merely in order to compete in the race – threats and risks don't stand still in the change continuum.

DAPR: Policy and Plan

Now that we've established an understanding of awareness, preparedness, and recovery, let's discuss policy and plan in further detail. It is policy that will help the organization at-large adopt and adhere to the appropriate level of awareness. It is the plan that will translate the organization's awareness into achievement of proper preparedness. Let's look at policy first:

Policy: Your policy defines and sets the mission. Your DAPR policy has to acknowledge some realities. If money were no object, all organizations, and each of us as individuals, would maintain a comprehensive "mirror" of our computing platforms, content, and systems. It's been said that Lehman Brothers were back online, conducting full business, 20 minutes after losing their primary business site in New York on 9/11. They maintained a staffed, duplicate, physical site across the river - essentially a comprehensive "backup" of all content, platform, business systems, people, and real-time transactions as they went along. From a pure business perspective: Loss of their primary site simply meant a few technical changes to throw the alternate site online, as the new primary.

It may seem a cruel example to discuss the continuity of business in the face of catastrophic human loss, such as that which occurred on 9/11 in America. But what we can realize here is that if we're able to make business recovery as rote and as painless as possible, we're able to focus that much more on helping *people*. The need for a job, a solid place of employment, and the sustaining of an economy are not going to melt away in the face of disaster. Taking care of survivors, and surviving family members, does not go away. Indeed, meeting those needs will be of extreme importance to the organization. Therefore we can think of it as a manifest duty to secure the relatively "mundane" continuity of business in the face of human disaster – to have the path cleared of competition for attention of our bruised minds, as it were, so as not to blur or obscure our focus for taking care of people.

Setting Priorities, Apportioning Resources: The Lehman Brothers example is one of extremes: extreme disaster, and extremely good recovery (fast, comprehensive, and according to plan). Understand too that their recovery from disaster presented a prevention-face to the world: they prevented the loss of their ability to conduct business, in the face of an extreme impact. Certainly if you're part of an organization that has the resources to mount a security and recovery posture such as Lehman Brother's, all to the good. The larger challenge is for the majority of organizations that have limited resources. It can be difficult to know how to apportion critical resources for DAPR vis-à-vis the daily concerns. Too, it can be difficult to know how to apportion resources *within* DAPR. After all, there will be competing business concerns even in this arena.

There is competition for all resources in sustaining the overwhelming normalcy of conditions: the daily business grind. It is a challenge just to meet those requirements in keeping up, and remaining functional and competitive. Even if you feel you have no real competition (perhaps you're a non-profit with a unique set of products and services) you must still remain functional in an ever-changing world. Within the demands of the real-world day-to-day, and in planning the future of the day-to-day, how do we responsibly apportion and balance critical resources for something that *might* happen, and which "probably won't"?

Rank and Document Key Business Areas: A logical start is for a DAPR team to identify, list, and rank key business areas. This way, the policy will guide Business' application of resources. As we've said before, your BIT team can begin DAPR planning, or DAPR may be delegated to a subset of this group – whatever is efficient and effective. As with all projects engaged by BIT, the DAPR planning team will further assign responsibilities as necessary. This team will also bring other people onto the team where appropriate, or invite them into specific discussions as the planning goes along.

Assembly of coherent business documentation for each of these areas is crucial. We don't need to provide a generic list here of functional areas: each organization should have a good start on this documentation. You can also find sample lists and ideas on the web for areas of inclusion to your own list, if your concern is that you're overlooking something. With simple diligence, this ranking will not be difficult to do – particularly if you survey your department heads for their ideas to DAPR.

Remember too that your organization has likely already identified and described key business areas, and associated values, standards, and practices. Where this documentation exists, it can be appropriated and *repurposed* to DAPR (here is where content management can assist and streamline this process) – no need to reinvent the wheel. Even if you are not yet maintaining critical business documentation, you may still find surprising information in this regard: You can dig for important detail regarding business processes, and associated values and standards, in such things as job descriptions, RFPs, and sales and marketing literature. Consider other areas too; these often have comprehensive descriptions of business process and associated needs. Collect, repurpose, create, and build the documentation as necessary.

Once you have identified major business areas, your team can begin to rank the areas in order of importance to the organization. Your list should include a description of each business process, and its relation to other processes (its dependencies on, and its supports to, any other processes). Also document whatever other dependencies exist: internal systems and resources, external systems and resources, and personnel, for example. The list will reveal important interdependencies, many of which have never been known, formally recognized, and documented.

Leveraging Documentation: In some cases, you may be rediscovering knowledge, and this is extremely important. As many of us are painfully aware, there are countless systems out there that were put into place by people long gone from the organization. These are mystery systems – the people utilizing them and counting on them hope that they keep working. Often, no one knows how to service them, or how to upgrade them for currency. Perhaps associated vendors and companies have gone out of business, or sold their product to someone else. Maybe you have systems that were developed in-house, and that were never properly documented. Some of these systems' technical concerns are too complicated to understand in the fast moving environment of the usual business day – imagine trying to recover them following a disaster.

These systems drifted so far off the maintenance map that only through Herculean effort can we bring these systems back into the zone of the known: A nice benefit of DAPR is that it often helps your ongoing business efforts by identifying and documenting all areas so that you have comprehensive, "bullet-proof" knowledge that is independent of employee turnover and other change. Therefore, DAPR should also prevent any business process or system from drifting into an undocumented and poorly maintained state. The DAPR posture and the documentation you build also contributes to content, and its management.

Assessing Risk: Once these key business areas have been ranked, they should be assessed for risk. Risk can influence how you direct your resources, and can even re-order some of your key areas in terms of priority for protection and recovery. You may have an internal business process that is critical, and which, at first glance, occupies a high order on your list for protection, recovery, and resources. However, this process may be in the exclusive control of internal, trustworthy, personnel, within a physical security space. Perhaps equipment and process are in a secure laboratory at a business site. The site may already have local departmental control and protection that already makes demands on resources, and which are sized to protection in accordance with DAPR. In this circumstance, the DAPR policy can nod to this condition, and better utilize the organization's resources elsewhere on the list.

Other conditions may take seemingly lower-priority areas to a greater elevation on the list. Let's say you're transferring data on a daily basis to business locations that have unreliable connectivity due to surrounding, relatively undeveloped, infrastructure. Here you may choose to place alternate, backup, means to transport data to these locations. You may employ redundant point-to-point connections that rely on different service providers and transports, for example. In this example, you may allot greater resource to the external business locations than you would have at first surmised necessary – having assumed data-transfers to be mundane.

There are other influencers as you develop your plan. For example, you may have a critical business function that is an absolute necessity for business continuity. However, if that process is hosted – that is, if it is being supported mainly by a vendor, at their site - it largely falls under their DAPR-equivalent plan. The continuity of business mission, beliefs, values and standards would translate as a service level agreement (SLA) within your contract with that vendor. That vendor should provide test results, and also conduct any testing in concert with your organization, to your satisfaction. Thus, realize that your DAPR resources will not always weight in direct proportion to risk, or even importance, of key areas. There will be many influencers that will evidence themselves as you plan – another important realization for the need to bring DAPR into focus. Once the organization has a good understanding of how to rank process and systems within the scope of critical business functions, their dependencies, and risks - a definition of the mission will begin to take shape, and an assignment of resources can be made. Resources such as money, personnel, equipment and time must be fairly and proportionately budgeted according to accurate requirements for prevention and recovery.

People: In the review of various organizations' "disaster recovery" postures, and even when appraising model plans on the web, we will notice something curious. Many plans don't account for the loss of *people*. Likely, it is because of the simple fact that we don't like to think about losing co-workers, friends, and other associates. We also don't like to think about our own risk in this regard. Yet, this omission is surprising, and we should expand on a concept here: People are our biggest challenge, our biggest resource, and, from a pure business perspective, they are a huge investment and a critical asset. We hope that we never lose people, but none-the-less have to plan for their loss – not planning for this contingency would be irresponsible.

Hopefully your organization already has a model in place to cover for absences. Vacations, arrivals of new children, emergencies, promotions, dismissals, turnover, all contribute to the necessity for a plan of coverage to essential duties and support of systems and processes. Here again DAPR assists in the normal course of business by helping us to establish an awareness, and subsequent construction of a "weave" of backup. We have personnel who are trained to a necessary degree and who know enough to step in as an alternate player to cover absences to positions. In the formal case of the DAPR policy and plan, people know what their duties are regarding recovery, and they know how to shift given specific absences of personnel. Let's note here that unavailability of personnel doesn't have to be related to death or injury during disaster. You may find that key people simply cannot *reach* the worksite due to environmental problems, as an example.

Plan: The DAPR Plan, and its actualization, is the manifestation of your policy. Your policy should set the overall mission, beliefs, values, and standards for prevention – as well as recovery, when recover is necessary. The mission and its associated quality will be actualized in detail by the plan. In this way, prevention is defined, and a schedule and level of recovery is established. And, when prevention and recovery are performed according to plan, they satisfy the policy.

Threats and Risk: The condition of threat is the thrust behind planning. Threats enter your awareness, you assess associated risk, and where necessary you make a plan of action in order to deny threats' delivery of harm. You also plan recovery actions when threat manifests as actual harm.

As you consider your DAPR policy and plan, you must assess various threats for consideration of risk to your business, and to what level you need to accommodate these risks. The same threat may pose different risks to different organizations. For example, an organization that serves reference material to customers can possibly afford to be off of the web for an hour or so. However, for an organization that relies heavily or solely on real-time, time-sensitive online transacting, such as stock brokering, or something like ebay, being offline for even a few minutes can cause extreme inconvenience or even damage to customers. It can also hurt that organization's reputation tremendously – imagine if AOL was offline.

Also realize that the same threat may represent differing demands on resources to differing organizations. For example, some organizations will be in a sole location – they may store their offsite backup data within that same city or general geographic area. We know this to be a condition for many organizations. A catastrophic disaster could conceivably wipe out the whole of their business intelligence – or ready access to it, and hence would impede their whole recovery effort. They may have to consider the expense of offsite storage to another city.

Another organization may be more dispersed, and may be able to afford and secure more redundancies (of data, and complete business platforms) because of already existing alternate business locations. Indeed, each discreet business location within a chain could be a backup to another location. A citywide disaster at one of their locations would, from a strictly business point of view, be far less threatening to their continuity of business. The former organization at the sole location may have to allocate a larger proportion of their total resources to DAPR than the latter.

Therefore, you must get the issues on your table for threat evaluation of the risk imposed, against ranked business processes. Even if you feel that some items are beyond your capacity or resource to deal with, you should still document them; set the reasons why their scope of treatment is as it is; and document whose authority set the scale of treatment.

Apportion your resources for DAPR against a sanctioned policy and plan that is understood and agreed to by all relevant parties.

Harming Events and Circumstances: By no means comprehensive, these things should be accommodated by your DAPR policy and planning process:

- *Environmental Events*
  - Weather
    - Snowstorms
    - Floods
    - Lightning
    - Tornado
    - Hurricane
    - Rain

  - Natural Hazards/Danger
    - Fire
    - Drought
    - Landslide
    - Contamination
    - Epidemic

- *Deliberate Acts of Disruption*
  - Terrorism
  - Sabotage
  - War
  - Theft
  - Arson
  - Disputes

- *Utilities*
  - Loss of electrical power
  - Loss of gas
  - Loss of water
  - Oil shortage or unavailability
  - Loss of local or National communications system

- *Equipment and Systems*
  - Internal loss of power
  - Loss of air conditioning or heating
  - Production, plant, or equipment failure (excluding IT)

- *Information Security and IT Equipment*
  - Exposure of sensitive content
  - Damage from Cyber crime (attacks, hacks)
  - Damage to content and/or systems from malware (viruses, keystroke monitoring, tracking software, malicious code to destruct data, etc.)
  - Loss of content, or loss of access to content
  - IT system failures
  - Loss of connectivity to the Internet
  - Loss of eCommerce capability
  - Unavailability of e-mail
  - Damage to main business system(s)

- *Other*
  - Legal issues
  - Mergers or acquisitions
  - Emerging and impacting business, health, and safety regulations
  - Workplace violence
  - Public transportation, public utility, neighborhood hazard, and other like-issues that can impact employee availability
  - Negative publicity
  - Employee morale
  - Harm from inadequate care, or mistakes

Any of these things represent a threat to the effective conduct of business. Your organization must assess your specific vulnerabilities relative to likelihood, threat, risk, and business priorities. As you examine each area, consider the impact to functional business areas. When planning protection to, and recovery to, specific business areas, it may help to simplify or focus things by keeping this in front of you:

- *Loss of All Centralized Processing and Systems*

- *Loss of Some Centralized Processing or Some Systems*

- *Loss of Content*

- *Damage to Content*

Remember that in addition to the core business systems that you use and "see" every day, there are other systems supporting your business that you may not think much about. You need to reestablish e-mail connectivity to the world. You need to reestablish any eCommerce, web traffic, and domain presence that you have. You've got to get voice communications going, and you need to reestablish customer service endeavors. You may need public relations, or perception management, help in communicating the organization's status to the public.

Also, don't overlook the fact that following disaster, DAPR does not go away during the challenge of continuing business: you must reestablish your backup and recovery scheme; if you're in a new location, you may need new solutions partners, etc.

KEY DOCUMENTATION

Begin to assemble the information you'll need to reestablish business in any circumstance:

- Organization charts, key staff, staff disaster responders, emergency contact information
- Business process documentation
- eCommerce
- E-mail
- Other real-time transactions and services
- Production lines
- Human Resources Management
- IT services
- Marketing
- Public relations/perception management
- Maintenance and support services
- Quality control, quality of service, terms of service, etc.
- Customer service
- Sales and related administration
- Finance, treasury, accounting, and auditing
- Research and development
- Strategic initiative and planning activities
- List of vendors, suppliers, contractors, and contact information.
- List of emergency services and contact information
- Business locations, premises, addresses, maps and floor plans

- Evacuation procedures
- Fire, health and safety regulations and procedures
- Operations and administrative procedures
- Inventories
- Systems documentation and specifications
- Maintenance and service level agreements
- Offsite storage and recovery procedures
- Alternate business location information
- Insurance documentation

When planning protection and recovery from disaster, you must go to the highest levels of disasters and their impact, and your reasonable dispersal and application of available resources against the threats and risks. Don't be afraid that you'll sound ridiculous. Don't cripple your definition of disaster – disaster is disaster. In fact, a starting position of *"This will never happen, but..."* is perfect. You may not apportion much, or any, of your precious resources against the "never happens," but by putting them on the table for discussion, Business and IT have acknowledged them, and have made certain that senior management, boards, governance, customer expectations, and any and all regulatory requirements are in complete satisfaction with the DAPR posture of your organization as regards all contingencies.

Also, by examining the largest disaster you can imagine, and by ticking down incrementally through various scenarios, you are less likely to miss an important accommodation to your recovery posture – *as opposed to starting or stopping in some "reasonable middle."* (And, it saves the team the time of batting around what the "reasonable middle" is; it should also prevent a discounting of disaster, assuming proper sanction for appropriate disaster planning).

Some Plan Fundamentals

We can and should discuss some fundamentals that apply to any organization. Starting with, and accommodating, the largest form of disasters will allow us to speak to everyone. It also grooms everyone's mind toward the condition that the standard here is to ferret out all threat and risk, for purpose of prevention of harm, protection, and defined recoveries when necessary. As importantly, it forces the organization to acknowledge its overall posture and any exposures.

As you go through your plan, and tackle smaller issues, your organization can decide how high on the scale of threat and risk it can afford to go or not go, specific to your situation. Regardless, our exercise here will expose the critical thinking and faculties necessary for examining issues large or small, and in establishing awareness, preparedness, and recovery for them.

Take the following awarenesses and apply them in your discussions:

COMPLETE LOSS OF PREMISES: Here the assumption and contingencies are made that you have permanent loss of your premises – you'll never return. Again, we're going to focus on those organizations that need the most DAPR help – those that cannot afford the luxury of a shotgun approach to complete business site mirroring.

Here we can consider two basic conditions for contingencies within a loss of physical premises:

- *Loss of an entire geographic area*: In these cases, an entire geographic region, such as a city or county, can no longer support business, resulting in a loss of your premises. Whether a natural or human event, it can be brought by such things as radiation; long-term loss of infrastructure like roads; or loss of ability to produce power, sustain utilities, provide police protection services, etc. During conditions of disaster, there is also the prospect of Government-ordered long-term evacuations, whether the general Public is in a position to anticipate such a move, or not -

    -and -

- *Loss of a limited, specific, business location*: In these cases, a business suffers the loss of their location through some localized disaster: maybe your building is removed by earthquake, or bomb, or access is lost through environmental hazard such as biological, chemical, or radiological contamination. In this case, your surrounding supports (infrastructures, utilities, police protection, etc.) remain intact. Only your primary business premises are removed from your use.

Let's look at these conditions in-turn:

LOSS OF AN ENTIRE GEOGRAPHIC AREA: If your organization has multiple locations dispersed across a Nation or around the world, you can have a designate sister organization for each location. Each location would provide reinforcement to a designated site – and vice versa. This way one of your remote organizations, removed from the disaster, would take up the business of the location that was lost. Each local DAPR planner works with the sister location regarding preparedness for restoration of content and systems.

It is possible to have these multiple locations serving as backup-up, real-time transactional processing sites: essentially a complete mirror of your location. In other words, all accounting, sales, services, communications, inventories, statuses, contracts, websites, etc., are maintained to the same degree - and are transacted, updated, and stored simultaneously at the sister site. Important hardcopy information would have to be mailed or pouched there, and maintained. In the event of disaster, the sister site initiates action to activate this mirror as the primary business platform for the lost site: changing over customer service phone lines, activating e-mail, contacting internet service providers and other solutions partners, administering reports, performing month end closes, performing maintenance to systems, etc. To maintain this posture of preparedness, the sister site needs necessary processing power, bandwidth, storage, and staff.

More affordable and suitable to the average dispersed organization may be to have the sister sites serve largely as offsite storage for their counterparts in the plan. This can mean a complete duplicate set of electronic business systems for ready install, associated documentation, and data: the sister site can procure additional hardware, infrastructure, and personnel at the actual time of disaster, and restore these systems to a platform for the conduct of the inoperative location's business. In this scenario, the organization sends initial copies of business systems and documentation to the sister organization where it is maintained on backup media, ready for implementation. Any time systems or documentation changes, comprehensive updates are sent to replace the old versions. Data – content - should be sent nightly: it doesn't have to be all content each night – only that content which has changed over the course of the past day.

This data-send can be done as a replication via broadband, can be a file transfer that is administered through a web portal (or site), or can even be a type of courier or mail transfer – many organizations have regularized pouches going back and forth between sites. Whatever suits your organization according to affordability and necessity. Some organizations may be comfortable with weekly transfers, for example. Your plan should also identify and make allowance for the dispatch of key personnel to the sister location to lead the resumption of business.

For these sorts of circumstances, the local DAPR planners would likely (hopefully) be operating within a guide established by, and with assistance from, a higher headquarters. The BIT team at higher headquarters would lead this project by creating a project team comprising other BIT members at all other locations.

The Single-Location Organization: What if your organization is a sole location enterprise, and can never return to its physical premises? If a large geographical area surrounding your location is rendered inaccessible, you must have a plan to get business up and running in a place that is likely to be quite a distance from your former premises. You'll have to relocate key staff in the days immediately following disaster. That means you must not only identify staff, but you must certify their flexibility and commitment to this move beforehand.

We need to understand that disasters of large magnitude can remove a professional commitment that was made in the comfort of a conference room, coffee in hand. Personal and family concerns can and will take over in many instances – in some instances that will be necessary and correct – but where does that leave disaster awareness, preparedness, and *recovery*? DAPR poorly staffed is no DAPR at all. So – you must select the disaster responders carefully, according to character, commitment, and the ability to do what is required. If a requirement is to pack up and move on a moment's notice, think about what that means, communicate it to the team, and seek and find those that you feel can best adhere to that commitment – to ensure the *organization* adheres to the plan. A plan is no good if you can't execute it for predictable and successful outcomes. In fact, it's worse than no good – it was a waste of time and effort, and stole the place of proper efforts.

Your contingencies here must be examined closely. If the whole region is suffering the same calamity as your business location, keep this in mind: Yours will not be the only business competing for new space. Space will command premium prices, and competition for space with supports for business (power, lighting, data wiring, physical security, communications, etc.) will be fierce - for those who have not planned in advance. True contingency planning in this case involves the reservation of guaranteed space at an outsourced location – it becomes a part of your overall business insurance- and there are many solutions partners who suit this need.

You need to decide how far away this location can be while still being practical. If you lose an entire area, such as a city, you'll need to quickly assemble key people at the remote reserved office space. You may have to quickly assemble and train some measure of new hires at the new location – therefore, ensure that there are sufficient contractors or temporary staffing agencies in that location. You must also have prior arrangement for the delivery of necessary equipment, systems, and data in order to reconstitute business. If available, and if your budget supports it, you can reserve business-ready spaces – they come populated with an appropriate measure of guaranteed equipment that suits your near-term recovery need according to a contracted service level agreement. Things such as office furniture, central computing equipment, fileservers, workstations, phones, routers, switches, firewalls, internet connectivity, etc.

Don't purchase your own stock of equipment for a backup business site (unless the site is a functional mirror) – it will quickly go out of date: never purchase equipment to sit on a shelf. Leave equipment concerns to vendors who "roll stock." You can reserve space, and leave the equipment concerns to your backup and recovery vendor. Have agreements in place for the necessary equipment, and a deadline for emplacing it and enabling it for the conduct of business. Your recovery vendor should be the one who stores your offsite data. A fully integrated plan for space, equipment, and systems/data recovery, regardless of the number of solutions partners engaged, should involve planning and discussion through real-time collaboration of all recovery parties.

For organizations that are unable to apportion resources to these sorts of scenarios, there are still ways to improve your chances for continuity of business. At least identify potential solutions partners and support vendors in a remote location, and build a contact list. Have your recovery personnel make contact with these service providers, and identify what will be necessary to establish business with these providers on a quick-term basis should you have to move operations. Most of these vendors will be willing to accept a credit application, and will be willing to exchange a business agreement with you in anticipation for future business. In other words, do what you can to avoid cold starts in the face of disaster.

Certainly identify all no-cost, low-cost, actions and allowances you can take and make beforehand. Identify systems, process, resources, personnel, documentation, and actions – store this information with your offsite backup vendor. Be imaginative and creative in doing the best that you can within whatever limitations exist. No one can expect more than your organization's best. Make absolutely certain that you present a status regarding preparedness to those authorities with responsibility for continuity of business. This way, any limitations and risks imposed cannot be overlooked – or disavowed.

LOSS OF A LIMITED, SPECIFIC, AREA AND BUSINESS LOCATION: If a catastrophe is limited to your building, or to some measure of city blocks for example, your business can trigger a plan to occupy nearby business space. Here you could satisfy convenience by remaining local, but things can be tricky. If you're paying for reserved, guaranteed remote space – just how remote is it? Should you move into that space? Or is it better to have guaranteed local space in the first place, as opposed to remote? Should you have both?

Only your organization can answer these questions. Again, these are the things that the organization must decide based on the assessment of threats, risks, *acceptable risks*, and available resources. If your organization has a sole location in a city, and is providing goods and services that are somehow specific to that city, you may come to the realization that there's no sense making contingency for a disaster that *removes* the city. Therefore, if your decision is to reserve contingency space, you can apportion your budget to guaranteed reserve *local* space – remote space will do you no good! Also recognize that if a loss of premises is due to very specific local considerations, there will be no real competition for alternate space – it should be easy to find.

Whether you decide to pay for a reservation of guaranteed space or not, you need to make an informed decision: your plan should cover the estimated level of competition you can expect for nearby, readily accessible, space for various degrees of disaster. This can be done by first uncovering just how much available space exists generally, the density of business in your region, and your own estimation for a prudent budget against a likelihood of events - against acceptable risk.

Again, in coordination with your disaster recovery partners (likely beginning with your offsite storage vendor), you can have a model in place for delivery of the necessary technical platforms for business: centralized computing; workstations; phones; internet connectivity; restoration of data, applications, and processes; etc. A pre-identified, representative proportion of people from critical departments and business functional areas would report to the designated location to perform essential business functions and services in the days following disaster. Having fundamentals identified, however rudimentarily sketched, will offer tremendous leverage in getting business up and running in the face of disaster.

Temporary Loss of Access to Premises: A temporary loss of premises can be a matter of an hour - to a few hours - to days, weeks, or months. Anything approaching weeks or a month probably kicks your plan into the same gear as would a permanent loss of premises, except that the plan is executed for a limited duration of loss.

For loss of access to premises in the duration of hours - such as during fire drills/events, bomb threats, false alarms of some sort, etc., it is helpful to have an identified sequence of action to be taken. For example, the central reception authority should change to an organizational voicemail indicating that the organization is temporarily unavailable, with an expected return later in the day. IT should collect and exit with the prior night's backup, and any other pre-identified media and documentation that requires removal in case a "temporary" delay turns into a prolonged one. An e-mail notification list can exist to alert clients, customers, members, etc., that some or all elements of business may be suspended, and an expected duration.

At the same time, alternate means of contact can also be identified and communicated. Members of the BIT team should imagine themselves in several roles: their own formal role in the organization, the role of customer, the role of subordinates, etc., and determine valid expectations and requirements for various levels of events and disasters. Gradually, your plan of action will fill in, and it will become as comprehensive a disaster-proof weave as you can make it.

You may think these things obvious – but organizations frequently fail in basic actions – either in their planning, or in their execution. They don't necessarily fall short because they've failed to identify, but rather because there is a lack of awareness, training, testing and refreshers. Fire drills are fairly routine: Who in your business has ever approached IT in the street or parking lot and asked "who has the backup?" Many organizations fail this simple test. No one thought to grab the backup, or a designate forgot. If you suddenly find yourself outside, can you confidently know that clients, constituents, customers, etc., will receive an appropriate notification that routine business is offline for the moment? Or will they be left to wonder…

In the future - as security takes a higher position in everyone's awareness – your customers, clients, members, etc. will take a dim view of you if they are unable to contact or transact with you for some duration, or are unable to receive basic information regarding services. Woe to you if you're not tracking critical business processes or deals or services that require time-sensitive activity – activity that will not tolerate hours' or a day's delay. If your clientele find later that it was a mundane fire drill, technical outage, or simple evacuation caused by hoax causing their frustration, they'll be left to wonder: What is these peoples' preparedness for a *real* emergency?

DAPR Provides Comfort and Confidence

Everyone's DAPR training and documentation should reinforce an escalating series of actions for escalating events. For example, if a power failure lasts longer than the duration of your backup power supplies, your systems will do a hard crash. In this circumstance, you don't want your sensitive equipment and systems simply snapping off when the batteries run out of power. Potential for corruption of operating systems, business applications, and data is too great. Therefore you must have an ability to assess a situation according to the best information at-hand, and to shut down systems, and consequently business, according to your best judgment.

If the area is experiencing intermittent power during your evacuation, someone has to evaluate the risk to systems against the benefit of leaving them online. Therefore, for any level of impact, you need a concise document that can help to steer action. At some threshold of event, a part of your documentation will be a set of identified players for quick-time consultation upon an emergency, for rapid decision-making. The document and its contents must support prior disaster awareness training; this way, your disaster recovery team will be able to execute the appropriate actions according to the scale of events, in a timely fashion, and under potential duress.

A Word about Checklists: Checklists for different impacts should exist. You must build your particular checklists for consideration of every reasonable "possible," in accordance with your organization's specific needs, approvals, and resources. At the same time, a checklist cannot supplant common sense and good judgment. The checklists should help to make certain that necessary actions are not overlooked – they should not be a straightjacket that forces a sequence of activity that ignores evolving circumstances or better judgments. Also, checklists are not plans - they are tools within plans.

Getting There: The Organization has What it Needs: Model or sample DAPR plans are beyond our scope here (grab some disaster plans off the net if you like), simply because there are too many organizations and too many variables to cover all situations. Further, it is dangerous for anyone to presume that they can craft a solid plan from afar – for this reason, make certain that those charged with developing your policy and plan are fully aware, engaged, and understand their mission.

Your organization has what it needs to create a strong DAPR posture. Developing your policy and plan requires close inspection by those present; requires intelligent analysis; requires difficult compromises and decisions; and you must end with thoroughly understood agreements by everyone involved (governance, policy makers, planners, staff, vendors and solutions partners).

The goal is to establish a formal process to be followed during disaster – one which allows the organization to prevent business failure from disruptive incidents, is understood by all concerned as to how it is to be executed, and is up to date. By "up to date," we mean that your DAPR posture reflects current circumstances; those *within* the organization (state of the business and technology, associated risks and vulnerabilities), and *with-out* (threats, conditions, variables, etc.).

Remember: Your organization has everything it needs to mount DAPR: a group of people who should thoroughly understand business process, a group of people who understand the supports, and there will be a group of people with a prudent understanding of threats. There will be individuals in your organization who have a measure of all three understandings. Mesh the proper people into a weave within the BIT forum so that you can deliver the ultimate success in mounting DAPR.

Don't forget that you must regularly review and test your protection, contingency and recovery arrangements. This is the only real way to ensure that your policy and planning are up to date, and are comprehensive. Only through test can the organization satisfy itself, and report to others, that it can withstand or recover from a given major incident. Realize too: DAPR has a payout outside of the direct disaster considerations. An effective DAPR posture means that you can protect and maintain business during normal business conditions – a new scale of reliability, general quality, and service should evidence itself in the course of the routine – which leads to the other side of security: the *routine*.

Managing the Balance between Security and The Routine

Beyond disaster or harmful events, we find that security requires simple, steady management of the day-to-day, and prudent evolution into the future. A fair number of organizations look upon security from a limited view of malicious intent or some unanticipated disaster. Of course, this view misses the fact that most business failures occur during relatively benign times.

We can consider business failure a couple of different ways. We can view it as a cessation of existence, as when an organization "goes out of business." In these cases, we don't want to miss the fact that non-profits and like organizations go out of business too. Even government agencies go by the wayside through reorganization or closures if there is a failure to perform and deliver, or if an overarching mission moves beyond what a specific institution can effectively deliver. On the other hand, we can consider business failure as shortfalls within a continuing organization, such as when an organization misses targets or objectives; when it loses market share; when profits fall; or by failing to attract and retain quality personnel.

A business failure can result from poor planning, yielding poor execution, and poor outcomes. It can be failure to achieve an effective Business-Technology Weave, for example, and the unwitting sustaining of divides – everything we've talked about. Regardless - whether we talk about comprehensive failure of the organization (resulting in its demise), or specific failures within, you must recognize that all failure is a threat to security to one degree or another: security of mission, project, people, product, and organization. If a business cannot articulate and plan its guard for its continued existence within the normal business swim, it is certainly not secured. *It has no security.*

Here we won't regrind *The Success Culture,* or belabor your need for one-year, five-year, even ten-year plans… We know we need defined missions, discipline, accountability… beliefs, values, standards, and so on and so forth. But an important point is made: In a world of increasing risk and exposure, you cannot afford to short-change daily attention to security. All "normal" conduct of business must be viewed and discussed through the security prism too. You must realize the importance and relevance of everything the Weave represents, offers, and requires from the security standpoint.

All of this leads us to an acknowledgment: we must balance the force of business against prudence. We must balance security awareness between DAPR and the "day." It won't do any organization much good to have a robust security awareness and DAPR posture as they spiral steadily down through broken service models, poor products, ethical challenges, or general obsolescence, etc. Did Enron's larger security apparatus overcome their ultimate challenges to business security? No.

The aware organization has the advantage of maintaining and enhancing security through every initiative, every project, every policy, every plan, every investment, every compliance, and every action. It is the organization's duty – *any* organization's – to examine the security of business considerations inherent within every element of action, and it has the responsibility to maintain security by virtue of this broad weave. When overall conduct of business is viewed this way, security and DAPR almost become a roll-up. When every member of the organization is security-aware, it becomes an efficient process for managers to collect concerns, to deliver them to the parties on the BIT and other teams, for inclusion to overall security planning.

We will further discuss the routine daily relationship between security, success, and balance in the upcoming chapter *The Heart of It All (Turning the Crank).* For now…

Managing the Edge – Make it Routine Too: We must manage the Edge in contribution to security. We've already defined the Edge as a responsible forward posture whereby we have our plans clearly defined, sanctioned by IT and Business, and properly balanced according to change, resources, expectations, and needs. We know that your organization is always changing: its business (even if just by nuance), the staff (through turnover, promotion, training, etc.), associated technology, and support. And, we know the surrounding environment changes and influences you too. Therefore, a secure edge is really a comprehensive view of many Edges. Each initiative, group, individual, vendor, competition, etc., has its own Edge – that leading element of change and progress. Keeping the Edge in mind, and what you do to maintain it, keeps the present from completely crowding out those things you need to do in serving the future.

In fact, if you can make The Edge a routine part of considerations, you've achieved an important perspective and balance. Assessing any initiative's impacts to the future is an important part of the present. And, as we've stated earlier, anything that can be made routine, must be made routine, in order to make room for the coming challenges. Whether those challenges are unanticipated demands on business, or entirely new disciplines, emergencies, threats, etc., it should be obvious that anything we can do to "regularize" things strengthens our posture.

When examining any part of the Weave, always consider the next step. It's almost like playing pool – the best players make their shots with their next one already in mind – sometimes their next two, three, or more shots. They not only consider their shots, but they are aware of the potential actions their partners or competitors may take. In the course of business, "competitor action" can be defined beyond business competition, to include any adverse reaction or activity that may come your way in competing for your attention, and your contingency for it.

The further into the future you can see, with an accurate and effective forecast for what you and others will be doing, and with an appreciation for all of the interwoven dependencies, the better off you'll be. Let's take a look at how this next-step perspective factors into our awareness of The Edge. A few simple examples will help to groom your thinking, and should get you primed so that you can take a further, more comprehensive look at your own situation. You can leverage the awareness we're developing here to your advantage in your own organization.

- *Sharpening the Edge to Your Advantage*: Let's consider something pretty straightforward that every organization does periodically, whether you're a sole-proprietorship or Ford Motor Company. You buy new computer equipment. For most organizations you likely have some kind of schedule for the rotation of PCs, maybe replacing a third of them, the oldest, each year. Every three years you have a complete turnover of PC workstations. Many organizations are on this rigid schedule of workstation replacement. What if we could extend the useful life of at least some workstations to four or even five years? Why would we do this?

Well, the obvious reason would be to save money by extending their life, and reducing our purchase of new machines through extension of the cycle of replacement for these select machines. But there's another reason, and it involves The Edge. Everyone and everything has an Edge – systems, equipment, manufacturers, vendors, government agencies, people, etc. Everyone and everything is moving forward in time. By extending the life of some PC workstations, we not only get more service out of them, but when they do get replaced, a better, less expensive, machine replaces them. This is because that as time goes by, the same products come down in price. As time goes by, technology and products get better – you get more bang for the buck. Here you've examined the Edge, and doubled its effectiveness.

Here's a related awareness that you can weave into this part of The Edge. Perhaps you're worried that as you extend your cycle of replacements, for whatever equipment you choose to consider, you'll run the risk of increased maintenance costs. Or that as equipment falls out of warranty periods, you'll be at risk. But you can always reject a cost of maintenance; you can procure an outright replacement - you've already achieved use of something beyond the usual expectations. Further, consider this: you likely have a backoffice support contract with a vendor; covering everything from advanced network support to contingencies of catastrophic equipment failure, to outright disaster recovery efforts. You're paying good money for this piece of mind, but like a lot of insurance, it represents expense without a lot of actual "delivery."

In other words, you're paying for coverage in case of a lot of "what ifs," and the vast majority of the time the what-ifs don't happen. You are therefore obligated to shove as much peace of mind into this bubble as you can. Get your vendor to throw in even more peace of mind by agreeing to deliver a workstation or two on X hour's notice. It can be something they have lying around the shop – your technicians can prep it once it's in the door, so vendor effort is minimal. Overcome any vendor objections by indicating that you're going to find someone to provide this service as an add-on, feel-good to the next contract you execute – and it might as well be them.

This is not to suggest that you jettison quality vendors. But many organizations live with a "suite" of vendors that have survived longer than the organization's allied managers. There are IT and Business environments that have turned-over in their entirety multiple times – and yet the same vendors remain. It's time to take a hard look at your support players, and certainly under these conditions: If a vendor is not in the mood to negotiate these things, it may be a good time to find a new vendor who is hungry for business, and who will offer better overall coverage for the money.

Here's another take on vendors and your Edge. It is no sin to have a sharper Edge than those around you. Vendors are going to profit from you. You are going to profit too – in your use of their product, and its service to you. You are duty bound to pull as much return as you can – you must go to the outer limits of what their service or product offers. In other words, gain concessions within sound business.

Seek out and partner with the vendors that are doing what we're doing here: maintaining and managing *their* Edge so as to move themselves into their future - with the least resistance and the appropriate effort. They will be the ones with the best-cost efficiencies and managed resources so as to offer you, their customer, the best deals. They will have the best ideas for sharpening *your* Edge.

- *Managing the "People Edge"*: Let's look at another element of Edge maintenance. We said every person has an Edge. What are the considerations as each moves into the future – both from their perspective and that of the Weave?

Let's consider an apartment building for a moment: Every month, the building's monthly revenue increases. Each month some number of people achieve an annual anniversary of occupancy, and they experience a hike in rent. Hence, each month's revenue is more than the prior month's. That's pretty powerful.

Using this example of a steady cycle and a one-way progression, let's appropriate it to staff. Every year a staff member achieves an annual occupancy of sorts in your organization. However, unlike a tenant, they don't pay the organization in direct revenue – the organization pays them. Generally, the organization pays them more each year. Without sounding too clinical, the organization is therefore obligated to get more from staff, as a balance against staff's increased compensation. In an appropriate success culture, staff also wants to contribute more – a happy match. In fact, staff should want to better the organization's position as much as their own, as these are mutually reinforcing. But further, the organization is obligated to create the path and the means whereby staff *can* contribute more.

Let's create a cycle of wealth in the Business-Technology Weave. You can create many cycles of wealth – they just require definition, effort, and discipline. Some will be monthly, some will be quarterly, and some will be annual. For example, the fruits of our annual plans are delivered through a cycle of wealth. For now, let's discuss a regularized, recurring goal – one we'll set for your user population, whereby we'll create a knowledge-wealth cycle. This cycle will assist the maintenance of individuals' Edges, and in maintaining a comprehensive Knowledge Edge for your organization's user body at-large.

- *A Cycle and a Progression – A Knowledge Edge*: Any Business and IT leader should desire to increase the staff's knowledge of Business, and their facility with the supporting technology. They should be endeavoring to do that with a plan to make it happen, and measures of survey to ensure that it is happening. This is because your business and information technology systems are changing on their own cycles of progression; standing still relative to them will mean that people are regressing. Therefore everyone needs to be on a regularized schedule of education, or familiarization, with existing and upcoming systems. This includes those very leaders. Making knowledge gains routine, and an accepted part of the organization's culture, prevents it from being seen as an imposition, or something unusual.

Further, no individual, group, or organization should wait for formal training or formal tasking in order to progress. Formal training and direction has its place, but at the same time strong encouragement must be made to individuals for self-train, self-awareness, self-motivation – a progression of self in a moving world. You can direct your people to your vendors' websites for free online training. Vendors also have newsletters that can be very valuable. Appropriate people should also seek vendor-sponsored groups and seminars. Leverage the use of the world's general online library of business/technical reference and resource material. Any self-progression on the part of individuals or groups means that the organization has that much more resources available for other challenges. There should be a stated expectation within job descriptions for self-acquired knowledge, and performance evaluations should detail the direct contributions resulting.

- *The LeadUser*: Another thing that's helpful, and available to the Business manager on an immediate basis, is the assignment within his or her department of an appropriate LeadUser. That person is tasked to head a knowledge-share group, and over time ferrets out the end-use tips and tricks for all manner of desktop resources – from main business applications to shelf software. The LeadUser can concentrate on those levers that best help their department in its use of those resources. This person then convenes the regularized knowledge-share sessions within the department to share these tips and tricks, as the other members are encouraged to share *their* knowledge – remember, they are self-motivating within a larger requirement to progress their knowledge.

In this way each department can leverage their collective staff knowledge. Much of this knowledge will benefit the organization at-large, and therefore should roll up to an organizational Users Group. We'll talk more about the idea of an in-house Users Group in the next chapter –a properly functioning Users Group can go a long way toward maximizing efficiency and productivity.

Understand that standing still for any length of time means you'll drift backward relative to the world's progression. Of course, we can take breaks. But maintain the awareness regarding the nature of time and changes, and in the necessity of effort in maintaining The Edge. There should never be any mystery as to how a quality organization, department, project, or person went downhill. It was a lack of leadership, and a lack of channeled, managed energy, effort and work. Knowing we can't stand still, not for long, you should always have something cooking in order to advance your staff's Knowledge Edge.

In this manner, like the monthly increases to the apartment complex's revenue, your organization's knowledge will grow by leaps and bounds as it ticks up each month, each quarter, each year. You must make it predictable – a given. You only have to define the groups, expend the effort in setting them up, set the expectations, and ensure the discipline is in place to congregate the users for participation. It is well worth it.

Specifically for the IT leader: It is important that you get your technical staff into this routine. Theirs is not only a burden to stay current with the hard-core technology concerns, but they must also be educating themselves regarding the organization's business. They can read and review materials, they can meet with department heads, they can meet with groups of staff. They should be dropping into the occasional knowledge-share group, where they can answer questions that those users cannot answer for themselves. IT should also be keeping abreast of general business developments through online resources. IT members need to participate in their own departmental technology-oriented and business knowledge-shares.

Remember ~ Anything you can successfully hook onto a schedule is going to zoom in terms of reliability and accrued wealth. Think for a moment about this: How does your organization create wealth within your requirement for secure data? Well, for one thing, your backups are on a schedule. There is an effort to administer and maintain the backup and its routine according to defined standards. There is a discipline of channeled energy in meeting standards: to perform the backups according to this schedule, and to back up data with integrity. You accrue wealth in the form of safeguarded, recoverable, data – a wealth of data safeguarding your standing at the end of each business day. This accrual becomes a steady, reliable, routine asset in your security posture. Think about this example when casting about for other ideas.

It's important to state that everyone and everything has an Edge: think of it as the bow of a ship, plowing through the water. The ship can represent an organization, a department, a project, a task, and an individual. No thing's and no one's circumstances are standing still. The forward momentum of the ship is your movement through time. The water is your changing environment – you'll encounter smooth water, new water, rapids, reefs, obstructions – hopefully you won't go over any falls or hit any icebergs! So, your Edge is always moving – cutting the way into the future - and that's why you must manage that Edge – point it, steer it, pilot it so that you go where you need to go, not where the water decides to push you.

When you update your plans - the one-year, five-year, individual action, projects - you are directing and sharpening The Edge so that you cut your way into the future with the least resistance, in the appropriate direction, and with the appropriate effort. You adjust the speed, direction, and force, and you bring whatever resources necessary to bear in pushing The Edge. In this manner, you securely manage the future.

ZEROING BURDENS – ENSURING SURVIVAL

We've talked about the competition for resources with the Business-Technology Weave. We know there's going to be a steady advance in the burden for maintaining business. The general, collective, advancing burden in maintaining our Weave requires up-to-date knowledge; best, vetted, practice; and intelligently applied effort for maximum affect and return.

Let's also take this opportunity to mention that we don't mean to imply a negative connotation to "burden" here: we're talking about the weight, or load, of work – it is *work* we're discussing, after all – so by all means let's talk about burdens. In the face of tight resources, possible reduction of resources, and expansion of need – what can we do regarding the non-stop advance of burdens?

We can be bold: When we can offset a zooming consumption of resources in one area by virtually eliminating the consumption of resources in another, we can achieve an overall parity between the onset and offset burdens. We can even get ahead of the game. This is going to be very important in the coming years as you balance your ever-changing Business-Technology environment's consumption of resources. Consider this: In most organizations, there is a natural resistance to change, coupled with inefficient change management and action. There's inertia. This inertia exhibits itself in individuals, and in the organization at large. Why does it exist? Often, a go-slow (or even a no-go) approach is considered safe. Frequently a go-slow approach is necessitated by ignorance: no one is qualified to go at a better speed. In these circumstances, the organization has created a self-fulfilling requirement for the go-slow approach. How can you be bold when you're ignorant? How can you sustain confidence in a changing Weave? You can't.

The Divide between That Which You Must Do, and That Which You Can Do: When you combine this go-slow situation with new requirements that constantly stream into the face of business/technology, you have a divide. That is, the organization struggles to close the gap between what it is able to do, and the seemingly constant elevation of what it must do. This is often because the organization finds itself performing relatively obsolete chores, or chores in a manner that deliver appropriate return for yesterday. Concurrent with this inherent lag in fixing or tuning wasted, inefficient, or outdated efforts, is the forced assumption of new burdens. In the absence of planning on your part, new burdens don't bother to align with your condition of limited awareness or preparedness. These new burdens may be necessary in the advance of business – or they may be necessary just to keep up.

Burden Management: Burden management can be an umbrella concept for the modern organization: it entails the review of work, resources, and returns. The essence of burden management goes on to some degree everywhere, by various names and reviews, in various formal and informal manners. Those things should continue – but burden management here is an aggressive, but responsible, effort to identify and stamp out foolishness. Just as there are false solutions to problems, there are "false burdens."

The False Burden: False burdens present real burden – they are false in the sense that they are falsely assigned and falsely borne. They are false in the sense that they have no merit – they don't deliver, or protect, or advance anything. Many of us have discovered thick reports that are generated on a regularized basis, delivered to some location, and thrown away without any sort of attention. Many organizations conduct mandated training that is poorly attended, or which delivers little in the way of real knowledge. Cloaked criticism of the busy-work variety, and its attendant destruct of efficiency, yields false burdens. And of course we have probably all experienced the wasted effort of projects that go nowhere, and even of implementing burdens of the False Solution.

When we become practiced at making objective, successful, arguments for doing away with wasted work, we find that we can maintain headroom to tackle unforeseen changes with aplomb and efficiency. Zeroing and reducing burdens provides a yield: It means that we can fill any new slack in resources with support to the emerging demands of the Weave. It also should grant time for research into those things necessary for a better business-technology future.

Use the zeroing of burdens principle to grant space to your efforts so that you can make more fully informed and therefore more intelligent, more accurate, forecasts and planning. Seek to size burdens appropriately (new *and* old), to seize and implement best practices as soon as possible in order to resize (reduce) burdens, and to even *eliminate* (zero) burdens as we can. The result will be more accurate implementations and supports to the Business-Technology Weave.

Zeroing and Managing Burdens the Right Way:

Burdens have Sponsors Too: When seeking to reduce burdens, based on the assumption that they are unnecessary or inflated, we may run into a familiar problem. Someone sponsored the burden. Someone has a vested interest in this burden, and won't appreciate it being exposed as a time-waster, or as something poorly sized or fitted. This is why it is important to make an objective case for reduction or elimination of the burden, and to show the benefits to be had. At the same time, the organization must ensure there is no liability in reducing or closing the burden. Remember the rules of valid, justified, criticism when tackling burdens that are being improperly managed and sponsored.

Burdens can be Born of Larger, Natural, Biases: We've been making a sale here: A twin track to performing work more efficiently is to eliminate certain work entirely. This is a tricky affair, for it goes against a natural grain. Most of us have an upbringing that includes a heavy indoctrination regarding hard work. Work in general is presented as laudable and necessary: the key to "getting ahead." And it is. Work builds character.

Therefore, it too often follows that a reduction of work, an elimination of work, or some combining of work for reduced effort, gets automatically labeled as a short cut that imperils quality. It's a shirk of responsibility; or a flat "get out of work" scheme. Any or all of these things can be true – in the correct context. However, we often times misapply these general feelings about work. Governance, managers, and individuals have a natural bias toward believing specific work necessary simply on the basis that if we're doing it, there must be a good reason for us doing it. At the very least, doing it will build and support character. Don't let this bias influence an objective examination of specific work's actual contribution to productivity, efficiency, security, and desired results.

Burdens as Sustained by Inertia: There too is the inertia that is imposed by fear, ignorance, or just an unwillingness to examine a new way of doing something – again, all that stuff we've been discussing. Fear of change, too. It's important for the organization to take an ongoing objective look at the expending of various efforts – where effort is being applied, to what end, and the usability of that "end." Often times we find that were producing very little of value for our efforts.

Beware the "Trendy": Gone down a path because it's popular? Trendy? "Everyone's doing it" because it's the latest buzz? There are all sorts of panaceas that look good to people – particularly to managers who don't do the actual work in implementing the panacea; the work in maintaining them, and the actual work in attempting the payoff. Those that *do* do the work, however, frequently see through these endeavors for what they are: resource hogs that deliver little return on the efforts.

None of this is a bash on managers, or those in the trenches who may be reticent to expose unnecessary work or procedure: we're all one and the same, as pulling in the same direction for positive business. In other words, we *all* have to look at ourselves and what we're doing.

AN EXAMPLE

E-mail has become a parallel universe for storage. Users have now constructed (that is, all of us have been allowed to construct) elaborate file structures within Inboxes, Sent folders, etc. This is so that we can file things, find things, reference things, respond to things, etc. Contributing to the problem are vendors who are writing their business applications so that reports' data can be delivered into e-mail folders. The thinking is: the one application that most senior executive types are able to navigate is e-mail - and indeed the one app that everybody uses and is best familiar with is e-mail. So, why not deliver reports into folders inside e-mail, conveniently marked: *4th Quarter Finance Report, Current Membership Count*, etc., etc.

This distortion of the e-mail system is a poor idea. E-mail has now been compromised – its focus blurred. E-mail should remain a communication vehicle. It's overlap into the area of storage, retrieval, and its feeble content management capability is redundant, confusing, and inefficient. Retrieving deleted e-mail content for reinsertion to a user's e-mail environment can be an enormous chore – even putting the stability of the production mail system in jeopardy.

Why store long-term content in the e-mail system, which is comparatively volatile? After all, there already exists a stable system of data locations, access control, and securities in your organization, which happily does not burden one of your prime electronic communications systems. It's your network folder environment.

Realize that with appropriate training, everyone will make better use of systems and applications without bastardizing e-mail. Also, realize that as time moves by, staff will be more facile in their use of systems. This will happen through formal training and their self-motivation – it will also happen through the process of attrition and replacement. Therefore, you should be building expectations of use with a bias toward efficiency. As everyone is becoming more tech savvy as time goes by, we should expect people to file, manage, and retrieve the information they need directly to and from respective business applications according to systems' best use.

The Misplaced Burden: Managing e-mail has now become an elaborate endeavor for IT and Business: notifying users about system deletions and when to archive; running reports; reviewing mailboxes for size, content, number of items, size of items, age of items, inappropriateness, etc. Sometimes this oversight spills out of IT: there are Business people who review mailbox reports. This may seem like a disciplined approach to managing e-mail, but in fact it is not disciplined. It's an example of a runaway, uncontrolled, system of over-management. This approach is a poor idea. All of this "managing" out amongst the leaves of the tree is inefficient, and expensive. All of this human oversight and forced activity robs us of the resources that we have a crucial need for elsewhere. Let's get - not to the trunk - to the *root* of the situation.

Realize that e-mail is primarily about communication. The e-mail system should not be a records or content storage system. (The introduction and growth of content management systems, and their position relative to e-mail and other content, is an important exposure and lesson within the changing Business-Technology Weave). An e-mail system and its contents should be lean and mean. Any e-mail content that is important enough to keep should be filed elsewhere for whatever longer-term storage suits the item. If it's related to budget, put it into a network budget folder; if it's contract related, put it into an appropriate contract folder, and so on.

Put the Burden Where It Belongs: Most e-mail should be answered quickly, generally within the window of the most aggressive cleanup policy. Most e-mail is answered within hours, and business etiquette dictates that e-mail is at least acknowledged within a *day*. E-mail should be dispatched within 30 days –

answered (within a day or two), any contents saved as (and where) appropriate, and original e-mail deleted. When you do have e-mail contents that can serve as reference, or require keeping, groom your users to offload e-mail to appropriate network folders. It will be easy enough to retrieve and provide relevant prior info as a future attachment. The user can also choose to cut-and-paste relevant electronic material into an e-mail.

Even if a chain of communication is thought to be important, it can be saved outside of the mail system, as content, and tagged accordingly. But keep this in mind: You should not be relying on e-mails, in an e-mail system, to document agreements, commitments, or obligations. Any supporting e-mails to those kinds of things need to be stored outside of the e-mail system as support to relevant contracts, service agreements, policies, and other documents. Getting the Weave under control will greatly aid the return of e-mail to what it is supposed to be.

So, rather than archiving mail, or merely keeping it around forever, users should be encouraged to Save mail to network folders, according to content, whereby the resulting file will undergo the assignment of metadata. The file will experience subsequent management according to its <u>content</u>, not the whimsy of some e-mail system and/or administrator's whack of data according to an arbitrary <u>date</u>. Remember – in an e-mail system, content is disposed of according to a date that serves the administration of the system; content is not treated according to its value. Once former e-mail content is filed appropriately on the network, you're managing content according to value, which reduces not only a burden in the e-mail system, but the opportunity for mistakes. Advantages far outweigh any disadvantages.

Once you get a new policy in place, and once the users get the hang of it, you will get important content *out* of the e-mail system. With discipline, it is possible to have everyone efficiently offloading relevant e-mails to folders within the network folder structure – where permanent and semi-permanent data belongs. It will now be managed from content and storage considerations along with all other content – a leverage and an efficiency. This satisfies our drive of all content to an appropriate, centralized, network repository.

Try to manage e-mail the same way voicemail gets managed: You listen, you call back or forward when necessary, you write something down or type notes where necessary, then you *delete the voicemail*. Get users to administer their e-mail in a similar fashion: They read the e-mail (analogous to the "listen"), they respond to and possibly forward the e-mail, they file to a central network folder *if necessary* (analogous to writing down or note typing), then they can *delete*. A properly managed mail system will be far more cost effective, easier to use and administer, and be far more secure.

Swapping Burdens

Another way to "zero" burdens is to move them. In this case, a burden isn't really zeroed from an overall organizational perspective. However, it is zeroed from a department or practice perspective - by repositioning the burden in an area that can better perform specific work. To the organization, efficiency increases as the burden is lessened; work achieves proper distribution and placement according to whom is best positioned to do it.

This positions the original department to better tackle its emerging burdens, and clears the work for which it was not optimally suited. Now, many organizations shuffle burdens, resources and people during major reorganizations, and reorganizations are necessary from time-to-time. But what we're talking about here are things that can be achieved between departments, without a lot of research and analysis. These are things that are large enough to be viewable through a common sense lens.

Often times organizations find that they've placed work, not according to where it is supposed to reside, but rather, where the organization found someone willing or able to do it. Over time, these sorts of placements wobble out of balance as personnel change or move up in the organization. These placements of work are not even prudent at the outset – placing work based on personalities, or a reason other than appropriate business discipline, is shortsighted and does not build a solid foundation.

Giving Security a Break: In the Weave, there is a growing burden associated with the sheer weight of effort in maintaining and securing technology – a large part of business' indispensable foundation. IT will need breathing room. With the expanding power and knowledge at the desktop, you can look for burdens that can be shifted out of IT to the Business arena. Are there information service endeavors going on in IT that can be shifted to your users? Perhaps you can train administrators in each department to run regularized reports that are being handled by IT. You can and should train users to craft and run ad hoc reports from your main business systems, as one example.

You can also build a network of user support out amongst the users. As we'll see, a users support group, *led by a user*, meeting on a regular schedule, can help users not only push through difficulties with common problems, it gives them the ability to maximize their use of office technologies. At the same time, it can free your IT department for the more challenging problems, and give them more space for researching a better future.

I.T. WARS

An Absence of Wasted Effort: Capitalize on the absence of wasted effort. Your potent efforts now translate more *directly* into continuous improvement, increased quality, productivity, and delivered service. We want our efforts to maximize the bottom line – to maximize *success*. You're not operating in burn-out mode – you have a store of energy for the challenges that spike. Remove the tax on success invoked by wasted effort. Remove the divide between effort and reward. Make these contributions to security and the Weave.

Remember ~

This is how we manage security: We avoid the falls, the icebergs, and the bad water by actively surveying for risk and potential harm – we point our responsible forward Edge accordingly. We maneuver past and build protections against threats. We can take appropriate action to prevent harm by knowing what to do, and doing it.

With basic security in place, we chart our course across the best water, further insuring our security by knowing how to manage our organization into top productivity and efficiency – building and managing a secure routine. We acknowledge our Weave, we protect our foundation, and we manage burdens in maximizing returns. Within the stability of the routine, we have the time to plan and evolve to our secured future.

Finally, we know what to do if something unforeseen, or beyond our control, pushes us into bad water. Through the properly maintained DAPR posture, we stand our best chance for recovery, our best chance for the continuity of business, and we maintain our ability to maneuver back to good water – that place where we again achieve the stability of the routine; where we again mount the plans to our sound, secured, future.

19

THE USERS GROUP
(THE POWER WITHIN)

Knowledge is Power

Francis Bacon

These days an organization cannot afford "hidden" assets. Who would want to hide, or be unaware of, and under-utilize an asset? Yet many organizations fail to leverage assets that essentially hide in plain site. In the coming years, doing your best will take on a whole new meaning –an *unqualified* meaning. That is, it will no longer be acceptable, prudent, or possible to take a position that "we're doing the best we can, given the circumstances."

We must change and bias circumstances to favor everything we do in order to achieve our objectives. We need to achieve success on an ever-expanding basis, in the circumstances of the change continuum. When we consider people, we have in each individual a considerable set of circumstances – and the potential for many optimizations. For any manager, don't we owe it to people to help them actualize and optimize their contribution to the organization? For any individual, manager included, don't we desire to work smarter, making greater contribution, in forwarding the organization and ourselves?

CONTENT AND PEOPLE

Just as we expose and leverage content contained in various systems of storage, we must expose and leverage content (knowledge) as contained in people. From a planning and implementation perspective, this is what the BIT forum presents – an opportunity to expose and leverage collective knowledge and talent in managing the present and future. There is always more knowledge and talent to be leveraged, and it involves every user at every level – each and every WorkOn, WorkWith, and WorkFor.

As your business information is stored in various databases and repositories, every organization has a collective *knowledge base*: There are those individuals who know how to do things that others do not, or who know how to do things better than others: things that are common requirements for all staff, or things that all staff can use. Because individuals have strengths and weaknesses, we should strive to propagate strengths in overcoming weaknesses. After all, it's not like transferring water from one bucket to another: we don't lose strength in one individual who imparts knowledge or training to someone who gains those things. Further, the imparting individual can gain training skills, communication skills, and other collaborative skills. The receiver gains the new knowledge and abilities. Of course the organization gains by having a more knowledgeable, able, staff. This is a win-win-win for all involved.

Maximizing the collective knowledge in your organization requires a forum where this knowledge can be shared, where training can be conducted, and where questions can be addressed for resolution. This effort also strengthens your HelpDesk posture, in freeing them for support to new challenges. Just as your HelpDesk imparts knowledge, with the objective of maximizing the utility and use of your office technologies, so too should your users share and impart their knowledge amongst themselves. Technologies are better leveraged, and users are more effectively served, as they help themselves and each other.

This can be done through knowledge-share events and user-led training sessions. The schedule for these events is whatever best works in your organization – a balance of need and priority. In essence, your HelpDesk frontier expands across the entire organization. Instead of a single locus, you establish HelpDesk loci in various departments, and eventually turn every user into a HelpDesk of sorts – to themselves and to others. User-led sessions can be within and across departments –in various sizes and with various specificities to departments. There can be varying degrees of formality – and indeed there is much power in the ad hoc, one-on-one help that users provide each other. However, on top of these endeavors there should be a comprehensive, organization-wide, group - The Users Group.

The Users Group and its Leader

The Users Group must be led by a user. Having a user at the head of the group has a primary reason: this user sets an example simply by *being*. We desire a user body that is as self-standing and as self-reliant as possible – office applications and automation tools are designed for the *end user* – not for the HelpDesk, not for IT, not for a support vendor. Therefore, by having a user conducting and leading the Users Group meetings, you set the collective user mind toward ownership of, and responsibility for, keeping up. There is a requirement for making effective use of business technologies, and users own that responsibility.

Naturally this leader can't be any user – this has to be a TechnoShine. However, this particular TechnoShine has to be user-friendly, as opposed to inhibiting. Seek a friendly, helpful, person. This person should be a quick learner, and must have the time to prepare the meetings and to conduct them. Occasionally, the Users Group leader can solicit other users in the organization to lead a meeting. Many users in the organization will have a known strength: someone in Accounting may be recruited to conduct a meeting regarding spreadsheets for example; someone from Marketing can present training on slideshow presentations; someone from the Customer Service department can expose some facet of the main business application, and so on.

Occasionally, a member of the IT team can present something regarding the e-mail system, or file/content management, etc. Generally, IT's involvement should be reserved for those things that are new to the organization, or are of a more advanced or technical nature – therefore something that no user, no matter how advanced, would be particularly qualified to know, learn or teach very well.

THE USERS GROUP MEETING

The Users Group meeting can be set up quite simply with the following in mind: It should meet at least once a month. It should meet on the same day, and at the same time, with very few exceptions. It should reserve its place by virtue of a respect imbued by the organization. Senior-most management should refer to the Users Group occasionally, and spotlight its important role in maintaining the organization's currency and forward-posture.

The meeting should have a formal length of one hour. The leader should devote the first 20 to 40 minutes to a lesson, depending on the nature of the individual lesson: the lesson should deliver empowering knowledge to the other users. It may be a lesson to aid better use of an application in looking up information for a customer faster. Maybe a lesson can help users design and deliver better reports. An important lesson could help to understand proper security procedures when using remote computing equipment on the road – there is no end to knowledge. The remaining time is divided between questions on the lesson delivered; general questions, shared ideas, quick answers; and a solicitation for the next month's lesson.

When you select the right user for the lead of this group, you'll notice something: this user will prepare and be qualified to teach. If someone requests training that is not in the leader's experience, he or she will procure the necessary training materials, will do the research, the practice, and familiarization, in order to deliver the lesson. This is where the example of a user "self-empowering" can be extremely influential: by being proactive, by utilizing online Help, by seeking web tutorials, and through self-train, the leader shows that a proactive, largely self-maintaining posture is not only possible in our Business-Technology Weave – it is becoming increasingly important and necessary.

THE GUEST LEADER

There will be cases where there is a request for training that is beyond what the lead user can accommodate. Here this person needs to have the judgment to involve another person – someone in the organization with the knowledge, experience, qualification, and *authority* to impart specific material.

For example, users may ask for guidance and clarifications regarding applications and use that spills into legal areas, or into matters of policy and regulation. Now, there are other forums where these sorts of formal dictates are addressed, by their appropriate sponsors and authorities. However, if there is enough critical need and interest between these other forums, there is nothing wrong with addressing them in the Users Group. In these cases, the group leader would approach the appropriate authority to solicit a session to be led by that authority. We can note here too that even if that authority deems the Users Group an inappropriate or less efficient forum, the Users Group has served an important purpose even here: it has brought an important need to the attention of the organization, and the organization can review that need for information and training and make the appropriate arrangements.

THE USERS GROUP: A GRASSROOTS AID TO SUCCESS AND SECURITY

The Users Group helps current staff beyond the immediacy of any specific meeting, even beyond the specifics of particular training. The lead user needs to instill a philosophy of self-start and self-train amongst all levels of users – this is extremely important in today's fast changing world, with the attendant user tools and paired expectations for fulfillment in using these tools. Therefore, your Users Group can start with effective demonstrations and lessons for using various applications' built-in, online Help; for using web-based help and tutorials; and for using other training channels such as CD-ROM, DVD, or live web-hosted seminars (webinars). Your internal Users Group should also pair and partner with external users groups in the area as appropriate: your main business application vendor may sponsor a relevant group, for example.

In these regards, the Users Group supports positive outlooks – what else? The group itself represents a solutions-bias – it fosters an ability to overcome obstacles by instilling a collective belief that obstacles can be overcome, and gives people the confidence to do what they should be doing. In making efficient the solving of short-term problems, the Users Group widens the organization's ability to address long-term challenges. The group should build LeadUsers – TechnoShines who seek as much knowledge and leverage as possible – who can be leveraged in their respective departments, helping to sustain knowledge-shares there. These LeadUsers can also be leveraged during times of change and stress.

The Users Group leader can contribute to change in another important way: a hiring authority can invite the leader to sit in on interviews when they feel that is appropriate. The leader will be ideal in helping any manager perform a hire-to-fit in meeting the general needs of your business-technology environment's office automation tools.

REMEMBER ~

The benefits of the Users Group are available to everyone. When the group assumes the correct placement in your organization, you'll find that even senior people drop in for lessons from time-to-time. Remember that applications' sophistication and use keeps expanding. Constant innovation of business systems and technology requires people to adapt to new methods quickly: everyone must be nimble and flexible in their use of systems and information.

Information sources and resultant content are expanding. The organization needs to determine appropriate and reliable use of these, and the Users Group helps enormously. Similarly, people harbor "content" – knowledge. The group helps to uncover knowledge that is often silo'd in individuals and departments – and helps to disperse and leverage this knowledge throughout the organization.

The Users Group is not only a powerful way to dispense knowledge, it also is a team-builder, and builds morale. Everyone in the organization has the necessity of merging and weaving their business with technology – therefore, everyone in the room, regardless of formal standing in the organization, becomes aware of having something in common. The group should be fun and productive: when run properly, users at all levels look forward to the next meeting.

20

The Heart of It All
- Turning the Crank Day-by-Day

It doesn't work to leap a twenty-foot chasm in two ten-foot jumps.

American proverb

We know that we can eliminate most divides. We have to: Even in a business sense, falling into chasms is painful, damaging, and frequently fatal. We also recognize that the better our posture and strength in the course of the day-to-day, the better positioned we are to make any unanticipated "twenty-foot" leaps with ease, reliability, and in accordance with necessity.

One of the most fertile areas for the germination of divides is in the area of routine IT activity. All too frequently, IT takes action that breaks a business process – something goes offline unexpectedly, with the attendant unavailability and inconvenience. What could present a starker divide: the gap between the expectation that IT-supported business services will just be there, and the condition whereby a service is "missing in action"? And it's really a two-way street; we also recognize that Business activities often present a gap of their own: if sudden changes within business process occur, IT scrambles. In all of our managing, we can't lose sight of the day-to-day.

Today – and All of Our "Todays"

Today, we need an alignment between Technology and Business Process. Our daily business, and its fit to the future, can be illustrated like this: Have you ever been lost while driving in an unfamiliar city? You're seeking the entrance to an expressway, thinking "If I can only find the expressway, I can get to my destination." However, you're being impaired by the streets directly in front of you. Your destination, no matter how carefully understood as a route from the expressway, is out of reach so long as you're lost in the immediacy of the streets in front of you.

The advance of your Business-Technology Weave requires you to know the "streets" directly in front of you. You must know what you're doing today, if you're to know what you're doing tomorrow (you must know Where You Are to know how to get to Where You're Going). Today's activity (today's negotiation of streets) is our agreement to an immediate and best alignment between IT activity and business process. That is the largest part of our means for reaching the expressway; for getting onto an efficient route to achieving the organization's near and long term goals.

We need to understand this alignment, and ensure a steady ongoing alliance, through the chain of "todays." Our success here is dependent on our understanding of how IT process affects business, and how business process impacts IT. We know this requires more than any single-point alignment between Business and Technology, such as executive level oversight, or a few constricted pipes of communication between silos. We need a steady effective partnering of Business and Technology at all levels so as to support, effect, and enable business critical services. This partnering needs to be a contiguous, broad, and effective engagement – hence our analogy of the Weave. Because technology now touches virtually everything in the organization, from top to bottom, from side-to-side, we could also say that your alignment should be as comprehensive and as close as paint on a wall. There needs to be a touch, an understanding and fit, at each level of business-technology practice, process, policy, and plan.

DEFINING THE HANDLE

This daily awareness allows a Weave so as to prevent the lurch from one challenge area to another. But what is the handle that we can grab and crank, on a secure, day-by-day basis, so as to ensure successful attention, in the proper measure, to *all* areas? As we chart and pilot our way into the future, how do we keep things from falling off the table *this afternoon*? What are the general missions in managing any Weave right now in sustaining and dispensing service?

In a dynamic environment, we must build a routine. One that exists as our reference, our hold on reality, our tether to something fixed. This serves as our platform, traction and support in managing the ever changing Business-

Technology Weave. It allows us to maneuver into the future without slipping and falling. This foundation is comprised of identified practices that must be exercised in supporting your organization's business. Setting this foundation gives everyone a better sense of purpose – always a good thing. Now we show up and feel that we know what to do *today*. Our daily purpose and actions are the "handle and crank" of the day-to-day.

Let's illuminate what virtually every organization needs to do day-in and day-out, and to do with excellence. Let's note that these areas don't include such things as DAPR, futures planning, change management, or people management, etc. Rather, these are the things that are today's focus, right now – which support those larger business and technology goals we just mentioned. At the risk of one too many analogies, there's another way to think of this: You may be planning a dinner party for next week, and assessing your best china and silverware; in the meantime, you need to eat something today. Below is the "food" and "utensils" the organization needs today, to support all the "todays":

We need to manage:

- Identity
- Service Levels
- Problems
- Platforms
- Events
- Assets
- Configurations
- Resources

Some of these areas will require more or less formality in each organization. Some areas lend themselves to application tracking or monitoring software: For example, a large HelpDesk endeavor can benefit from a system of problem tickets, to support their tracking for event resolution, and documentation of fixes for future reference. Another example is web traffic monitoring; or monitoring of network resources. The idea here is not to craft a specific system for everyone – recognize that some organizations can discuss manual systems of oversight and documentation, others will require and be able to afford automated assists.

Our intention here is to indicate the awarenesses and considerations that *every* organization must accommodate. These considerations can be addressed in your BIT sessions, and should be presented to IT for solution. In organizations where it is appropriate, these requirements can be brought before your solutions partners, in sizing your organization's awareness and systems in managing these areas successfully. Each area is not only managed within itself, but must be managed as a fit to the surrounding areas – a comprehensive management of the "manageds" - so as to present a cohesive, successfully managed Weave to your business process and platform.

Let's take a look at each:

IDENTITY MANAGEMENT: In the course of the day-to-day, identity management pretty much leads. Certainly one of the very first, leading, things you do for new hires is to create an identity for them in your computing and business systems: a User ID; an e-mail account; associated authorities; associated access. To the organization, this identity is as important as a person's name: think of HR's dispensation of material and communication to the new hire in the first days – as much, or more, of it is electronic as face-to-face. This creation of identity can, and usually does, happen in the days before the new hire even comes on board.

For business users, IT users, and invited users (authorized users from allied organizations, vendors, customers, members, or other guests, etc.), identity is a golden key. It must be protected and secured: a compromise of identity and associated security opens the organization to catastrophic harm. Establishment and management of identity yields uniqueness within a system: This, in-turn, yields discrete recognition, authentication, authorization, access, and grants the ability to work and to produce on a secure basis.

Identity management can and should include the managing of your *organization's* identities. For example, your organization is identified by company name, domain, web presence, and e-mail address(es). Managing this level of identity is also essential to security.

SERVICE LEVELS: Most, if not all, discussions treat service level management as agreements within contracts in order to ensure appropriate services from vendors. However, the modern organization must look at the quality and nature of service that it dispenses to *itself*, as well as the type and level of service it demands from others. You must examine both in strengthening the organization's own posture for delivery of its business output to others.

The organization needs a strong method of defining metrics for services; the means of measuring and assuring that service meets our requirements and expectations. Too, you must identify possible liabilities posed by service, particularly poor service, and methods for avoidance on the part of all parties - provider and recipient alike. Not the least of our concerns is the actual actions to be taken according to circumstances and requirements.

Service Within: Levels of service within the modern organization must deliver on-target results, with efficiency, accuracy, and with an associated Quality of Service (QOS). You even have formal Terms of Service (TOS), and Service Level Agreements (SLAs) for internal relationships, if only through standards and expectations that are spelled out in job descriptions. This holds true for individuals in primary service-provider roles (such as computer HelpDesk), or for the internal service-provision aspects of virtually every other job: Most modern organizations understand that everyone within is a customer at moments, and a customer service agent at others. It's another method of achieving a success culture - by working together, not just in the same place.

For example, folks in Accounting are prepared to answer questions about timesheets, expense reporting, etc., for their customers. Governance has customers. Your board has customers. Everyone has people that they must service and satisfy - both in a formal sense, and in an informal one. (Think again about the PowerPrism, and WorkOns, WorkWiths, and WorkFors).

The service within concept is a crucial one. In one global company, an IT team failed to perform meaningful backups of data for 3 months. Tapes were rotated through drives, but nothing was written to them. The backup application and related scheme was broken. What was the service within – that to the organization? Well, there was no protection, no prevention of harm (in the case of a necessary data recovery), no security, and thus no real service.

Every organization should examine service within, and in accordance with the values and standards we've been discussing. Test, observe, measure – to determine that service is actual. Reports of poor service should be corrected quickly. The service culture should be an understood, primary value in any organization: it is necessary to getting the job done. If your organization seems to struggle with deliveries (of any kind); in meeting expectations; in planning and execution - look to your service ethos. Slipshod service is not only costly for the organization, it is frustrating, impairing, and even a challenge to your security efforts.

Service Received: Many organizations seem to have difficulty achieving a proper relationship with, and a proper return from, vendors. Some SLAs seem to be written for the advantage of the vendor: the definition of "this" is limited to "that"; we don't do the following things under these conditions; this circumstance will bill at 1.5x rate; and on and on. Many support contracts are missing fundamentals: a defined schedule for delivery of items in support of equipment failure, to cite one example.

In a specific instance, involving an organization of international stature, the organization's recovery vendor spent 3 days trying to locate critical replacement parts for a centralized computing platform. This platform's failure took significant business offline. The organization's reputation suffered in the eyes of customers and members. That vendor had to be dismissed, the contract cancelled, and another vendor was able to procure and install the drive from their own stock. Of course, the internal IT team was deficient too, in that they didn't have the proper redundancies and protections in place to grant a space in time for procurement while normal operations continued. There was no prevention of harm, here. This was a security impact. The associated Business oversight was lax too, in that they did not have even a fundamental awareness for standards that would have ensured continuity of business through modern, *boilerplate*, configurations.

Therefore, it was not at all surprising that this divided environment had the further divide between quality service and the actual loosely contracted services. Every organization should make periodic review of SLAs - Business should review them, and IT should review them - with an eye toward making them *better*. What is "better"?

- *Solutions Partners*: All vendors today should be considered from the "solutions partner" perspective. A qualified vendor thrives when a supported organization/customer thrives. Indeed, where would the vendor be without you, and other organizations like yours? Hence, any real solutions partner must understand that the better *you* do, the better they do. As your organization succeeds and grows, the greater will be your demand for services and products, and the better positioned your organization will be to pay for those services and products. Therefore, any vendor, and any agent of a vendor, should always view each and every transaction, relationship, and deliverable as a contiguous effort, a continuum of support. This is a leveraged success for both parties.

This abolishes the shortsighted sale; the staggered stand-alone sales perspective; the "ka-*ching* - let us know when you want to spend some more money" sort of relationship. This helps you avoid relationships with vendors who sell product and services with a near-term outlook – the mere "how do we make today's sale?... We need to make this month's numbers." You want a true partner with your long-term interest at heart.

This kind of relationship comes with strong vendors who have solid, successful, client bases that they've helped to establish and support. In other words, they've helped their clients achieve success by selling long-term solutions: appropriate capacities, scalable products, reliable products, products that deliver solid performance and returns, with longevity. That vendor has built a foundation of successful clients, and is positioned solidly on that when they come to you to partner. They have a large bank of favorable references. They are anxious for you to talk to their clients, and will want you to visit local clients.

When interviewing and reviewing vendors as potential solutions partners, *you* set the expectations. You let the vendor know what the terms of service and quality of service expectations are. If your negotiations with a particular vendor feel like a see-saw (if I'm up, you must be down), you need a new vendor. When a vendor echoes, understands, and even amplifies your values, standards, and expectations, you'll have a good indication that you've found the right one. You are each on the same side, that side is up, and your combined strength is leveraged as an advantage to both organizations.

Events: Incident and Problem Management: When we discuss incidents here, we mean occurrences not of our desire or directed making. We're talking about the kinds of incidents that have negative outcomes of some degree, and which, if left unattended, lead to problems of varying magnitudes – up to and including disaster. Most organizations have systems and supports for handling incidents and the resolution of problems. In supporting business through the modern weave of technology, we've given rise to the HelpDesk. This is our front-line dispatch of services to the needy through a virtual "desk" that you approach for... help.

The HelpDesk can be one person in a small organization, and can be a team of people as organizations increase in size. Whether a phone call, e-mail, or walk-in request for service of some sort, the HelpDesk is probably the largest, most common experience that nearly everyone in the organization has with the IT department. Beyond the HelpDesk, there exist other structures of support, such as the Network Operating Center (NOC), where most of a centralized computing platform resides, with attendant monitoring, maintenance, and building. (Your organization may call it "the computer room"). This is where the guts of what's supporting your front-end user experience resides, and where much of incident and problem resolution occurs.

Your organization too may have a programming team, and changes to software and related coding often creates incidents and problems. Regardless of a specific problem's origin, users will generally alert IT through the HelpDesk.

Prevention: Dispatching incidents and fixing problems ties in with service, obviously. The better your overall service ethos, the better will be your structure, attitude, and efficiency in fixing what's wrong. As importantly, the better will be all of that in *preventing* incidents and problems. Many organizations make the mistake of brainstorming problems from the perspective of "Ok, Problem 'X' has happened – what do we do? Let's make a list..."

While it's important and necessary to plan for the contingency that something has already happened, we cannot lose sight of our opportunity to put into place those things that can *prevent* Problem "X" from happening at all.

In other words, when developing services for incident and problem management don't focus exclusively on response to incidents at the expense of preventing problems in the first place. Incident and problem management in your organization should foremost be a proactive problem prevention initiative.

"Leveraging Problems": When we do have problems, it is important that with our resolution of them, we undertake proper effort to eliminate, or at least reduce, the likelihood of them happening again. Organizations will employ their own systems, but all will need to record incidents and problems for proper documentation. They should be classified – in essence, you're managing problem *content* by classifying them, and aligning them with past similar problems. In this manner, you can review and leverage past solutions. You can also review this collective content to achieve ever better preventive maintenance measures so that, again, you can prevent problems in the first place. You can expose common cause, and you can effect more comprehensive solutions.

Learn, and Spread the Wealth: Once you diagnose a problem, document it, and resolve it for any recoveries necessary, you can make closure. Closure means not only resolving the immediate problem, but should also mean that you have emplaced a fix in order to prevent a recurrence. There should also be a *furtherance*: a leveraging of the insight gained. You should apply lessons to surrounding business systems and supports in preventing like problems in other systems, or even in allied departments and agencies. Problem resolutions should be shared in the appropriate Users Groups, knowledge-share forums, and with various solutions partners.

PLATFORMS - INFRASTRUCTURE, SYSTEMS, AND APPLICATION MANAGEMENT: Let's start with another helpful analogy: You live in a home: a house, a condo, an apartment. Laying a foundation, putting up four walls, and emplacing a roof to keep the rain off of your head are relatively easy. The hard part is building or finding a house that you will be comfortable living in. One that accommodates the size of your family, suits your style, and is located near the amenities you seek. When you get all of that in alignment, we like to think that the prior "foundation/four walls/roof" part is a given. You have all of that solidly in place – because if you don't, the rest of the alignment doesn't matter.

Today, snapping networks together, dispensing desktop applications power, and wiring up connectivities is supposed to be the easy part. This is foundational, supporting our daily crank. After all, elementary school kids are doing this; setting up their own computers and even networks in their homes. The "hard part" is the sizing, comfort, and amenities. That is, the building of your Business-Technology Weave as you size solutions, align technology support to business process, emplace security, manage the future, etc. Your infrastructure and application management is the raw foundation and house in your organization.

From the Business perspective, it's supposed to just be there – like plumbing and electricity, like four walls and a roof. It's what allows you to tweak and size and build your total Business-Technology Weave as you grace it with the proper "amenities" – the customizations, configurations, and overall fit to your business. Therefore, we need to make your infrastructure and applications as sound as possible. We need to make their steadiness routine, so that we can spend our time on aligning them. We need to ensure availability, reliability, and appropriate capacity of critical hardware, software applications, and overall business platforms – at all times.

Ensuring Routine: Here again, that which can be routine, must be made routine - so as to create the space to engage and handle the emerging burdens of the evolving Business-Technology Weave. You must automate repetitive tasks. You must install instruments and measures that accurately deliver information regarding capacities, performance, and productivities of systems. These measures help forecast evolving needs, and leverage the productivity and cost-effectiveness of the IT staff. This posture also helps staff to identify and handle issues before service levels top out, or are otherwise impacted. This is just one more way of preventing problems before they happen.

Staying Current: You must be proactive, not reactive, in these regards: You must grow and evolve your support platforms to maintain currency, while at the same time sustaining solid support to business. The organization must survey and manage technical platforms and applications components not within some IT bubble, but in a context of the whole infrastructure and business operations environment. This will yield an obvious and comprehensible view to the impact on business services, and also the view to what is necessary in terms of maintenance. Too, you stay ahead of needs, ensuring that capacities have a necessary lead on demands. Things don't get overlooked, or unassigned. We can go even further: this view will grant you the means of leveraging assets: instead of harboring redundant methods, products, and even hidden expertise within departments, you leverage applications, supports, and knowledge across the enterprise.

Once you have this comprehensible view, Business and IT can achieve true efficiencies, reductions in cost, and greater returns on investments.

Event and Impact Management: When we discuss "events," we are defining something other than an incident or problem, as earlier. Here, events are proceedings of our design, instigation, and inspiration. They are undertaken as necessary to further our business. They can be large-scale projects, such as the migration to a new accounting software (falling under the formal purview of change and project management), or they can be smaller events, such as an upgrade to your wordprocessing, spreadsheet and other applications suite.

They can be routine, regularized events, such as the rollout of new PC workstations. Events can be almost anything you want them to be, depending on what proceedings the organization deems worthy of event management. Any event represents change and challenge to some degree. Therefore, we must not only manage the event; we must manage its impact.

Many organizations have a divide between IT priorities, and the associated business-impacts. IT activity should be prioritized as best as possible according to business-impact priorities. IT is, after all, providing business-relevant services and support. It's important to recognize connections and map them between IT elements, the business services they deliver, and the constituents who use these services. The organization should seek to eliminate divides, essentially boundaries, which can separate IT's and Business' perception and experience with events. This way you can create an intelligent, joint appreciation, and a combined enablement for event planning according to business impact and priorities.

Asset Management: Managing assets is a challenge when there is high turnover of assets. Business technical supports tend to get replaced relatively quickly. What we mean here is that assets in the Weave, unlike some others, don't remain in service until they age and begin to break or fail at a rate that makes their repair a poor return. In the Business-Technology Weave, technical components - as functioning and reliable as the day they went into service – are routinely removed and replaced.

You may have perfectly serviceable furniture that is 10 years old, but you won't have many, if any, PCs kicking around at that age. Your servers, routers, switches and other supporting infrastructure will not remain that long – they may have turned over 2, 3, or even 4 times in that period. In this area, assets are overcome by newer assets that represent greater efficiency, an ability to support higher productivity, and hopefully a reduction in cost in the form of less maintenance and oversight vs. the rate of production that they directly support.

The Right Assets – Again, What You Need is What You Get: Asset management can involve all kinds of things in all sorts of organizations, but the fundamentals are essential for the most sophisticated environment. You need an ability to emplace the right assets in the first place; understand what you have and make the most of it; and replace assets at the right time. In achieving this, we can think of asset management as being similar to content management. Here again is an opportunity to leverage our understanding of the Weave involving all things Business and Technical: everything touches everything. Systems of management and advantages to be had in one discipline can translate quite effectively into another discipline.

Just as we leverage a collective understanding of content, we can leverage a collective understanding of all organizational assets. As appropriate, the more you can share any asset across the organization, the better the organization is served by that asset, and the greater that asset's return. Given the high turnover of assets in a modern environment, and the mobility of many assets (laptops, PDAs, portable printers, projectors, test equipment, etc.), suitably sizing your array of assets involves a tight understanding of what you have, what it does, who uses it, when (or when not) it's used, and even where it specifically resides at any given moment.

Know What You Have: For an environment that has had poor asset management, a period of discovery is necessary to make a comprehensive inventory of assets and an understanding of them. Even after this, periodic discovery will be necessary: no matter how successful an initial survey of assets, no matter how tightly controlled are inventories, and no matter how strict the record of addition and removal of assets over time, nothing can be perfect. That fact alone necessitates the occasioned comprehensive asset review (to be determined by the organization). But there are yet other reasons. Theft, unreported loss, unreported breakage, unrecovered loans, etc., required these comprehensive reviews and assessments.

Essentially, over time circumstances will arise whereby certain equipment and assets are on record as being available and in a contributing posture, when in fact they are *not*. The organization determines the schedule of full asset assessment based on the success of overall asset control and management, and how close to reality it remains between the comprehensive reviews. The comprehensive reviews can be made more or less regular depending on the level of successful day-to-day management: the organization, as in all other things, will determine the best return on effort. Some organizations may need annual reviews of certain assets, others may require quarterly reviews, and others may need monthly or even weekly review. Different types of assets will require differing schedules of accountability too – this is something we all largely know, but it's worth mentioning here: is your organization using today's best practices and best available systems of accountability?

Leverage Assets: Once assets are inventoried (essentially identified, located, and understood) they are categorized (much like content gets categorized) their lifecycle is managed (again, this should seem familiar), and further they are identified and made known to all elements of the organization that may have purpose and use for the asset (*very* familiar) – this then becomes a lever that you can employ for better return to business. This identification, record, categorization and management of lifecycle ensures that we retain assets that are performing and delivering a proper return, and enables us to move the asset out of the production environment when its return falls below a cost effective threshold.

For any organization, those are the considerations: whether you're small and feel that you can handle asset management through BIT, and with internal documentation and procedures - or whether you're large and require the formal engagement of a solutions partner, with attendant levels of service, contractual guarantees, and installation of formal management systems. For any organization, keep in mind that automated systems exist that can manage lifecycles to include contractual and financial controls. These systems help to automate configurations and can expose relationships, such as dependencies and supports, between assets. Also exposed is any surplus of assets, for purpose of redistribution, or adjustment in sizing particular inventories of assets. Often times the organization finds that it can eliminate manual or inefficient business processes with the discovery and proper management of assets it already possesses.

Configuration Management: We've addressed change and its challenges. Here we're focused on rather specific changes, but ones that are no less comprehensive in their impact. IT finds that it must constantly configure and reconfigure systems and services in response to changes in business process. That is it must tweak, or adjust things. IT also must reconfigure when responding to changes in business policy. These adjustments are generally the setting of variables and values in tailoring systems and applications to your specific business environment. It could be a turn-on or turn-off situation, such as an area of content access for a user, or class of users. It could be values in a reference table, such as prices in an eCommerce area. It could be the enablement of a secure application for someone new.

At the same time, IT makes changes within technical configurations, or must configure entirely new systems – in a more or less transparent support to business. These are necessary within evolving IT practices, services, and products. For example, things such as a new backup system; perhaps configurations to better distribute network traffic; to monitor inbound/outbound electronic traffic; or to provide other enhancements to security. It could involve configurations surrounding a new Internet service provider (ISP), for purposes of increased bandwidth. Consider changes and configurations that happen within the support of remote access capability, and all manner of other business supporting systems. IT configurations in these regards must be achieved effectively, and should not represent "events and impacts" to business.

Complexities and Requirements: Because the IT environment is increasingly complex, it can almost be viewed as fragile – it requires a steady and unremitting increase in care and effective knowledge. These things are necessary in maintaining its daily purposefulness, its reliability, and its security. It can be hard to know exact IT components' relationship to critical business services, and changes to one area can break something in another. Configurations must be carefully understood and managed.

A very similar circumstance exists to the one we exposed in *Security*, where we realized that most business failures occur during routine, stable times – as opposed to disaster or extraordinary circumstances. Here too we can note that 80% of system outages happen due to unmanaged change, and resulting *errors in configuration*. Further, within planned, carefully managed change, there is system failure 20% of the time. Any of us are probably well aware of systemic changes in our work environment that don't go as planned: the network is suddenly unavailable, or perhaps e-mail is down, or we must remain "out of" some specific application until further notice - and so on.

These sorts of unintended events and impacts also affect us in our personal lives: Any time you attempt to reach your bank and are told that their computers are down, any time your home Internet connection is unavailable, any time your cable television (or a station) is out, any time an ATM is "out of service" – it is almost certainly due to poorly managed change and configuration.

Understanding Where We Are: To fix this problem, we must understand its genesis. Often times, IT makes unapproved changes, or unwitting ones, which can lead to unsupported configurations. IT may not realize it's making a "change." Often times someone will perceive a change as being a routine maintenance action, not realizing that they are creating a breakage within or between systems - and the larger business. An IT action may have the best motivation and intention, but if there is a limited view to impacts, a lack of awareness for the upstream and downstream interrelated dependencies (that enable your interwoven business supports), you will suffer harm from unmanaged configurations.

For these reasons, any organization needs effective management of IT configuration in support to business. This management is crucial whether IT necessitates change in accordance with new practices and procedures in the IT realm, or whether IT must mount change in order to support requirements in the business realm. We also need to remember that the organization that handles change effectively has a competitive advantage – beyond that, adaptability is necessary for survival. Therefore change, and its push on further change, *and* any push on rippling configurations must be managed to an extremely high standard. There simply is no way to overemphasize that.

Aiding Routine Control, Routine Security: All change is driven by something else that is changing. Configuration Management helps the organization to improve responsiveness to change, and to maintain a *controlled* IT environment as it undergoes change. As the IT environment is controlled, so too is support to business during its change – business is secured. All of these dynamics must be carefully managed, and they fit squarely within the other disciplines in this section – everything is self-reinforcing in the Weave. Again, just as we must be aware of things like content, security, assets, etc., we must be aware of changes, configurations, and impacts to those things and overall process.

In these regards, we can understand some fundamentals as we *Discover, Act, and Manage*.

- *Discover*: As we manage the Business-Technology Weave, and discover and remove divides, we find that we achieve seamless understandings. In discovering and documenting your changes and configurations, you'll begin to map all systems and supports to direct business outcomes. With this illumination comes a huge reduction in the chance for unintended business impacts due to change, and change in configurations. Discovery also involves the uncovering of necessary change in order to better support the entire organization's business and technical environment.

- *Act*: Action is required to handle changing and evolving IT circumstances, and changing business requirements. Taking action involves the protection of business continuity and wherever possible, effecting a complete transparency to business as the change or modification to configuration is happening. In achieving this, IT must develop a system where people operate within their respective areas of assigned control; within the limits of their judgment and authority; and within their scope of knowledge.

- Manage: Managing here involves the documentation, understanding, and control of all critical configurations in the IT environment. This includes a total knowledge as to where those configurations map to business, the assignment of those authorized to make changes in configuration, and the control of changes in protecting solid, reliable business process. This also means protection and prevention against a loss of knowledge or capacity. In other words, you must document configurations and their understandings – you can't afford to have the one person who manages a system being absent at a critical juncture of need.

This management can be assisted by various vendor solutions, which help to discover, document, streamline, and even automate key activities. Large business environments will require such systems, particularly where configurations span multiple agencies or organizations with combined projects and missions. As built and maintained properly over time, these systems help track a comprehensive set of configurations along with their relevancy to various business systems and services.

Remember that any "automated" system requires human input, oversight, and reportage on its performance. Manual systems have their place too. Smaller organizations can maintain key configurations by printing various setup files and notes, and securing them. You can even maintain statuses on secure whiteboards on the wall of the computer room. With any manual system, it is obviously essential to document the new configuration(s) and post any immediately to the documentation sets. In all cases - automated and manual - changes to configurations must be communicated to the relevant team members.

Resources - Capacity Management and Provisioning: The demands of business are dynamic. In a moment's notice, IT must be ready to provide resources necessary to sustain an increased capacity for utilization. This can be processing power, bandwidth, storage, outputs… even the dispatch of personnel. This is another area of managed risk: we need to avoid risks associated with crimps to utilization. Who hasn't experienced the pain of rushing to produce a huge volume of printed output on a looming deadline? Often this means seeking available printers, and tying them up for hours with someone's dedicated output. What about anemic bandwidth, and painfully slow data transfers, or even interruptions? How about queries, sorts, and reports on data that take forever to resolve? Have you ever run out of room in your allocated disk space? There is no opportune time to discover these crimps, and they have a negative impact on efficiency, on productivity, *on business*.

As importantly, over-provisioning an area is wasteful. A shotgun of capacity and utilization potential so as to constantly ride above spikes or cycles of heavy business is not cost effective – and certainly does not represent best practice or intelligent management. This creates large amounts of idle time for idle resources. We need a rise and collapse of provision that is a tandem trace of each business area's dynamic demand, whether demand is high or low, increasing or decreasing. In this way, we avoid underutilized or unused resources, and we avoid under-served areas. When we dispense resources according to dynamic need, we find that we can reduce cost over the entire enterprise.

We must therefore employ some sort of predictive model and system so that the impact of moving demands can be accommodated. So that known cycles of business, with their varying demands on resources, can be handled in sustaining service on a managed basis. Analysis of usage trends can help to avoid response-time problems before they occur. Centralized management of resource provisioning allows an enterprise-wide view to what is being utilized where, and how effectively.

IT needs to ensure that performance and capacity exist that is reliably and properly sized, so as to effectively support business services as those needs flex. Further, resources need to be allocated and redistributed according to a structured, reliable process, based on the dynamics of various areas' changing demands. The business rhythms and cycles must be interpreted for the requirements they represent, and there must be an on-time delivery of resources. Where possible, an automated distribution of resources based on real-time demand would be ideal.

The payout comes in an increase to the organization's return on investment. By optimizing resource utilization and allocation, we can reduce capital costs. We sustain systems that are properly sized based on true understanding of demand. In addition, when we ensure the delivery of properly sized capacities, we improve efficiency and productivity, as well as aiding security and reliability.

REMEMBER ~

The tie between business services and IT provision is direct. You can afford no divide. Therefore, comprehensive understanding is required along the full length of that connection. We find that we must eliminate a common view that alignment of technology to business services rests solely with the IT leader and that department.

As we seek to achieve the IT Enlightened Organization, and the Business-driven IT strategy, so too must we achieve a combined strength of purpose. Together, we crank and maximize technology's *daily* service to business. When Business and IT combine to understand service requirements and supports, we have a strong handle on a leveraged management for ultimate service success, and daily business success.

21

- What's At Stake -
Lessons of the Business-Technology Weave:
The 4-1-1 on 9/11, Katrina & Beyond…

The dogmas of the quiet past are inadequate to the stormy present. The occasion is piled high with difficulty, and we must rise with the occasion. As our case is new, so we must think anew and act anew.

    Abraham Lincoln

The most important failure was one of imagination.

    The 9/11 Commission Report

The best way to predict the future is to create it.

    Unknown

The overall rise of the Business-Technology Weave has enabled all manner of human progress. While not a perfect world, the Weave has advanced our medical care, has granted the ability to communicate with far-away people, and allows us to travel almost anywhere in the world. It has provided immediate access to information in support of better knowledge, has created an ability to dispatch services to people in peril and need, and so on. Truly, to any modern society, the Business-Technology Weave is a necessary foundation. This means that the modern society has built crucial business and support systems that are almost totally dependent on technology: banking, commerce, communications, national security, transportation, manufacturing, construction, food production, water treatment, distribution, health care, policing - the list could probably go on and on.

There are some who would argue that the advance and steep of technology into all facets of business and general life isn't necessarily good. We need not take issue with that here. This is because, whether we like it or not, this advance is unlikely to stop anytime soon. However, as in any advance, people have built crucial dependencies on these advancements. Extreme vulnerabilities have mounted over the course of progress. What can the "local" organization observe and learn from all of this? Also, is there a contribution for the local organization to make, in supporting itself, through its support to the larger public security? Let's set the background:

Understanding What's At Stake – A Background to Where We Are

Dependencies must be protected and vulnerabilities exposed and managed. There is never a divide between dependency and vulnerability: there is only our protection, efforts of prevention, and postures for recovery, as relates to potentials of harm. The increasing mesh of business and technology has presented extremely large dependencies and vulnerabilities, which in-turn have presented entirely new scales of burdens for management, maintenance, and protection.

These burdens are generally not adequately addressed, and efforts regarding them are found lacking – in stunning ways. This is because there's more excitement in developing new systems, and more attraction in their implementation for use, than in the routine matters of maintenance or appropriate protection. Absent new awareness, the passion remains with the creation side of systems and enhancements, which leaves maintenance in a continual catch-up condition. Too, development naturally precedes the establishment of maintenance and protection protocols. Something must exist before you can maintain it. And, it's only upon true delivery and use of a system whereby all of the necessary supports evidence themselves. By then, resources are already going to the next creation.

This natural order of things means that there is a divide between that which exists to serve - and the fulfillment of its true requirement for protection. Look again to the levees in New Orleans: they existed, they served; however, they were not managed, maintained, nor protected appropriately (by increasing their strength). And, they were not managed according to standards and values of prevention. New Orleans itself suffered the divide.

If we consider 9/11 under this model, we can see the divide too. We've built large buildings, bridges, and all manner of infrastructure and systems. In the face of escalating threats, these must be maintained to standards of prevention from harm. Standards of so-called recovery will not always suffice.

Within emerging challenges of priority and scales of effort, there are new burdens of necessary awareness, skill, and action. These burdens continue to change dramatically – and quickly - in today's world.

A Sobering Reliance: In securing any Business-Technology Weave – which today includes organizations, cities, nations, and our individual lives (they have become Weaves too) - we are forced to rely on many external givens. Givens that are fundamental and generally taken for granted.

We need stable external physical infrastructure such as roads, landmarks, and airports; we require steady, reliable utilities for power, availability of water, and removal of waste; we need solid policing of our environment to maintain our safety and our health. Our own security initiatives - that is, our proactive posture for the prevention of problems; our DAPR policies and plans; our business and homeowner's insurance; our faith that we can handle and overcome any situation - are based on a presumption. That presumption is that we'll have the larger public environment to help enable and sustain our security. And, when necessary, it will be there to support any recoveries.

We have a rising awareness that specific organizational and individual protection, no matter how perfectly secured at any local level, is increasingly vulnerable to extremely large risks and extremes of catastrophic loss. Potential for catastrophic harm can also include huge geographic areas – even a nation itself – and is managed beyond the organization's level. These conditions can happen from deliberate attack, or natural forces.

This divide between the organization's control of internal security - and its relative non-control reliance on a larger public security, means that any organization and its people can find themselves quite impotent as concerns their DAPR. How many businesses in New Orleans had disaster recovery plans that were washed away in the flood? How many homes had the security of doors, locks, and insurance, but were yet vulnerable within the inadequacies to the larger public protection? A new awareness here is being manifested by a deepening appreciation of the facts: by individual people, as well as an increase in the breadth of individuals who are now grappling with deep feelings of vulnerability, and new understandings of dependencies and divides.

From either an organizational or personal perspective, managing protection from these large forces is outside the local scope of direct control. For the average business organization, no DAPR plan can much accommodate a jet bringing down a building, or a flood coming over a levee. We know that no organization's DAPR plan can match a nuclear bomb going off in its vicinity, or a large-scale release of chemical or biological agents, or even a suicide bomber. Also, business – whether private or public, individual or organization – is vulnerable to the larger economy, which itself is completely dependent on security. This would seem to be the Achilles heel of any organization's DAPR posture.

New Realities, New Awareness: We need a new, almost provocative awareness: If you're a person in the next New Orleans or the next Twin Tower, there is not much use for a standard understanding of security, or disaster recovery. We will attempt to open a path of influence for the individual and the organization. We'll take the approach that we must, and can, prevent disaster from potential terror attack. At the same time, we must and can mitigate harm from naturally occurring disasters. After the lessons of 9/11 and New Orleans, we don't have to enable or compound disaster. Nor can we afford to. And, we'll note that "unaffordability" has taken on a whole new meaning.

There have always been large-scale threats, and delivery on threats, yielding events of horrendous directed harm: world wars, atomic bombs, genocide… we don't need a comprehensive list for perspective. Also, there has existed for some years the power to deliver large-scale Unrecoverability to a society: comprehensive nuclear attack, for example. However, this power has been within traditional states and systems, which thus far have managed to hold this power in check. Some collective of more-or-less reasonable minds communicated, cooperated, compromised, prevailed, and co-existed.

Too, even in the case of world wars and other cataclysmic events, there was some measure of a surrounding society and civilization that was ready, and willing, to pitch in and help make recoveries to whatever disaster occurred – natural or man.

Today there are uncompromising minds that are acquiring the power to deliver, and are willing to deliver, catastrophe from which there will be no real recovery. For the reader, there can be no failure of imagination here. Conditions of Unrecoverability can be had in any machine or system. A Nation itself can find itself in an unrecoverable posture when disaster is large enough.

A state of Unrecoverability is frequently reached through a condition of *Runaway*. We can define *Runaway* simply: It's a condition where an entity and its actions become irrelevant within the scope of an inevitable outcome. Consider that statement carefully: we'll provide a very simple example of Runaway shortly that will put it into a proper perspective and make it readily understood. We'll also arrange Runaway and Unrecoverability with some other important concepts from the Weave.

TERROR ATTACK: Today, possibilities of comprehensive national catastrophe (to any nation) are no longer in the realm of Science Fiction, or held in abeyance through *MAD* (Mutually Assured Destruction, as during the *Cold War*). We face extremely large harm from asymmetrical sources: Sources that are weaker than their opponents in conventional terms. They can't compete through strength in numbers: neither by membership; number of conventional arms; or even in the numbers of their sympathizers. Their goals can be anathema to the vast majority.

But these asymmetric forces' business and objectives (that which they'll do, in support of their desired outcomes, respectively) are as strong as they can possibly be. In fact, their business trumps any concern for survival of any specific individual of their own. And, their objectives include the stated destruction of whole societies. We must realize too, that with these groups, an effective internal check-and-balance on unreasonable actions diminishes rapidly as the size of the considered group diminishes.

However, tremendous will - even infinite will - means nothing without some form of power. Today, power is moving closer - closing a divide - with this tremendous will of the relative few. Soon, if not now, weapons representing delivery of catastrophic harm will be available to the few - no matter how vile their agenda, no matter how onerous their task in procurement. Our argument here is not the specific who – that is not necessary in setting the awareness. For the present, we can emphasize a keen awareness that asymmetric attack forces are closing a divide: Until recently, the achievement of their objectives was denied because of the simple divide between their will to dispense widespread destruction, and their means to do it.

It is reasonable to assume that once closing a divide between will and means, a complete dedication to "business" will be paired with extraordinarily damaging technology. One group or another will pull the trigger once closing this divide. So, at the risk of getting ahead of our discussion, we need a solution. As we will see, a solution will require a project, and that project will require a proper definition. Let's briefly consider our other large threat:

NATURAL DISASTER: Let's look at natural disaster from the perspective of recent events. Natural forces, such as hurricane Katrina, represent further threat to local efforts of protection. But even wrapped in these natural, unpreventable, disasters are oftentimes further disaster of man's own making: poor recovery plans, delayed help, and inaction on prior preventables.

When we consider the overriding (known) preventable element in the loss of New Orleans (prevention of flooding through the strengthening of levees), sadly, we are able to ask: *Who can afford to enable and compound disaster?* We can also ask another question: Where is the next Katrina-New Orleans hiding?

Today's Reliance Requires Assurance, Conviction, and Trust: We spoke of a lack of matching public participation to today's security challenges. In scale to enormous threats, some of which have already been manifested, we merely rely on the expectation that a surrounding whole of public safety will exist.

Yet, if reliance is to remain, it is those authorized agencies and individuals – those government elements that have their hands on power and influence - who must now perform and be accountable in a whole new way. This must be a way that satisfies the standards and values of the local stakeholders. To paraphrase from earlier: Government will have to jump, perform, and deliver with an immediacy that wasn't required 10 years ago, or even five. They must do their jobs in a much more imaginative, rapid, and effective fashion than has ever been done.

At the same time, it is a fair question to ask: "Can government really secure us?" To prevent misunderstanding, this is not an indictment of government, nor will there be one. Absent new thinking, it is fair to examine where we are, and where we're likely to be. Government is not known for its imagination, efficiency, and quickness (comparatively speaking). Therefore we must know: Can government achieve a necessary agility to match the agility of today's man-made threat, and today's considerations of natural disaster?

We will answer the question. In the meantime, you may well ask yourself: "Has government assured me? Has government convinced me? Can I trust government to secure me?"

Qualifying the Discussion: National and International politics is beyond the scope of our discussion here. All that follows is based on an empirical understanding of risk – risk to any nation, society, group, endeavor or person. The author also believes there can be no political liability in a discussion of such universal values as the prevention and elimination of tragic outcomes, and the insured safety of innocents – as long as we are sincere in our effort to move the business of those things forward.

Also, our discussion is for a world audience; and the lessons we've noted apply to people in governments, as well as the people who choose, or live under, those representations.

Advancing the Discussion: With our accrual and broadening of awareness, we must realize that risk of harm from with-out has thus far had a corresponding enabling and compounding risk from within. That is, by definition there is a risk, so there must be some inadequacy within that can enable, or compound, the risk of delivery on the threat (whether directed or naturally occurring).

Post-9/11, Americans have heard from a variety of U.S. political leaders, from virtually all levels and backgrounds, that another large terror strike in America is inevitable. This belief is reflected in polls of the American people. As carefully as we can, we must note that these statements and attitudes are counter to the position of a success culture. They are not very hopeful. There remains hope, however, as these statements and attitudes are in opposition to the prudent position we've taken here: that it is possible to secure the safety of business and its supporting technology – and therefore our livelihoods and lives - through proper planning, activity, and results. Given what's at stake, we too should make allowance for a realization: Statements of inevitability are a conceded loss, as opposed to a confident posture of a win. (This is where the inadequacy of the "within" enables the threat from "with-out").

But because such statements are made today, and with a seeming lack of challenge, we must face them at the local level.

CLOSING A DIVIDE: NEW THINKING FOR NEW REALITIES

- IDRU -

IDRU (Id`-roo) is an acronym:

Inadequacy, Disaster, Runaway, and *Unrecoverability*.

And IDRU is:

Inadequacy: Inadequacy is manifested as lack of awareness, lack of planning, lack of action, lack of results, and dire consequence. On a local scale, we're aware of inefficient, ineffective, and inadequate attention, inadequate business, and inadequate technology (or use of it), leading to poor business outcomes.

We needn't belabor inadequacy's national influence: in America, we've achieved a large yield from inadequacies: 9/11, and the loss of New Orleans, as well as many others.

Disaster: Today, disaster can manifest itself as a relatively new phenomenon: an individual, or small group of individuals, can dispense catastrophic harm through the actualization of Nuclear, Biological, or Chemical elements (NBC). Because relatively small groups now can possess a formerly disproportionate amount of power to harm, already possess the will to harm, and can exploit inadequacy on the part of those they desire to harm, we have a prevailing threat of disaster.

Beyond NBC, there are new threats of disaster so monumental, that their prevention is not just some measure of abeyance in the style of a 9/11; their prevention is necessary to deny a state of total Unrecoverability. A massive, generalized state of Unrecoverability has to be of overriding concern to the collective Business-Technology Weave, of any Nation, group, endeavor and person. To serve our example of IDRU, we will use the most prevailing of these threats. This threat, and its ability to deliver Unrecoverability, is that of *EMP: Electro-Magnetic Pulse*. We will discuss that in some detail shortly.

Runaway: A simple analogy will serve: You are the driver of a car. You are speeding on a wet and winding road. There are signs, and they are warning: one gives the Speed Limit. One indicates Slippery When Wet. One indicates Dangerous Curve Ahead. Given the nature and conditions of the road, you should have an adequate awareness of danger, and you should have enough information to take action: to slow down, to drive with care, to prevent a bad outcome.

However, you fail to do these things. Your attention, concern, and actions are inadequate. You fail to imagine and plan for the contingency that soon happens: you cannot make the dangerous curve; you break through a guardrail; and you begin a plummet down a cliff. Your predicament was preventable, but now this, for you, is disaster.

But - you yet have systems at your disposal. You mash the brake. There is no effect. You turn the wheel to the left, to the right - again, your action has no effect. In fact, your fall accelerates. You pull the emergency brake. You are in an emergency and beyond: You are in a condition of Runaway. You, and any action you take, are irrelevant to an inevitable outcome. It is, simply, too late.

Here, prevention wasn't some part of a disaster plan – it was all of it. Once you begin Runaway, there is no meaningful action to be taken, and - regardless of remaining plan - no executable part of a plan that contains any meaning.

Unrecoverability: Once you're in the zone of an inevitable bad outcome, you are in a position of Unrecoverability. Our car is in a Runaway condition, and the car and its occupant are now Unrecoverable – they will be smashed and killed, respectively.

Any Business-Technology Weave, and any measure of it, is susceptible to unrecoverable situations. Enron became unrecoverable. The specific case tracking system, VCF, of the FBI's found itself in an Unrecoverable position. A nation can be Unrecoverable.

Understanding IDRU's "value": As we will shortly see, when Unrecoverability imperils nations and societies, there can be no good reason to risk even the beginning of IDRU: Inadequacy. As everything starts with awareness, we must push on in our discussion to remove the inadequacy of awareness: The whole concept of IDRU, and its inclusion in this book, is driven by relatively new mainstays and awarenesses regarding Unrecoverability. Asymmetric threat is aligning itself with the capability to deliver catastrophic harm. There is an infinite, and expressed, will to do this. Further, within IDRU, we must consider:

♦ Unrecoverability can manifest itself across an entire Nation – crashing its basic existence.

♦ Unrecoverability on this large scale can happen in an instant.

How?

THE THREAT OF ELECTRO-MAGNETIC PULSE (EMP)

Our concept of Unrecoverability aligns with some realities that have already emerged: existing means of accomplishment; the will of those who wish to accomplish it; and inadequate recognition of the threat. Hence, there is no real plan, project, definition, and solution to thwart those who are working at this moment to deliver Unrecoverability. This lack of recognition, and the risk associated with it, falls not only on "government," but also on each of us. So too will responsibility.

The easiest means of defeating a modern country - a country that relies on a Business-Technology Weave at the highest, lowest, and broadest levels - is through an Electro-Magnetic Pulse attack. An EMP attack could be something as simple as a scud missile carrying a single nuclear warhead. This missile need not be accurate for any specific target. It need only be detonated at a suitable altitude: the weapon would produce an electro-magnetic pulse that would knock out power in a region – all power.

Not only would some measure of a nation's power grid be out, but also generators and batteries would not work. There would be no evacuation of affected areas: Cars would not work, and all public transportation would be inoperable. Even if trains, planes, and other mass transit were operable, the computers that enable their safe use would not be. This would be due to the loss of all electronic data, rendering *all* computers useless. There would be no banking, no stock market, no fiscal activity of any kind, and there would be no economy.

Hospitals would fail without power. There would be no electronic communications: no mobile phones, no land phones, no e-mail, no television transmission, nor even radio. There would be no refrigeration of food, which would quickly rot to become inconsumable. Potable drinking water would quickly be expended, and the means to create more would not exist. Fires would rage, as the ability to deliver and pump water would be virtually nonexistent.

No Federal Government would be able to govern – nor would any State or local government command any control over events. No police department could be able to know where events were happening requiring response. Priorities would be non-existent. The only actionable situations would be those in a direct line of sight. The Military would not be able to communicate. Hence, there would be no chain-of-command; no control. Scattered commands and units would soon begin operating autonomously in the vacuum.

The affected society, on all levels, would be sliced and diced into small groups and factions hell-bent on survival – the situation would be an almost immediate chaos. As we've seen during New Orleans and other disasters, breakdown of the social order is rapid and deadly. In this circumstance, it would also be prolonged, and possibly permanent – until the arrival of an enemy control. Imagine, if you will, a peak, sustained, New Orleans breakdown, coast-to-coast.

AN AMERICAN PERSPECTIVE

A Grim Knowledge: In America's case, a burnout of large scale, created by an extensive EMP attack, would create damage to equipment that takes years to replace. Today, there are massive transformers in our power grid that are no longer manufactured in America. This represents a very wide divide: the conduct of business on a crucial support structure - that has no ready replacement in the event of failure. These transformers can take a year to build – they then have to be transported, delivered, and installed.

At a recent Senate subcommittee hearing on the threat of EMP, scientific testimony yielded this statement: "The longer the basic outage, the more problematic and uncertain the recovery of any [infrastructure system] will be. It is possible – indeed, seemingly likely – for sufficiently severe functional outages to become *mutually reinforcing* [emphasis added], until a point at which the degradation… could have irreversible effects on the country's ability to support any large fraction of its present human population." This should sound familiar. This is Runaway, resulting in Unrecoverability.

Here in America we also have to recognize that a nuclear-generated EMP attack can quite easily be mounted so as to affect the entire continental United States, parts of Canada, and parts of Mexico. An EMP attack would not kill many people outright. However, the comprehensive wallop of systems disablement would ripple and self-reinforce, having been characterized as throwing any receiving nation back to the mid-1800s. But, people in the mid-1800s relied on paper for records; horses and buggies for personal transportation; operated and maintained sewage and water systems without computers; fed themselves largely without refrigeration through local production of food; had not yet built reliance and vulnerabilities on comprehensive, instantaneous communication; and were in the middle of a reasonably ordered, stable, and progressing society.

Throwing today's America, or any industrialized country, instantly back to the mid-1800s will result in a catastrophic loss of all social order. It will also make that country a walk-in for assumption of control by others.

The threat of an EMP attack is a real risk: a part of where we are.

NATIONAL SECURITY: "WHERE WE REALLY ARE"

In knowing where security stands, it is helpful to consider some statements from leading representatives. Congressman Roscoe Bartlett (R-6-MD), Chairman of the House Projection Forces Subcommittee, stated on his website:

> …America is vulnerable and virtually *unprotected* against a *devastating EMP attack* [emphasis added]. That's the bad news. The good news is that we can significantly reduce both the threat and impact of an EMP attack with relatively inexpensive steps that can be taken *in the next few years* [emphasis added].

The Congressman's website does not detail a solution to the threat of EMP; rather, noting that we must develop "insurance" against the threat, and to "reduce" its impact once already occurring. There is no suggestion of a mission or a project here. Prevention is absent.

There are also those in government who propose guarding sensitive equipment from EMP attack by building some equipment to new EMP proof standards. For example, Senator Jon Kyl (R-AZ), Chairman of the Senate Judiciary Subcommittee on Terrorism, Technology and Homeland Security, states:

> Fortunately, hardening key infrastructure systems and procuring vital backup equipment such as transformers is both feasible and – compared with the threat – relatively inexpensive, according to a comprehensive report on the EMP threat by a commission of prominent experts. *But it will take leadership by the Department of Homeland Security, the Defense Department, and other federal agencies, along with support from Congress, all of which have yet to materialize* [emphasis added].

Here we may sense a false solution, as explained shortly.

The Best We Can Do? These statements seem representative of the Federal government's posture. Recognize that these are the government representatives who are proactive, and leading, voices on EMP (comparatively speaking). In other words, they represent our best at the moment. What can we glean from these statements?

- ♦ The limit of hardening "key" infrastructure: Some infrastructure is left out of EMP protection. Just as during New Orleans, there will be the perception that certain areas were left off the protection grid according to some devaluation of human life, or through a prioritization of certain regions' protection over others. Indeed, some areas will be left out, partly based on prioritizing others, in order to protect food stores, water, larger populations vs. smaller ones, and so on. In any event, the difficulty will be how we set the standards for who and what gets protection, and who and what do not. Recognize that following an EMP attack, "key" priority infrastructure assets will be like unstrung beads: some areas will have power, many won't – and all that goes with that.

- The threat has been characterized by people in government, as well as Science, as being <u>now</u>. The "solution" could be ready in "the next few years" (assuming immediate start, and a perfect project). Government's estimation of the threat and solution yields a divide that is difficult to exaggerate.

Because the divides are so large, and the consequence so dire, let's direct our focus to this: there is a tremendous inadequacy here on government's part in the face of this threat, and our current response to it. Given the stakes, we are already too far into IDRU.

WHERE WE'RE GOING: UNMANAGED POSSIBILITIES BECOME PROBABILITIES

Government has shown that it has difficulty handling emerging threats, where they are most affordable, and where the lever is on the side of efficiency, effectiveness, and prevention. Government typically handles threats on the back side – post-catastrophe. Even if we consider the war on terror to be proactive, we have to acknowledge that the war's existence is a response - a post-trauma event. There was no overarching proactivity that escalated, moved ahead of, and thwarted, the gathering threat of 9/11. Further, the creation of the Department of Homeland Security did nothing to help secure New Orleans: pre- or post-Katrina. Will this repeat? Consider:

- Government's current "solution" to EMP requires coordination between agencies that have so far failed to demonstrate adequate leadership, standards, and cooperation – in spite of escalating disasters. Even a new agency, specifically designed and tailored to overcome these failings, has itself failed recently - that of Homeland Security. Congressmen Kyl and Bartlett's statements, and the conclusions of the EMP commission, tell us that government knows of a dire, manifest, and fatal threat, but leadership and support has not materialized within the primary government bodies for taking action against this threat.

- The "solution" does not prevent EMP attack, nor discuss prevention as a desirable, a considerable, or a possible. Because prevention is discounted, or dismissed, it has been devalued. We have crippled our chance to zero-out risk right at the starting gate. There is talk of "reducing" the threat (not eliminating it), and talk of reducing the "impact" of EMP.

Going forward, we must also ask: Is it affordable to trust loose standards and the dubious success in reducing threats and impacts (whatever that may mean), to a general populace's uninvolvement? We don't even know when these diminished "successes" are to be delivered on their behalf.

When we talk about prevention here, we must truly know the stakes: As in the loss of New Orleans, a so-called cleanup after EMP will be exponentially more difficult, expensive, and in that case potentially impossible – as compared to the simple act of prevention. In the case of a large EMP burst, there would exist no national or large geographic unity. Society would plunge into war between those divided: Ones with power, food, water, shelter – and those without. It is quite possible that all would be without.

NO SHORTAGE OF DIVIDES

On the Precipice of a Runaway: New York City took action recently to warn the public of a possible subway attack. They also boosted their transit security based on intelligence they received regarding this potential impending attack. Based on this same intelligence, the Department of Homeland Security did not agree that a public warning was necessary, and did not find the threat "credible." This divide is stark. We must have an adequate awareness that the divide between Federal, State, and local authorities continues to evidence itself.

In the course of the recent New York subway action, it was reported that New York City has its own "CIA." New York maintains a foreign intelligence agency, with agents in over a dozen countries. This represents inefficiency and a huge divide – although that's not to say that this isn't necessary at the moment. New York may have good reason to budget and staff its own CIA. However, this is an overlapping mission with the nation's Central Intelligence Agency. There can be no good reason for New York to have its own foreign intelligence agents, other than the divide of mistrust: NYC does not trust that the Federal Government can collect and impart the necessary intelligence in order to help New York remain secure.

Whether New York's agents are empowered to take action beyond intelligence gathering is not known here. However, given what we do know, we have an extreme risk of competing, duplicitous systems. If New York City feels that they cannot rely on Federal resources to do the job overseas, how will they trust them, share information with them, and prevent protectionism and jealousy? How can Federal and City agents pursue the same sources, and not step on each other's toes? Realize too that NYC tax dollars that are supposed to apply locally, are now being applied against the same requirements that Federal tax dollars are. This overlap is an inefficient use of resources all around.

When we consider that NYC and the Federal Government each have foreign intelligence agencies, and when we examine such things as the FBI's challenge in tracking and leveraging information regarding terror, we can readily see efforts that are not efficient. Government efforts are not producing the best return on investment, and we are entitled to examine whether or not we can really afford that. In the present model, America is just a few disasters away from a condition of ever expanding efforts, and ever diminishing returns – perhaps only one.

Government is deliberative: it moves with deliberation and caution. While this deliberateness is a strength in most circumstances, it is not a strength when facing impending, agile, threats.

Today, government is spending an inordinate amount of time and resource going back to fix the *last* failure - removing precious time, attention, and resource from the imagination and proactivity of going forward. With both the implied and stated discount for prevention, we can only assume that an escalating set of attacks will ensue, with the attendant look back to see what went wrong. When this is paired with increasing recovery efforts to ever-greater impacts, we can fairly predict the ensuing stagger in attempting to move forward in a meaningful state of security.

This model of address presents a very readily seen gateway to Runaway. Without the adequate awareness and activity on the front edge of threats, we can easily "connect dots" and see that Unrecoverability could be right around the corner.

TRUE UNDERSTANDING OF "WHERE WE ARE" YIELDS THE RIGHT QUESTION – AND AN ANSWER

We know where we are, and based on that the right question is this:

"How do we create an avenue to results, as delivered by collective common sense, for purpose of collective security?"

This is an interesting question. It can have different versions (Just as our "Does this move business forward?" question did: "Does this have business value?" etc.). For the individual, it translates as "What do I do, and where can I do it?" For the organization, the question is, "How do we exercise meaningful DAPR in a volatile world?"

We must fully understand the need for the question (and its versions), in determining the correct answer for getting to where we need to go. The necessities for the question, its answer, and resultant action are well exemplified by any government's inherent inadequacies:

Government alone cannot secure us in today's world. Government has already asked each individual person for his and her help. Security now is a sustained, progressive, grassroots force that is an obligation to be leveraged by all who would be secured.

The Real Responsibility: As we project the loss of New Orleans, for example, onto the screen of a maximum national drama, the finger would have to point back at you, the reader, and me. Therefore, we must now recognize that there is not a one of us who can afford to risk a society's Runaway and Unrecoverability to some half-measure of awareness – on anyone's part.

Poorly managed governmental, or any other, half-measures are the Inadequacies and run-ups to Disaster that will precipitate Runaway and Unrecoverability in today's world.

An Answer

One answer may well be a network of teams. We'll call each team a Business Security Team, or *BizSec*. In addition to BIT-like attributes, and awareness of success culture values and standards, *plus* deep appreciation of security requirements, BizSec will need a public profile, and true influence. BizSec will be proactive, and preventative.

The Stake: We, as individuals, have at our disposal "the organization." As individuals, we may not feel that we have much leverage in our current discussion. However, our places of business can and will. Because any organization's security is wrapped in the larger public vulnerability (just as the individual's), the organization - every organization – has a stake in the security of its public surroundings. Appropriate individuals can make contribution to their organization's larger BizSec contribution.

The Qualification: Too, the organization has been forced in recent years to accommodate the safety of its personnel in a whole new way: some have safe-rooms, some have stockpiles of food and water, and organizations are exploring their burden and liability in advising personnel on actions during emergencies (whether to stay put, or leave, for example). Most have plans for staffing during emergencies. Increasingly, the organization must know how, and must maintain the means, to communicate as best they can with civil authorities during emergencies, so as to best advise employees.

These sorts of qualifiers for the organization's interest and activity regarding public security correspond with existing models and means for all kinds of other activity: Unlike any individual, the organization has tremendous resources in outreach, liaising, constructing and reporting. The organization has contacts in governments and other organizations; has ability to plan, to schedule and to administer meetings; and has the ability to weigh and judge results based on business needs and associated metrics. These abilities translate to many parallel things within large scale security.

A Voice: Every organization needs to consider having some kind of security voice, and therefore influence, at a larger table. This table is external to the organization, and is made up of representatives from other organizations in a defined locality. It should have as its focus and agenda an overriding objective for helping to define public security requirements and solutions, while at the same time holding people accountable whom are charged with the public's protection from harm.

A Team: This almost surely has to be a new team, as recent and past evidence suggests that local security's vulnerability to large-scale harm is not being addressed in accordance with true needs; either locally, at State, or National levels. The consolidated concerns and best ideas, as collected and developed at the table, from this team of organizations would roll up to a city or county agency, or commission, that is tasked with disaster prevention and preparedness. Ultimately, these concerns and ideas would roll up to State and Federal level awareness, helping to define and evolve a National DAPR posture (in accordance with IDRU-driven considerations). Accountabilities would be determined for each level of BizSec effort and anticipated results.

An Influence: Your organization's representation ensures that your economic and physical security concerns are represented, and leveraged with other organizations' concerns. At the same time, you bring the requirements, leverages, and lessons of the Business-Technology Weave to bear at that table. BizSec is a diverse set of people, from various backgrounds and experiences, from diverse organizations.

BizSec

BizSec will help us to our destination by closing a divide: BizSec will help to create a comprehensive public security system that matches the local organization's DAPR.

In order to make a difference, any BizSec that we're defining here will need to move the business of security forward in a real sense, constantly and consistently. All of the things we've discussed in maintaining Business-Technology Weaves will apply. We should not need to re-examine those here, but simply realize that a BizSec team will be patterned after the BIT model that we've established for any organization – in order to bias energy toward closing divides, directing purpose, and achieving results.

However, where BizSec will differ is that it will need a public profile, so as to assume a mantle of public power and influence. Local BizSec teams can announce themselves to local newspapers, so as to gain exposure through a featured article. They should gain television exposure, and will. Local BizSec teams, once structured and positioned, should have leverage and influence because they *are* the business community: that is significant stake, influence, and power. They can align themselves into a National Association of BizSecs. This is the self-interest of business: to secure public safety on behalf of its own safety – therefore BizSec, once existing, can make a difference.

BizSec will be efficient in that it will only require a few hours a month from its participants, as the agenda is planned and exercised. What would BizSec do? Let's consider the New Orleans BizSec, and the job it "did" in the winning of New Orleans' security against Katrina and negligence. Far from a 20/20 hindsight exercise, many people knew about New Orleans' peril.

The New Orleans BizSec Team: The New Orleans BizSec team has identified the levees' problem in simple, stark terms. The levees' inadequacies have been well-known, but the information has been ignored through the years, and sheltered by those who would rather not address the problem.

But now this overriding security breach has been well positioned in that locality's collective consciousness through the BizSec Team's due diligence, in accordance with their charter: A BizSec report is available on the web, is in local libraries, has been in the newspaper along with relevant reportage, has been profiled on radio and television, and the citizenry are well-informed. Because this is a Sword of Damocles-type issue of impending, complete, and *guaranteed* catastrophic harm people are waking up, thinking: "this levee thing is making me very uncomfortable. What can I do?"

In this climate, the BizSec team and their allied resources make it their primary business to lobby and call to account their local, State, and Federal representatives - until the levees are the top priority construction project, and underway. In this manner, people – any and most people – are spurred to some kind of action in order to remove an escalating discomfort - in order to prevent a catastrophic disaster. Whether that's lobbying, letter writing, a vote, talk-show appearances, establishment of public address forums, or other involvement, we can see that activity will level itself according to the quality of awareness and size of the threat – once there is a supporting structure to deliver concerns and force action on the part of those in seats of power, influence, and trust.

In New Orleans, a BizSec team would have defined New Orlean's overall security as virtually non-existent. Further, it would have been in Business' interest, and everyone's, to juxtapose a proactive $30 billion levee upgrade project against a $400+ billion recovery of a lost city. Hopefully, too, this team would feel an overwhelming obligation to a simple value: that of human life.

Further Value in BizSec: To truly understand the value of this, and the need, let's examine something else: It's interesting to note that no one has asked why the Department of Homeland Security hadn't connected the dots before the New Orleans disaster and facilitated a solution to its vulnerability. All factors were known well for decades, and we can safely presume that a major American city, in an ongoing, precarious, security posture – at risk for total loss – would be a large profile target for a Department of Homeland Security.

Perhaps we can make allowance that DHS was concentrating on terror vulnerabilities – and yet – New Orleans was lost. It was lost just as surely as if it had been blown up. Here it should be easy to see that a local team of BizSec would make no distinctions of threat's source: Security is security.

Here, we should pause to say that BizSec's purpose is not to sustain a permanent state of scare. To the contrary, BizSec's purpose is to bring peace of mind through the established state of best possible security. A solid BizSec posture will bring confidence by delivering the means to control and emplace true-value security. When we define actions for purpose of directing outcomes, we lower stress. However, in achieving peace of mind, BizSec cannot collude in a false peace of mind. It is in circumstances of plainly understood threat, with readily seen solution, that BizSec must go after.

Furthering BizSec: Another powerful aspect to BizSec can be its ability to rate a local state of security on a scale, according to established categories of safety. This can help businesses to size their insurance, and their various scales and balances of organizational preparedness. BizSec can stay abreast of law and rulings regarding business obligations to employees in the face of disaster, and can help businesses plan their own DAPR postures.

A community's BizSec team can collect the public records of any agencies and persons who inhabit positions of public trust, and assemble their relevant stance on community security. Relevant agencies will benefit from a public oversight, and any agency or individual in a fulcrum position regarding public security should be rated against all others.

This way, BizSec can rate communities according to their present security postures and awarenesses by collecting and assessing this information. All of the information collected by BizSec will represent *managed content*. This is where our understandings can leverage to tremendous purpose: any concerned party can access information concerning their community's overall position and participation regarding security, and they can measure any functionary's or agency's awareness and activity against any security issue. BizSec can make this information available to the public on its website, through reports accessible in local libraries, and in public forums, such as community meetings. Therefore, we can leverage any general public's concern through the lever of a collective of organizations.

BizSec = Privatization? In helping government, BizSec could almost have the mantle of privatization. However, there would be no direct profit component; BizSecs in and of themselves are not profit-making entities. Government wouldn't be ceding the ownership of anything, other than certain responsibilities. Government would possibly extend greater information and levels of control to qualifying BizSecs. The profit would come to government in offloading a certain amount of the burden for creativity, agility, and efficiency in addressing all of the pieces of national security's aggregate local components. BizSec's profit would be a direct influence on the nature and level of security resources to be dispensed to the region, based on qualified, locally identified threats and conditions. Depending on BizSec's ultimate operational role and scale of participation, this could be a powerful Weave across a nation's security requirements.

BizSec Is Not A Panacea

BizSec teams are not a total answer to society's security. They may be the final 5% emphasis that's lacking in putting the picture in place, and in securing the whole. Or, they may simply be a fertile ground from which springs a nation's best hope for generating entrants to public office and other areas of service who possess proper awareness (and will do something real about today's security divides).

We also have to realize that there will be issues of security that will, when properly addressed by government and society at large, put a tax on business, so to speak. There may also be issues within certain security needs that go against the political grain of some organizations and individuals. Issues like those may be resisted by certain organizations within specific BizSecs. However, if we seek the most diverse representation possible within our BizSecs, we stand the best chance of a fair evaluation of risks, threats, and solutions. At the very least, we can certainly get all facets of issues into a focus of awareness. That awareness alone helps; eliminating inadequacy of awareness is the first step to a more comprehensive security posture for the at-large Business-Technology Weave.

TODAY'S ADJUSTMENT IN THINKING – IF BUSINESS AND TECHNOLOGY LEAD, WE ALL FOLLOW

If your business were moving from the middle of the country to a hurricane zone, you would hopefully consider altering and tailoring your security awareness and activities. Any enterprise would have to provide protection to its business against a new standard of threat. You would have to now consider a new scale of potential wind damage. Would this influence the sort of building you'd inhabit? You would have to consider and enact flood control around your premises where possible. Would you make special accommodations in equipment for the increased risk for the loss of power, and for the sustained loss of power? Would you perhaps begin to participate in your locality's larger, surrounding, security efforts – ones that would help protect and guard your community, and therefore your business? Would you contact BizSec for information and help?

All of us are moving into a hurricane zone. That hurricane zone is one of directed threat from extraordinarily large forces, wielded by the relative few. The weather is changing rapidly, and we need to strengthen our shelter. It is beyond prudent - it is a looming responsibility for the individual and the organization to become involved in the new security realities that have direct bearing on individual, organization, and nation alike.

DAVID SCOTT

NO NATION CAN AFFORD TO MOUNT THE GRANDEST FALSE SOLUTION IMAGINABLE.

An expectation for a government solution is faith in a false solution. Government has already asked for our help: our vigilance, and our reportage of suspicious activities. Therefore - if we don't help government - we straddle the divide of reliance without corresponding assurance, conviction, and trust.

Until now, public questions and even public blame have not contributed to a solution to today's "what's at stake." It poses no solution to point the collective public finger at the comprehensive diversity in those who failed during New Orleans: Homeland Security. FEMA. Republicans. Democrats. Black representatives. White representatives. A President, a Governor, a Director, and a Mayor. And, whomever else the public squares in its sights, while somehow hoping for better outcomes.

These represent a broad spectrum of the specialists and representatives charged with the resources and power to deliver success. Regardless who populates these agencies and positions, we risk failure right up until, and through, our exposure to the maximum national disaster – unless - a grassroots effort addresses the present inadequacy.

- The World Trade Center was bombed in 1993. It was destroyed in 2001.

- It took four days for delivery of Federal aid to Florida after 1992's Hurricane Andrew. It took even longer in post-Katrina New Orleans.

No Divide: Comprehensive Failure, on Comprehensive Cycle: Because today's security-awareness and associated burdens are so different, and changing so quickly, we cannot fault government, per se. Blaming "government" for its cumbersomeness relative to today's fast-breaking world realities would be like blaming the desert for having no water: it's the immutable nature of the situation. Thus, we must recognize that as things stand now, these same agencies and systems will fail us again: no matter who populates them, and no matter what we call them.

We need improvement on security to be a one-way ratchet – ever better, ever more comprehensive. Security cannot be a one-step forward, one-step back outcome. In fact, in determining where we truly are, we should consider this question regarding EMP that casts today's situation in bare terms:

Representative Roscoe Bartlett, R-MD, has asked,

> Will government and industry heed the recommendations of the EMP commission? Or will the pattern of America's growing vulnerability and collective denial by our leaders repeat, until, as with Pearl Harbor and 9/11, an unimaginable catastrophe teaches us the hard way?

Here we ask: Teach us how to live in an 1800s society?

Or worse?

REPURPOSING PAST EXAMPLES

From past examples, we know that we can do many things thought impossible by the many. When the few stand up, stand firm, and work to expand their numbers, we succeed. We can mine these past examples as content, and repurpose that content: We can look to lessons from the Civil Rights Movement; we can look to the Wright Brothers; we can look to the moon landing. What we take from these lessons is that objectives that were deemed by the majority to be unlikely or impossible, were achieved.

We should be able to look to how those people of the past brought about changes in hearts, minds, and systems – and now leverage that knowledge for today's challenge. As America's past has shown, and many others, any stated goal that is ethical, meritorious, and of supreme importance, is achievable. The goal or objectives do not have to be convenient.

AfterWord

The Big Conundrum – The Simple Solution

The Conundrum is this:

> Unrealistic - But Necessary - Expectations.

This statement seems to be contradictory. However, those four words describe business very accurately in many organizations. How?

All business environments, at all times, find themselves in positions of need. The needs generate expectations: of fulfillment. However, many organizations find that they cannot realistically deliver on these needs in an effective way: they have not built and maintained the standards necessary to deliver.

Needs now pop up faster, in ever-greater volume, and needs will require ever-quicker fulfillment than they did in the past. Most organizations are qualified to deliver on the last set of needs; in accordance with their past character, and as things existed at the time of the last major initiative. As the unqualified organization struggles to deliver on expectations for emerging needs, it often finds that it fails, and starts over – any number of times as are necessary to getting things right.

To the organization that doesn't maintain its Weave appropriately, or even understand what the Business-Technology Weave is, this reality has the appearance of an unmanageable acceleration. Going back to the FBI: they failed to qualify and emplace appropriate IT leadership, and they failed to process business and technology planning in an effective arena. They failed to maintain their infrastructure, their standards of project management, and their overall understanding of technology's fit to business. They had no combination of vision and pragmatism. Within that "where they were," they mounted their VCF initiative: They could not reach where they were trying to go, because they had a broken route. They were not qualified for change, thus their expectations of success at the outset of VCF were unrealistic. Yet, their expected change was absolutely necessary. A condition of very "necessary" but wholly "unrealistic" expectations.

Like most organizations, they *did* know that they had to go somewhere. The present was not working according to today and tomorrow's needs. For any of your organizations, we know that without a strong Business-Technology Weave, your present will begin to fail those needs. We can see potential pain, futility, and danger in what is the *ultimate* divide – one that is in fact, infinite: Unrealistic, but Necessary, Expectations. This divide leads to Runaway and Unrecoverability. In these circumstances, waste just might *waste you*.

We can plainly see divides now, and we can understand what imperils many business-technology endeavors and organizations. We also know what makes things right. You must remember that the future of successful business-technology planning and implementation will involve a holistic understanding: One of reciprocal reinforcements involving people, knowledge, communication, corporate culture, attitudes, relationships, content (information), infrastructure, applications, needs, and expectations – all tuned and balanced in accordance with the continuum of change. Within that continuum of change will be ongoing challenges, and the contiguous nature of technology's support to every corner and crevice of your business process. Everything in the preceding chapters supports and helps you to maneuver to an appropriate Business-Technology Weave, and to its best maintenance going forward.

I hope this book helps those who find themselves struggling to align business and technology, and to weave it to best purpose. Weave it to real world standards and values. The sooner you get a comprehensive handle on all areas of the Weave, the sooner you can employ the principles in this book to closing divides within areas, between areas, and the sooner you can maximize the entire woven environment's return for best outcomes.

Find out what you need in your organization, and join the growing collective of the *true* Business-Technology Weave.